A PILGRIM'S GUIDE TO THE

Camino de Santiago

✝

St. Jean – Roncesvalles – Santiago

The

The ancient pilg— ... Francés

*A Practical & Mystical Manual
for the Modern-Day Pilgrim*

John Brierley

First published as A Pilgrim's Guide to Camino Francés in 2003
This new fully revised **14th** edition published in **2017**.

ISBN: 978-1-84409-711-1

British Library Cataloguing-in-Publication Data.
A catalogue record for this book is available from the British Library.

All photographs © John Brierley 2017
Author photograph Gemma Brierley
All maps © John Brierley 2017

Printed and bound in the European Union

Published by
CAMINO GUIDES
An imprint of Findhorn Press Ltd
117-121 High Street
Forres IV36 1AB
Scotland

Tel: +44(0)1309-690582
Fax: +44(0)131-777-2711

Email: info@findhornpress.com
www.findhornpress.com
www.caminoguides.com

Download our Mobile Application

Available on iOS, Android and Windows Phone 8

eCamino

www.ecamino.eu

Contents:

A **Acknowledgements**

B **Before You Go**

Planning – *Route*

Preparation – *Outer*

Preparation – *Inner*

Maps – *Waymarks*

C **Camino – *En Route***

33 Stages to Santiago

X **Useful addresses**

Y **Bibliography**

Z **Returning Home**

A ACKNOWLEDGEMENTS:

This guidebook has been a lifetime in the making and a decade in the mapping. It is an on-going journey with many deep valleys and high peaks. Countless individuals have crossed this path and each one, in their own way, has helped to shape it. This is no less true today as I finalise this latest update of the original guide. So, apart from my earlier mentors and helpers, I want to thank the many Friends of the Way *Amigos del Camino* and the various associations whose voluntary efforts to waymark the route means that, today, we need only the barest details to get us safely to our destination. And finally I acknowledge Don Elías Valiña Sampedro of O Cebreiro whose vision set in motion the revitalisation of the modern camino de Santiago. I heard his call and was inspired.

And a special thanks to pilgrims who took the time to feedback comments, many of these are incorporated in this latest edition. Your questions and feedback help to keep these guides relevant and up-to-date so do please continue to email me at: **jb@caminoguides.com**. Likewise before setting off on the camino please *check in* at: **www.caminoguides.com** for latest news and amendments under *Updates*.

I am often asked why I endorse 'cheap' air travel to and from Santiago when it is so costly for the environment. Details have been included on how to offset damaging greenhouse emissions and travel *carbon-neutral*, whether this be by air, rail or bus. My conscience is also clear because I know that walking the caminos can be a powerful catalyst for positive change so that the means (of getting there) fully justifies the end (expanded awareness). A central tenet of these guides is that pilgrimage starts the moment we become conscious that life itself is a sacred journey, carrying with it the responsibility to act accordingly.

And finally, I thank you, fellow pilgrim, for travelling the path with me. Let us remind each other that every step is a prayer – for good *or* ill – so let us manifest goodwill in all our thoughts, words and actions.

Buen Camino John Brierley

IMPORTANT NOTE TO THE 14th EDITION:

This 14th edition incorporates several improvements. It is smaller and lighter yet with additional town plans to help find lodging swiftly at the end of each day. To meet the differing needs of pilgrims all routes are colour coded for quick selection at option points. Several new 'scenic' routes have been introduced such as the routes into Pamplona and Burgos which have delightful riverside options *parque fluvial*. These are marked as 'green' paths ● ● ● ● and might be considered by pilgrims seeking more solitude along *the way less travelled*. An additional category of very remote 'purple' pathways ● ● ● ● is shown for experienced walkers seeking the silence of nature and a more solitary and reflective experience. The main camino, carrying around 80% of all pilgrims, is shown with the familiar yellow marking ● ● ● ●.

The biggest change continues to be the rise in the number of pilgrims travelling the camino – over ¼ million in 2015. Inevitably this puts a strain on resources and some hostels at bottleneck locations were *completo* by noon, before they were even officially due to open! This is no reason *not* to go during the extended summer period but we need to stay flexible and have enough energy in reserve to search out alternatives if necessary. The addition of new hostels continues to help meet the ever increasing demand and relieves *some* of the pressure on lodging. Upgrading of facilities is also welcome, such as the addition of washing *and* drying machines *secadoras*, the latter can be a real boon in wet weather. The one piece of advice that I would pick out from the first edition is simply this: *'There are no guarantees in this life and a pilgrim is well served by offering gratitude for all experiences encountered along the path.'* Welcome the unknown, keep an open mind and heart, let go expectations and feel the freedom to be found along this ancient pilgrim path.

A snapshot of modern Spain has been included at the end of the historical sketch to provide a cultural and political context for pilgrims visiting Spain for the first time. As an aide-mémoire essential Spanish words are shown in italics with the exception *excepción* of camino that has now effectively become anglicised. A self-assessment questionnaire has also been included to help formulate and, hopefully, answer some of the deeper questions that often bubble to the surface when we clear space and head off along a path of enquiry.

Introduction:

Welcome to The Way of St. James *el camino de Sant Iago*. Unlike many other routes to Santiago de Compostela, the waymarking on the French Way *camino francés* is now very extensive. The familiar yellow arrow *flecha amarilla* will become a source of great comfort to you along the way – popping into view just when you think you are lost. This said, an accurate map and guidebook is useful to help you plan your itinerary and excursions and to put you back on the path when your mind wanders and your feet follow!

I generally found guidebooks were either too big (and full of information that I could gather elsewhere along the way) or too small (with inadequate data). There was also a wide variation in the distances provided, exacerbated by the total absence of details of the start and end point for measurements, 'Burgos 12 km' is meaningless without specifying *where* in Burgos – the new pilgrim hostel is 7.8 km from the start of the city environs, a very long way at the end of a day's walk! But what inspired me to write *another* guidebook was the almost universal absence of any reference, yet alone waymarks, to the *inner* path.

I urge you to find a spiritual purpose for taking this journey. If you have difficulty with this term, find one more meaningful to you, and check out your local bookstore – you'll find a wealth of literature on the subject. The words 'significant journey' threw up 63 million suggestions on my web browser – so you get the idea! But attend to this promptly so that you have time to mull over your motivation *before* you travel. A core question arises: what turns a walking holiday into pilgrimage? When you receive an answer you may find a fundamental change in how you approach the journey – from intention down to what you put in your backpack. The strategy is not to feel pressurised to follow any particular 'way' – you will know when something rings true for you – learn to trust that resonance. Some suggestions are listed in the bibliography.

I have endeavoured to find a balance between the *inner* and *outer* journey by paying equal respect to both. That is why these guides are subtitled *a practical and mystical manual for the modern-day pilgrim*. That we might find a place to lay our weary head at the end of the day but also, and crucially, that we might feel supported and encouraged to dive into the mysteries of our individual soul awakenings, without which all journeying is essentially purposeless. Along every path of enquiry there comes a point that requires a leap of faith, where we have to abandon the security of out-dated dogma handed down to us over millennia. When we reach that point we have to let go of the safety of the familiar and dive into the unknown, with nothing but our faith to support us.

The traditional pilgrim way is on foot, carrying all your 'worldly goods'. This allows the freedom to choose where to stop and tests your faith that there will be room in the inn! This flexibility is lost if you have your backpack transported as it requires that you book ahead. You can also obtain a certificate of completion *compostela* by going on bike but you may miss some of the beauty of the outer landscape and the spirit of the inner journey. Pilgrimage takes the time it takes. Travel alone if at all possible – this way you are more likely to meet the country folk and absorb their wisdom and local lore. You will learn the native language as you go and you will also meet other fellow pilgrims along the way. But above all, you may meet your *Self* and find that you are never alone – and that is surely a primary purpose of pilgrimage and perhaps of life itself.

This guidebook is dedicated to awakening beyond human consciousness. It was born out of a mid-life crisis and the perceived need for a time to reflect on the purpose and direction of life. We have a sacred contract, a divine function and reason why we came here. Pilgrimage provides an opportunity to delve deeper into that purpose and time to re-orientate our lives towards its fulfilment. We have been asleep a long time but alarm bells are ringing for young and old and there are signs that we are collectively waking up. The Call of the Camino is being heard all around the world – the call to move beyond that which separates us and to find that common bond, that spiritual thread which binds us together and, by extension, connects us to the Source of all that is. There is a yearning to break free from our self-imposed imprisonment and isolation so eloquently captured in the words of Christopher Fry in *A Sleep of Prisoners*:

> Thank God our time is now when wrong
> Comes up to face us everywhere,
> Never to leave us till we take
> The longest stride of soul folk ever took.
>
> Affairs are now soul size.
> The enterprise is exploration into God.
> Where are you making for?
> It takes so many thousand years to wake,
> But will you wake for pity's sake?

May your journey along your chosen path be blessed – rough or smooth, long or short – whichever route you take, know that you are loved and your destination is assured. God speed *Ultreia!*

❶ Travel – A Quick Guide:

• **When?** Spring is often wet and windy but the route is relatively quiet with early flowers appearing. Summer is busy and hot and hostels often full. Autumn often provides the most stable weather with harvesting adding to the colour and celebrations of the countryside. Winter is solitary and cold and many hostels will be closed.

• **How long?** The route is divided into 33 stages each one corresponding to an average days walk – but find your own pace and overnight at intermediate hostels as required. Clear the decks and allow some spaciousness into your life – 5 weeks is ideal but join or leave the route to fit in with your schedule.

❷ Preparation – *Outer*: **what do I need to take** *and* **leave behind.**

• Buy your boots in time to walk them in before you go.
• Pack a Poncho, Spain can provide downpours at any time of year.
• Bring a hat, sunstroke is painful and can be dangerous.
• Look again if your backpack weighs more than 10 kilos.

What *not* **to bring:**
• Get rid of books (except this one – and all the maps you need are included.)
• Don't take 'extras', Spain has shops if you need to replace something.
• If you want to deepen your experience, leave behind:
  – your *camera* – you'll be able to live for the moment rather than memories.
  – your *watch* – you'll be surprised how quickly you adapt to a natural clock.
  – your *mobile phone* – break the dependency (excepting solo pilgrims travelling in the winter months when a phone may be useful and a compass necessary to navigate especially in snow when waymarks may become obliterated).

❸ Language learn it now, *before* you go.

❹ Pilgrim Passport, Protocol & Prayer

• Get a *credencial* from your local confraternity – and join it.
• Have consideration for your fellow pilgrims and gratitude for your hosts.
• May every step be a prayer for peace and an extension of loving kindness.

❺ Preparation – *Inner*: **why am I doing this?**

Take time to prepare a purpose for this pilgrimage and to complete the self-assessment questionnaire. Start from the basis that you are essentially a spiritual being on a human journey, not a human being on a spiritual one. We came to learn some lesson and this pilgrimage affords an opportunity to find out what that is. Ask for help and expect it – it's there, now, waiting for you.

Whatever you do – for heaven's sake don't forget to start.

B   **Before you go:** This section has more detailed notes on preparation. Once you have finalised your packing consider cutting out these pages along the dotted line to leave extra space for your *credencial* or other personal papers – every ounce needs to be accounted for!

When to go? If you like peace and quiet, the **spring** months of March and April will provide fewer other pilgrims and tourists. Hostels will be opening and flights and ferries should be operating, at least on a limited basis. You will be accompanied by early spring flowers and cool conditions for walking, although the nights are likely to be cold and rain plentiful, especially in the mountain areas and Galicia. Pack additional wet gear and warm fleeces.

The **summer** months can be very hot and accommodation, even water, in short supply. July & August are bedlam and, if this coincides with a Holy Year (any year when St. James Day, 25th July, falls on a Sunday) it can turn into a nightmare for those wanting an introspective time. These 2 months alone account for almost half of all pilgrims arriving in Santiago for the whole year. May / June and September are also becoming very busy.

The **autumn** season from late September through October often provides more stable weather than spring, the fierce heat of summer is over, the snow hasn't yet arrived and most hostels are still open. However, this period has also become busy. If you are an experienced walker, the depths of **winter** can provide some of the most mystical experiences. There may be fewer flights and many hostels will be closed, but I have never wanted for a bed or floor to sleep on at this time of year (see page 16 for list). Costs will be lower and you'll have much of the camino to yourself. Bring warm waterproof clothes and remember that daylight hours are restricted, so the daily distance that you can cover is reduced.

The **weather** in northern Spain, particularly Galicia, is very unpredictable. The **summer** months may see temperatures soar to over 35 Celsius (95 Fahrenheit) and the nights are often uncomfortably warm. Sun protection is vital, especially on the high plateau *Meseta* much of which has no shade of any kind. Plenty of water is essential to replace fluids lost through physical exertion and the heat. In **winter** the higher ground can be blocked with snow with temperatures dropping below

freezing. At the shoulder seasons, you can expect anything in between. The worst weather I ever experienced was in May when it rained nonstop in Galicia for 9 days, accompanied by fierce storms and low temperatures – by contrast, early November was warm and dry. So be prepared for any eventuality. **Daylight hours** can be important when planning each day's stage. In the summer you have all the hours God made and certainly more than you could walk! In mid winter, your daylight is reduced to 8 hours.

When does everyone else go? The following graphs might help your decision. Whilst clearly not everyone arriving at Santiago will report to the pilgrim office, 262,458 pilgrims collected a *compostela* in 2015. 66% of all pilgrims arrive in Santiago via the *camino francés* (down from 95% 10 years ago) and 55% arrive in June, July and August. However most start in Galicia, the majority in Sarria (67,408) 26%) entitling pilgrims to a compostela being just over 100 km from Santiago so the Galician stages are particularly busy. The next major gateway to the Camino is St. Jean Pied de Port (31,052 – 12%) and Tui (13,799 – 5%).

The number of pilgrims has more than doubles over the past decade with pilgrims from 140 different nationalities arriving in 2015. The first graph shows the number of pilgrims collecting compostelas over the last 12 year period. Holy Years (in yellow) increases the numbers on the route and the visit by Pope Benedict during the Holy Year in 2010 saw the number pass ¼ Million for the first time in the modern history of the camino at 272,412. The next Holy Year *Año Santo Jacobeo* will not be until 2021.

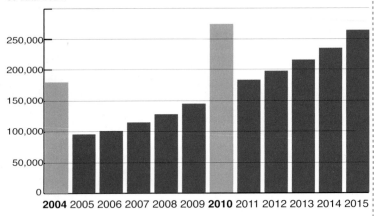

The second graph is based on average monthly figures. Pilgrims are now spread out more evenly from May to October (over 20,000 each month) although August (54,796) still tops the list with 1,217 braving the journey in January.

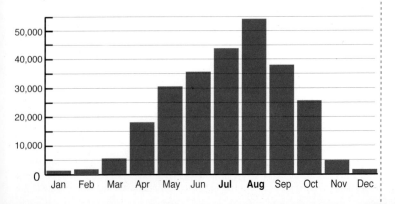

How long does it take? This depends on many factors such as level of fitness, which varies between individuals and within individuals (your biorhythms don't just affect mood swings!). When you add in variations in weather, detours (planned and otherwise) and different motivation and time constraints all this results in a heady mix of possibilities. I once met a manic pilgrim in Finisterre who had just arrived from Seville. He had walked 1,000 kilometres in a staggering 19 days: that's over 50 km per day! He just had time to proudly show me his *credencial* to 'prove' the fact, before heading off down the hill again! It appears that many people allow completion of the journey in the minimum time to become the main focus. You are the only one who can evaluate your purpose and, if sporting achievement is yours, so be it, but it is unlikely to be a pilgrimage.

Statistics are limited, but my sense is that most people take 4 weeks to walk the entire *Camino Francés* 776.2 km (482.3 miles) or 809.5 km if you include the scenic routes and detours to the monasteries at San Millan and Samos). This fits (just) into a month-long 'holyday' period with a day either side to fly in and out. These 33 days represent something of a minimum and would require averaging 23.5 kilometres (14.6 miles) a day with no detours, no rest days, no strains or sprains and no alternative travel plans. By the time you have found a bed, had a shower, massaged your feet, washed your socks, had a meal... there will be little time to attend mass, meditate, write-up your spiritual journal, reflect on your purpose...

Find your own pace but the one described here will allow you to reach Santiago *gracefully* in 5 weeks. This allows for an average of 22.2 kilometres (13.8 miles) a day for 33 days with 2 rest days. I like the idea that I walk one day for every year that Christ lived on earth. It connects me to a bigger picture and slows the pace to allow the inner alchemy of introspection to work. Pilgrimage takes the time it takes – 6 weeks (40 days and 40 nights) invites a deepening of the experience and would allow for the inclusion of the pilgrimage to Finisterre returning to Santiago via Muxía (see *Camino Finisterre*) and still provide time to integrate lessons and insights learnt along the way. Others start along one of the waymarked routes that commence further back in France (see map inside back cover) and there is now a waymarked route all the way from Budapest (via Hungary, Austria, Switzerland, France!). However, many people work within a 2-week framework and so will need 2 or 3 trips to complete the entire camino. The commencement of daily budget flights from the UK and Europe to midpoints such as Madrid, Valladolid & Santander makes access to Logroño, Burgos and León an easy option and rail and bus connections within Spain are reliable and inexpensive.

In reality we have all the time in the world, but most of us don't believe it (especially our employers, employees, partners and peers). Come back to the 'real world' is a phrase that is often heard – and where, in heaven's name, might that be? And even if we know we have all the time there is, if we are honest perhaps we are afraid to take the time to reflect on our life and its direction. I know people who have cleared the decks and opened up a whole summer for pilgrimage, only to return within days, terrified of having time to contemplate their lives and the changes that any soul-searching might prescribe. Pilgrimage, like life, is experienced on many different levels. What makes sense for one may seem strange to another. We each have our reason for going. Whatever you do, don't put off starting as it might just prove to be the major turning point in your life.

Safety: The camino offers a remarkably safe environment in an inherently unsafe world. Very few cases of unsettling behaviour are reported but it is wise to be cautious when travelling alone especially late in the evening or at night. Incidents of theft are likewise rare but picket-pockets are to be found all over the world, especially in the larger towns and cities where the disparity between rich and poor is most noticeable. *Trust in God and tether your camel* seems like sensible advice.

How to get there – *and back*: (See **map** on inside back cover for airports and ferry terminals). Note that schedules and prices are liable to change and reduced services can be expected during the winter months. **Carbon Neutral Travel:** All travel has an impact on the environment; none more so than air travel. We can, however, minimise the damaging emissions of greenhouse gases by offsetting the amount produced in what is effectively a carbon sink. <www.climatecare.org/home.aspx> will calculate the amount of emissions produced from your departure point and what you would need to contribute to offset this. A return flight London to Santiago will produce 0.33 tonnes of CO_2 *(rail reduces this by around 90%!)* but the stakes go up if you're coming from the west coast of the USA or Canada where you produce 2.04 tonnes (based on 80% seat occupancy). Carbon offsets don't solve the problem but help orientate us towards finding solutions. The key aspect here is about raising awareness – not about producing guilt trips. In these harsh economic times the cancellation of flights by airlines that haven't enough passengers booked to make the flight economic is an increasing trend. *The following schedules are liable to change at short notice – stay flexible!*

•AIR: From the UK the easiest access to St. Jean Pied de Port is to fly to **Biarritz**. Ryanair & Easyjet have a direct service from London and Flybe twice weekly from Birmingham. These schedules usually allow time to catch the airport coach (regular departures with journey time ½ hour) to Bayonne *Baion* rail station in time for the mountain rail to St. Jean. The scenic rail journey takes 1½ hours and a 5 minute walk into the town centre. Landslides can render the track impassable but in that event a bus is laid on either from Bayonne from or Cambo-Les-Bains. Alternatively consider taking a taxi direct from the airport to St. Jean, a distance of 55 km and check out any other passengers with scallop shells who might share the cost or contact Express Burricot ℂ +33 0661 960 476 a pilgrim travel company based in St. Jean who will collect. **Bordeaux** direct flights from the UK and rail and bus connections to Bayonne. **Bilbao** direct flights from the UK with Ryanair, EasyJet, Vueling, BA & Iberia with rail or bus connections to Bayonne (or Pamplona for Roncesvalles). Other access points along the camino with direct Ryanair flights from the UK include **Madrid**, **Valladolid** and **Santander** with easy onward bus or rail connections to Logroño, Burgos or León. Easyjet fly London to Oviedo (Asturias) with easy access to León. **From Ireland by Air:** Ryanair fly Dublin (+ Knock) to Biarritz also Madrid and Santander. Aer Lingus fly Dublin to Bordeaux, Bilbao or Madrid. Iberia has an extensive service to regional airports. **From USA and Canada:** Madrid or Paris offer the best onward connections.

•BUS: National Express/Eurolines London to Bordeaux depart 14:00 arrive 10.45 next day with onward travel by bus or rail. **•RAIL:** raileurope or Seat61 show daily schedule London – Bayonne (via Eurostar Paris) and TGV taking around 10½ hours (e.g. 09:12—19:46). **•FERRY:** P&O sail Portsmouth to Bilbao – journey time 36 hours. **•CAR HIRE:** It is very competitive *within* Spain and this makes a good option for onward travel especially when car sharing. However, a pick-up in one country with a drop-off in another is usually prohibitively expensive.
From the rest of Europe: There are extensive and inexpensive rail and bus connections from all parts of Europe. The budget airlines have also extended their networks within Europe – check out appropriate websites.

Returning from Santiago: Increased services by rail, bus and air have made departure from Santiago easier than previous years. Travel costs vary widely but increasing competition between national and budget airlines has helped to minimise costs. Generally the sooner you commit to going the cheaper the ticket – but staying flexible on a return date can sometimes be rewarded with a last-minute promotional fare. Galicia currently has 3 international airports at Santiago, A Corunna & Vigo.

•**AIR** *Ryanair* fly direct from Santiago to London Stansted, Frankfurt and Milan and a wide selection of cities within Spain (with possibility of onward connections). *Easyjet* fly from Santiago to London Gatwick and Geneva. *Vueling (Click Air)* fly direct to Paris and Zurich. *Air Berlin* has flights to major destinations throughout Europe from Santiago or via their hub in La Palma Majorca. *Aer Lingus* fly Santiago – Dublin (summer schedule) and *BA* and *Iberia* and other major airlines offer regular services throughout the year via connecting airports in Spain, mainly Madrid. **Note:** Direct daily rail / bus links from Santiago to Vigo, A Corunna, Porto and Lisbon airports, which widens the possibilities of return flights.

•**RAIL** Book online with Spanish rail network RENFE *www.renfe.com* or with Rail Europe *www.raileurope.co.uk* also *www.seat61.com*
•**Bus** you can book online with National Express (eurolines) for connections throughout Europe: *www.nationalexpress.com* or via Alsa *www.alsa.es/en/ (online payments via Paypal).*
•**FERRY** The advantage of sailing home is that you get a chance to acclimatise slowly: Santander & Bilbao offer regular sailings to the U.K. Check with Brittany Ferries (Portsmouth to Bilbao and Santander to Plymouth).

•**CAR HIRE** If you can find other passengers to share the cost then this is often a relatively cheap and convenient way to travel on to such places as Santander or Bilbao and flying or sailing home from there.

TRAVEL NOTES:

_____
_____
_____
_____
_____
_____
_____
_____
_____
_____
_____
_____
_____
_____
_____
_____
_____
_____
_____
_____

Pilgrim Passport *credencial* **and Protocol:** In order to stay at pilgrim hostels and to receive a *compostela* (certificate of completion of pilgrimage to Santiago) you need to provide proof that you have walked the route (at least the last 100 km from Sarria). This is done by having a pilgrim passport *credencial* impressed with a rubber stamp *sello* primarily by the wardens *hospitaleros* in the pilgrim hostels but you can also have it stamped at cathedrals, churches, hostels, bars and town halls along the way. You need 2 stamps per day from Sarria.

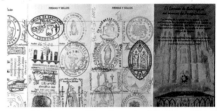

You can obtain a pilgrim passport or record before travelling from the Confraternity of St. James in London or possibly from a local Confraternity in your country of origin (see useful addresses at the back) alternatively you can obtain a *credencial* on arrival at the pilgrim office in St. Jean Pied de Port / Roncesvalles (or Sarria as a last resort). Every effort should be made to join and support the work of the Confraternities who do so much to prepare and maintain the route and its facilities. Apply in good time (an internet application may speed processing.)

Pilgrim Hostels: *hostales, refugios* or *albergues de peregrinos* are reserved exclusively for pilgrims on the camino. They are provided throughout the route at convenient 10 – 20 km intervals (frequently less, never more) and all are on, or adjacent, to the camino. This includes youth hostels *albergues juvenil* generally available to pilgrims holding a *credencial*. Accommodation is usually in bunk beds with additional overflow space on mattresses *colchonetas* on the floor *suelo*.

Bedbugs *chinches* are an increasing source of concern and any accommodation where people sleep in close proximity has added risks. Bedbugs live in mattresses etc. feeding at night, so until the accommodation is treated the problem remains. Carrying a pretreated pillowcase and bed sheet (e.g. LifeAventure 3X) can be a useful preventative measure. If affected (3 or more bites in a row is a good indication) you need to [1] immediately advise the establishment of the problem and also the next hostel(s) so that they can take preventive measures. [2] wash and/or tumble dry all clothes at highest settings for 2+ hours and [3] Seek medical attention in severe cases (Hydrocortisone). Vinegar is reported to reduce itchiness. Advice is often contradictory so seek help from those who have experience of the problem. The local chemist may be able to help.

Hostels are generally open from March (Easter) through to end of October. Some open all year (subject to holidays and maintenance) and these are indicated where known but even those listed as closed may be open and vice-versa – be prepared for the unexpected. **Winter pilgrims** check www.aprinca.com/alberguesinvierno for list. With increasing demand new hostels are opening every year and existing ones extending their season and the greater problem is finding lodging in the summer rather than the winter! Names and telephone numbers have been included for emergency use (busy wardens will not thank you for idle requests) and to aid pilgrims travelling off-season to establish whether or not a hostel ahead is open. It is generally not possible to book official pilgrim hostels in advance.

Albergues fit into one of 6 main categories – the shortened form appears on the maps Private *Priv*. *Nº of bunk beds ÷ Nº dormitories [20÷2] additional private rooms where available are marked with a plus sign +. Prices can change at short notice and are provided as a guide. Some include breakfast and this is shown as € incl.*

❶ *Mun.* **& Xunta. Municipal** hostel *albergue municipal* a basic hostel with limited facilities owned and maintained by the local authority. The warden *hospitalero/a* often lives next door (average cost €5). In this category are the Galician government hostels *Xunta. albergues Xunta de Galicia* (€6).

❷ *Par.* **Parish** hostel *albergue parroquia* these are generally owned by the local diocese and run by the parish priest. Some offer a regular pilgrim mass and they tend to be more informal and relaxed than municipal hostels with a communal meal and blessing. Generally welcoming but basic €5 often by donation *donativo*.

❸ *Conv.* **Convent or Monastery** hostel *monasterio o convento* (*mosteiro* in Gallego) *Convento* on its own is a monastery (monks) while *convento de monjas* (nuns) is a convent! The atmosphere in each is often markedly different so check the details provided (av. cost €5 or *donativo*).

❹ *Asoc.* **Association** hostels are owned and run by local Spanish or other national confraternities, sometimes in conjunction with the local authority. They tend to be particularly well equipped for the needs of the pilgrim and are generally staffed by former pilgrim volunteers (av. cost €7).

❺ *Priv.**(star) **Network** hostel *red de albergues* are private hostels that have formed themselves into a loose association. They are often owned and maintained by an individual but are increasingly being handed over to a management group engendering greater confidence in on-going availability. They have a similar sense of brotherhood/sisterhood as in confraternity hostels but often provide additional facilities such as washing/drying machines, internet access, dinner and breakfast and many have single/double rooms for higher price (bunk bed €10+).

❻ *Priv.* **Private** hostel *albergue privado* similar to the network hostels (above) but with no overall code or regulations. They tend to be more flexible (commercial realities) with a full range of facilities and more flexible opening hours (€10+) additional private rooms +, where available, from €20+.

Opening Hours: vary but are generally cleaned and ready again from around 13:00 to welcome pilgrims. Many hostels have a policy of holding places for those travelling by foot until around 18:00, cyclists not being admitted until after that time. Hostels generally close their doors and turn off lights around 22:00. The morning routine will find early birds discreetly, or noisily, leaving their beds from 05.30 with the main rush hour between 06:30 and 07:30. Most hostels close for cleaning at 08:30 when the last stragglers will be sent on their way. Any special arrangements, such as the provision of breakfast, will generally be notified on arrival but it is good practise to scan any notice boards.

Opening times for tourist offices and museums are generally from 10:00–13:00 and again after *siesta* from 16:00–19:00. Shop hours are generally a bit longer. Note that many public buildings, including churches, are **closed on Mondays**.

Warden *hospitalero/a* every hostel has at least one person whose job it is to ensure that the place is open at the appropriate time in the day and doors are locked and lights turned off at night. Resident *hospitaleros* are generally voluntary, live in the hostel itself and have probably walked the route in previous years and therefore know the needs of their fellow pilgrims. Nonresident wardens will live locally and can provide reliable local information such as where to shop, restaurants, times of Mass, etc. Non-resident wardens are generally on hand between 16:00 and 20:00 to allocate bed spaces, collect the overnight charge and to stamp *credenciales*.

Facilities and levels of cleanliness vary widely, but hot showers are now standard everywhere. Don't forget that hot showers do not mean limitless hot water. If you are last in a group early in the afternoon, the water may have run cold. Conversely if you are last in during the evening it may have heated up again! There is a welcome increase in the number of hostels now providing automatic washing machines *lavadora* rarer but often more practical is the addition of a clothes-dryer *secadora* (not to be confused with the less useful spin-dryer *centrífuga*) – it can rain for days on end and a *secadora* can make a big difference to personal comfort (note machines are sometimes out of order). Most hostels provide a kitchen with (some) basic utensils and cutlery and a lounge that often serves as the dining area.

Standards – vary greatly and constantly change so grading can often set up false expectations. However, you will find an objective note of facilities offered which includes the number of bed spaces (usually bunks) and the number of rooms. Simple division will indicate how many roommates you are likely to be sharing with – up to 110 beds in one dormitory (Roncesvalles overflow) *[110÷1]*! and down to 2 *[60÷30]* (Azofra). + sign indicates additional private rooms available.

Gratitude for mercies small and large is a trait to be developed by all genuine pilgrims. This is nowhere more apparent than in the offering and acceptance of a place for the pilgrim to lay his or her head. Tired at the end of a long day or caught out in a storm *tormenta* any port may induce a feeling of gratitude for the humblest of abodes and the most casual of welcomes – this is entirely as it should be.

The best way to establish the standard of a hostel is from the welcome you receive at the door and from comments made by fellow pilgrims in the *guest book*. There is an erroneous belief that all 'true' pilgrims must stay at the pilgrim hostels. Mediaeval pilgrims used every available bed regardless of whether or not it was an official *hospital de peregrino*. Yes, by all means stay in the recognised hostels and meet up with fellow pilgrims and share news, but don't become reliant solely on these hostels. Spread your inner and outer wealth!

Eating out: A basic pilgrim menu or *menú del dia* starts from around €9. Once you go off the set menu costs rise out of all proportion. *Tapas* (small snacks available from many bars and cafés throughout the day) or the more generous *raciones* are appetising but expensive. Vegetarians *V.* have a really hard time as Spain, which is firmly carnivorous, has little understanding of the needs of the *vegetariano/a*. Vegetable soup is often made on meat stock and don't be surprised to find ham in your potato omelette! Breakfast equates to *café* and *croissantes*. Another cultural challenge posed to northern European and North American pilgrims are meal times. Lunch *almuerzo* (or simply *comer*) is the main meal and rarely ends before 15:00 and dinner *cena* doesn't usually start before 20:00. It helps to think laterally (*tapas*), to speak clearly (*en español*) and to prepare meals of your choice and time in the hostels from provisions bought in the local shop *mercado*.

Hotels: If hostels are full **alternative accommodation** is generally available in the immediate area. These also vary in facilities offered and priced (generally per room – not per person) accordingly. The Spanish tourist board categorises all 'official' accommodation. **'r'** in each category denotes *residencial* (no dining facilities beyond breakfast). The main defining feature in cost is the number of stars awarded. The cost of accommodation also varies between seasons (add 25% during peak holidays) and regions (add 25% in cities). Some smaller hotels and hostels, particularly in rural areas, offer a pilgrim discount but ask at reception *before* booking.

Price: During off-season the price of a room can often be less than that officially displayed. At the lower end (from €15) we find simply beds *camas* and guest houses known variously as *fondas*, *hospedajes* or *hospederías* without any star category. Moving up the scale (from €20) are *pensiónes P* and *hostales Hs* with one or more stars and the smaller rural *hoteles H* and hostals *Hs.* In the middle bracket (from €35) are up-market B&B's usually presented at a high standard and known variously as rural houses *casa rural CR*, rural tourism *turismo rural TR* or agricultural tourism *agrícola turismo AT. Then come the hotels from 1 star in rural areas H° (€25+) up to 5 stars H***** in the city (€100+).*

Costs: allow a basic €25 a day to include €5 for overnight stay at a basic municipal hostel and the remainder for food and drink. Some hostels provide a communal supper (dependent on the warden *hospitalero*) for a small contribution and many have a basic kitchen where a simple meal can be prepared and shared. Alternatively most locations have a restaurant serving a *menú del peregrino* for a fixed price of around €9 for 3 courses including wine. If you want to indulge in the gastronomy of Spain and sample its finer wines then expect to double this basic cost. A few parish hostels still use a donation basis with the underlying philosophy: *leave us what you can and if that is only your prayers that will be sufficient.* We must be careful not to abuse this trust in our individual circumstances – unless you are a genuine mendicant, plan to leave at least 5 euros towards basic costs of a bed. Private hostels average around €10–€15 per night but often provide additional facilities such as internet access, washing / drying machines and dining facilities (supper and breakfast at extra cost).

Payment: all pilgrim hostels, most small pensions, rural B&B's *casa rurales* and local shops operate on a **cash only basis**. That being said, even the smallest town and many of the villages have automatic cash dispensing machines *cajeros automáticos* that accept most international bank debit or credit cards. Traveller's cheques are difficult to exchange and also rely on inconvenient bank opening hours. Consider settling your bill the night before if you plan an early departure and check that doors will be open!

Respecting nature: Please don't leave waste behind you. Orange peel can take 20 years to decompose; plastic bottles 500! Collect some rubbish along the way each day with the intention of leaving the path *better* than you found it. If a sense of superiority arises, visualise yourself cleaning up the mess that you left behind at other times in your life when you were, perhaps, less aware. Pilgrims are not hikers *per se* and many will not be familiar with the country code. Human waste is a particular problem so check out café stops for toilet breaks and discipline your bowels. Don't dump on the path! Re-use tissues where possible and dispose responsibly later. It only takes a few unaware pilgrims to create the problem... and only a small band of conscientious ones to inform and  help alleviate it. You might also like to try a psychic cleansing after experiencing any negativity in your own thoughts or in any interaction that you witness en route that is unloving. Simply shake out the negativity from your mind and invite loving thoughts to replace them. These simple practises will help to keep both the physical and psychic environments clean and unpolluted.

Respecting fellow pilgrims: facilities such as showers and kitchens have a limited supply of hot water and utensils and these, especially during the summer months, can be stretched. Be aware of your own needs but also of the needs of others and try and find a balance that feels right. If you have arrived early and bagged the best bed keep an eye on who comes in later – if you are on a bottom bunk and someone arrives late with a damaged knee you could move to a top bunk. Observe your reactions but don't judge yourself. There is already enough guilt in the world to engulf it and we certainly don't need more! Awareness is the starting point for change.

Preparation – *Outer*:

Physical – what shape is the body in? Any reasonably fit person can accomplish this journey without undue stress. I walked from Seville to Santiago (1,000+ km) with a Japanese grandfather who celebrated his 80th birthday en route, 94 is the oldest I have met! However, if you have recently had an illness or are otherwise concerned about your state of health then go and have a medical check up. It generally takes the body a week to adjust fully to the regular walking with full backpack. Give body, mind and soul time to acclimatise. Don't push yourself at the beginning – remember that most injuries, such as strained tendons and blisters occur in the early days.

It is always advisable to put in some physical training before you go. I would be surprised if more than 10% of pilgrims actually act on this advice. If you are one of the 90% who haven't then *please* heed the advice to take the first week slowly. I know many pilgrims who have had to deal with the mental, let alone physical, anguish of having to pull out of the pilgrimage because they did too much in the early days. Lightweight walking poles, if used properly, can greatly reduce wear and tear on the body. If you don't have a pair (one in each hand creates better balance and is twice as effective) consider buying a set. They are likely to prove a good investment for this walk – and future ones!

A related matter is the weight you carry, both your backpack and body weight. If you are 2 stone overweight and are going to be carrying an additional 2 stone on your back, the resultant stress factor is likely to show up in cracks, literally, in the body (1 stone = 14 pounds = 6.4 kilograms). While you will inevitably lose weight on the journey, try and reduce before you start out. Pilgrimage is a great metaphor for life. What are you carrying that is not really necessary?

"From contentment with little comes happiness." African proverb.

Equipment and Clothing: *Think quality not quantity*

Your pilgrimage starts at the planning stage. So start by invoking the highest intention for your journey and bring awareness to what you buy. There is so much exploitation of human and natural resources supported by our unconscious consumerism. Become informed and use your voice and money to support those companies who genuinely try to make a positive difference in the world. To walk a pilgrim path for peace in gear produced from exploitative business practises or oppressive regimes is not congruent – we must make very effort to *walk our talk.*

What to bring? You will bring too much; everyone does! Be prepared to give away, leave behind or post back items you don't need and notice which option you choose, why and at what stage of the journey. Aim to carry no more than 10% of body weight with an ***upper limit of 10 Kilos (22 lbs)***. Whatever you carry your knees and feet will absorb most of the shock and will be the first to buckle if you carry more than essentials. Buy materials that are essentially: (a) lightweight and non-bulky (b) that wick away moisture from your skin (c) are easy to wash and quick to dry.

Essential equipment from the feet up includes:

walking shoes / boots: should provide good ankle support, be breathable, lightweight and yet have strong soles for the rough ground you will encounter. Heavyweight boots are not necessary but consider trail shoes with waterproof lining if travelling in the winter season. **Sandals** or lightweight shoe for use in the evening and to give your walking shoes time to dry out and have a chance to breathe.

socks: bring several pairs as it is a good idea to change socks and massage your feet half-way through the day (even if you don't think they need it).

trousers, skirts and shorts: for most of the year shorts are ideal and your legs will dry out much more quickly than fabric if you walk into a rain shower. Rural Spain remains very traditional – a sarong is ideal for women to wrap around bare legs when visiting churches, etc., and also cool and easy to wash and dry.

fleece: a lightweight fleece is useful – you will need to increase the thickness the closer into winter that you plan to travel. If you intend travelling in mid-winter you will need proper thermal clothing and a sleeping bag for the subzero temperatures that you may encounter, particularly on the higher ground where you can expect snow and ice.

waterproofs: even allowing for obvious seasonal changes the weather in northern Spain, particularly in Galicia, is notoriously unpredictable (see Weather). There are many lightweight rain and wind-proof jackets and trousers, Paclite® by Berghaus are ideal, but expensive. A cheaper option is a plastic poncho that covers not only the body but the backpack as well. This can be rolled out during rain showers and the loose fitting nature of the poncho means you don't get *too* much build up of sweat as with most tight-fitting plastic or nylon garments. A popular model is the Altus available from www.barrabes.com or pilgrim shops en route.

hat: in the summer months your main consideration will be protection from the sun. Wear a wide brim hat to protect your head and neck and any other exposed areas. Sunstroke can be painful and, in extreme cases, dangerous.

rucksack: 50 litres should be ample, avoid a large capacity rucksack (70 +litres) as you may be tempted to fill it with unnecessary items. An essential element is the waist strap that must allow you to adjust and carry the weight on your hips – *never* off your shoulder. You will need dry bags (not plastic bags which can actually pool water!) to ensure dry kit at the end of a wet day. If you are not using a poncho then a backpack cover is also recommended for heavy downpours.

sleeping bag: essential for all pilgrim hostels. If you are travelling in the summer months a lightweight 1 or 2 season bag will suffice (or just a sheet bag). A zip will allow you to open it up in very hot conditions. Most hostels, especially in the mountain areas, have blankets.

first aid: All hostels are obliged to carry first aid boxes and there are innumerable chemists *farmacia* along the way. However, some essentials should be carried with you. While prevention is better than cure, unless you are well seasoned you will get blisters! Each to their own, but *Compeed*® is readily available, easy to apply and acts as a second skin. Whatever you bring apply it as soon as you feel a hot spot developing (don't wait until it has developed into a full blister). Many make the mistake of loosening shoes to relieve the pressure but this can aggravate the friction – the cause of the problem in the first place. Make sure your footwear fits snugly.

Other essentials are plasters and antiseptic ointment for cuts and pain relief tablets such as Paracetamol for toothache etc. and Ibuprofen for relief of muscular pain. Bring a high factor sun protection and apply regularly or, alternatively, try Calypso or P_{20}® by Riemann which binds to the skin and only needs to be applied once each day. You will also need lip protection and after sun lotion. Be sure to bring an adequate supply of any prescribed medication, e.g. inhalers for asthmatics, as these may be difficult to obtain en route without prescription. Elasticised tubing can help support a sprained knee or ankle.

For the **homeopathically** inclined, essentials might include: Arnica for muscular sprains and bruising, Calendula for cuts and Combudoron for insect bites. For those using chemically based products, bring equivalent treatments.

toiletries: Apart from the usual take a small scissors with needle and thread for draining blisters and essential repairs.

water container: many people prefer carrying two ½ litre bottles rather than a bulkier 1 litre that can be harder to pack and unpack. **Water is essential** and evidence supports the view that a minimum 2 litres a day can significantly reduce fatigue, blisters and other common ailments of long distance walking as well as avoiding dehydration. There are drinking fonts *fuente [F.]* all  along the way – fill up at every opportunity especially in high summer when drinking fonts can dry up. Non-tap water is often OK to drink but not guaranteed *sin garantia* – check with locals if in doubt. You may notice a difference between the quality of water around the main cities with their chemical additives, so empty and refill from the purer waters of the mountains and rural villages whenever possible.

Optional Extras:

walking poles: while not essential, they are highly recommended and will greatly reduce the impact on your body, around 25% if used properly, e.g. taking the strain on the strap, don't clutch with your fingers (use blister pads if necessary). They will steady you over rough patches and may create confidence when passing barking dogs. Take two to avoid becoming lopsided and try and get ones with the handles angled to avoid wrist strain. Most pilgrims opt for a wooden staff collected along the way and that is certainly better than nothing.

sleeping mat: useful if you want the freedom of experiencing life under the stars or if you are travelling in the busy season as it allows you more options – there will always be a floor somewhere! *Therm-a-Rest®* is the most comfortable but is heavier and more expensive than a basic foam-style mat.

cooking utensils: many hostels have basic kitchen equipment and creating a meal is a great way to bond with other pilgrims. If you intend cooking regularly it is advisable to bring your own utensils. A small plastic container with lid will make it easier to carry soft fruit (such as tomatoes) and sandwiches made from leftovers.

camping equipment: there is no need to carry a tent; however, if you enjoy and are experienced in the outdoors you will know what to bring. Campsites en route are few and far between and few hostels have facilities for tents.

books: be *very* selective as books add enormously to weight and you'll be surprised how little time you have for reading. Try bringing something inspirational and uplifting that you can read over again such as a compendium of your favourite poems. Historical notes and more detailed information on the many artistic treasures to be found along the way are often issued free of charge from tourist offices or as part of the price of an entry ticket.

camera: a *compact* camera may allow you to share some of your experiences with friends and family on your return. But don't forget that you can't photograph an *inner* experience, so don't set up a disappointment for yourself! A well-known travel author, writing in *The Times* states, *Photographing local people is selfish. It takes much and gives little.* The camera not only creates a physical barrier but also insulates the photographer from the reality of the experience. I have taken several thousand slides for this guidebook and regret any offence I may have caused – but perhaps they will suffice for your purposes also.

binoculars: a *compact* set will enable you to pick out the detail of some of the many fine monuments and buildings along the way. It might also help to identify alternative paths and help pick out directional signs, etc. I would prefer to take a pair of binoculars to a camera, but better still:

monocular: weighs less than half that of a pair of binoculars. It is easy to use, won't go out of focus and fits easily into a pocket. It might be a compromise for leaving behind the camera and binoculars.

mobile phone: consider leaving it behind – your experience, and that of your fellow pilgrims, will be enhanced by so doing. Break the dependence. If you feel the need to travel with a phone consider only turning it on at the end of the day or only when in cafes etc. Don't 'walk and talk' or you will miss the bird song... and much else.

A checklist with Spanish translations is provided on the next page to help strengthen your vocabulary and assist you to buy or replace items along the way. This is not necessarily a recommended list, as this will vary through the seasons. Highlight your essential items and then tick them off as you put them into your backpack.

Clothes:	***Ropas:***
hat (sun)	*sombrero*
sunglasses	*gafas de sol*
shirt(s)	*camisa(s)*
T-shirt(s)	*camiseta(s)*
travel vest	*chaqueta de viaje*
jacket –	*chaqueta –*
waterproof	*chubasquera*
breathable	*transpirable*
underpants	*calzoncillos*
shorts	*pantalones cortos*
trousers	*pantalones largos*
handkerchief	*pañuelo*
socks	*calcetines*

Shoes:	***Zapatos:***
boots (mountain)	*botas (de montaña)*
shoes (walking)	*zapatos (de andar)*
sandals (leather)	*sandalias (piel)*

Size:	***Tamaño:***
larger	*mas grande*
smaller	*mas pequeño*
cheaper	*mas barato*
more expensive	*mas caro*
model	*modelo*

Essential documents	***Documentos esenciales:***
passport	*pasaporte*
pilgrim record	*credencial de peregrino*
wallet / purse	*monedero / cartera*
cash	*dinero en efectivo*
credit card	*tarjeta de crédito*
travel tickets	*pasaje de viaje*
diary	*diario*
emergency addresses	*dirección de emergencia*
phone numbers	*números de teléfono*

Backpack	***Mochila***
rain cover	*protección de mochila*
sleeping bag	*saco de dormir*
towel	*toalla*
water bottle	*botella de agua*
penknife	*navaja*

Toiletries:	***Artículos de tocador:***
soap	*jabón*
shampoo	*champú*

tooth brush	*cepillo de dientes*
toothpaste	*dentífrico*
hair brush	*cepillo de pelo*
comb	*peine*
sink stopper	*tapón de fregadero*
shaving cream	*espuma de afeitar*
razor (blades)	*maquinilla de afeitar*
face cloth	*guante de aseo*
sun cream (lotion)	*crema solar (loción)*
after sun cream	*leche solar (after sun)*
moisturiser	*crema hidratante*
toilet paper	*papel higiénico*
tissues	*pañuelos de papel*
sanitary pads	*salva-slips*
tampons	*tampones*

First Aid Kit: *Botiquín*

painkiller	*analgésico*
aspirin / paracetemol	*aspirina / paracetamol*
plasters	*esparadrapo*
blister pads	*apósito para ampollas*
compeed-*second skin*	*compeed-segunda piel*
antiseptic cream	*crema antiséptica*
muscular ache (ointment)	*(pomada) dolores musculares*
homeopathic remedies	*remedios homeopáticos*

Medicine (prescription):   *Medicina (prescripción):*

asthma inhaler	*inhalador para el asma*
hay fever tablets	*medicina para las alergias*
diarrhoea pills	*pastillas para la diarrea*
other (doctor)	*otros (médico)*

Accessories: (optional)   *Accesorios: (opcional)*

walking poles	*bastones de caminar*
pilgrim shell	*concha de peregrino*
monocular	*catalejo*
binocular	*prismáticos*
camera	*cámara*
torch	*linterna*
wrist watch	*reloj de pulsera*
alarm clock	*despertador*
poncho	*poncho*
sleeping mat	*esterilla*
clothes pegs	*pinzas para la ropa*
clothes line (cord)	*cuerda para tender ropa*
earplugs (against snoring)	*tapones para los oídos (ronquidos)*
cutlery	*cubiertos*
knife	*cuchillo*
fork	*tenedor*
spoon	*cuchara*
mug / cup	*taza / vaso*

Language *Lenguaje:*

The Spanish are proud of their national identity and language, particularly in rural areas. It is a matter of extreme discourtesy to assume that everyone will automatically speak English. To walk into a shop or to stop and ask directions in anything other than the native language of the area you are travelling through is clearly insensitive. It behoves pilgrims to have at least a few basic phrases and to make the time to learn and use them. English is *not* widely spoken in the countryside. Ideally get a language CD a month or two *before* you travel and spend a few minutes each day practising this lovely lyrical language – the third most widely spoken in the world. Be sure to take a small dictionary and phrase book with you. Below you will find some basic pilgrim words and phrases that may not be included in a general phrase book.

As all place names and directions will, of course, be in Spanish (or Galego when in Galicia) all maps have been prepared accordingly. Some common phrases and words have also been scattered around the text as a reminder that you are a guest in someone else's country. For the real novice, I have included words that have a similar resonance between English and Spanish. This should enable you to more readily bring to mind the required word, even if it isn't exactly *exactamente* the word that a professional translator might have used. An example is vigilance! with the Spanish counterpart ¡*Vigilancia*! One might more properly use the word danger *peligroso* but this bears no resemblance to the English word at all. For those of you who are *elocuente*, please *omitir* the following *sección*! Spanish is placed in italics immediately following the English word or phrase. You will make progress if you follow these fundamental conventions *convenciónes fundamentales*:

Nouns are gender specific. words ending in *e* are (generally) masculine and those in *a* feminine. Plural (generally) add *s* or *es* at end of the word *el* or *la, los* or *las*; the man *el hombre,* the men *los hombres,* the woman *la señora,* the women *las señoras.* **Vowels** are always articulated; **a** pronounced (pron:) as in far; **i** as in deed; **e** as in bed; **o** as in obey; **u** as in food. **Emphasis** is on the penultimate syllable Melide, pron: Meh-**lee**-deh; unless denoted with an accent; Nájera, pron: **Ná**-kher-a, *not* Ná-**kher**-a.

Consonants are similar to English excepting: 'c' pron: th as in then. Centre *centro* pron: **then**-*tro* – 'd' at the end of a word is pron: th as in path. You *usted,* pron: *oo*-**steth**. Note here the emphasis is on the last syllable, an exception to the rule! – 'g' and 'j' have a guttural kh sound similar to a Scottish loch: urgent *urgente* pron: er-**khen**-*tay* or garden *jardín* pron: *khar*-**deen** (note emphasis on last syllable because it has an accent) – 'h' is always silent. Hotels *hoteles* pron: oh-**tel**-*es*. –'ll' is pronounced with a lyeh sound / full *lleno* pron: *lyeh-no*. –'ñ' is pron: as in onion / tomorrow *mañana* pron: *man*-**yahn**-*ah*. –'qu' is pron: as in k for key / fifteen *quince* pron: **keen**-*thay*. –'v' falls between v and soft b sound / journey *viaje* pron: *bhee-a-khay*. 'X' in Galego as 'sh' / Xunta pron: Shunta. 'Z' as in 'th' / Zumo pron: thoomo.

Verbs are more complex but follow 3 basic forms: [1] those ending in **-ar** as in *habl**ar*** to speak. I speak ***hablo***, you speak ***hablas***, he/she speaks ***habla***, we speak ***hablamos***, you all speak ***habláis,*** they speak ***hablan***. [2] those ending in **-er** as in *comer* to eat. I eat ***como***, you eat ***comes***, he/she eats ***come***, we eat ***comemos***, you all eat ***coméis***, they eat ***comen***. [3] those ending in **-ir** as in *vivir* to live. I live ***vivo***, you live ***vives***, he/she lives ***vive***, we live ***vivimos***, you all live ***vivís***, they live ***vivan***. Use the irregular verb 'to go' for the future tense. I am going to mass tomorrow *Voy a misa mañana*. We are going to León *Vamos a León*.

Basic Phrases: so here are a few simple phrases to get you going. A new language can't be learnt in a day; but it is really important that you *try* whenever the opportunity arises – everyone loves a trier.

Greetings / *Saludos*

Yes / *Sí*	No / *No*
Please / *Por favor*	Thanks / *Gracias*

How are things? / *Qué tal?*   Have a good trip / *Buen viaje*
Hello! How are you? / *Hola! Cómo está?*
Good day / evening / night   *Buenos días / Buenas tardes / noches*
What a splendid day / *Qué día mas espléndido!*
Goodbye! Until later / *¡Adiós! Hasta luego*

Welcome / *Bienvenida*

What's your name? / *¿Cómo se llama?*	My name is ... / *Me llamo ...*
Where do you live? / *¿Dónde vives?*	I live in London / *Vivo en Londres*
Are you English? / *Es usted Inglés?*	I'm Irish / *Soy Irlandes(a)*
I'm single / *Estoy soltero(a)*	I'm married / *Estoy casado(a)*
I have 2 sons / *Tengo dos hijos(as)*	I have no children / *No tengo hijos*

I'm here on (pilgrimage) / *Estoy aquí de peregrinación*

Excuse me! / *¡Disculpe!*   Pardon? / *¿Perdone?*

What did you say / *¿Cómo dice?*	It's not important / *No importa*
Do you understand? / *¿Entiende?*	I don't understand! / *¡No entiendo!*

I speak very little Spanish / *Hablo muy poco español*
Do you speak English? / *¿Habla usted Inglés?*
How do you pronounce that? / *¿Cómo se pronuncia eso?*
Please write it down. / *Escríbamelo, por favor*
What does this mean? / *¿Qué significa esto?*

Where is it? / *¿Dónde está?*

Here / *Aquí*	There / *Allí*
On the left / *a la izquierda*	On the right / *a la derecha*
Outside the bank / *Fuera del banco*	Beside the cafe / *Al lado del café*
Near the centre / *Cerca del centro*	Opposite the market / *Enfrente del mercado*

Where are you going? / *¿A dónde vas?*
Where is the pilgrim hostel / *¿Dónde está el albergue de peregrinos?*
Where are the toilets / *¿Dónde están los servicios?*
Where can I change some money? / *¿Dónde se puede cambiar dinero?*
Where do I get the taxi to the airport? / *¿Dónde se coge el taxi al aeropuerto?*
How do I get to the centre of León? / *¿Cómo se va al centro de León?*

What time is it? / *¿Qué hora es?*

It's midday / *Es mediodía*	Five past one / *Es la una y cinco*
Ten past two / *Son los dos y diez*	Half past three / *Son las tres y media*
Quarter past five / *Son los cinco y cuarto*	Twenty to five / *cinco menos veinte*
Quarter to six / *seis menos cuarto*	Five to seven / *siete menos cinco*
Today / *Hoy*	Yesterday / *Ayer*
Tomorrow / *Mañana*	Day after tomorrow / *Pasado mañana*
Last week / *la semana pasada*	This month / *este mes*
Next year / *al año que viene*	Every year / *todos los años*

What day is it today? / *¿Qué día es hoy?*
Lunes / Martes / Miércoles / Jueves / Viernes / Sábado / Domingo
What is today's date? / *¿Qué fecha es hoy?*
It's April 10th / *Estamos a diez de abril*
Saturday, September 25th / *sábado, veinte cinco de septiembre*

spring / *primavera*	**summer / *verano***
autumn / *otoño*	winter / *invierno*

enero / febrero / marzo / abril / mayo / junio / julio / agosto / septiembre / octubre / noviembre / diciembre

Room / *Habitación*

Do you have any vacancies? / *¿Tienen alguna habitación libre?*
I'd like a room for one night / *Quería una habitación para una noche*
There's a problem with the room / *La habitación tiene un problema*
It's too hot (cold) / *Hace demasiado calor (frío)*
There is no hot water / *No hay agua caliente*
Where can I wash my clothes / *¿Dónde puedo lavar mi ropa?*

Doctor / *Médico*	**Dentist / *Dentista***

I need a dentist (doctor) / *Necesito un dentista (medico)*
Where is the health centre? / *¿Dónde está el centro de salud?*
I have blisters / *Tengo ampollas*
I have a tendinitis / *Tengo tendinitis*
My leg/knee/foot/toe...hurts / *Mi pierna/rodillo/pie/dedo del pie...me duele*
My ankle is swollen / *Mi tobillo está hinchado*
My lower back is in spasm / *Mi espalda tiene una contractura*
Where is the pharmacy? / *¿Dónde está la farmacia?*

Food / *Comida*	**Menu / *Menú***
breakfast / *desayuno*	lunch / *la comida*
savoury snack / *tapas*	dinner / *cena*
meat / *carne*	**fish / *pescado***
beef steak / *bistec*	trout / *trucha*
fillet steak / *filete*	salmon / *salmón*
pork / *cerdo*	sole / *lenguado*
lamb / *cordero*	hake / *merluza*
veal / *ternera*	prawns / *gambas*
chops / *chuletas*	squid / *calamares*
ham / *jamón*	mussels / *mejillones*
chicken / *pollo*	seafood / *mariscos*
vegetables / *verduras*	**(tomato) salad / *ensalada (de tomate)***
desert / *postre*	fruit / *fruta*
sandwich / *bocadillo*	cheese / *queso*
I am hungry / *Tengo hambre*	I am thirsty / *Tengo sed*

red wine / *vino tinto*	**white wine / *vino blanco***
water / *agua*	milk / *leche*

What time is dinner (breakfast) / *¿A qué hora es la cena (el desayuno)?*
Is there a vegetarian restaurant? / *¿Hay un restaurante vegetariano?*
What's today's special / *¿Cuál es el plato del día?*
Do you have a menu in English / *¿Tiene un menú en Inglés?*
This food is cold (too hot) / *La comida está fría (demesiado caliente)*

Train / *Tren*   **Bus / *Autobús***

Have you a timetable? / *¿Tienen un horario?*
What time do we get to León? / *¿A qué hora llegamos a León?*
How much is a single (return) ticket? /*¿Cuánto cuesta un billete de ida (y vuelta)*
I want to cancel my reservation / *Quería anular mi reserva*
When does the museum open? / *¿Cuándo abre el museo?*
When does the bus arrive at Arcos? / *¿Cuándo llega el autobús a Arcos?*
When is the next train to Bilbao? / *¿Cuándo sale el próximo tren para Bilbao?*

Shoes / *Zapatos*   **Size / *Talla***
I take size 8 / *Calzo el cuarenta*
footwear / *calzado*   shoelace / *el cordón*
shoemaker / *zapatero*   shoeshop / *zapatería*

Clothes / *Ropa*   **Size / *Talla***
I take size 40 / *Mi talla es la 40*
Have you a bigger (smaller) size? /   *Tiene una talla mas mayor (menor)*
big / *grande*   small / *pequeño(a)*
(See under check list for other items)

Books: (limited)   ***Libros: (cupo lim.)***
spiritual texts   *textos espirituales*
inspirational quotations   *citas inspiradoras*
poetry   *poesía*
phrase book –   *libro de frases –*
  Spanish   *Español*
  French   *Francés*
post office / *Correos*   Stamps / *Sellos*

Map / *Mapa*   **Plan / *Plano***
option / *opción*   crossing / *cruce*
castle / *castillo*   church / *iglesia*
chapel / *ermita*   cathedral / *catedral*
wayside cross / *cruceiro*   drinking font / *fuente*
bridge / *puente*   rise or height / *alto*
park / *parque*   town square / *la plaza de la ciudad*
town centre / *centro de ciudad*   ruins / *ruinas*
river / *río*   street / *calle* (written c/)
sun rise /*salida del sol*   sun set / *puesta del sol*
waymarking / *indicador*   yellow arrow / *flecha amarilla*

_____
_____
_____
_____
_____
_____
_____
_____
_____
_____
_____
_____

The Camino – Past, Present & Future

The Past – *The Changing Course of History*

•**Pleistocene Age c. 1,000,000 B.C.**

The earliest human remains ever discovered in Europe are to be found on a small hill directly on the camino (see stage 12 – Atapuerca). So we follow in the footsteps of our ancestors who have been accorded the scientific name *Homo Antecessor* and dated to over 900,000 years B.C. In recognition of the unique part Atapuerca plays in our understanding of the way of life of the first human communities the site was accorded World Heritage status by UNESCO in 1998.

•**Late Palaeolithic period c. 10,000 B.C.**

During this period we see the arrival of hunter-gatherer clans *Homo sapiens* from central Europe. They settled along the north-western fringes of Spain in the Cantabrian Mountains where we can still find some of the best examples of their rock art in the cave dwellings at Altamira. These have been described as the 'Sistine Chapel of the Paleolithic period' and led the site to be added to the UNESCO World Heritage list in 1985. (The caves are situated 30 km west of Santander.)

•**Megalithic period c. 4000 B.C.**

This period is best known for the building of great *mega* stone structures sometimes referred to as Dolmens or Mamoas. They are the early 'cathedrals' of our ancestors and were aligned to the winter solstice sun and connected to sun worship. Some of the best examples can be found along the *camino* in Galicia. This megalithic culture was deeply religious and left a powerful impact on the peoples who followed.

•**Early Celtic period c. 1,000 B.C.**

Central European Celts settled in north-western Spain and Portugal, inter-marrying with the Iberians and giving rise to the Celtiberian tribes. Remains of their Celtic villages *Castros* can be seen dotted around the remote countryside, especially in Galicia, but examples also exist along other parts of the camino. These fortified villages were built in a circular formation usually occupying some elevated ground or hillock. The extensive mineral deposits of this area gave rise to a rich artistic movement and bronze and gold artefacts of this period grace many museums.

•**Early Roman period c. 200 B.C.**

The Roman occupation of the Iberian peninsular began around the 2nd century B.C. The Romans were attracted by the rich mining potential of the area. Decimus Junius Brutus was the first Roman general to break the fierce resistance of the Celtiberian tribe known as the Lusitani who occupied the area around the Miño valley. Brutus fought his way to the end of the world *finis terrae*, a place of immense spiritual significance at that time.

•Early Christian Period c. 40 A. D.

While there may be no historical evidence to support the contention that St. James preached in Galicia, there is some anecdotal testimony to that effect. It appears that some years after Christ's crucifixion St. James sailed to Galicia (probably Padrón and Finisterre) and commenced his ministry amongst the pagan population there. It is reasonable to assume that he and his followers would have known about the importance of Finisterre as one of the foremost places of Druidic ritual and initiation. It was common practice for the early Christian church to seek out such sites on which to graft its own message. It appears that St. James' mission met with only limited success and he returned to Jerusalem where he was summarily beheaded by Herod in 42 A. D. Following his martyrdom, St. James disciples brought his body back via Padrón in order to be buried at World's End *Finis Terre*. The legendary Queen Lupa conspired with the Roman Legate based at Dugium (present day Duyo in Finisterre) to destroy St. James's body and that of his disciples (see *A Pilgrim's Guide to the Camino Finisterre*). In a story reminiscent of the Biblical Red Sea flight into freedom, they managed to escape over the river Tambre with the bridge collapsing just after they had passed over. Libredon (now Santiago) was not far away and it was here they finally laid St. James body to rest. This period marks the beginning of the San Tiago story in Spain but the mists of time grew over these remarkable events, until they finally disappeared from collective memory. This period and place also saw the martyrdom of the Gnostic master Prescillian who lived in Galicia and some legends suggest he was buried in Libredon.

•The Middle Ages c. 476 – 1453

The decline and fall of the **Roman Empire in Spain** was hastened by the barbarian invasions and the arrival first of the Franks and Suevi tribes and then the Visigoths from Gaul, although their chaotic influence was felt most acutely in Toledo. Incessant internal squabbles resulted in one faction seeking support from the Muslims based in Morocco, who duly obliged, arriving in rather larger numbers than anticipated! Islam had spread at breathtaking speed across northern Africa and less than 80 years after Muhammad's death in Medina in 632 the Moorish conquest of the southern Iberian peninsular, spearheaded by Tariq of Tangier in 711, was virtually complete.

The relatively benign rule of the Moors (the name given to the Arab and Berber settlers from Morocco) appears to have been much more favourable than life under the Visigoths. The latter had initiated the first expulsion of Jews from the peninsula while the Moors allowed complete freedom of religious and artistic expression. Indeed the *western Islamic empire*, centred at Córdoba, was amongst the most tolerant and enlightened administrations to be found anywhere in the known world at that time. *Mozarabic* was the name given to freely practising Christians under Moorish rule and this period saw a great flowering of the sciences, art and architecture in Spain. Some of the finest example of the Mozarabic style (Christian churches built using the typical Moorish horseshoe arch) can be seen at San Miguel de Escalada near León and at Santo Tomás de las Ollas in Ponferrada.

While this period was not without resistance to Muslim domination, alarm bells began to ring when they advanced northwards and in 778 Charles the Great *Charlemagne* crossed the Pyrenees to stop their advance at Zaragoza and greatly upset the volatile Basques by breaching the walls of Pamplona on his return (having given assurances that the town would not be damaged) setting in motion the famous battle of Roncesvalles and the defeat of the rear-guard of the army under the command of his 'nephew' Roland. This in turn spawned the epic poem of chivalry *La Chanson de Roland*. The story of El Cid a century later has a similar chivalric vein (see under Burgos).

The Santiago story re-emerges in 813 when a shepherd named Pelayo was drawn to a field in Libredon by a 'bright light' or star. Thus from Latin we have, the field *compus* of the stars *stellae* of Saint James *Sant Iago*, which gives us *Santiago de Compostela*. Other accounts suggest the name comes from the Latin for burial *componere,* as there was evidence of a Roman cemetery on this spot built over earlier Celtic remains. Either way, the Bishop of Iria Flavia (Padrón) *Theodomirus* seized the moment and 'confirmed' the discovery of the tomb of the Apostle and so the story of St. James was resurrected in perfect timing to spearhead the re-conquest *reconquista* of Spain for Christianity, starting with the mythical battle of Clavijo in 844 to the decisive victory at Las Navas de Tolosa in 1212 and each time St. James appeared at the crucial moment to turn the tide of battle.

Thus we have the image of St. James the Moor-slayer **Santiago Matamoros**, depicted as the knight in shining armour astride a white charger decapitating Moors with his sword (as opposed to the gentler image of the pilgrim saint –see below). Following these military successes, St. James became patron saint of Spain, a position that he enjoys to this day. The first written record of pilgrimage to Santiago also belongs to this period when Bishop Gotescalco journeyed here in 950 and in 1072 Alfonso VI abolished tolls for all pilgrims travelling up into Galicia through Val Carce.

Between the 12th and 14th centuries Santiago de Compostela grew in importance and prestige, at times even eclipsing the pilgrim routes to Rome and essentially taking over from the pilgrimages to Jerusalem once the crusades had collapsed and the Holy Land was lost to the Christian cause and no longer accessible. It is remarkable that tens of thousands of pilgrims chose to suffer the hazards of this route every year during the Middle Ages. A combination of the relative accessibility of the route and the miracles associated with the relics of the Saint beneath the magnificent cathedral were certainly contributing factors in its popularity. The *Camino de Santiago* was now firmly established and from this period we see the gentler image of St. James the Pilgrim **Santiago Peregrino** portrayed all along the route with staff, bible, wide brim hat to keep off the sun and scallop shell *concha*. The *concha* survives as the single identifying symbol of the pilgrim to Santiago, hence the term *concheiros* to distinguish them from *romeros* and *palmeros* which were applied to pilgrims going to Rome and Jerusalem respectively. One of the great exponents of the camino in the 12th century was Pope Calixtus II who instigated the privileges of the Compostelan Holy Years. It was at this time that the French priest Aymeric Picaud from Parthenay-le-Vieux near Poitou travelled the pilgrim road. He recorded his experiences in detail in 5 volumes that became known as the **Codex Calixtinus** in honour of the incumbent Pope. Book 5 is known as the Book of St. James *Liber Sancti Jacobi* and is essentially the first travel guide to the camino dividing it into 13 stages commencing at Saint-Michel by St. Jean Pied de Port.

The increasing activity gave rise to many religious and chivalrous orders dedicated to the protection of the pilgrim and the furtherance of the aim of the Crusades to re-establish Christianity now diverted away from the Holy Land and specifically towards Spain. While there has been extensive research into the Camino de Santiago and the background events that helped to shape the physical route we walk today, its esoteric heritage is less well documented. For many, the Knights Templar with their links to the contemporary Western mystery tradition became a corner stone in this 'hidden' heritage of the camino. Their secret initiation rites and Gnostic (as opposed to literalist) interpretations of biblical events coupled with their rising influence throughout the Western world, became a threat to the power base of the Papacy and the Catholic Monarchies and led to their eventual downfall. Pope Clement V and King

Philip IV of France joined forces and on Friday 13th October 1314, **Jacques de Molay**, the Grand Master of the Order, and the majority of the Knights Templar were arrested and many subsequently put to death. The legacy of this massacre lives on in our collective folk memory as the reason why Friday 13th is considered unlucky. With the demise of the Knights Templar there disappeared one of the original protectors of both the outer pilgrim pathway and its inner mysteries. One of the best preserved Templar castles lies directly on the camino at Ponferrada (see photo).

Much of the property and commanderies of the Knights Templar along the camino were transferred to the **Hospitallers of St. John** who already had a strong presence in Spain. This illustrious order influenced the development of many of the towns and cities we travel through today, such as Pamplona, Burgos, León, Santiago, not to mention the many villages and hamlets that maintained pilgrim *hospitals* to house and protect the pilgrims that travelled this route and the many other caminos that snaked their way across Spain to Santiago. In this way the caminos provided a framework for the re-emergence of Catholicism throughout Spain.

•The Catholic Monarchs 1479 – 1808

Spain's 'Golden Age' sprang from the union of Isabel I of Castile and Fernando V of Aragón. Isabel *la Católica* is widely regarded as the most influential ruler in Spanish history. She oversaw the *reconquista* and the collapse of Islam and Moorish rule in Iberia. More notoriously, Isabel instigated the Inquisition and ruthlessly stamped out all 'heretical' sects, expelling the Jews from Spain in the process. She then set about financing and promoting the 'discovery' of the new world and the plunder of its ancient riches. 1492 marked both the Discovery of the Americas by Columbus and the final re-conquest of Granada under her rule. She must have regretted marrying off her daughter, Catherine of Aragon, to Henry VIII but would, no doubt, have been pleased that her grandson Charles V became Holy Roman Emperor and married, rather more fortuitously, Isabel of Portugal. This deft move added the considerable wealth of Portugal to her overseas dominions and an already impressive list of assets.

The only surviving (legitimate) child from the marriage of Charles and Isabel acceded to the throne in 1556 becoming Felipe II of Spain (and Philip I of Portugal) and effectively the first King of a united Hispanic peninsular. This marks the high point of Spanish influence abroad. Things began to go downhill from here on, starting with the ill-advised Spanish support of Mary Queen of Scots claim to the English throne and the ensuing ill-fated Armada in 1588. The power and influence of the monarchy continued its downward spiral over the next century and in 1700 Felipe V came to the Spanish throne, starting the War of the Spanish Succession between the Bourbon dynasty of France and Charles of Austria whose claim to the Spanish throne was supported by the British. Spain suffered badly in this long drawn out dispute, losing Gibraltar in the process.

•The Peninsular War and the First Republic 1808 – 1810

Events turned from bad to worse with the arrival of Napoleon's army in 1808 and the abdication of King Carlos IV. Spanish resistance was supported by British troops under Sir John Moore and the French were finally ejected and in 1810 a newly formed Parliament *Cortes* prepared a constitution. This first effort at parliamentary rule was short lived and was quickly followed by the Carlist Wars and a series of military coups lasting for another century.

•The Franco Years 1936 – 1975

In 1936 General Franco seized power leading to the one of the bloodiest civil wars in history. The Republican northeast enlisted thousands of volunteers in the International Brigade but was no match for the Nationalist army in the southwest under Franco that had the support of Nazi Germany and Fascist Italy. The ensuing carnage is hauntingly portrayed in Pablo Picasso's painting *La Guernica*. The Pact of Silence or Forgetting *el pacto de olvido* attempts to suppress the painful memories of the Franco dictatorship when tens of thousands were summarily shot and buried in mass graves around the countryside. Monuments to the dead of the Civil War are found all along the camino and its legacy still casts a dark shadow over Spain.

•Modern Spain 1975 – 2017

Franco's carefully groomed successor, Admiral Carrero Blanco, was assassinated by Basque separatists in 1970 and on Franco's death in 1975, King Carlos nominally succeeded and appointed political reformist Adlofo Suárez to form a government. This proved widely popular with the people but the liberal approach of Suárez was not supported by the military. The Suárez government drew up a new constitution and in 1978 Spain became a full democracy under a cumbersome and decidedly expensive system of self-rule with its 17 autonomous communities *autonomías* (the larger ones are subdivided into provinces) which each elect representatives to the central government based in Madrid. The camino passes through 4 of these *autonomías* viz: Navarra, La Rioja, Castilla y León (Burgos, Palencia and León provinces) and Galicia (Lugo and la Coruña provinces). The only hiccup in this progress towards democracy was an attempted military coup in 1981 but Spain regained her composure and democracy was swiftly re-established and the Franco years put firmly behind.

In 1982 the socialist party (PSOE) won a sweeping victory under Felipe González who successfully steered Spain into full membership of the EEC in 1986. In 1996 José María Aznar, leader of the right wing *Partido Popular* (PP), came to power but in 2002 the oil tanker Prestige ran into a storm off Finisterre and the ensuing ecological catastrophe sank not only the livelihood of scores of Galician fisherman but, in time, the right wing government as well. The disregard for the environment displayed by the President of Galicia and the Spanish environment minister resulted in a popular cry up and down the country of 'never again' *nunca mais.* It only took the government's deeply unpopular support of the invasion of Iraq coupled with the retaliatory Madrid bombings in March 2004 to put the socialists back in power under the youthful leadership of José Luis Rodríguez Zapatero. The new government set in motion an immediate change in foreign policy and, more controversially, a sudden but decisive shift from a conservative Catholic to a liberal secular society that led to one newspaper headline, *Church and State square up in struggle for the spirit of Spain.* The Euro crisis in 2011 led to a crushing defeat of the Socialists and a return to the conservative PP under Mariano Rajoy who was elected on a promise to reduce Spain's public deficit. But with austerity measures getting increasingly unpopular we begin to see the swing back to the left and the rise of the 'We can' *Podemos* party... and seemingly immune to all these social and political upheavals, the camino quietly goes about her gentle spirit of transformation.

• **The Present:** *Breakdown and Breakthrough:*

Two centuries of rampant materialism have resulted in a spiritual aridity unparalleled in human history. Statistics reveal a collapse in church attendance matched by a significant fall in the numbers entering the priesthood. Recent surveys indicate that Spain, until recently a deeply religious society, now has less than 20% of its population practising Catholicism. Yet here is the rub – in this same period the numbers entering the Camino de Santiago have soared and the pilgrim figures have risen tenfold in a decade. How do we interpret these trends? There seems little doubt that there is a great thirst for genuine spiritual experience and a deep desire to refresh and enliven our religious life. It has been suggested by a leading Christian moderator that we have become bored and disillusioned with the religion we have been fed since childhood and this is leading to a collapse of formalised religious practice.

• **A Future Perspective:** *A New Age of Pilgrimage:*

There are many explanations for the anomalies and sweeping changes confronting us today. Each of us will read the signs and interpret these to develop our own future scenarios. I favour the emerging concept of a new and unprecedented flowering of human consciousness that is so positive and profound that we have no collective idea where it will lead us. We have become so spiritually dehydrated that we are now desperate to drink directly from the Divine Well and our thirst will no longer be slaked by drinking from a substitute or tainted source. We are awakening to a new spiritual age – one less dependent on an outer authority and more attuned to the God within. Conjecture is rife, but we cannot deny the statistics that point, on the one hand, to collapse and, on the other hand, to renewal. While the death of the old can be alarming the birth of the new is always exciting. Something is undoubtedly 'astir in the land' and what we are witnessing is, perhaps, a collective emergence to a new spiritual reality directing our lives. Of course, the more cynical might point to tourism, now the single largest industry in the world, as the reason for the sudden rise in the interest in the Camino de Santiago. Truth is relative and human nature such that we each will tend towards a theory that reinforces our individual belief systems.

Today, Santiago flourishes as a centre of both tourism and pilgrimage, but the ancient path itself is less susceptible to commercialisation. *El Camino* is rousing itself from centuries of slumber and its potential to exert a positive influence on the changes confronting us at every turn along the way is enormous. The spirit of St. James and the camino is alive and well and ready to assist each one of us in formulating a new and positive future quite unlike anything we have manifested in the past. 'Time for Change' was Barack Obama's platform – ours too.

PREPARATION – *INNER*: *Why am I doing this?*

A majority of those setting out on the *Camino de Santiago* give a religious or spiritual reason for going, yet few appear to undertake any conscious inner preparation for the journey. It is so easy to allow the demands of our secular life to rob us of time for such preparation. We take our tired bodies and neglected souls and dump them at the start of the camino and trust that all will be well. And of course, all will be well and our physical and spiritual muscles will become rejuvenated – it's just that warm-up exercises will maximise the benefits and speed our rate of recovery. A pilgrim travels on two paths simultaneously and must pay attention to both. When we place ourselves on the pilgrim path we sow the intention to stretch and expand soul consciousness so that we can lift ourselves out of the mundane in order to journey back to God or whatever name we give to that nameless Source whence we came.

And how, in this busy secular world of ours, do we prepare for such a journey? A useful guideline is to spend at least as much time on inner preparation as general logistics. This way we balance the inner and outer realities and give equal account to both. Spirit seeks to inform all those who sincerely ask the deeper questions behind our existence. These questions may arise from some crisis; diagnosis of a life threatening disease, death of a loved one, loss of employment, marital breakdown or just deep dissatisfaction with life for no apparent reason. All of these events can awaken in us a desire to understand the context as well as the content of our lives. Existential loneliness will not disappear by finding or replacing partners, changing jobs, moving house. Of course, in discovering who we are these outer circumstances may change but it is our ability to observe the changing dramas of our life, and the life of others around us, against a larger backdrop that will bring a united purpose to all our journeying.

We all have different psychological, spiritual and emotional needs and pathologies. While pilgrimage can be a way of breaking through resistances (releasing blocks and realising insights as to what prevents us being all that we truly are) it is wise to start off with a relatively balanced state of mind. If you feel you need psychotherapy, counselling or other help, seek it. It will be disturbing enough when previously dearly held belief systems start to break down. A mental and emotional check up might be useful, even necessary, before you start embarking on an inner quest.

When asked to describe a personal experience of the sacred, an overwhelming majority refer to a time alone in nature, 'A sunrise over the sea; animal tracks in fresh powder snow; a walk under the full moon'. It was not the sun or the moon that created any shift in perception but they acted as a reflection of a larger perspective, a distant memory of something holy – something bigger than, and yet part of, us. This is where the camino can provide such a powerful reminder of the sacred in our lives and the desire to reclaim our spiritual inheritance.

As we set out towards the fabled city of Santiago we need to be mindful, as *A Course In Miracles* suggests, that the true temple is not a structure at all. Its true holiness lies at the inner altar around which the structure is built – yet the real beauty of the inner temple cannot be seen with the physical eye. An emphasis on beautiful structures can be a sign of unwillingness to exercise spiritual vision. As we walk through the *landscape temple* that is the *camino* and through the towns and cities spread out along the way, we pass some of the most physically striking religious buildings to be found anywhere in this world. But let us not confuse the messenger with the message and so help each other to search out and find that elusive *inner altar*.

Risks: Apart from the obvious precautions, especially in the larger towns and cities, it is hard to conceive of a safer environment within which to reflect on life and its direction. The people along the camino have been welcoming pilgrims for centuries. The needs of medieval pilgrims were looked after by *hospitallers*, today they are called *hospitaleros* which is a much more welcoming word than the English equivalent of warden. And this distinction goes to the heart of the camino. Countless millions have walked this path with a high purpose in mind and many return to serve the on-going needs of the pilgrim. That elevated intentionality and goodwill is embedded in this route and available to each of us as we pass along it.

There are of course exceptions to every rule. We live in a fearful world and this is nowhere more obvious than in Spain where military and armed police presence is noticeable everywhere you go and many homes have guard dogs. However, we need to put crime in perspective and realise that our privilege to have the freedom, time and money to be able to walk a pilgrim path can be resented by a tiny minority who see pilgrims as a legitimate target for rich pickings. We need to remind ourselves that an attack is really a cry for help and calls for understanding and a loving response, not a counter-attack. If you find yourself becoming fearful for yourself or your belongings, you might find the following words of *William Ward* a source of encouragement:

To laugh is to risk appearing a fool
To weep is to risk being called sentimental
To reach out to another is to risk involvement
To expose feelings is to risk exposing your true self
To place your ideas and dreams before a crowd is to risk their loss
To love is to risk not being loved in return
To live is to risk dying
To try is to risk failure.

But risks must be taken
Because the greatest hazard in life is to risk nothing.
The people who risk nothing may avoid suffering and sorrow,
But they cannot learn, feel, change, grow or really live.
Chained by their servitude they are slaves who have forfeited all freedom.
Only a person who risks is truly free.

SELF-ASSESSMENT *INNER WAYMARKS*

This self-assessment questionnaire is designed to encourage you to reflect on your life and its direction. View it as a snapshot of this moment in the on-going journey of your life. In the busy-ness that surrounds us we often fail to take stock of where we are headed and our changing roles in the unfolding drama of our life story.

You might find it useful to initially answer these questions in quick succession as this may allow a more intuitive response. Afterwards, you can reflect more deeply and check if your intellectual answers confirm these, change them or bring in other insights. You can download copies of this questionnaire from the *Camino Guides* web site – make some extra copies so you can repeat the exercise on your return and again in (say) 3 months time. This way you can compare results and ensure you continue to follow through on any insights that come to you while walking the camino.

❏ How do you differentiate pilgrimage from a long distance walk?
❏ How do you define spirituality – what does it mean to you?
❏ How is your spirituality expressed at home and at work?

❏ What do you see as the primary purpose of your life?
❏ Are you working consciously towards fulfilling that purpose?
❏ How clear are you on your goal and the right direction for you at this time?
❏ How will you recognise resistance to any changes that might be necessary?

❏ When did you first become aware of a desire to take time-out?
❏ What prompted you originally to go on the camino?
❏ Did the prompt come from something that you felt needed changing?
❏ Make a list of what appears to be blocking any change from happening.

❏ What help might you need on a practical, emotional and spiritual level?
❏ How will you recognise the right help or correct answer?
❏ What are the joys and challenges in working towards your unique potential?
❏ What are your next steps towards fulfilling that potential?

How aware are you of the following? Score yourself on a level of 1 – 10 and compare these scores again on your return from the camino.

❏ Awareness of your inner spiritual world
❏ Clarity on what inspires you and the capacity to live your passion
❏ Confidence to follow your intuitive sense of the right direction
❏ Ability to recognise your resistance and patterns of defence
❏ Ease with asking for and receiving support from others

MAP LEGEND *OUTER WAYMARKS*

This guidebook provides you with essential information in a concise format. The maps have been designed so you can instantly see how far it is to the next place of interest etc. without having to scale the distance. All pilgrim hostels and the location of alternative accommodation are clearly shown. Distances on the maps correspond to those in the text and are generally spaced at around 3 km intervals corresponding to approximately 1 hour of walking at an average pace. For clarity and accuracy each stage begins and ends at the front door of a clearly specified pilgrim hostel or other clearly defined 'end point'. These maps are one directional *to* Santiago; if you intend to walk the route 'in reverse' source conventional maps.

Familiarise yourself with the map symbols and note that: ❶ the **Main Route** (c.80% of pilgrims) generally follows the most direct path and is indicated by a line of yellow dots ● ● ● ● symbolic of the yellow arrows that will be your guide throughout the journey. Distances along this route are shown in **blue.** ❷ **Scenic Routes** (more remote with fewer facilities and waymarks) are recommended for pilgrims seeking a more contemplative time in the relative silence of nature. These quieter paths are shown with green dots ● ● ● ● indicating the natural landscape they travel through and the text appears on a green panel. ❸ **Road Routes** follow on or close to asphalt roads and are marked with **grey** dots ● ● ● ● symbolising asphalt and distances provided are also coloured **grey** and the text appears on a grey background. ❹ **Detours** to places of special interest are shown with **turquoise** dots ● ● ● ● and the text appears on a turquoise panel. Finally there are very remote routes ❺ shown with purple dots ● ● ● ● with few, if any, facilities and waymarks and *less* than 1% of all pilgrims. On this account they can offer some rewarding experiences immersed in the silence of the natural landscape but should only be attempted by seasoned pilgrims with hiking and orienteering experience who are seeking a meditative experience along 'the path less travelled'.

Waymarks: Thanks to the voluntary efforts of the various associations and 'friends of the way' – waymarking is now so thorough that we need only the barest information to get us safely to the end of each stage along the way. If you get 'lost' it is invariably because you have let your mind wander and your feet have followed! – stay present and focused especially at points shown with an exclamation mark [!]. If you find yourself temporarily off-course be careful when asking directions as locals are not generally familiar with the waymarked paths but may direct you along the public roads – it is often best to re-trace your steps until you pick up the waymarks again. A sun-compass has been provided on each map as an aid to orientation.

Should you become 'lost' the **sun compass** will help re-orientate. Even in poor weather we can generally tell the direction of the sun so, for example, if you are walking from St. Jean to Roncesvalles you are heading south/west and the morning sun will be on your left (east). At midday the sun will be straight ahead (south) and by late afternoon it will be on your *right>* (west). If you find yourself in the late afternoon with the sun on your *<left* – stop and re-assess as you may be following some other track *back* to St. Jean. Those of us who decide to leave our wristwatch at home the sun will also become our natural clock. It is surprising how quickly we get to know the time of day by the length of

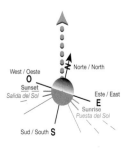

our shadow and our body will tell us when it is time to eat or drink. The sun can also help us shift our focus away from self-aggrandisement. We like to identify ourselves as being at the centre of the universe and say that the sun rises in the east because that is our experience but it is entirely wrong – it is of course the earth turning on its axis that turns us towards the sun in the morning and away from it at night. This is no mere semantics. It was considered a heresy, as Galileo also discovered!

Each day's stage is measured from the front door of one albergue to the next, i.e. daily distances are between sleeping accommodation. Intermediate hotels or hostels are also shown, those directly on the route in a solid panel and those *off* route with a border only. The number of available beds is also shown [in brackets]. The maps have been designed to show relevant information only and are therefore not strictly to scale – instead accurate distances are given between each point marked on the map and this corresponds to the text for ease of reference. Distances in between these points are shown bracketed in the text as follows: **[1.0** km] plus **[0.2** km] add up to the boxed figure in blue **1.2 km** Note <left means *turn* left – (left) means *on* your left – right> *turn* right etc.

[?] indicates an option – green 'scenic' routes follow the less travelled tracks so as to minimise the time spent on asphalt. The main (N-*National*) roads are shown in red, symbolic of their added danger and volume of traffic. Every effort has been made to minimise exposure to these 'red' routes and extra care is needed on the few stretches where they simply cannot be avoided. [!] Indicates a dangerous stretch of road, a steep descent or an area where the waymarks are not clear. Use the 'sun compass' to help orientate yourself through cities and other poorly waymarked areas.

Text and place names on the maps are generally in Spanish *Castellano*. However, on entering Galicia, place names are provided in *Galego* unless they appear 'on the ground' in Spanish. The Church of St. John may, therefore, appear as *Iglesia San Juan* or *Igrexa San Xoán*. Villages in Spain, particularly Galicia, tend to straggle without any defined centre and even the local church is frequently located outside the actual town. Distances are usually measured to the albergue or other clearly defined feature, such as a drinking font *[F.] fuente*.

Contour guides are shown for each day's walk. This will give you a thumbnail sketch of the day's terrain and help you prepare for the uphill stretches and anticipate the downhill ones. They are drawn to an exaggerated scale to emphasise steep inclines.

Equivalent distances are given for each stage adjusted for height using the common factor of 10 minutes for every 100 metres climbed and then applied to the slower (leisurely) pace of 20 minutes per kilometre. **Note: 1 km = 0.6 mile.**
3 m.p.h. (1 mile every 20 mins) is equiv. to 4.8 k.p.h. (1 km every 12.5 mins).

Based on the following chart a very fit (fast) walker can accomplish up to a *maximum* of 40 *adjusted* kilometres in an 8-hour day. This drops to 35 km for an average walker and 25 km for a leisurely pace.

Fitness Level	**kph**	**minutes/km**	**25**km	**30**km	**35**km	**40**km
			The above distances (kilometres)			
			will take the following time (hours)			
Fast walker	5 kph	12 min's/km	5.0	6.0	7.0	8.0
Average pace	4 kph	15 min's/km	6.3	7.5	8.6	—
Leisurely pace	3 kph	20 min's/km	8.3	—	—	—

■ **Average pace** depends on many other factors, apart from gradient. Awareness of the following additional factors will help you plan your itinerary. **Time of day will also affect your speed and endurance.** Ideally start each day early and either (a) finish by lunchtime or (b) plan a midday stop, rest in the shade, and continue on when the worst heat of the day is over.

■ **End of day pace** will produce the biggest variations. On the longer stretches you may find your pace slowing considerably and you should allow *half* the normal pace (*double* the time) in calculating whether to continue onwards at the end of a long day. *(Pilgrims tend to only query measurements for the last section of a day that they feel must be longer than that published! That is why it is misleading to publish time rather than distance for any section).*

Traversing cities along the route. The more time you spend on the quiet country sections the greater is likely to be your vulnerability to the noise and bustle of the cities. If you are travelling as a solo contemplative pilgrim you might plan your itinerary to walk through the city on the relatively traffic free Sunday or during siesta times. Waymarking in cities has to compete with consumer advertising, traffic lights and other distractions, so allow time to retrace steps if you take a wrong turning.

Traffic can be dangerous and draining. Spanish driving is no safer than in any other country (some would maintain it's worse!). Regarding the energy drain often experienced as a result of the noise and air blast or suction, especially of large articulated trucks, it can help to understand the dynamics of subtle (and not so subtle) energy. One way of working with this is to try 'singing' into the roar as it passes you by. As you hear traffic approaching, start humming your favourite tune. As it draws nearer raise your volume until, at the moment of passing, your roar matches that of the vehicle's engine. This is one simple method of dispersing negative inner and outer vibrations! You can also use the sudden screech of a car passing at speed (or noise of a cycling pilgrim or barking dog) as an alarm call – a rude awakening and reminder of your purpose for being on pilgrimage. Whatever reaction you have, try and stay focused and shake out angry reactions immediately they arise.

Senda: These modern gravel paths offer a practical but somewhat soulless modern addition to the camino. They generally run alongside and parallel to the public road and are 'softening' with time.

Future Scenarios: Over the past few years, bus-loads of tourists on 'pilgrim' holidays have begun to appear along the route. Some well-deserving charity organisations also organise group tours that threaten to overload the capacity of the camino to cope gracefully with the increase in numbers. I have been forced off the path by a 4 wheel drive 'pilgrim safari' from a UK adventure holiday company – a humbling but not particularly edifying experience! *Mickey Mouse* dressed as a pilgrim complete with skip and staff makes an appearance in Castille & León, one of the areas most affected by officials unaware, perhaps, of the simple needs of a pilgrim. We need to stay vigilant and give feedback to local authorities and travel organisations of any concerns we might have and remind ourselves that overcrowding was also a problem of the medieval period.

Map Legend: Symbols used in this guide:

Total km — Total distance for stage map

Adjusted for climb (100m vertical = additional 0.5km)

(850m) Alto ▲ — Contours / High point of each stage

< Ⓐ Ⓗ > — Intermediate accommodation (*often less busy / quieter*)

◀ **3.5** — Precise distance between points (3.5 km = ± 1 hour)

•50m > / ^ / < — Interim distances •50m turn right> / s/o=straight on^ / <left
     c.=circa (about) / adj.=adjacent / incl.=including

‧‧‧‧‧‧‧‧‧‧‧‧‧ — Natural path / forest track or gravel (grey) *senda*

Secondary road (*grey*: asphalt) / Roundabout *rotonda*

N-11 — Main road [N-] *Nacional* (*red*: additional traffic and hazard)

A-1 — Motorway *autopista* (*blue*: conventional motorway colour)

+++++++● — Railway *ferrocarril* / Station *estación*

●●●●●● — Primary Path of pilgrimage; inner path of Soul

●●●●●● — Main physical route (*yellow*: ± 80% of pilgrims)

●●●●●● — Alternative Scenic route (*green*: more remote / less pilgrims)

●●●●●● — Optional detour *desvío* (*turquoise*)

●●●●●● — Alternative road route (*grey*: more asphalt & traffic)

Ⓧ ❓ 🜹 — Crossing *cruce* / Option *opción* / Extra care *¡cuidado!*

🜨 ⚶ ⍑ — Windmill / Viewpoint *punto de vista* / Radio mast

‧—‧/‧—‧ — National boundary / Provincial boundary *límite provincial*

∼ / ∼ — River *río* / Stream *arroyo*

◯ / ◯ — Sea or Lake *Mar o Lago* / Woodland *bosques*

⛪ ⛪ ✝ — Church *iglesia* / Chapel *capilla* / Wayside cross *cruceiro*

Ⓕ 🍴 🏪 — Drinking font *fuente* / Café / Shop *minimercado*

menú V. — *menú peregrino* 3 course meal + wine / V. *Vegetariano*

🅩 🏠 ✕ — Tourist office *turismo* / Manor house *casa señorial* / Picnic

➕ ⊕ ✉ — Pharmacy *farmacia* / Hospital / Post office *correos*

✈ 🚌 ⛽ — Airport / Bus station *estación de autobús* / gasolinera

⁛ XII — Ancient monument / 12th century

Ⓐ❶ Ⓙ — Pilgrim hostel(s) *Albergue Alb.* / Youth hostel *Juventude*

Ⓗ Ⓟ Ⓒ — Hotels *H-H***** €30-90 / Pension *P*** €20+ / CR (B&B) €35+

Ⓗ Ⓐ Ⓙ — (off route accommodation *alojamiento fuera de ruta*)

[32] — Number of bed spaces (usually bunk beds *literas*)

[÷4]+ — ÷ number of rooms / + additional private rooms €20+

Par. — Parish hostel *Parroquia* donation *donativo* / €5

Conv. — Convent or monastery hostel *donativo* / €5

Muni. — Municipal hostel €5+

Xunta — Galician government *Xunta* hostel €6

Asoc. — Association hostel €8+

Priv. (*) — Private hostel (network*) €10+

*Average price (low season) for comparison purposes **only***
Rest'=Restaurant / Hs.=Hostal / R.= Residencial (camas=beds)
½-b. half-board / media pension (dinner+bed+breakfast)

▭ — Town plan *plan de la ciudad* with page number

(Pop.–Alt. m) — Town population and altitude in metres

▨ — City suburbs *suburbios de la ciudad* (*grey*)

▨ — Historical centre *centro histórico* (*brown*)

33 STAGE SUMMARY – ROUTE MAPS & TOWN GUIDES

St Jean Pied de Port – Santiago de Compostela 776.2 km (482.3 miles)

Page	Map	Km	From	To	*Town Plan—page*
			NAVARRA ----------		
48	01	25.1	St Jean	Roncesvalles	***St Jean**—45*
56	02	21.9	Roncesvalles	Zubiri	
60	03	20.9	Zubiri	Pamplona	***Pamplona**—67*
68	04	23.8	Pamplona	Puente la Reina	***P. la Reina**—74*
76	05	21.9	Puente la Reina	Estella	***Estella**—81*
84	06	21.5	Estella	Los Arcos	***Arcos**—89*
90	07	27.8	Los Arcos	Logroño	***Logroño**—95*
			LA RIOJA ----------		
98	08	28.9	Logroño	Nájera	
106	09	21.3	Nájera	Santo Domingo	
112	10	22.4	Santo Domingo	Belorado	
			CASTILLA Y LEON *(BURGOS)* ----------		
118	11	24.2	Belorado	St Juan Ortega	
124	12	26.1	St Juan Ortega	Burgos	***Burgos**—131*
134	13	21.0	Burgos	Hornillos	
140	14	20.1	Hornillos	Castrojeriz	
			CASTILLA Y LEON (*PALENCIA*) ----------		
146	15	24.9	Castrojeriz	Frómista	
152	16	19.3	Frómista	Carrion ‘Condes	
158	17	26.8	Carrion los Condes	Terradillos	
162	18	23.5	Terradillos	Bercianos *—via—*	***Sahagún**—167*
			CASTILLA Y LEON *(LEÓN)* ----------		
170	19	26.7	Bercianos/Calzadilla	Mansilla	***Mansilla**—175*
176	20	18.1	Mansilla	León	***León**—181*
184	21	21.3	León	Villadangos/Mazarife	
192	22	28.5	Villadangos	Astorga	***Astorga**—199*
202	23	20.6	Astorga	Rabanal	
208	24	25.6	Rabanal	Molinaseca	
214	25	30.6	Molinaseca	Villafranca *—via—*	***Ponferrada**—219*
224	26	28.9	Villafranca Bierzo	O’Cebreiro	***Villafranca**—223*
			GALICIA (*LUGO*) ----------		
236	27	20.7	O’Cebreiro	Triacastela	
240	28	18.7	Triacastela / Samos	Sarria	***Sarria**—245*
248	29	22.1	Sarria	Portomarín	
254	30	24.8	Portomarín	Palas do Rei	
260	31	25.6	Palas do Rei	Ribadiso (Arzúa)	
			GALICIA (*LA CORUÑA*) ----------		
266	32	22.8	Ribadiso	Pedrouzo (O’ Pino/Arca)	
270	33	19.8	Pedrouzo	Santiago	***Santiago**—279*

ST. JEAN PIED de PORT *(pop. 1,800 – alt. 170m)*: The ancient capital of the Basque region of Basse-Navarre retains a delightful medieval atmosphere in its narrow streets and the language is retained on signs and place names which appear in both French or Basque (and across the border in Spanish or Basque). This attractive town nestles in the foothills of the Pyrenees at the 'foot of the pass' *pied de port* to Roncevaux *French*, Orreaga *Basque* and Roncesvalles *Spanish*. A population of 1,800 serves the many tourists, hill walkers and pilgrims that converge on this small enclave in the summer months. Activity gravitates towards the central square *Place du-Gaulle* where we find the **Office de Tourisme** © 0559-370 357 along with a range of hotels and cafés where you can wine and dine amongst the traffic fumes or…

Explore the historic walled town where the pilgrim office and hostels are located. St. Jean Pied de Port has become the modern gateway to the camino and the traditional starting point for pilgrims from all over the world with the exception of those in Spain, where the main starting point is Roncesvalles (for the whole route) or Sarria in Galicia (100 km from Santiago and thus entitling pilgrims to a compostela).

Porte Saint-Jacques & Pilgrim Hostel

❏ **Monuments historiques:** A basic tour starts in the medieval *rue de la Citadelle*. This is a continuation of the Way of St. James through France *Chemin de Saint Jacques* and part of the camino itself. From this ancient cobbled main street there are several access points to the old ramparts. At the very top of the town is ❶ *Porte St Jacques XV* St. James Gate (UNESCO World Heritage status) through which pilgrims arriving from Le Puy, Vezelay and Paris, via Ostabat, enter the town. From here a steep climb takes us to the imposing ❷ *Citadelle (Table d'Orientation)* with a fine view over the old town and the Pyrenees. *[A steep climb down on the eastern boundary (269 steps!) brings us to the narrow Porte de l'Echauguette that opens onto the river Nive – see below].* Continuing down the rue de la Citadelle we pass ❸ *La Maison des Evêques XVI* Prison of the Bishops with museum displaying artefacts from the Camino de Santiago. Just below we find the pilgrim office *Accueil pèlerins* at no 39. Further on down (right) is rue de France leading to one of the 4 medieval gates to the town ❹ *Porte de France* and rue Eglise leading to ❺ *Porte de Navarre*. At the bottom of the street (left) we arrive at ❻ *Notre Dame du Bout du Pont XIV* The church of Our Lady at the End of the Bridge – a fitting place, perhaps, from which to bless the beginning of your journey and that of your fellow pilgrims who will pass under her protective arch *Porte Notre Dame* on the way out in the morning. From the church you can take a peaceful 1 km circular detour up river, past the wooden footbridge, to the Roman bridge *Pont Eyeraberri*. Cross over and return via the Pelota court *Frontón* and the Spanish Gate ❼ *Porte D'Espagne* leading into the rue d'Espagne back to the Porte Notre Dame (See town plan).

■ **Pilgrim Passport** *Carnet de Pelerin / Credencial del Peregrino* available from the **Pilgrim Welcome Office** ■ *Accueil pèlerins* © 0559 370 509 *rue de la Citadelle (Nº39)* 07:30–12:30 / 13:30–22:00 providing local weather and accommodation information. **Pilgrim equipment and guidebooks:** ■ *Boutique du pélerin (Nº32)* © 0559 379 852 open daily 06:30–19:00. **Backpack transfer & transport from Biarritz airport:** ■ *Express Burricot (Nº31)* © 0661 960 476 07:00–10:00 /16:30– 20:30. Caroline Aphessetche www.expressbourricot.com

■ **Accommodation** *Logements*. © **France +33.** ■ *Albergues:* •*Rue de la Citadelle* *Nº55* ❶Municipal *[24÷3]* €10 incl. *Nº50* ❷Azkorria *Priv.[8÷2]*+ €16+ © 676 020 536. *Nº40* ❸Bellari *(L'Esprit du Chemin) Priv.[18÷4]* €26 ½-board. © 0559 372 468. *Nº36* ❹Au Chant du Coq *Priv.[15]*+ © 0674 310 283. *Nº25* ❺L'auberge du pèlerin *Priv.[43÷4]* © 0559 491 086. *Nº8* ❻Gite Ultreïa *Priv.*[15÷4]*+ €16+€44 © 0680 884 622. •*Rue d'Espagne Nº21* (adj. L'Atelier du Chocolat) ❼Le Chemin Vers L'Etoile *Priv.[20÷5]* €15 incl. / €25 ½-board. © 0559 372 071. *Nº43* ❽Maison Kaserna *Par.[12÷1]* © 0559 376 517 €-donativo. *Outside the old town:* ●9 Zuharpeta *Priv.[22÷2]* © 0559 373 588 rue Zuharpeta 5. ●10 Compostella *Priv. [14÷2]* © 0559 370 236 rue d'Arneguy. ●11 Refuge Esponda *Priv.*© 0679 075 252 place du Trinquet €14.

■ *Hotels €60+:* H*Ramuntcho © 0559 370 391 rue de Citadelle 24. *Gîte d'Étape* Etchegoin © 0559 371 208 Rue d'Uhart, 9. H**Les Remparts © 0559 371 379 Place Floquet 16 and @Nº15 H**Etche Ona © 0559 370 114. Maison Ziberoa €60+ © 661 235 944 route d'arnéguy 3. H**Central Place du Général de Gaulle 1 © 0559 370 022. H**Itzalpea © 0559 370 366 Place du Trinquet 5. H**Continental © 0559 370 025 Av. Renaud (rue du Gare). *€120+*H****Les Pyrénées © 0559 370 101.

■ See p.17 for average cost of hostels and p.19 hotels – within Spain.

Choice of routes: This first stage is one of the more strenuous and a veritable baptism of fire into *El Camino* and Spain. Don't worry: millions of pilgrims have gone before you to pave the way! You do, however, have a choice of 2 different routes to reach Roncesvalles and your choice will be dependent on 2 main considerations: [a] prevailing weather conditions and [b] your personal level of fitness and experience. Whichever route you take is likely to stretch both physical and spiritual muscles that have, perhaps, become atrophied over time with our increasingly sedentary and secular lives. This stage represents one of the steepest ascents of the whole pilgrimage. However, the climb is rewarded with the great panorama of the Pyrenees. So have all your gear, food and water prepared for an early morning start so you can sleep soundly holding your inner purpose for this journey, rather than your worldly goods, clearly in mind. If that purpose remains obscure – ask for clarity now. *[If you are not fit or otherwise doubtful of your abilities consider staying in accommodation en route such as Orrison or Valcarlos. See map for stage 1.]*

❶ **Route de Napoléon: 25.1 km** *(adjusted for climb 32.0 km allowing for a cumulative ascent in the day of 1,390m equivalent to an extra 6.9 km of time and effort expended over and above that required for a level walk).* This is the steepest and most arduous route but arguably the most beautiful and spectacular. It was the way favoured by the great French general to get his troops in and out of Spain during the Peninsular War and by pilgrims anxious to avoid the bandits hiding in the trees surrounding the lower route. It should only be attempted in good weather but it makes the most of the early morning sun, which doesn't penetrate into the Valcarlos valley (alternative route) until later in the day. The steep climb up onto the high plateau is rewarded with wonderful views back over St. Jean de Pied Port. The first 11.4 km is mostly by quiet country lanes (asphalt) but the last section up through Col de Bentartea and Col de Lepoeder is entirely on natural pathways.

Unless you are an experienced hill walker, you should not tackle this route: [a] in winter when daylight hours are diminished and weather more extreme, or [b] during any other season if the weather is bad or forecast to deteriorate. Note that during late autumn and early spring there are frequent snow showers and these can obliterate waymarks. At any time of year hill fog can cause poor visibility. Fog should be distinguished from early morning mist, which usually burns off in the first few hours long before you reach the high plateau and have to leave the relative security of the road. If you are unsure or anxious, enquire at the pilgrim office as they have access to local weather forecasts and regular updates. Guidebooks are duty bound to sound cautionary notes! Be sensible, but know that any reasonably fit person can cover the ground and is likely to have a peak experience in so doing. Remember to take food and water with you, as there are no facilities beyond Orisson and drinking fonts are few and far between. If the weather is very unsettled then it might be preferable to stick to the road route parallel to the N-135 with its cafés and hostels. *N.B.* Local authorities on both sides of the border discourage walking the Route Napoleon in winter and in 2015 it was officially closed between November and March effectively putting the cost of any mountain rescue on any pilgrim ignoring closure notices!

[1a] A little known (and used) variant on route ❶ is the GR65 from Mayorga on the outskirts of St. Jean. This alternative adds 1 km to the recommended route which it joins at the 1,000m contour close to the Pic d'Orisson. While it avoids most of the asphalt section of the D428 it is poorly waymarked and it is easy to get lost along the remote mountain paths. If you are an experienced hill walker and want to use this route obtain the IGN 1:25 map 1346 OT available in St. Jean or any good map shop – otherwise stick to the main routes.

❷ **Valcarlos route: 24.0 km** *(adjusted for climb 28.9 km allowing for a cumulative ascent in the day of 990m, equivalent to an extra 4.9 km).* Charles' Valley *Val Carlos* was the way chosen by the Holy Roman Emperor Charlemagne to get his troops in and, somewhat disastrously, out of Spain. You cannot avoid the main road completely, but you can save 6 km of it before Arneguy and a further 10 km of it after Valcarlos. This alternative route runs parallel to the main road and follows quiet country lanes into Arneguy. However, the waymarking is not so clear and there are several side roads that could delay you unless you stay alert and vigilant. 6 km after Valcarlos a path leaves the road and climbs directly to the Ibañeta pass through a mixture of pine and beech trees. This is a very steep pathway but it eliminates the innumerable bends on the main road.

[2a] A little used variant on route ❷ is to follow the main road all the way to Roncesvalles 27.5 km, adjusted for climb 32.0 km (allowing for a cumulative ascent in the day of 890m equivalent to an extra 4.5 km). The road route is the longest and goes through the villages of Arneguy and Valcarlos with their shops, bars and hotels. However, this is a main route into Spain and is designated an N *(nacional)* road and is not recommended. Today, the road carries an ever-increasing amount of tourist traffic and is noisy and dangerous particularly in wet or windy conditions. Note that apart from the noise and danger of traffic it can also be very chilly in the early morning, as the sun does not penetrate the deep-sided valley until later in the day.

Preparations for next day – Outer: As you will need to leave early in the morning to get to Roncesvalles, you should shop for snacks the evening before as there are limited facilities and shops won't be open when in the early morning. An exception is the *Boutique du pélerin,* which opens at 06:30. The rue d'Espagne has several food outlets including *Alimentacion* (opp. patisserie *Barbier Millox*) and a supermarket *Le Relais des Mousquetaires* on the corner of the rue d'Uhart and just before Porte d'Espagne is the *Boulangerie Iriart* (also opens around 06:30) Fill your water flask before you leave town and top up as you pass drinking fonts en route.

Preparations for next day – Inner: Take time now, again, to reflect on the purpose of your pilgrimage. Try the church for some quiet space or take a walk along the river loop. Look again at your personal journal or self-assessment notes and ponder on the journey of your life that has brought you this far – reflect on your purpose for now. You may yet meet Jesús Jato, but in the meantime you can walk with his words in your heart *El Camino es tiempo de meditación interior, no itinerario turístico.*

REFLECTIONS:

❏ **Personal Journal:** *"... The stress of arriving at St. Jean combined with the urge to begin the pilgrimage resulted in a false start. I had fallen straight back into my familiar mode of active doing and the simple act of Being was lost to me. In my haste and confusion I had forgotten to pause and to dedicate this first leg of the journey to my purpose – 'to find and inhabit that place within me that touches God'. Tears welled up from deep within me at this prompt from my guides, 'Start anew', they urged...*

...It was hard to retrace my steps but I knew it was meaningless to continue in this frame of mind. Lost in the busy-ness of past and future, I had forsaken the present, the only place I could find what I was looking for. I write these notes on a tiny balcony above the camino with the church tower just visible against the darkening sky. Tomorrow I will follow my inner guidance and start afresh..."

❒ **A journey of a thousand miles begins with a single step**. *Lao Tzu*

01 **776.2** km (482.3 ml) – Santiago de Compostela

ST. JEAN PIED-de-PORT (Pays Basque) – RONCESVALLES (Navarre)
❶ *Route de Napoléon (recommended route – weather permitting).*

┈┈┈┈┈	--- ---	12.4	--- ---	*49%*
───────	--- ---	12.7	--- ---	*51%*
▮	--- ---	0.0		
Total km	--- ---	**25.1 km**	(15.6 ml)	

◣ 32.0 km (^1,390m+6.9 km)
Alto ▲ Col de Loepeder 1,450m (4,757 ft)
< Ⓐ Ⓗ > Huntto **5.4** km – Orisson **7.8** km

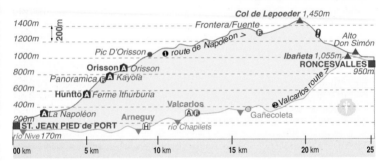

❶ **Route de Napoléon:** A strenuous uphill walk is rewarded with stunning views in all directions (provided we are spared the hill fog). The first part, as far as *Huntto*, is along a steep country lane rising to open hill and moorland, with some woodland (mostly beech) on the Spanish side. While the uphill section will stretch the cardiovascular muscles, injury is more likely on the steep downhill stage into Roncesvalles when mind and muscles will be tired – stay focussed.

❒ **The Practical Path:** While we start with one of the more demanding walks of the entire route, you will doubtless be full of energy and the sense of adventure ahead. Don't let euphoria force a pace in these early days that you and your feet have not adequately trained for – walk lightly and easily within your physical capabilities. The hospitals of Logroño (about a week away) specialise in treating foot and leg injuries sustained by over-eager pilgrims some of whom are forced to abandon the journey at this early stage. If you are with a companion(s) then find your own walking speed and don't allow yourself to be forced into someone else's stride. Stop at the intermediate hostels as needed, you can always catch up later and in the meantime you will make new friends and experience the rich camaraderie that develops along the way. For general emergencies (medical, police etc.) ℘ 112.

❒ **The Mystical Path:** A sharing from the heart can be reflected in a simple smile; words are not needed. If the eyes are the windows of the soul, then words are often the blinds that shut out the light. We yet may see the handcrafted crosses by the remote boundary marker but will we stop awhile to reflect on the truth behind this ancient symbol? What else will our awareness reveal to us along the way?

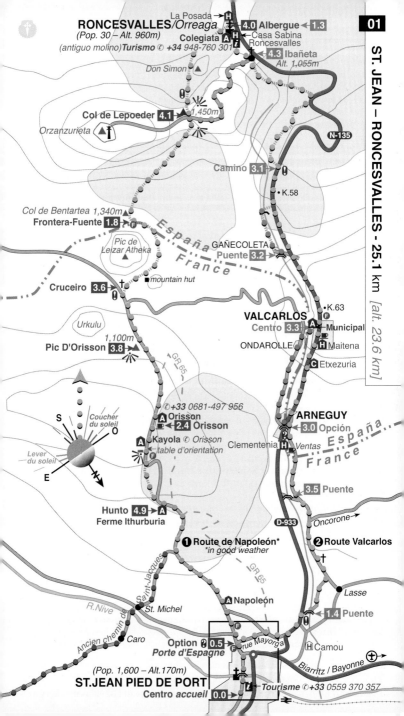

RONCESVALLES/Orreaga
(Pop. 30 – Alt. 960m)
(antiguo molino)Turismo © +34 948-760 301

La Posada → H
Colegiata A
Casa Sabina
Roncesvalles

4.0 Albergue ← 1.3

4.3 Ibañeta
Alt. 1,055m

Don Simon ▲

Col de Lepoeder 4.1
1,450m

Orzanzurieta ⛪

N-135

Camino 3.1

• K.58

Col de Bentartea 1,340m
Frontera-Fuente 1.8 ← F

España
France

Pic de
Leizar Atheka ▲

GANECOLETA
Puente 3.2

■ mountain hut

Cruceiro 3.6 †

• K.63
F

VALCARLOS
Centro 3.3   A   Municipal
ONDAROLLE   H   Maitena
                 C   Etxezuria

Urkulu

1,100m
Pic D'Orisson 3.8 →

GR 65

S

Coucher
du soleil

Lever
du soleil
E

O

© +33 0681-497 956
A Orisson
2.4 Orisson

Kayola © Orisson
A   table d'orientation
F

ARNEGUY
3.0 Opción

Clementenia H Ventas

España
France

3.5 Puente

Hunto 4.9 A
Ferme Ithurburia

D-933

Oncorone →

❶ Route de Napoleón*
*in good weather

❷ Route Valcarlos

†

Saint-Jacques

GR 65

A Napoleón

Lasse

R.Nive
St. Michel

Ancien chemin de
Caro

1.4 Puente

Option ? 0.5
Porte d'Espagne

rue Mayorga

H Camou

Biarritz / Bayonne ✠ →

(Pop. 1,600 – Alt.170m)
ST.JEAN PIED DE PORT
Centro accueil 0.0

i → Tourisme © +33 0559 370 357

❐ **Personal Reflections:** *"... The deep sense of peace that surrounds me is in stark contrast to the stress I felt when I first set out. It is All Saints Day – an auspicious start to my journey and a moment of tenderness as I recalled burying my father in Spanish soil on this very day all those years ago. I record these thoughts in the silence of my own company, surrounded by empty chairs and empty tables. I am the only pilgrim in this enormous building but I am not alone as the ancient Celtic prayer reminds me, 'Christ before me. Christ behind me. Christ all around me... Christ within me."*

Fauna: Take time to take in the magnificence of the natural landscape that surrounds you. Watch out for the Griffon Vultures that soar in the mountain thermals alert for any signs of carrion, its staple diet. These majestic birds have a wingspan up to 2.5m (8 feet) and there are 1,800 pairs in the region, the biggest concentration in the world. We will also see a variety of birds of prey including the Kite, Buzzard and smaller and swifter Sparrow hawk. This area is an important flight path for many species of migrating bird, hence the ornithological information centre at Ibañeta. You may encounter a rare Pyrenean chamois *izard* and almost certainly see many of the hill ponies running 'free', source of much of the French horse meat *viande de cheval*. The black-faced sheep roaming the high pasture are *Manech* bred for the quality of their milk and famous *Etorki & Ossau Iraty* cheese. **Flora:** Depending on the season, you will see many varieties of wild flowers in particular the Merendera Montana (Liliaceae) so emblematic of the camino with its purple and yellow hues that carpet the path all the way to Santiago. Also the similar Crocus Nudifloras, with its softer colours and identified by its longer stem.

Leaving the pilgrim office and central albergue in St. Jean we turn down the cobbled rue de la Citadelle passing the parish church *Notre Dame du Bout du Pont*. Drinking font *Fuente [F.]* (left) and pass through the archway and over the river Nive. This is the lowest point of the first stage at 170m above sea level. By this afternoon we will have climbed to 1,450m through the Col de Lepoeder! *[*As we look back from the bridge we will find the Virgin and Child watching over us as we take our first steps on the journey].* Proceed up cobbled rue D'Espagne to the ancient gateway into Spain **Porte D'Espagne [0.4 km]** *[F.]* (left). Continue straight on (s/o) past school (right) to **option point [0.1 km]**.

0.5 km　Option *Opción* [?] The last opportunity to decide which route to take. *For the **alternative road** route via Valcarlos and Puerto de Ibañeta turn right>*

For **Route de Napoleon ❶** over Col de Lepoeder continue (s/o) *[F.]* (right) last chance to fill water bottles before the ascent. Continue up into the Chemin de Saint Jacques (*Jondoni Jakobe Bidea* in Basque) along the minor road D-428. Past *Auberge* **La Coquille Napoleón** *Priv.[10÷1]* €15 (dinner €12) ☎ 0662 259 940 where Lorna, Bixente & menagerie await **[0.8 km]** with Gite opp. **Villa Goxoki** ☎ 0559 491 773. Continue s/o veering <left at Villa Etchea Kalavainea and up to grove of chestnut trees at **Etchebestéa [2.1 km]**. Here the road from St. Michel joins from the left. *[*This was the ancient route taken by pilgrims coming from France – Stage I of the Codex Calixtinus].* Keep s/o uphill on the asphalt road to Huntto **[2.0 km]**.

4.9 km　Huntto *Auberge* **Ferme Ithurburia** *Priv.[22÷4]+* ☎ 0559 371 117 where Mme. Ourthiague offers a variety of meal options with 22 pilgrim bed spaces from €14 *Gites d'Etape* +priv. rooms *Chambres d'Hôtes* ½-board €32. Shortly afterwards turn <left onto grass **track [0.3 km]** to re-join **road [1.1 km]** with *[F.]* and viewing table *table d'orientation. Gite* **Kayola** *Priv.[12]* €15 run by auberge Orrison (see next panel). Continue on asphalt road for **[1.0 km]** to:

2.4 km　**Orisson** *Auberge* **Orrison** *Priv.* [18÷3] ℂ (France +33)* 0559 491 303 m: 0681 497 956 www.refuge-orisson.com network* hostel. *(photo right)*. popular bar and restaurant. Note lodging is ½-board only €35. Panoramic viewing platform *[F.]* & toilets (left). *[Next albergue: Roncesvalles – 17.1 km].* Continue s/o up the steep asphalt road and break through the 1,000m level to arrive at:

3.8 km　**Pic D'Orisson** (1,100m) with statue of the Virgin *Vierge d'Orisson Vierge de Biakorri* (see photo previous page) set against an impressive backdrop of the surrounding mountains and valleys. *[*Marian shrines to Our Lady appear all along the route and are one of the most common symbols of devotion on the camino].* Nearby (not visible) are the ruins of the ancient Chateau Pignon on the hill d'Urkulu. This remote area once had a medieval pilgrim hostel. Continue on the asphalt road with turn off (right) to Arneguy **D-128 [1.7 km]**. Keep s/o <left and turn off right> at *Le Croix Thibaud* a modern memorial **cross [1.9 km]** [!].

3.6 km　**Cruceiro** a bleak wayside cross leads us onto a rough grass track that cuts through a gap in the ridge ahead between *Pic de Leizar Atheka* and *the Col de Bentarte*. We leave the road at this stage. *Note: if the weather has deteriorated and you are not confident of proceeding, your options are: return to Auberge Orison, St Jean or take the D 128 to Arneguy. In an emergency there is a tiny mountain hut 50m (right) just through the gap ahead.* Pass through the gap in the ridge **[0.5 km]** (mountain shelter right) onto a woodland path turning <left at wire fence **[0.8 km]** along a heavily eroded gully passing a stone marker (No. 199) to a cattle grid **[0.5 km]** that marks the Spanish border.

1.8 km　**Frontera** *[F.] Fontaine de Roland* (left) cross over the cattle grid into Spain with stone border marker (ahead left) confirming that we are now in Navarre. *(Don't stray onto the GR10 the long-distance route over the Pyrenees from the Atlantic to the Mediterranean that crosses the path down to the left)* continue up right> on the GR65 to pass the ruins of an ancient border post (left). The camino now continues in a gentler climb through scattered woodland (mostly beech) up along a wide track until we reach the highest point at:

4.1 km　**Col de Lepoeder** (**1,450 metres**) from here we have our first view southwards over Navarre with the roof of the abbey at Roncesvalles and the town of Burguete in the valley below. **[?] Option:** *If you are tired or it is getting late (dusk) and/or it is wet and slippery underfoot, you can take the less steep (but longer) option by turning right> downhill on the asphalt road to Ibañeta 4.0 km and a further 1.3 km to Roncesvalles.* Otherwise, keep s/o over the road to the pathway that drops steeply down [!] through magnificent beech woods *bosque de Irati* one of the largest remaining beech forests in Europe, around Alto Don Simón to:

4.0 km　**Roncesvalles** *Orreaga Albergue* **Colegiata** *[183÷4].* Also 2 hotels, Casa Rural and Apartments. All immediately adjoining the monastery, collegiate church, bookshop, museum and ***Turismo*** *ℂ* 948 760 301 (see details overleaf).

ST. JEAN PIED-DE-PORT – RONCESVALLES
(Pays Basque)   (Navarre)

❷ **alternative road** route *Via Valcarlos
and the Puerto de Ibañeta*
Preferred option in bad or deteriorating weather.

	Path / Track	--- ---	6.8	---	*29%*
	Quiet Road	--- ---	10.6	---	*45%*
	Main Road	--- ---	6.2	---	*26%*
Total km	**Total distance**		**23.6 km** (14.7 ml)		

	Adjusted for climb	28.5 km (accrued ascent 990m = 4.9 km)
Alto ▲	High point: Ibañeta pass 1,055m. (3,460 feet)	
< Ⓐ Ⓗ >	**Intermediate accommodation:** Arneguy **8.4** & Valcarlos **11.7** km.	

The Practical Path: This is another strenuous uphill climb with less open views but more shelter from wind and rain in the woodland areas. While providing the security of the main road with shops and hotels along the way (Arneguy and Valcarlos) it also contains the hazards and noise of traffic and the harsh asphalt that is so tiring underfoot. Half the journey is on or parallel to the busy National Route N-135 but, notwithstanding, it also has peaceful woodland sections.

The variant [2a] is not recommended as it follows the main road all the way to Roncesvalles a distance of 27.5 km (32.0 km when adjusted for the cumulative ascent of 890m). Note: many pilgrims inadvertently take this option as they miss (a) the turn-off right> onto the quieter country lanes just outside St. Jean (b) the turn-off <left above Valcarlos onto the woodland path.

0.0 km **St. Jean** from central pilgrim office and albergues turn down the Rue de la Citadelle passing the parish Church of Our Lady at the End of the Bridge *Notre Dame du Bout du Pont* and out under the archway, over the river Nive and proceed up the cobbled rue D'Espagne to **Porte D'Espagne [0.4 km]** *[F.]* (left). Continue straight on (s/o) past the school (right) to **option point [0.1 km]**.

0.5 km **Option Opción** [?] This alternative road route via Valcarlos is recommended in bad weather. It is no less strenuous but the woods provide some shelter from rain and wind although the sun doesn't penetrate into the valley until late in the day. To access this route continue up for 100m past the school and turn right> into Chemin de Mayorga (signposted) to join the main road to Pamplona *Pampelune* on the D-933 (the N-135 once you cross the border into Spain).

1.4 km **Puente** [!] (1.9 km from the centre / albergue) as you leave the suburbs behind the main road takes a sharp left hand bend *down* to a slip road (right) [!] **Be Vigilant** *Vigilante*. Here, barely visible from the road and identified by a **3t** sign (3 tonne weight restriction) with red and white posts, is a short slip road to a concrete bridge over the river Chapitel (sometimes called petite Nive). Many pilgrims plod on along the main road, oblivious of this quieter parallel route.

You now continue on quiet lanes that wind their way up and down the pleasant rolling countryside parallel but away from the dangerous N-135. Veer <left at T-junction **[0.5 km]** continue and turn sharp <left at hairpin bend **[1.8 km]**. We now continue along a steeply undulating road for **[1.2 km]** down towards the main road over stream (bridge to the N-135 left) with sign to Oncorone right:

3.5 km   **Puente** (left) Turn up right> and then down <left and up again! to finally emerge onto the first short stretch of track where you cross the border into Spain at the modern shopping development *Venta Xabi & •café [F.]* Continue s/o through the car park (don't cross the river) and take the delightful riverside path all the way into Arneguy and:

3.0 km   **Arneguy / Option.** Several hotels and restaurants in Arneguy including *H°°* **Clementia** © 0559 371 354. Continue straight on along the main road *or* turn <left over the bridge (back into France!) and take the quieter scenic route (green) via Ondarolle (recommended) to cross the bridge and turn immediately right> up along the far bank of the river all the way into **Ondarolle [2.6 km]** and turn down right> to re-cross the river and take the steep path up **[0.7 km]** to:

3.3 km   **Valcarlos** *Luzaide Alb.* **Municipal** *[24÷2]* © 646 048 883 below main square €10 incl. (open all year). Continue past the public toilets turn <left on the main road. *[F.]* pilgrim monument opp. church dedicated to St. James with statue of the Saint as slayer-of-the-Moors *Santiago Matamoros*. *Ardandegia café & shop.* Other Lodging: *Hs°* **Maitena** © 948 790 210 adjoining the square and *Hs* **Casa Marcelino** © 948 790 186. The village takes its name from Charlemagne, who camped here on his return home and to lick his wounds after the defeat of his army rearguard and the death of Roland at Ibañeta. *[F.]* (right) as you leave the town **[0.5 km]**. Stay on the main road for another **[2.0 km]** and take a new turn off down <left (km.61) for **[0.7 km]** into:

3.2 km   **Gañecoleta** (no facilities) cross the river and take the riverside path cross back again up to the main road **[1.0 km]** continue up past (km.58) and take the slip road <left **[2.1 km]** to leave the main road for the last time.

3.1 km   **Camino** after **[0.4 km]** leave the track and take the narrow footpath up right> as it winds through beech and hazel woods to join the main road beside a house & dog kennels *Casa Borda Guardiano* **[2.2 km]**. Leave the road again after 90m and turn <left and continue through pine plantation for **[1.5 km]** to:

4.3 km   **Puerto Ibañeta** (1,055m) formerly the site of the Church and Hospice of San Salvador built in 1127 to serve pilgrims to Santiago and moved shortly afterwards to Roncesvalles. The pass now has a modern chapel and a stone monument to Roland (*Song of Roland fame, to mark the point at which the wail of his horn* Oliphant *was heard, too late to be rescued by Charlemagne*). There is also a bird observation post with information on the many species and flocks of birds that use this pass on their migrations. Turn <left down by the side of the observation centre along the path through the beech woods to:

1.3 km   **Roncesvalles** *Orreaga*

Albergue **Colegiata** *Conv.[183÷4]* © 948 760 000 recently renovated and housed in a quiet courtyard to the rear. The accommodation is spread over 3 floors with bunk beds in cubicles of 4 €12. Excellent modern facilities and open all year (separate building for use in the winter months). Summer overflow in the original medieval hostel *Itzandegia* on the main road with 110 beds in one room!

Albergue: Admission to the hostel and the official pilgrim passport *credencial del peregrino* can be obtained from the new pilgrim office in the albergue reception in the rear courtyard. Open daily 10:00–22:00. **Other accommodation:** *adj. monastery* **Casa de los Benficiados & *H**** Roncesvalles** © 948 760 105 part of the original monastery buildings with ind. rooms *from* €60 and pilgrim dinner (prior booking). On the main road: *Hs* **Casa Sabina** © 948 760 012 ind. rooms *from* €40. *Hs* **La Posada** © 948 760 225 *from* €45. *Next accommodation: Burgete (3.1 km).*

RONCESVALLES 'valley of thorns' (*Orreaga* in Basque) is still cloaked in its medieval atmosphere and provides another gateway to the camino. This is the major entry point for Spanish pilgrims travelling via Pamplona and was one of the earliest and most revered pilgrim refuges connecting the Augustinians' with the care of the Santiago pilgrims. Since the 12th century it has received, *'All pilgrims... sick and well. Catholics, Jews, pagans, heretics and vagabonds...'* this open hospitality continues today with one judicial agency offering the opportunity to walk the camino as a way of purging offenders of their misdeeds in lieu of a custodial sentence – finding self respect engendering a reformed life (details of this inspiring *last chance* concept can be found on the web; see New Internationalist *Redemption Road; Oikoten*).

The Royal Collegiate Church of Saint Mary *Real Collegiata de Santa María* was built at the behest of the Navarrese King Sancho the Strong *Sancho VII el Fuerte* but not consecrated until 1219 (after his death). It houses the beautiful 14[th]c. statue of Our Lady of Roncesvalles *Nuestra Señora de Roncesvalles*. There is a bookshop with pilgrim literature, maps and souvenirs and an interesting museum which includes the fine enamel / silver relic known as Charlemagne's chessboard *ajedrez de Carlomagno*. Adjoining the church is the cloisters *claustro* rebuilt in the 17th c. after they collapsed under snow! Access is via an inconspicuous door opposite the bookshop. Off the cloisters is the splendid *Sala Capitular XIV[th]c.* with its evocative mausoleum *XIII[th]c.*housing the tomb of Sancho VII and his wife Clemencia. The iron chains that Sancho broke in the defeat of the Moors at the famous battle of *Navas de Tolsa* in 1212 are located here and appear in the crest of the Government of Navarra. There is a small admission charge for the museum and cloisters.

Beside the Hostal La Posada is the Romanesque chapel of the Holy Spirit *Capilla de Sancti Spiritus XII[th]c.* otherwise referred to as the *Silo de Carlomagno* and reputed to be the burial place of the slaughtered rear-guard of Charlemagne's army and a medieval pilgrim burial site. Adjoining is the tiny Gothic chapel of St. James *Capilla de Santiago XII[th]c.* whose re-positioned bell (from the chapel at Ibañeta) once guided pilgrims through the swirling mists often experienced around the Ibañeta pass. Adjacent is a monument commemorating the battle of Roncesvalles and the death of Roland in 778.

Lying at an altitude of 950m, Roncesvalles has a resident population of only 30. The helpful *Turismo* © 948-760 301 is located in an old mill *antiguo molino* behind Casa Sabina. A simple pilgrim dinner is obtainable after mass (book *before* 18:00) at Hotel Roncesvalles, Casa Sabina or La Posada and provides an opportunity to meet other pilgrims and share experiences.

Pilgrim Mass: Mon-Fri at 20:00, Sat & Sun and festival days 18:00 (check times at the pilgrim office) in the *Iglesia de Santa María* with special blessing for all pilgrims of any faith. Note: pilgrim mass is often available at parish churches along the camino, generally around 20:00 but check availability and times at the local hostels.

PROVINCE OF NAVARRA: A fiercely independent mountainous region, its turbulent past has been influenced most notably by the French. Charlemagne's army damaged the walls of Pamplona despite an assurance that the city would not be harmed and so the Basques subsequently massacred the rear-guard of his army at Roncesvalles in retribution – but break no promises here and you will find a generosity of spirit and loyalty second to none. The hospitality of this region is graphically captured in the writings of many foreign authors, notably Ernest Hemingway who stayed for extended periods in Burguete and Pamplona. Fighting bulls and horses are bred in the hills and trout from the mountain streams and local game make up much of the cuisine of this area. Pork products find their way onto most menus with *chorizo* predominating (pork sausage marinated in various local spices, especially paprika) and often found in stews and soups. Vegetarians *vegetarianos* have a hard time here but on the lowlands further west we find widespread asparagus *espárrago de Navarra* and the bright red peppers *pimientas del piquillo* often stuffed with olives and other non-meat delicacies and eaten as snacks *tapas* along with the ubiquitous Spanish omelette *Tortilla de Patatas* made with thinly sliced potato and onion. The Navarrese love a sense of occasion and this is no more apparent than in the running of the bulls held during the festival of San Fermín in Pamplona in early July (to be avoided like the plague if you are on a solitary pilgrimage).

REFLECTIONS: *"I am doing the camino once again, looking for something I left behind or perhaps never found. It's like coming home."* Notes from a returning pilgrim from New Mexico recorded in the Pilgrim book in Roncesvalles. What are your reflections for this opening day to write in your own diary?

_____
_____
_____
_____
_____
_____
_____
_____
_____
_____
_____

❏ **Whatever you can do, or dream you can; begin it.**
Boldness has genius power and magic in it. *Goethe*

02 **751.1** km (466.7 ml) – Santiago

RONCESVALLES – ZUBIRI

▓▓▓▓▓▓	--- ---	17.5	--- ---	*80%*
━━━━	--- ---	3.2	--- ---	*15%*
▬▬▬▬	--- ---	1.2	--- ---	*5%*
Total km		**21.9** km (13.6 ml)		

▲▲▲ --- --- 23.1 km (^250m + 1.2 km)
Alto ▲ Alto de Mezquíriz 955m (3,133 ft)
< Ⓐ Ⓗ > Burguete **3.1** km – Espinal **6.7** km – Viskarreta **11.8** km.❏ **The Practical**

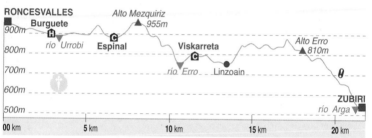

Path: Don't over extend yourself on these first few days. This second stage leads downhill across the fertile plain of the río Erro that flows southwards to join the río Ebro that we meet in Logroño. The Alto de Erro forms the ridge that separates the Erro from the Arga river valleys. There is good woodland shade and plenty of drinking fonts along this delightful section of the camino 83% of which is natural pathways that follow the N-135 which it crosses at several points. Close gates *cierren el portillo* as you pass through and be careful of the steep descent into Zubiri – the exposed rock makes it slippery, particularly in wet weather.

Note: *If you are feeling strong when you reach Zubiri you could continue to Larrasoaña 5.5 km (allow 2 hours at 'end of day pace'). This would allow extra time to explore Pamplona next day or the possibility of continuing to Cizur Menor.*

> *Decide where to stop according to your individual level of fitness. The maps in this guide are designed for an 'average' pace and based on what fits neatly on one page. Alternatives are limitless by using interim accommodation; e.g **Roncesvalles –Burgete 3.1 km – Pamplona 42.8 km! Or ❶ Roncesvalles–Larrasoaña 27.4 km. ❷ Larrasoaña–Cizur Menor 20.2 km. ❸ Cizur Menor–Puente la Reina 24.2 km...***

❏ **The Mystical Path:** The *Pasos de Roldán* are said to represent Roland's footsteps. Other legends have this melancholy place as scene of his failed attempt to summon Charlemagne to his rescue. Perhaps, in the silence of your own heart, you may still hear the wail of the Oliphant – symbol of that clarion call to spirit. Will you rest awhile at the old pilgrim well and hear a different horn break the woodland silence, a harsh and urgent note of warning from the fast moving traffic – a reminder to pilgrims that we travel now at a slower pace; one that allows awareness to expand.

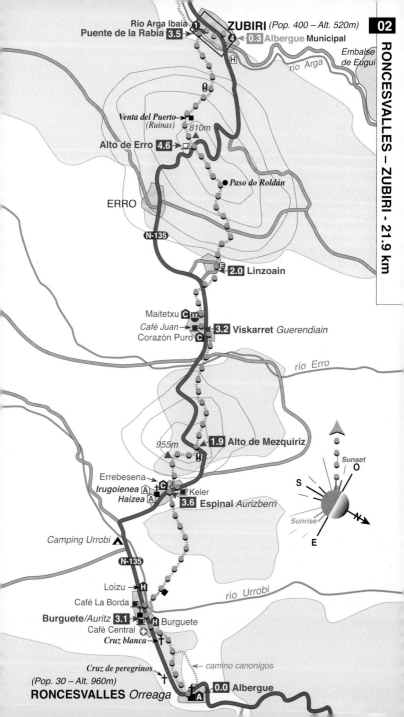

Río Arga Ibaia 1
Puente de la Rabia 3.5
ZUBIRI *(Pop. 400 – Alt. 520m)*
4 ← 0.3 Albergue **Municipal**
Embalse de Eugui

río Arga

θ

Venta del Puerto *(Ruinas)*
810m
Alto de Erro 4.6

● *Paso do Roldán*

ERRO

N-135

2.0 **Linzoain**

Maitetxu C m
Café Juan → C
Corazón Puro C
3.2 **Viskarret** *Guerendiain*

río Erro

955m
1.9 ← **Alto de Mezquiriz**
θ

Errebesena →
Irugoienea A C F
Haizea A ● Keler
3.6 **Espinal** *Aurizberri*

Camping Urrobi

N-135

río Urrobi

Loizu → H
Café La Borda
Burguete/*Auritz* 3.1
H **Burguete**
Café Central
Cruz blanca → ✝

Cruz de peregrinos ✝
(Pop. 30 – Alt. 960m)
RONCESVALLES *Orreaga*
⚓ A 0.0 **Albergue**

camino canónigos

Sunset O

S

Sunrise

E
N

❏ **Personal Reflections:** "…I have a blister on my heel and a bruised shoulder. Was it arrogance or absentmindedness that made me ignore the advice to stop and tighten my shoelaces and backpack – 60 seconds of adjustment would have prevented the friction and saved days of unnecessary suffering. I have become so conditioned to travelling in the fast lane, always trying to get somewhere in the shortest possible time, that I forget that the present moment contains the only time there is to actually act – all else is psychological time leading to stress… and unnecessary blisters."

0.0 km **Roncesvalles** *Orreaga* leaving the albergue proceed over the N-135 by hostal Posada onto woodland path parallel to the main road. Pass 14[th]c pilgrim cross *Cruz peregrino* **[0.5 km]** (left) on far side of road erected in honour of *Sancho VII. [*The dense woodland here held secret covens in the 16th century. Sorginaritz translates as 'Oakwood of Witches'. On the outskirts of Burguete we pass the White Cross Cruz Blanca* **[1.5 km]** *[symbol of divine purification erected as 'protection' against the witches healing arts!]*. Turn right on **N-135 [0.3 km]** continue long the main road into the village centre *centro del pueblo* **[0.37]**.

3.1 km **Burguete** *Auritz* Navarrese village at the start of which is *Hs*** **Burguete** €45+ ✆ 948 790 005 where Ernest Hemingway used to stay (it still has the piano bearing his signature 25/07/1923). The sombre central square of the town is overshadowed by Saint Nicholas church. *[*San Nicolás de Bari was closely identified with the camino and protector of pilgrims; but alas no help to the wise women of the area who were found guilty of witchcraft and burnt at the stake here in the village square]. Café Frontón* serves breakfast to pilgrims arriving from Roncesvalles. Public toilets adjoin (or try *Cafe y Panaderia La Borda* +100m). Other lodging: *CR* **Txikipolit** ✆ 948 760 019 *from* €30 (behind restaurant Txikipolit on main road). *Hs** **Iturrialdea** ✆ 948 760 243 *from* €30. *Hs** **Jaundeaburre** ✆ 948 760 078. *Hs** **Jauregui** ✆ 676 665 693. *P** **Iturrialdea** ✆ 948 760 243. *CR* **Pedroarena** ✆ 948 760 164 c/ Berexi 6 rooms from €38. At the far end of town the up-market *H**** **Loizu** ✆ 948 760 008 ind. rooms *from* €50. Turn right> [!] by *Banco Santander* over river Urrobi onto a wide farm track. At far end ford a small stream to enter a delightful woodland path to join a new asphalt track *[F.]* into:

3.6 km **Espinal** *Aurizberri* traditional village with *Iglesia de San Bartolomé* (left) at entrance (AT Irati not available for overnight stays). 200m left *Alb. Hs* **Haizea** *Priv.[30÷3]*+ €10 +€35 ✆ 948 760 379. *Alb.* **Irugoienea** *Priv.[18÷2]*+ €10 + ✆ 649 412 487 credenciales and free transport to Roncesvalles. Continue right along main street *Café-bar Keler* in central square (right). *CR* **Errebesena** ✆ 948 760 141 *[F.]* (left) and turn off <left onto quiet road which merges into a track and continues up through young forestry plantation, climbing steps into mature beech woods at the high point 955m and finally down through open fields to:

1.9 km **Alto de Mezquiriz** (Alt. 930m) cross N-135 [!] by stone plaque to the Virgin and Child and continue on the path down steeply through beech woods running above and parallel to the main road (path has been resurfaced and can be slippery when wet so watch your step [!]). Cross the río Erro on stepping-stones before finally crossing the N-135 into:

3.2 km **Viscarreta** *Bizkarreta / Guerendiain* ancient hamlet 13[th]c Church of St.

Peter and beginning of stage II of the Codex Calixtinus. Pensión 'Pure Heart' at entrance ♥ *P* **Corazón Puro** ✆ 948 392 113 B&B+dinner €18x2=36 (5 rooms). *CR* **La Posada Nueva** *from* €25 ✆ 948 760 173 directly opposite *Café Juan*. At village exit is a useful *supermercado* (left) and *CR* **Maitetxu** *from* €30-50 ✆ 948 760 175. Turn <left onto path and <left again past cemetery onto woodland path and cross over **N-135 [1.2** km] and continue to Pelota court *frontón* **[0.8** km] in:

2.0 km Linzoain *[F.]* (right) and climb steep narrow defile (recently concreted) into dense mixed woodland above. This delightful shaded path continues along a ridge and the *Pasos de Roldán* until we meet:

4.6 km Alto de Erro (Alt. 810m) cross N-135 to camino information signboard (left) and mobile café *Kiosco* into woodlands passing a former pilgrim inn *Venta de Puerto* (ruins) and descend steep rock outcrop [!] (slippery in wet weather) to:

3.5 km Zubiri *Puente de la Rabia* medieval bridge over the Río Arga *[*Named Rabia because of the legend that any animal led 3 times around the⌐central arch would be cured of rabies. This is also the likely site of a former leprosarium. Chapels and hospices dedicated to San Lazarus were often located at the entrance or exit to towns along the way].* We will cross the river Arga many times over the next few days until we finally leave it at Puente la Reina.

If you are feeling strong *fuerte* continue to the next albergue in Larrasoaña (5.6 km) the busy N-135 bypasses this latter village. This would allow more time to explore the historic city of Pamplona next day before proceeding, perhaps, to Cizur Menor? ***Find your own pace and make your own itinerary***. If you are feeling tired or it is late in the day turn right> over bridge into the industrial town of Zubiri which offers good pilgrim facilities: *Albergue* ❶ **Río Arga Ibaia** *Priv.[8÷2]*+ €15-€40 ✆ 948 304 243 by the bridge. ❷ **Zaldiko** *Priv.[24÷3]* €10 ✆ 609 736 420. 100m from the bridge. Continue past the church and turn right> on main road to ❸ **El Palo de Avellano** *Priv.[40÷5]*+ €15-17 +€55 double ✆ 948 304 770 garden at rear. ❹ **Antigua Escuela** *Muni.[48÷2]* €8 (€4 on floor adj.) ✆ 628 324 186 Av. Zubiri *[+300m]*. ❺ **Suseia** *Priv.[22÷4]*+ €15 ✆ 948 304 353 C/ Murelu, 12 *[+500m]*. **ZUBIRI**: Industrial town (Pop: 400) straddling the N-135 and serving the adjacent Magna plant *Magnesitas de Navarra*. Facilities incl. Planeta Agua ✆ 948 304 063 (pilgrim equipment), grocery shop, bank and panadería centred on the parish Church of St. Stephen *San Esteban [F.]*. Popular *Bar Valentin* by the river & café *Ogi Berri* opp church. Other Lodging: *P*' **Zubiaren Etxea** ✆ 948 304 293. *P*' **Usoa** ✆ 628 058 048. *P*' **Amets** ✆ 948 304 308 popular (with garden onto river). On main road *P*' **Goika** ✆ 638 847 974. *P*' **Benta Berri** ✆ 636 134 781 & *Hs*' **Zubiri** ✆ 948 304 329 *from* €60-€100. *Hs* **Gau-Txori** €40 ✆ 948 30 45 31 Av Roncesvalles + 500m.

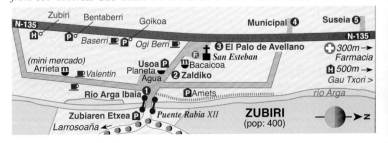

REFLECTIONS: *"Worrying is praying for what we don't want."* Pilgrim book.

❏ **I am not a human being on a spiritual journey.**
I am spiritual being on a human journey.
———————————————— *Spiritual maxim*

03 **729.2** km (453.1 ml) – Santiago

ZUBIRI – PAMPLONA

⬩⬩⬩⬩⬩⬩⬩⬩⬩	--- ---	13.3	--- ---	*64%*
———	--- ---	2.2	--- ---	*11%*
▬▬▬	--- ---	5.4	--- ---	*25%*
Total km		**20.9 km**	(13.0 ml)	

◣ --- --- 22.7 km (^360m + 1.8 km)

Alto ▲ Ilarratz 560m (1,837 ft)

< Ⓐ Ⓗ > Larrasoaña *(+0.3)* **5.3** km – Akerreta **6.0** km – Zuriain **9.1** km – *[Zabaldika* **12.7** *km (+0.3)]* - Trinidad de Arre / Villalba **16.1** km – *[Huarte* **16.6** *km].*

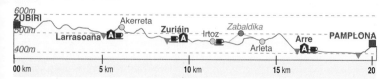

❏ **The Practical Path:** The first half of this section is a tranquil walk by the río Arga. The latter half is along busy main roads leading into and through the city of Pamplona. There is plenty of shade along the tree-lined riverbanks and a number of drinking fonts along the way. Be prepared for the noise and bustle of city life after the relative calm of the camino. City folk are forever in a rush, so tread warily amongst the traffic and watch your wallet. Petty theft has always been a problem in our unequal society. Medieval pilgrims were sometimes murdered for their satchels and sandals! *Trust in God, and tether your camel* feels like balanced advice and bears repeating. Pamplona is a beautiful city and the camino runs through its historic heart – so you can soak up some of the atmosphere and major buildings just by walking the waymarked route. Visit the cathedral & adjoining museum and explore the lively streets and sample some of the famous cafés and tapas *pintxos* bars.

❏ **The Mystical Path:** Santiago peregrino is carved into the ancient stone pillar and stands sentinel over the magnificent medieval bridge, gateway to this historic city. The sightless eyes have watched countless pilgrims wend their wary way over these self-same arches. And what of the invisible eye that sees beyond space and time, gateway to the inner realm of spirit. One path is full of distraction and decay. The other leads to peace and eternal truth. Which world we see depends on which we are looking for.

❏ **Personal Reflections:** *"...so many contrasting sensations – the quiet of the countryside, the bustle of the city, the warmth of the sun, the cool of the rain, the perfume of the wild flowers, the acrid smell of burning rubbish, the bright red of the ubiquitous poppy, the dull grey of asphalt road. I sit supported by my rucksack and watch the stalks of wheat swaying in the wind. My lunch is laid out before me like a royal feast. I feel an overwhelming sense of well-being and recite the beautiful Anthroposophical grace with which to bless the richness of this day and my simple meal...*

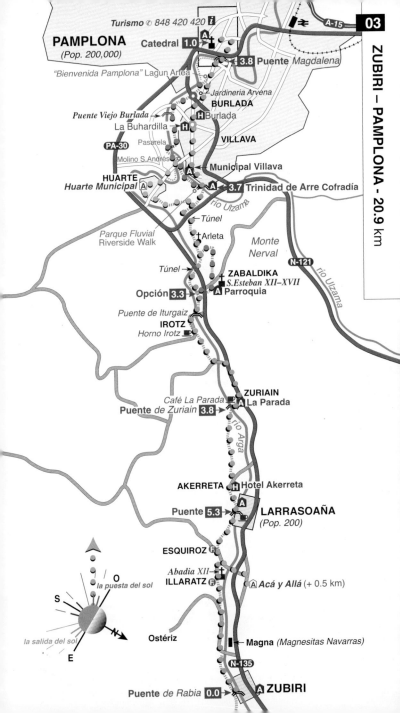

Turismo © 848 420 420 ℹ️

PAMPLONA
(Pop. 200,000)
Catedral 🅰️✝️ **1.0**

A-15

✈️🚉

✝️ **3.8** Puente *Magdalena*

"Bienvenida Pamplona" Lagun Artea

Jardinería Arvena

BURLADA

Puente Viejo Burlada →
La Buhardilla
Ⓗ Burlada
Ⓗ

PA-30
Pasarela

VILLAVA

Molino S.Andrés
→ 🅰️ Municipal Villava

HUARTE
Huarte Municipal 🅰️
🅰️ **3.7** Trinidad de Arre Cofradía

río Ulzama

Túnel

Parque Fluvial
Riverside Walk

✝️Arleta

Monte
Nerval

N-121

río Ulzama

Túnel →
✝️ **ZABALDIKA**
■ S.Esteban XII–XVII
Opción 3.3
🅰️ Parroquia

Puente de Iturgaiz
IROTZ
Horno Irotz ■

ZURIAIN
Café La Parada 🅰️ La Parada
Puente *de Zuriain* **3.8** →

río Arga

AKERRETA Ⓗ Hotel Akerreta
🅰️
Puente 5.3 → **LARRASOAÑA**
(Pop. 200)

ESQUIROZ Ⓕ

Abadía XII → ✝️
ILLARATZ Ⓕ
🅰️ *Acá y Allá* (+ 0.5 km)

O
la puesta del sol
S

Ostériz

E

la salida del sol

■ → **Magna** *(Magnesitas Navarras)*

N-135

Puente *de Rabia* **0.0** →
🅰️ **ZUBIRI**

The silver rain, the shining sun, the fields where scarlet poppies run
And all the ripples in the wheat are in the food that I do eat
So when I sit for every meal and say a grace, I always feel
That I am eating rain and sun and fields were scarlet poppies run.

0.0 km **Zubiri** *Puente de la Rabia* From the medieval bridge *Puente de la Rabia* keep s/o up concrete path *[F.]* (left) down over stream around the Magna industrial plant *Magnesitas Navarras* up into the peaceful hamlet of **Ilarratz** shelter and *[F.]* (right) past the Abbey ruins *XII (restoration project)* take road down to T-junction [with **Detour right Urdániz:** ● ● ● ● *(+ 0.5 km) Hs* **Acá y Allá** *Priv.[6÷1]* €15 / menú €10 + piscina © 615 245 439 (Jesús Góngora) c/ San Miguel 18. For main route turn left up steeply into **Esquirotz** *[F.]* (left) onto path parrallel to the rio Arga.

5.3 km Larrasoaña *Puente de los Bandidos* medieval bridge over río Arga. *If you don't plan to visit this historic pilgrim village keep s/o for Pamplona* ▼. *Otherwise turn right>* over the bridge past the Church of San Nicolás XIIIc to Taberna Perutxena. Turn <left *Alb.* ❷ **Bide Ederra** *Priv.[4÷1]*+ €16+40 c/San Nicolás 27 © 948 304 692. Continue into village square with town hall and *Alb.* ❶ **Larrasoaña** *Muni.[60÷8]* €6 © 605 505 489 beds spread over several rooms above the council offices and overflow in a converted barn in a laneway opposite; the basic facilities include a small open patio area; mixed reports. **Other Lodging:** *P*° El Camino *Casa Sangalo* €60 © 948 304 250 (350m past albergue) also *bar/ restaurant* Larrasoaña serving pilgrim *menú* and early breakfast. To the rear of San Nicolas church *CR* **Tau** €60 © 948 304 720 on c/ Errotabidea 18 and towards the far end of the village *Alb.* ❸ **San Nicolás** *Priv.[40÷8]* €11 © 619 559 225 (Luis y María Jesús) and adj. '*supermercado' Amari* also *P*° **El Peregrino** © 948 304 554 (often closed) and down side street opp. *CR* **Casa Elita** €60 © 948 304 449 c/ Amairu 7 (+ small shop).

LARRASOAÑA: Historic town (Population 200) has retained its links with the pilgrim's Way. An important pilgrim halt in medieval times with 2 pilgrim hospitals and a monastery (no longer evident) it achieved the status of *Villa Franca* (a settlement of pilgrims arriving from France). The town is full of Jacobean symbols and armorial shields on its traditional stone buildings.

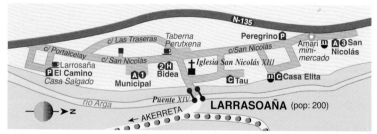

If you have been visiting Larrasoaña return to the **bridge** turn right> and ▼ climb to the hilltop hamlet of **Akerreta [0.7 km]** *H*°°°*Akerreta* © 948 304 572 well restored Basque house with rooms from €60-90. Continue downhill through open country to re-join the river Arga before crossing the bridge in **Zuriáin [3.1 km]** into:

`3.8 km` **Zuriáin** *Café & Alb.* **La Parada de Zuriain** *Priv.[4÷1]*+ €16-20 incl. ℂ 699 556 741. Turn <left on N-135 [!] and <left again *signposted Illurdotz* cross the río Arga and right> past houses and abandoned quarry climbing up a narrow path (fine views over the Arga valley) to **Irotz [2.1 km]** with rest area *[F.]* and *Horno Irotz* whose oven *horno* bakes fresh bread or pizza which you can eat on the terrace patio. Continue down to **Puente de Iturgaiz [0.5 km]**. Here a concrete track follows the river along a riverside park *parque fluvial* or take the original parallel path immediately above into **Barrio San Estaban de Abajo [0.7 km]** and option.

`3.3 km` **Opción** (down) left for main route or (up) right for Zabaldika. ▼

Option Zabaldika ✓● ● ● ● **(0.5 km shorter)** turn up right across the N-135 [!] and take the path (by access road) up to **Zabaldika [0.3 km]** ♥ *Alb.* **Zabaldika** *Par.[18÷2]* €-donativo ℂ 948 330 918 lovingly renovated and meticulously run by volunteers from the Federation of Friends. After a communal meal the RSCJ Sisters (Society of the Sacred Heart) welcome pilgrims to the adj. XIII *iglesia de San Esteban* with fine altarpiece *retablo* and statue of St. James. The sisters provide the possibility to pray and share together and to visit the ancient belfry. Take the high path out of the village and rejoin the main route just before Arleta **[0.7 km]**.

▼ For the main route continue along concrete river track and under the N-135 to picnic site **parque [0.6 km]** *[F.]* w.c. Take steep path up the side of Monte Narval *(alternative route from Zabaldika joins from above right* **[0.4 km]***)* continue through **Arleta [0.5 km]** manor house and capela de Santa Marina (private). Continue on path and take the underpass **Túnel [1.1 km]** steeply up the far side *Monte Miravalles* to optional detour to Huarte at the high point *alto* 495m **[0.3 km]**. ▼

Detour Huarte 1.3 km ● ● ● ● At the high point take the path <left down into the suburb of Huarte via calle San Esteban. Cross the wide main road into Plaza San Juan. The municipal hostel is located behind the church **[1.3 km]** *Alb.* **Huarte** *Muni.[60÷7]* €10 ℂ 948 334 413. Modern building with all facilities €10. Rejoin the river route at **Molino de San Andrés [1.0 km]**. (Note the route is waymarked either directly via the main road or by following the river loop) or continue into Av. Serapio Huici in Villava (a further 400m) and join the main route at that point.

▼ For the main route continue s/o down to the magnificent medieval bridge over the río Ultzama (tributary of the Arga) and **option [0.8 km]**:

`3.7 km` **Puente de Arre** *Opción Alb.* **Cofradía de la Trinidad de Arre** *Conv. [34÷4]* € 8 *Hermanos Maristas* ℂ 948 332 941 located behind the basilica church *Convento de la Trinidad*. Quiet location with peaceful gardens adjoining the river.

Note: for the next 9.7 km (until you reach Cizur Menor on the western outskirts) the waymarked camino is on hard city pavements and suburban streets with much traffic. There is an option to take the riverside path (recommended) see next page. Pamplona with population of 200,000 is a vibrant university city built around the historical old town and cathedral (with adjacent albergue) at its centre.

Option: Riverside Path *Parque Fluvial.* ✓● ● ● ● **Total from Arre 4.4 km** (*600m longer than the alternative route via the main road* calle mayor *through Burlada*). Delightful linear park where the rivers Ultzama and Arga provide the only necessary waymarks all the way to Puente de la Magdalena. To take this route turn <left along the river in Arre (*before* crossing over bridge). Continue (river on our right) past the municipal swimming pool *piscina* to next bridge and Saint Andrew's Mill **Puente y Molino de San Andrés [0.9 km]** with *Café Molino* mill museum (free) and outdoor recreation area. This is where the rios Arre and Ultzama join (also pilgrims from the Huarte detour). Continue along the river and cross over footbridge *pasarela* **[0.2 km]** through park passing (left) the 'old' bridge **Puente Viejo de Burlada [1.3 km]**. Keep s/o under the road **bridge [0.5 km]** and rejoin the main waymarked route by pelota court **Lagun Artea [0.5 km]** on c/ Burlada by Pamplona welcome *Bienvenida* sign. *[It is possible at this point to continue along the riverside path but it takes a wide loop away from our destination and is all on concrete].* Join main route to **Puente de la Magdalena [1.0 km]**.

Main waymarked route: Turn <left over the bridge at Arre into the pedestrian *calle Mayor* which we follow straight through **Villava** to Town Hall *Casa Consistorial* and Parroquia *S.Andrés* **[0.6 km]** with popular *Café Paradiso* and *detour**: *[200m (left) is the modern Alb.* **Villava** *Muni.[48÷5]* €9 © 948 331 971 c/Pedro de Atarrabia by the rio Ultzama (regular bus to city centre). On the far side of the river (near swimpool) P* **Etxea** *B&B* €25 © 696 597 140 c/ grupo martiket, 6]. *Continue s/o through the busy suburbs of **Burlada** to rotunda and *H°* **La Buhardilla** © 948 382 872 Av. Serapio Huici . Various modern hotels and cafés incl. *H°°* **Burlada** © 948 333 676 in c/Fuente. At the far end of *c/Mayor* **[1.5 km]** we turn diagonally right> by *Talleres Garysa neumaticos* at the corner of school *Hermanos del Amor Dios* and cross main road by garden centre *Jardinería Arvena* into c/Burlada past timber yard (right) and welcome *Bienvenida* sign and pelota court at **Lagun Artea [0.7 km]** (here river path joins) and finally to the medieval bridge 'gateway' to Pamplona **[1.0 km]**:

3.8 km Puente ❶ *Puente de Magdalena XII*th*C*. Cross the famous pilgrim bridge *[Note: Turn left over bridge for 200m to Alb. ❶* **Casa Paderborn** *Asoc.[26÷5]* €6 © 948 211 712 Playa de Caparroso, 6 located on the river and managed by a German confraternity. The bar in the adj. swimming complex Club Natación is open to the public and just beyond is a cliff side lift to the bullring].*

To proceed directly to the city centre veer right> over bridge, cross the tree-lined Playa Caparroso veering right> around the old city walls entering this historic city over the drawbridge and the splendid ❷ *Portal de Zumalacárregi* **[0.5 km]** also called *Portal de Francia* – a reminder that Pamplona has always opened its doors to pilgrims coming from France since mediaeval times.

[Note: immediately inside the city walls there is an option to turn up sharp <left to "one of the most charming spots in the city" ● *Baluarte del Redín* viewpoint and rampart walk overlooking rio Arga. Gossip corner & cross *rincón y cruz de Menidero* had a more sinister use as site of the city's executions! More benignly the *café Caballo Blanco* was a former pilgrim hospital where the lane to the rear gives access to the cathedral (see photo left) via the shaded Plaza San José.

The main route (from Portal de Francia) continues s/o into c/ Carmen *Karmen Kalea*. Here at the start @N°31 *Alb.* ❷ **Ibarrola** *Priv.[20÷1]* €15 incl. © 948 223 332 (Iñaki y César) ultra modern interior; can arrange next stage by horse! @N°18 *Alb.* ❸ **Iruñako Aterpea** *Priv.[22÷1]* €14 © 948 044 637. Proceed to the cross of 5 roads [0.3 km]. To continue through the city centre turn right into c/ de Mercederes or turn <left into c/Curia to visit the cathedral and the main pilgrim hostel [0.2 km] passing ■ *Caminoteca* at N° 15 © 948 210 316 where Itsván & Anita provide pilgrim support, information and a wide range of pilgrim equipment and maps...

1.0 km **Pamplona** *Alb.* ❹ **Jesús y María** *Asoc.[114÷2]* €7 © 948 222 644 part of the 17thC Jesuit church of *Jesús y María* adapted to provide beds in cubicles built into the naves with all mod cons (closed Dec/Jan and S.Fermin fiesta). Centrally situated on c/ Compañía good location to explore the old town and adj. cathedral. Also ❺ **Plaza Catedral** *Priv.[46÷5]* €15-18 © 948 591 336 c/ Navarrería 35 and the far side of the city *Alb.* ❻ **Ciudadela 7** *Priv.[24÷4]* €16 © 616 786 479 c/Ciudadela 7, 1°.

❸ *Cathedral of Santa María la Real XVthC*
An austere Gothic structure with neoclassical façade. Visit the interior (€2 with credencial) and alabaster mausoleum of Carlos *El Noble* and his wife Leonor in the main nave but pride of place is the beautiful south door *puerta preciosa* ascribed to Master Esteban who also carved the south door *Puerta de las Platerias* in Santiago Cathedral. The beautiful **cloisters** with their fine filigree 'silverware' *plateresque* stonework (see photo) adjoin the ● *Diocesan museum*; site of the original Roman citadel.

❑ Tourist office **Turismo**, Av. Roncesvalles, 4 (adj. the bull-running statue *monumento al Encierro*). © 848 420 420. Open Tues-Sat 10.00-17.00, Sundays & festivals 10.00-14.00. Mondays closed. *[Note: austerity measures in Spain have forced some tourist offices to close or reduce opening hours. Note also that most public offices (and many churches, museums etc) close Mondays. © Spain +34.]*
❑ *Other hostels:* (€15+ incl.): **Hemingway** c/Amaya,26 © 948 983 884. **Aloha** c/Sangüesa,2 © 648 289 403. **Xarma** Av. Baja Navarra © 948 046 449.
❑ *Other Lodging:* At entrance: *H°°°°* **Pamplona Catedral** €70+ © 948 226 688 c/Dos de Mayo (*Puerta del camino* former convent). Also in the old city around San Saturnino wide selection of small and inexpensive hotels and pensions including: *P°* **Lambertini** c/Mercadore, 17 © 948 210 303. *P* **La Viña** c/Jarauta, 8 © 948 213 250. *P°* **Eslava** c/Eslava, 13 (one star mixed reports) © 948 221 558. *P* **Escaray** (no star good reports) c/Nueva, 24 © 948 227 825. **On c/ San Nicolás:** *P°°* **Otano** © 948 227 036 at N° 5. *P°* **San Nicolás** © 948 221 319 at N° 13. *Hs* **Don Lluis** © 948 210 499 at N° 24. *Hs* **Aralar** © 948 221 116 at N° 12. **On c/San Gregorio:** *P°* **La Montañesa** N° 2 © 948 224 380. *P°* **Dionisio** N°5 © 948 224 380. *P°* **El Camino** N° 12 © 638 206 664. At the far end of c/Mayor (behind the Convento Recoletas) *Hs°°* **Hotel Eslava** overlooking the tiny *Plaza Virgen de la O* which forms part of the old city walls and leads directly into the spacious *Parque Traconera*. Back on Plaza del Castillo the newly refurbished *H°°°°°* **La Perla** €140+ © 948 223 000 (Hemingway used to stay here). During the hectic summer months additional dormitory accommodation *may* be available at: **San Saturnino** (city centre). **Catholic Scouts** (Puente de la Magdalena). **Seminario Diocesano** Av. de la Baja Navarra. **Ikastola Aimur** sports hall at c/Fuente del Hierro. **Juvenil** *youth hostel* c/Goroabe, 36.

Pamplona City 'Tours': If you are a *Hemingway aficianado* visit the Paseo Ernest Hemingway with a statue of the author outside the bullring *Plaza de Toros adj.* ● *S. Bartolomé Fort XVII[th]C Interpretation Centre and park].* Hemingway's novel 'The Sun Also Rises' published in 1926 made the bull runs *encierros* and festival world renowned. The festival of *Sanfermines* was started in the 13th century but may have pre-Roman origins and some legends suggest that San Fermín himself was martyred by being dragged by bulls thorough the streets. Alcohol is probably the biggest cause of injury and death today despite rule 6 that states, 'it is not allowed to enter the route in a state of drunkenness or under the effects of drugs.'! Return via *calle Estafeta* where the bulls run free during San Fermín from July 6th to 14th when the city goes wild, beds are impossible to find and the price of everything soars!

Off calle Estafeta is Pamplona's main square ● *Plaza del Castillo* a huge open space with covered arcades shading the shops, bars and cafés. Don't miss the magnificent and sumptuous *interior* of the art deco *café Iruña.* Bar Txoko (top corner - gets the last of the evening sun) but tapas *pintxos* here cost double what you might expect to pay elsewhere so try the bustling and evocative *c/San Nicolás* full of inexpensive *pensiónes* and *tapas bars* where you also find the fortified Romanesque ❹ *Iglesia San Nicolás XII[th]C* on the corner of c/San Nicolás and c/San Miguel.

At the start of c/Mayor we arrive at the geographical centre of Pamplona ❺ *San Saturnino XIII[th]C* another fortified church also called San Cernín and formerly a pilgrim hostel (now a pilgrim association office). If you are staying in Pamplona this is a good place to take your bearings. Just in front of the church (in the paving slabs down the steps) is a plaque marking the well from which San Saturnino baptised the first Christians in the city. Next we come to the town hall ❻ *Casa Consistorial* with its splendid baroque façade dominating the small square (the *encierros* are 'announced' from its balcony). Steps at the rear bring us down into c/Santo Domingo where we find the ❼ *Museo de Navarra* (free with credencial) with Roman artefacts from the 1st century. (the building was formerly a medieval pilgrim hospital).

On the way out of the city we pass ❽ *Iglesia San Lorenzo (y Capela de San Fermín)* and ❾ *Ciudadela* described in the next stage and we exit the city at ❿ the stone pilgrim bridge over the río Sadar ❿ *[3.9 km from Puente de Magdalena ❶].*

PAMPLONA with an ever-expanding population (currently around 200,000) is a vibrant university city that retains its close historical connections with the camino and whose patron Saint is San Fermín. The Roman general Pompaelo reputedly founded the city in the first century B.C. Its long and dramatic history has been closely linked with pilgrims, many of whom were enticed to settle in the city under special status. This migration often created petty jealousies between the native inhabitants and the favoured settlers, resulting in the development of separate districts, which later became fortified as open hostilities raged between the inhabitants and their differing cultures. In 1423 King Carlos conceded the Privilege of the Union, which extended the special status to all parts of the city and began an era of cooperation. Several other towns and cities along the Way such as at Estella (stage 5) followed a similar pattern of agreement and development. Pamplona marks the beginning of stage III of the Codex Calixtinus.

REFLECTIONS: *"The camino already feels like a pilgrimage and has developed a deeper significance than when I began. I am stronger and have more courage than I thought. I have already been given many blessings and gifts..."* Notes from an Australian pilgrim recorded in the Pamplona albergue.

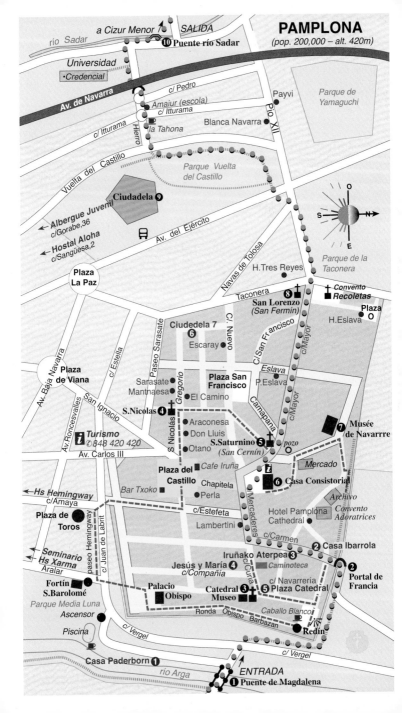

68

❏ **Be the change you want to see in the world.** *Mahatma Gandhi*

04 708.3 km (440.1 ml) – Santiago

PAMPLONA – PUENTE LA REINA

⋯⋯⋯⋯	--- --- 16.6--- ---	*70%*
▬▬▬	--- --- 4.1--- ---	*17%*
▬▬▬	--- --- 3.1--- ---	*13%*
Total km	**23.8 km** 14.8 ml	

▰▰ --- ---25.5 km (+1.7 km)
Alto ▲ Alto de Perdón 790m (2,590 ft)
< Ⓐ Ⓗ > Cizur Menor **5.0** km – Zariquiegui **11.1** km – Uterga **17.3** km – Muruzábal **19.8** km – Óbanos **21.6** km.

❏ **The Practical Path:** The first 5 km is mostly via city pavements and suburban roads which are hard underfoot. But beyond Cizur Menor we have pathways through the hill pass ahead. This is a steep climb through the middle of the wind turbines *parque ecológico* visible on the skyline at *Alto del Perdón*. As we ascend there are wonderful views back over Pamplona and to the south the conical peak of Higa at Monreal is clearly visible, behind which are the Sierra de Leyre and the Somport Pass through which the *Camino Aragonés* joins the route at Eunate. As we crest the summit the view westward over the Arga valley opens up with the villages we pass through now visible ahead. Be careful on the steep descent on the loose boulders.

❏ **The Mystical Path:** Will we notice the beehives? Each home to thousands of bees that collect nectar from the almond blossom that grace this fertile plain in the springtime. In the winter all is laid bare and the hives lie dormant waiting a time of renewal. What is the season of our inner landscape? Is it time to sow new seeds, a time of growth, of harvest or a time of reflection in the deep rich soil of the soul? The seasons turn in an endless cycle of life. After the dark of winter comes the light of summer and in between are the spring and autumn equinoxes when light and dark are perfectly balanced. Have we got the balance right in our life between the busy-ness of the ego and the being-ness of spirit?

❏ **Personal Reflections:** *"... I saw her ahead on the road to Cizur Menor, a diminutive figure walking alone into the dusk. She was a young mendicant carrying no money and accepting only whatever charity she received along the way. She accepted a simple pilgrim meal at the bar but refused to take any emergency cash. I was the one imprisoned by my fears – my wallet thick with euros. She was free, fearless and with an unshakable belief in the goodness of her fellow human beings. Her courage and trust leave me deeply humbled..."*

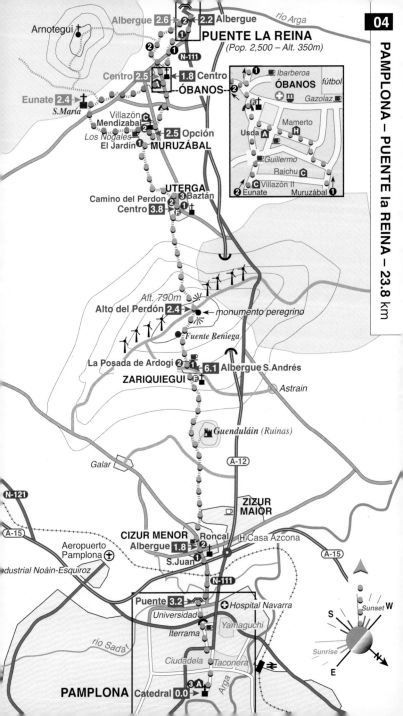

Arnotegui †

Albergue **2.6** → ❷ ← **2.2** Albergue

río Arga

❶

❷ ❶

PUENTE LA REINA
(Pop. 2,500 – Alt. 350m)

N-111

Centro **2.5**   **1.8** Centro

ÓBANOS

Eunate **2.4** †
S.María

Villazón
Mendizabal ❷   **2.5** Opción
Los Nogales
El Jardín   **MURUZÁBAL**

UTERGA
❸ Baztán
Camino del Perdon ❷
Centro **3.8**   ❶ †
F

Alt. 790m
Alto del Perdón **2.4**   *monumento peregrino*

Fuente Reniega

La Posada de Ardogi ❷   **6.1** Albergue S.Andrés
ZARIQUIEGUI   F

Astrain

Guenduláin (Ruinas)

Galar

A-12

ZIZUR
MAIOR

N-121
A-15

CIZUR MENOR   Roncal   H.Casa Azcona
Albergue **1.8**   ❷
Aeropuerto
Pamplona ✈
S.Juan
ndustrial Noáin-Esquiroz   N-111   A-15

Puente **3.2**
Universidad   ✚ Hospital Navarra
Iterrama   Yamaguchi
Ciudádela   Taconera
río Sada   Arga

PAMPLONA Catedral **0.0**   ❸ A

S   Sunset W

Sunrise

E

ÓBANOS inset

↑ ❶   ▪ Ibarberoa
F †   **ÓBANOS**   fútbol
✚ m   Gazolaz
❷
Mamerto
Usda A   H
Guillermo
Raichu
❷ Eunate   C Villazón II   C
Muruzábal ❶

70

0.0 km **Catedral** *Albergue* Continue down c/Curia (opp. entrance to the cathedral) into c/Mercaderes, past **San Saturnino** into the narrow c/Mayor which leads us into Plaza Recoletas (right) and **San Lorenzo** (left) with its chapel to the patron saint of Pamplona, San Fermín. Here we cross over the busy **c/Taconera** [**0.9** km] into c/ Bosquecillo alongside Parque de la Taconera (right). At the junction of Av. de Pio XII and Av. del Ejército veer <left over the junction (pedestrian crossings) through the relative calm of the park that surrounds the star-shaped citadel *ciudadela* (left).

Halfway round the park watch out for arrows that veer off right> over the busy c/Vuelta del Castillo into the wide tree-lined c/Fuente del Hierro. Follow this road to its junction with c/ Iturrama roundabout **Glorieta** [**1.4** km]. *[Note: this is the last opportunity for refreshments or shops before Cizur Menor.]* café La Tahona on the corner with sports hall of *Escola Amaiur* (red brick building on opposite corner (may house pilgrim groups during the busy summer months). *[For hotels in Iturrama area turn right off the camino into Av. Pio XII. There are a number of small pensiónes incl. P* **Payvi II / III** © 948 278 508 Av. Pío XII, Nº30 (adj. gasolinera). P* **Pasadena** © 948 177 650 Nº32 and H*** **Hotel Blanca de Navarra** Nº43 © 948 171 010 with pilgrim discount from €50].*

From the Iturrama roundabout pass *under* the busy Av. de Navarra ring road *túnel* along the university campus. Here on the left we can receive 'accreditation' from the university by having our *credenciales* stamped by the porter. Continue to the roundabout veering right> along main road and <left across the pilgrim bridge over the **Río Sadar** [**0.9** km].

3.2 km **Puente** *río Sadar Total distance from Puente de la Magdalena to Puente Sadar (entrance and exit to Pamplona city) 3.9 km.* Proceed over the river onto local road over railway line and A-15 autopista straight into the Cizur Menor with the church of St. John the Baptist (left at entrance) and the adjacent *Alb.* ❶ **Sanjuanista** *Priv.[27÷3]* €4 run by the Knights of St. John of Malta © 616 651 330 and up to **crossroads** with restaurant *Martintxo,* asador *Tremendo* Bar *Kariba* and farmacia.

1.8 km Cizur Menor ♥*Alb.* ❷ **Roncal** *Priv.[50÷5]* €10 Maribel Roncal © 670 323 271 located just up from the crossroads (below the church of San Miguel). Run by the dedicated Roncal family with all facilities including a garden offering tranquillity – very popular and fills quickly during the summer season open all year except Nov. (see photo right). *Note:* If the albergues are full your options are [a] retrace your steps and find accommodation in Pamplona or its  suburbs (a local bus service connects from here to the city centre). [b] continue on to the next albergue in Zariquiegui 6.1 km. or [c] Head over to Cizur Mayor *Zizur Maior (Basque)* to the popular H **Casa Azcona** €40+ © 948 287 662 Av. Belascoaín or the upmarket Marriott H*** **AC Zizur Mayor** €60+ © 948 287 119 or the more modest Hs **Nekea** © 948 185 044 Travesia S.Francisco (*Directions*: head uphill past the church over flyover (autopista) [1.1 km] into the modern suburb of Zizur Maior. For Hotel Azcona continue s/o for 0.5 km.

Cizur Menor is an affluent dormitory town of Pamplona with a rapidly expanding population that has quadrupled in the last decade and now stands at 2,200. It was formerly a commandery of the Order of St. John of Jerusalem and also provided a pilgrim hospice dedicated to Our Lady of Forgiveness *Nuestra Señora del Perdón,* who was, and remains, much venerated in this area. Occupying an elevated site is the XII[th]C Romanesque church dedicated to the archangel Saint Michael *Iglesia de San Miguel Arcángel.* Several restaurants, bar, shop and a chemist.

Keep s/o past albergue ❷ down to medieval well (left) and pelota court *[F.]* and continue through modern housing estate to a dirt road which skirts the suburbs *urbanisation* of Cizur Mayor *[Cafe La Tahona* far *end].* We now start the climb up to the village of Zariquiegui, below the wind farm on the horizon. The path winds through open arable fields crossing road to Galar, visible up to the left. *[*It was over this ground that Charlemagne's Christian forces defeated Aigolando's Muslim army in the 8th century. Today a more peaceful spot is hard to imagine as we leave the city behind us].* Further on the path crosses a stream with path to the ruins of the XVI[th]C Guenduláin palace, church and pilgrim hospital (200m) in the woods up to the right.

6.1 km **Zariquiegui** church of St. Andrew *San Andrés* Romanesque doorway and *[F.].* Crossroads with mini-market & *Alb.* ❶ **San Andrés** *Priv.[18÷2]* €10 © 948 353 876 with popular *café.* 50m *up* the street *Alb.* ❷ **La Posada de Ardogi** *Priv. [16÷2]* €11 © 948 353 353 also with bar & restaurant. Continue up steeply towards the wind turbines and just below the ridge is the ancient spring *Gambellacos* **Fuente Reniega** *(renouncement). [*A medieval pilgrim reached this spot dying of thirst. The*

devil, disguised as a pilgrim, offered to show him a spring if he would only renounce God. The pilgrim refused and St. James himself miraculously appeared revealing the spring and quenching his thirst with water in a scallop shell. Today, the well is often dry (a sign, perhaps, of the spiritual aridity of our times) but we can look back over Pamplona and the Pyrenees beyond them and reflect on our own journey to this point. The hum of the wind generators on the ridge above remind of us the possibilities of creating another, more sustainable future].* A final climb and we reach the summit:

2.4 km **Alto del Perdón** (altitude 790m) *Parque ecológico* wind turbines tower over a wrought iron representation of medieval pilgrims, heads bent to the west wind with the inscription: "Where the way of the wind crosses the way of the stars – *Donde se cruza el camino del viento con el de las estrellas.*" Looking ahead are the villages we will pass through spread out below lining the route westwards. The conical peak of Monte Arnotegui with hermitage atop is situated overlooking Puente de la Reina and is just visible ahead on the horizon. Descend [!] carefully over the loose stones and through the scrubland to the vineyards and almond trees below. Here the path winds along a delightful ridge running parallel to a quiet country road that you join at:

3.8 km **Uterga** *Alb.* ❶ **Municipal** *[2÷1]* opp. the fountain *[F.]* basic hostel in the main square 1 bunkbed with floor space (?) for 2 more in small room with shower & toilet off. ❷ **Camino del Perdón** *Priv.[16÷1]+* €10 +Ana Calvo © 948 344 598 c/Mayor with popular bar & restaurant and pilgrim menú. Opposite we find newly renovated ❸ **Casa Baztan** *Priv.[24÷1]+* €10 +€45 © 691 840 408 c/Mayor 46 email: mariamor827@hotmail.com. *[Next Albergue: Óbanos – 4.3 km].* If all else fails, the Gothic parish church has a wide porch and the *[F.]* in the centre offers pure fresh water (you might want to empty out the chemical residue from the water of Pamplona and refill here). The quiet country road continues to:

2.5 km **Muruzábal** *Alb.* ❶ **El Jardín de Muruzábal** *Priv.[14÷1]+* €10-€50 Ⓒ 696 688 399 (Alicia & Carlos) menú / bikes to visit Eunate! Camino Monteviejo 21. *Alb.* ❷ **Mendizabal** *Priv.[10÷4]* €18 incl. Ⓒ 948 344 631 c/ Mayor 7 – also provide bikes for Eunate. Church of St. Stephen *San Esteban* with statue of St. James. *[F.]* in the main square and near the pelota court *CR* **Villazón II** Ⓒ 630 767 346. Also *Bar/ restaurant Nogales* ... and Eunate option.

Detour ● ● ● ● ● *Eunate:* add 3.1 km to the direct route (around 1 hour). Directions: at the entrance to the village, just before the church, turn <left (signposted) around the back of the houses where the road turns down <left onto a wide farm track passing a small *Ermita* **[1.0 km]** before crossing the main road onto a tree-lined avenue to **Eunate church [1.4 km].**

2.4 km **Eunate** Beautiful XII[th]C Romanesque Church of Santa María de Eunate (see photograph below) one of the jewels of the camino. The church has been linked with the Knights Templar who long defended the pilgrim on the route to Santiago. There is a striking similarity with the church at Torres del Rio (see next stage) with its octagonal form, modelled on the Holy Sepulchre in Jerusalem, and its unadorned interior, a feature also associated with the Knights. But, uniquely, Eunate has a splendid freestanding outer porch with delicate twin pillars that surrounds the church. (Closed on Mondays, but its setting and external cloister is still worth the visit). It has been suggested that Eunate was also a burial place for pilgrims who had succumbed to the gruelling physical hardships experienced along the route. Standing on its own in the simple beauty of the countryside it evokes a powerful reminder of our own journey back to our spiritual source and Home.

Accommodation is no longer available in the adjoining hermitage *Casa de Onat* awaiting its next incarnation it is currently described as 'a house of prayer and reflection.' The church still provides background Gregorian chant and continues to weave its magic despite the bus loads of tourists that descend on this peaceful oasis. See map for alternative routes to Puente la Reina and Óbanos. A 'high level' walk *sendero* to the hermitage at Arnotegi (3.9 km) also starts from here.

For the waymarked route to Óbanos continue on path through the picnic site to the main road **[1.0 km]**. Proceed over main road past cemetery **[0.8 km]** onto asphalt over crossroads and up steeply into Óbanos to the central square **[0.7 km]** (church and albergue).

2.5 km **Óbanos** *Plaza Mayor / Iglesia* Main route joins from the right.

For the direct route to Óbanos from Muruzábal continue along the main road turning right> as you leave the village to follow the path parallel and under the bypass **[0.9 km]** and up steeply to the village of Óbanos clearly visible on the rise ahead. Turn right> at *[F.]* and make your way through the sleepy winding streets resplendent with their armorial crests emblazoned in the stone facades to the main square with albergue opposite the church **[0.9 km]**:

1.8 km Óbanos *Plaza* with the imposing parish church *[F.]* and shaded cloister in this historic village. Here the noblemen of Navarre met in the 14th century in an effort to limit the power of the monarchy. Their motto translates loosely as 'Liberty for people and country.'] The impressive neo-Gothic Church of St. John the Baptist *San Juan Bautista* has a splendid retablo and statue of St. James. The skull of St. William is also housed here in a silver reliquary giving zest to the mystical play enacted here every few

Plaza Óbanos & Albergue

years *The Mystery of Óbanos.* [*Legend has it that William (Guillaume) Duke of Aquitaine, killed his sister Felicia in a bout of fury at her refusal to return to court duties after her pilgrimage to Santiago. In repentance and riddled with remorse Guillaume also took the pilgrimage to Compostela and renounced his nobility for a life of poverty, penitence and prayer. He lived the remainder of his life in the hermitage of Arnotegui.]*

    Alb. Usda *Priv.[36÷3]* €8 © 676 560 927 situated on the corner of the main square and c/San Lorenzo with rear patio and lounge with open fire in the winter. ***Other lodging:*** *Hs* **Mamerto** €30-45 © 948 344 344 c/San Lorenze 13. *CR* **Villazón II** €35-50 © 620 441 467. *CR* **Raichu** €30-45 © 948 344 285 c/ Larrotagaña 2. Several bars & restaurants, shop and chemist on c/S.Salvador (adj. main square). Continue via the stone archway with choice of 2 routes to Puente la Reina.

Alternative route ❷ to albergue ❷ ● ● ● ● ● s/o steeply downhill on c/ Errotaldea and cross over main road **[0.5 km]** onto track and take sharp turn right> **[1.7 km]** *off* main track to cross stream up into the back of town **[0.4 km]**. **Total 2.6 km.**

For route ❶ to albergue ❶ veer right> *[F.]* past church on c/ S. Salvador down to track across **main road [1.2 km]** and s/o track to **Hotel Jakue [0.6 km]**. *Alb.* ❶ **Jakue** *Priv.*[40÷2]+ © 948 341 017 pilgrim reception pavilion on the outskirts of town. The hotel has reserved the basement as a pilgrim hostel with 40 beds in cubicles €10). Also kitchen, dining and lounge area with washing machine. The lack of outside window space is compensated by the addition of a sauna and library and generous *menú peregrino* €13 and *desayuno* €4. Part of *H**** **Jakue** (rooms from €45) adj. the hotel on the main road is the modern pilgrim statue erected to mark the joining of the Navarrese and Aragonés routes (which effectively join at Eunate). *Hotel El Peregrino (currently closed).* Continue along main road passing restaurant and *Hostal Zubi XXI (currently closed).* to church square and main **albergue** ❷ **[0.4 km]**.

2.2 km Puente la Reina *Alb.* Padres Reparadores ➋ *Conv.[96÷10]* €5 ℂ 948 340 050. adj. main road as you enter town on c/Crucifijo. All facilities and extensive rear garden. Well located opp. the Church of the Crucifixion ➊ *Iglesia del Crucifijo.* Originally known as the Church of St. Mary of the Meadows *Iglesia Santa María de las Vegas* under the auspices of the Knights Templar passing to the Order of the Hospitallers of St. John and renamed Iglesia Santo Cristo. Today, it is named after the unusual XIVth Gothic 'Y' shaped crucifix brought here by medieval pilgrims from Germany. It is now under the care of the Padres Reparadores in the seminary opposite (linked by a stone arch). To access the town, pass under the arch and continue over the busy N-111 into the historic main street *calle Mayor*.

A convenient *correos* on the N-111 adj. c/Mayor offers an opportunity to post all those extra items that you realise that you no longer need. **Calle Mayor** retains its medieval atmosphere with ➋ *Iglesia de Santiago* with its XII[th]C facade and portico and a gilded statue of Santiago Peregrino *Beltxa* adding some colour to the sombre interior. ➌ *Iglesia San Pedro Apóstol* close to the pilgrim bridge with image of N.S del Puy otherwise known as Our Lady of the Bird *N.S del Txori (pron: Chorri) – a reference to the lovely legend of a bird that took water from the river to wash the face of the statue when it was kept in a niche on the bridge.*

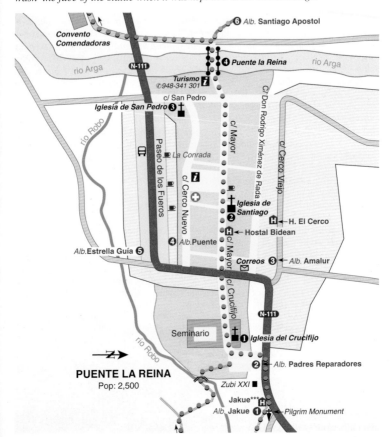

Convento Comendadoras

➏ *Alb.* Santiago Apostol

rio Arga   N-111   ➍ *Puente la Reina*   rio Arga

Turismo
ℂ948-341 301   Turismo [i]

c/ San Pedro

Iglesia de San Pedro ➌ †

rio Robo

Paseo de los Fueros

La Conrada

[i]

c/ Cerco Nuevo

➍ *Alb.*Puente

*Alb.*Estrella Guía ➎

c/ Mayor

c/ Don Rodrigo Ximénez de Rada

c/ Cerco Viejo

† Iglesia de Santiago ➋

[H] ← H. El Cerco

[H] ← Hostal Bidean

Correos ➌ ← *Alb.* Amalur

N-111

Seminario   † ➊ Iglesia del Crucifijo

→↗ 🌣

PUENTE LA REINA
Pop: 2,500

➋ ← *Alb.* Padres Reparadores

Zubi XXI ■

Jakue***   [H]
Alb. Jakue ➊ † ← Pilgrim Monument

❏ **Tourist office** ✆ 948 341 301 c/ Mayor adj. medieval bridge. *Alb.* ❸ **Amalur** *Priv.* *[20÷2]* €12 incl. ✆ 948 341 090 c/Cerco Viejo with popular bar & restaurant. ❹ **Puente** *Priv.[22÷3]*+ €12 incl (+€34) ✆ 661 705 642 with first floor terrace on Paseo de los Fueros,57 and rear access from c/Cerco Nuevo, 57. On the opp. side of main road: ❺ **Estrella Guía** *Priv.[6÷2]* €12 incl. ✆ 948 340 001 Paseo de Los Fueros, 34 / 2° piso adj. Bar Eunea. ❻ **Santiago Apostol** *Priv.** *[100÷5]* €8 ✆ 948 340 220 located at the far end of town across the river 1.1 km from albergue [1] but convenient for leaving the

Albergue ❷ *Padres Repardores*

next day. Industrial style building with swimpool bar and restaurant serving Menú. ❏ **Other Lodging:** *H* **Bidean** ✆ 948 341 156 c/Mayor from €50. *H* **El Cerco** ✆ 948 34 12 69 c/Rodrigo Ximenez de Rada from €45-60 + *H* **Jakue.** Wide selection of bars and restaurants on c/Mayor and Paseo de los Fueros (N-111).

PUENTE LA REINA (*Gares* in Basque) named 'Queens Bridge' ❹ in honour of Doña Mayor, wife of Sancho III. She commanded the magnificent Romanesque bridge to be built to support the safe movement of the increasing number of medieval pilgrims who joined the route at this stage from both the camino francés and camino aragonés. The bridge's six arches span the Arga that has now swollen to a powerful river since we first crossed it back at the Puente de Rabia in Zubiri. Charlemagne is reputed to have stayed in this town after his victorious battle against the Moors back in Cizur. Take an historical tour of Puente La Reina? (English / Spanish) with the passionate Miguel Perez Guterrez ✆ 677 036 655. With a population of 2,500 the town straddles the busy N-111 linking Pamplona with Estella and has a frequent bus service to both from outside Bar La Conrada adjoining panadería El Paseo on Paseo de los Fueros.

REFLECTIONS:

❏ **Practise random acts of loving kindness and acts of senseless beauty.**

05 **684.5** km (425.3 ml) – Santiago

PUENTE LA REINA – ESTELLA (Navarra)

▦▦▦▦▦▦	--- ---	16.5	--- ---	75%
▬▬▬	--- ---	5.4	--- ---	25%
▬▬▬	--- ---	0.0		
Total km		**21.9** km (13.6 ml)		

◣ --- --- 23.4 km (^300m + 1.5 km)
Alto ▲ Cirauqui 500m (1,640 ft)
<🅰 🅗> Mañeru **5.2** km – Cirauqui **7.8** km – Lorca **13.5** km – Villatuerta **18.0** km.

[Elevation profile diagram showing:]
500m --- Cirauqui, *Alto* 500m, Lorca
Mañeru 🅒, Cirauqui 🅐, Lorca 🅐, Villatuerta 🅐 ESTELLA ■
400m --- Mañeru --- *Río Salado* --- *Río Iranzu*
■PUENTE LA REINA
300m ---
00 km | 5 km | 10 km | 15 km | 20 km

❏ **The Practical Path:** Another quiet stage along gently rolling farmland and vineyards with few trees and little shelter. Some fine examples of Roman roadway between Cirauqui and Lorca and a glorious 75% is on natural tracks. The first section has steep climbs to the 3 hilltop villages before descending into Estella.

❏ **The Mystical Path:** Will we pause a moment to look on the ancient stone cross atop the rise and reflect at the speed with which the motorised travellers now flash past it? Can you see the beauty of the stonemason's craftsmanship that fashioned it, and the deeper meaning behind the symbol? In the rush of modern life we miss so much of true significance... and the waymarks Home.

❏ **Personal Reflections:** *"... I started today with the intention to practise loving kindness... and here I am 2 hours later seething with rage. Someone has stolen items from my rucksack. In this moment of anger I become judge and jury, condemning my fellow human being to damnation. Where have the loving thoughts I invoked at daybreak gone? It is easy to act in a loving manner when the sun is shining and body and kit are together. But can I bring myself to love in adversity? ..."*

0.0 km **Puente La Reina** Leaving albergue ❷ pass under the connecting arch of Iglesia del Crucifijo and Padres Reparadores and s/o over the N-111 into c/Mayor. Past the Iglesia de Santiago (right) and cross the famous XII[th]C 'Queen's Bridge' *Puente la Reina* **[0.8 km]** Turn <left over the bridge (albergue *Santiago Apostol* is up the track s/o) and cross the main road to the Nun's Neighbourhood *Barrio de las Monjas* with its convento Comendadoras del Espíritu Santo *[F.]*. Rejoin the Río Arga and pass under the new road bridge and along an earth track before striking off right> uphill along a steep ravine to pass the XIII[th]C site of the Monasterio de Bogota before we crest the top at 470m **[4.0 km]** XIV[th]C roadside cross *(at this point there are fine views back over the Río Arga valley).* Continue down past the roundabout at Mañeru with *[F.]* into the central village square **[0.4 km]:**

5.2 km **Mañeru** *Centro* Village linked with the Knights Templar and Order of

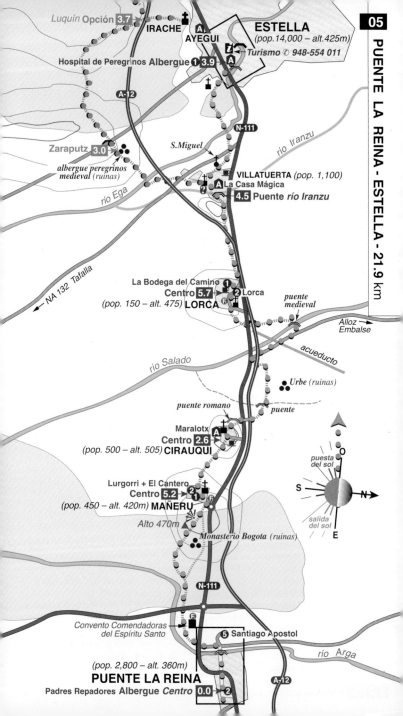

Luquín **Opción** `3.7`

IRACHE

ESTELLA *(pop.14,000 – alt.425m)*

AYEGUI

i ← *Turismo* © 948-554 011

Hospital de Peregrinos Albergue ❶ `3.9`

A-12

N-111

S.Miguel

Zarraputz `3.0` →

rio Iranzu

albergue peregrinos medieval (ruinas)

rio Ega

VILLATUERTA *(pop. 1,100)*
La Casa Mágica
`4.5` **Puente** *rio Iranzu*

← NA 132 *Tafalla*

La Bodega del Camino ❶
Centro `5.7` ❷ *Lorca*
(pop. 150 – alt. 475)
LORCA

puente medieval

Alloz →
Embalse

rio Salado

acueducto

Urbe (ruinas)

puente romano

puente

Maralotx
Centro `2.6`
(pop. 500 – alt. 505) **CIRAUQUI**

O

puesta del sol

S

N

salida del sol

E

Lurgorri + El Cantero ❷
Centro `5.2` → ❶
(pop. 450 – alt. 420m) **MAÑERU**

Alto 470m

Monasterio Bogota (ruinas)

N-111

Convento Comendadoras del Espíritu Santo →

❺ **Santiago Apostol**

rio Arga

(pop. 2,800 – alt. 360m)
PUENTE LA REINA
Padres Repadores Albergue *Centro* `0.0` → ❷

A-12

St. John whose influence in this area was considerable in the Middle Ages. Plaza *[F.] Alb.* ❶ **Lurgorri** *Priv.[12÷1]* €10 incl. © 686 521 174 c/Esperanza, 5 & @ Nº2 ❷ **El Cantero** *Priv.[26÷2]* €10 © 948 342 142 Roberto. Iglesia S.Pedro, bar, shop, farmacia and *CR* **Isabel** © 948 340 283. The sleepy meandering streets lead to the cemetery via the street of the 'inevitable' *calle Forzosa* from where a view opens up of the next life… or our next destination Cirauqui (see

photo). We now take a path through vineyards, interspersed with olive into:

2.6 km **Cirauqui** (*Zirauki*) medieval hilltop village beautifully preserved with narrow winding streets and houses bearing armorial crests and ornate balconies. At the entrance is aptly named *Café El Portal* (photo right) At the top is church of *San Román* with multi-lobed doorway and *Santa Catalina* both dating from the 13th century. *Alb.* ❶ *Par.[14÷1]* Basic parish hostel

donativo (summer only) accessed on the right just before entering the square adj. to *supermercado Teofilo* 50m (right). ❷ **Maralotx** *Priv.[28÷3]+* €11 © 678 635 208 adj. church in Plaza San Román with all facilities, dinner and breakfast available.

　　　Leave the village through an arch off the main square *(sello for credencial)* and out on to one of the best examples of **Roman road** on the camino continuing over a single span Roman bridge. Cross the N-111 and A-12 onto an earth track that meanders gently downhill through open farmland running parallel to the new autopista (left) which we pass under onto the N-111 and back again under the A-12 to take a quiet country road to pass modern aqueduct (canal de Alloz) turning <left over the famous medieval stone bridge (now restored) that crosses the Salt river *río Salado. [*Aymeric Picaud, in his epic journal written in the 12th century warns pilgrims not to drink from its deadly waters. It was here that he encountered Basques preparing to skin any pilgrim's horse that might drink from the river and die – his own horse falling victim!].* Veer <left up through an underpass (finished with attractive local stone) and up into the village passing XIIthC *Iglesia San Salvador* into:

5.7 km **Lorca** This quaint village is the site of a former pilgrim hospice with connections to the monastery at Roncesvalles and now boasting 2 private hostels both with bar & restaurant *Alb.* ❶ **La Bodega del Camino** *Priv.[30÷5]+* © 948 541 327 in restored stone building at the far end of the village on c/Mayor opp: *Alb.* ❷ **Lorca** *Priv.[12÷3]+* © 948 541 190. The route now goes back to the main road *Cafe Casa Julio* and veers <left onto track alongside the main road through farmland passing site of ancient pilgrim hostel *Hospital de peregrinos de Arandigoyen* founded in 1066, before taking a tunnel under the town bypass into the modern suburbs of Villatuerta (Note: 1.4 km until we pick up the path again at the far end). Continue past sports hall *polideportivo* on plaza Mayor passing *Café Marta* and chemist to cross the medieval bridge.

4.5 km **Villatuerta** 100m beyond the bridge popular albergue (signposted) ♥*Alb.*

Villatuerta *Casa Mágica Priv.**[30÷5]+ €12
(dinner €13) Simone & Miguel ℂ 948 536
095 network* hostel in restored medieval
building on c/ Rebote 5 with covered patio
for relaxing – massage and healing available.
Ayuntamiento with *Bar Jubilados* to the rear
adj. pelota court. Church of the Assumption
XIV with reredos of St Veremundo defeating
the moors. *[F.]* and raised flagstone surround

with views back over the route from Lorca and towards Monte Jurra to the south.
Note: Alternative (original) Route via Zaraputz begins at the church. ▼

If you intend to take this remote route all the way to Los Arcos via Luquín (see
next stage) note there are no (reliable) facilities en route (unless you detour back to
Estella). Before Estella was founded in 1090, early pilgrims travelled directly to the
monastery at Irache using this southern route via Novaleta, Echavarra and Zaraputz.
The route still exists and is marked as part of the GR 65. It is well waymarked and
makes a delightful alternative route.

Consider this option if you have walked the camino
francés before or if travelling with a companion
and want to experience walking alone and the joy
of meeting up again at the end of the day to share
individual insights. This alternative is still virtually
unused in comparison to the constant stream of
pilgrims on the main camino. Turn left around the side
of the church and s/o at T-Junction onto track and *first
waymark* [0.1 km]. The path now drops down at side

Zaraputz <left arrow

of factory and under access road to the village of *Noveleta* [1.6 km] and under *A-6*
[0.4 km] over *river* [0.5 km] where the track now climbs steeply for [0.4 km] to:

3.0 km Zaraputz ruins of XV[th]C pilgrim hostel occupying elevated site (440m).
Continue over a pedestrian bridge *pasarela* [0.7 km] climbing again to ridge (515m)
where the first views of Estella open up ahead. The path curves around a valley and
up again to **cemetery** [1.4 km] turn <left off asphalt road [0.4 km] and right> before
farmyard (signs may be defaced) and cross over old road [0.4 km] into Holm oak
woods. The path now drops down through woodland for [0.8 km] to route signpost:

3.7 km Option signpost with choice of routes: [a] continue by remote path direct
to Luquín / Los Arcos (described in next stage) or [b] take the route to Estella /
Monjardín by continuing under the A-6 to next option sign [0.4 km] (left for
Monjardín / Hotel Irache or right for Irache monastery [0.5 km]. The albergue at
Ayegui is [1.2 km] or the main albergue in Estella an additional [1.5 km] (see map).

▼ The main waymarked route continues s/o to rejoin path that bypasses the ruins of
the ancient pilgrim hospital and X[th]C hermitage and of Archangel St. Michael *ermita
de San Miguel arcangel (access gate is not generally locked allowing pilgrims to
offer prayers on the bare altar.)* Site of some the earliest Christian iconography in
Spain (now moved to the Navarra museum Pamplona). Continue along track, down
steps beside the main road to rest area *[F.]* and onto wide track that winds down to
pasarela over the rio Ega past *Camping Lizarra* (left) and on down to riverside park
and the XIV[th]C Gothic *Iglesia del Santo Sepulchro* (left) with the Convento Santo
Domingo behind it. Continue through the underpass (N-111) into c/la Rua and:

3.9 km Estella *Alb.* ❶ **Hospital Peregrinos** *Asoc.[96÷5]* €6 © 948 550 200 well located at the entrance to the town but close to the noisy N-111 on c/La Rúa, 50 (photo right) bunkbeds spread tightly over 3 floors. Kitchen/dining and small patio to rear provides some open space. Several new hostels relieve the pressure at this previous bottleneck. *Rst. La Aljama* also on c/Rua has a pilgrim menu and rear patio. 100m further we come to the lovely Plaza de San Martin with *Fuente de los Chorros* XVI[th]C and *Turismo* c/ San Nicolas, 1 © 948 556 301.

❏ *Other Albergues:* ❷ **San Miguel** *Par.[32÷2]* €-donativo © 615 451 909 cMercado Viejo, 18 parish hostel on ground floor of modern residential building. ❸ **ANFAS** *Mun.[34÷1]* €7 © 639 011 688 c/Cordeleros, 7 Bajo (ANFAS support of mentally handicapped). For both above cross the bridge opposite albergue [1] (see photo) and head s/o along c/Asteria and at 2nd crossroads (250m) – for albergue [2] turn up left into c/Mercado Viejo and the hostel is on the right after 100m (opposite Decora Hogar). For albergue [3] continue s/o uphill along c/Asteria and veer right to modern buildings 150m. The other 3 hostels are the opposite end of town on the way out. ❹ **Rocamador** *Conv.[28÷5]+* €15-18 +€40 © 948 550 549 Hermanos Capuchinos c/ Rocamador 6 *(capilla virgen de Rocamador XII)*. ❺ *Juvenil* **Oncineda** *Muni. [150÷20]* €9–13 © 948-555 022 – 300m *off* the route (right) at first roundabout in c/Monasterio de Irache mod. building with meals available and set in quiet wooded site. ❻ **San Cipriano de Ayegui** *Mun.[80÷2]* © 948 554 311 c/Polideportivo, Ayegui. left off the camino past the 2nd roundabout at the far end of town (1.6 km from albergue [1]) part of the Ayegui sports hall *Polideportivo*.

❏ **Other Lodging:** *Hospedería* **Convento Benedictinas** Monasterio San Benito adj. the Basilica del Puy with viewpoint overlooking the town. Single en suite rooms and a heavenly choir make up this 'antidote to materialism'. *P*[*] **San Andrés** €40 © 948 554 158 plaza de Santiago popular with pilgrims also nearby restaurant *Casa Nova*. *Hs*[*] **Cristina** €40 © 948 550 450 c/Baja Navarra 1 / c/Mayor. *P* **Fonda Izarra** €20-40 © 948 550 678 c/Caldería 20 better known for its pilgrim menú. *P* **Apartamentos Gebala** €50 © 606 980 675 plaza Fueros, 31 with special pilgrim price. *H*[****] **Chapitel** €70+ © 948 551 090 c/Chapitel, 1. Near Ayegui in modern suburbs c/Merkatondoa: *Hs* **El Volante** €40+ © 948 553 957 also *Hs* **Area-99** © 948 553 370. Further out past the bullring on the western outskirts. *H*[**] **Yerri** €45-€65 © 948 546 034 and just beyond Irache *H*[***] **Irache** © 948 551 150 and adj. campsite (both with pilgrim discount).

❏ **ESTELLA** *LIZARRA* (Basque) *(pop. 14,000 – alt. 425m)* a vibrant town with lots to do and see. Estella is big enough to provide reasonable facilities and yet sufficiently compact to easily explore its wonderful historic buildings, museums, interesting churches and its varied restaurants and bars (perhaps a good place to take a day's rest).

Opposite albergue [1] is the restored medieval bridge ❶ *Puente de Carcel* (photo right) and 200m past the albergue along c/ la Rua we find ❷ *Plaza San Martín* with its graceful fountain and the adjoining XIIthC Palace of the Kings of Navarre *Palacio de los Reyes de Navarra* ❸ now a museum and art gallery. Opposite are the impressive flight of steps to Church of *San Pedro de la Rúa* ❹ with its beautiful XIIthC cloister, two sides of which are missing, evidence of its troubled past. It was here that the Kings of Navarre took their oaths and is worth a visit despite the noise of traffic on the busy N-111 immediately to the rear (a lift *ascensor* is available to this point from c/San Niclóas). The church is open before evening mass and guided tours are available – check with the tourist office. On the other side of the river Ega we find the parish church of *Iglesia San Miguel* ❺ and the bustling main square *Plaza de los Fueros* filled with cafés and the austere church *San Juan Bautista* ❻ taking up the eastern side. A further 200m along the c/Mayor you come to the more intimate ***Plaza de Santiago*** with its ancient fountain. A variety of inexpensive restaurants, bars and hotels are located in the surrounding streets. The area to the north of the river was called Lizarra (Basque for ash tree) and was the original village built on the slopes of the hill of San Millán where today we find the modern Basilica of the Virgin of le Puy. Quick to realise the enormous potential of the pilgrim road to Santiago Sancho Ramírez created a separate Borough in 1090 for French pilgrim settlers on the other side of the river L'Izarra which became *Estella* (Spanish for star) with all its connections with the Milky Way *Via Lactea* otherwise known as the 'Way of the Stars' to Compostela. This marks the beginning of stage IV of the Codex Calixtinus.

As in other areas along the Way, artisans were encouraged to return and bring their skills with them. It was this inflow of stonemasons and artists that created the beautiful buildings, monuments and bridges, hospitals and cathedrals that we still admire and use today. However, the ever-present human characteristics of jealousy and greed also created disharmony, open warfare and mindless massacres. The unification of the different boroughs into one town in 1266 did not end the hostilities. The flowering Jewish colony was expelled in the 14th century and the destruction of the castle adjoining San Pedro also destroyed two sides of its exquisite Romanesque cloister (see photo). Even up to the last century, Estella was one of the strongholds of the Carlists in the conflict over the successor to King Ferdinand, no doubt contributing to the town's royalist reputation. Today, the fiery Navarrese blood is cooled in the Court of Justice *Juzgado*, which now occupies the original town hall immediately to the left of the steps to the church of San Pedro in Plaza San Martín.

REFLECTIONS:

❏ **To attain knowledge, add things every day.**
To attain wisdom, remove things every day.
——————————————— *Lao-tzu*

06 **662.6** km (411.7 ml) – Santiago

ESTELLA – LOS ARCOS (Navarra)

▥▥▥▥▥	--- ---	17.5	--- ---	82%
▬▬▬	--- ---	3.7	--- ---	17%
▬▬▬	--- ---	0.3	--- ---	1%
Total km		**21.5** km (13.4 ml)		

◣ --- --- 23.3 km (^370m + 1.8 km)
Alto ▲ Monjardín 690m (2,132 ft)
< Ⓐ Ⓗ > Ayegui **1.5** km – Hotel Irache **4.0** km – Monjardín **9.3** km.

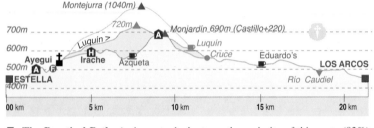

Montejurra (1040m) ▲

700m ------ 720m▲ --- *Monjardín 690m (Castillo+220)* ----- ⓘ
.... *Luquín >* Ⓐ .... *Luquín*
600m ------------------------------- *Cruce* *Eduardo's*
Ayegui ✝ Ⓗ *Azqueta* **LOS ARCOS**
500m Ⓐ Ⓕ *Irache*
■ESTELLA *Río Caudiel* ■
400m ---

00 km   5 km   10 km   15 km   20 km

❏ **The Practical Path:** As in yesterday's stage, the majority of this route (82%) is on delightful natural paths. The first section is through native holm oak and pine trees as we climb our way up to Monjardín. There are magnificent views southwards over the alternative route, which passes above Luquín. The two routes join for the last stretch into Los Arcos taking us through remote vineyards and open country but with little shade and few water fonts. Take food and water for the isolated day ahead, particularly for the remote alternative route.

❏ **The Mystical Path:** Will you find the fish that circle the stone fountain, symbol of the hidden Christian life? The fish are located at the centre of these ancient cloisters. How long will they remain? How long will we? This monastic community was founded here in 958 and it became one of the first monasteries to receive pilgrims on their way to venerate the recently discovered tomb of San Tiago. For over a millennium it was a respected seat of learning and hospitality. Today it is uninhabited, abandoned by the monks that gave it life for over a thousand years. Perhaps the ferns that gave these majestic buildings their name will yet reclaim them... or maybe they will become *un Parador del paraíso.*

❏ **Personal Reflections:** *"... Everywhere there are fountains. Some contain refreshing drinking water to hydrate the body; others wine to fortify it. I now find myself being offered a different water to quench a different thirst. In a display of loving kindness, offered without any expectation of anything in return, I am showered with generosity. I leave this oasis of service with the gift of a little booklet entitled* Living Water *and based on the Gospel of Saint John. Tears well up as I open the book and find a handwritten message from Anton. "I give this book you to find Jesus Christ. God help you!" I reflect on my purpose for this journey and smile at the exclamation mark. God help me indeed! ..."*

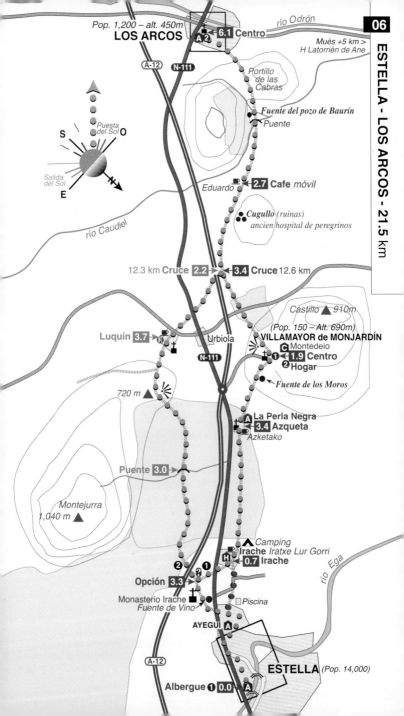

Pop. 1,200 – alt. 450m
LOS ARCOS
A **2** ← **6.1** **Centro**
río Odrón

*Mués +5 km >
H Latorrién de Ane*

*Portillo
de las
Cabras*

Fuente del pozo de Baurín
→ *Puente*

*Puesta
del Sol* **O**

S

**Salida
del Sol** **E**

Eduardo ■← **2.7** **Cafe** *móvil*

Cugullo (*ruinas*)
ancien hospital de peregrinos

río Caudiel

12.3 km **Cruce** **2.2** → ← **3.4** **Cruce** 12.6 km

Castillo ▲ *910m*

(*Pop. 150 – Alt. 690m*)
VILLAMAYOR de MONJARDÍN

Luquín **3.7**
Urbiola
N-111

C *Montedeio*
†**1** ← **1.9** **Centro**
2 **Hogar**

→ *Fuente de los Moros*

720 m ▲

A **La Perla Negra**
†← **3.4** **Azqueta**
Azketako

Puente **3.0** →

*Montejurra
1,040 m* ▲

▲ *Camping*
■ **Irache** *Iratxe Lur Gorri*
H **0.7** **Irache**

Opción **3.3** **2** **0**?**0 1**

*Monasterio Irache
Fuente de Vino* → ■ ● □ *Piscina*

AYEGUI **A**

río Ega

ESTELLA (*Pop. 14,000*)

Albergue **1** **0.0** **A**

0.0 km **Estella** from albergue ❶ s/o c/Rúa into Plaza San Martin *[F.]* past ***Turismo*** out through *Puerta de Castilla* and cross the busy junction of the **N-111** *[albergue 4 right]*. Veer right> at next roundabout *Avia* up through the modern suburb of Ayegui passing *[F.]* ***el Piojo*** **[1.5** km] & *Alb.* ❺ **San Cipriano de Ayegui** (left). Continue s/o to turn down sharp <left *opción* **[0.6** km] **[?]** *(see map for alt. route.)*
*[**Alternative** route direct to Hotel Irache continue s/o past play area to the hotel visible ahead (1.6 km) where the waymarked route re-joins from the left.]*

Turn <left downhill and cross over the **N-111** up the earth track to rear of the *Bodegas Irache* with its famous wine fountain ***Fuente del Vino*** **[0.6** km] where pilgrims can fortify themselves for the journey ahead at the generosity of the Bodegas. Continue to tree-fringed square *[F.]* and the entrance to the ancient Benedictine **Monasterio de Irache** **[0.1** km] (left) which has long been connected with Roncesvalles and the camino. A community of monks served pilgrims here

since the 10th century but were forced to vacate in 1985 due to a lack of novitiates. Now serving as a somewhat austere museum while it awaits its next incarnation, Parador? If it is closed you can still view the impressive XIIthC Romanesque door to the Benedictine Church of San Pedro, around to the left. The Bodegas Irache has a **wine museum** opposite. Continue along dirt track for **[0.5** km] to a fork in the path with wooden signpost.

3.3 km Irache *Opción* **[?]** Monjardín or Luquín.

Alternative scenic route ❷ via LUQUÍN (300m shorter but steeper). This route follows the *road less travelled* away from the bustle of the main camino and skirts the lower slopes of the mystical *Monte Jurra* (1040m). Entirely on natural pathways but facilities en route are limited so bring provisions. Veer left under A-12 up through delightful woodland to high pasture and fields of lavender. to:

Monjardín from Luquin route

3.0 km **Puente** wooden bridge across mountain stream (dry). Shortly afterwards the route breaks through the tree line to reveal the conical peak of Monjardín to the north. The track continues through the ridge ahead where a magnificent view south over Luquin opens up. This is the high point of the route at 720m. We now start the descent, crossing path and up again before final descent into:

3.7 km **Luquín** typical hill village with winding streets radiating out from the Basilica and the parish Church of San Martin. The latter has a finely carved portico and adjoins the main square with seating and *[F.]*. Community *café/bar San Isidro* (often closed). Wind your way down through the village and out onto an open path crossing over the N-111 (close to the village of Urbiola where the Knights of St. John maintained a medieval pilgrim hospice) continue under the A-12 to:

2.2 km **Cruce** Here we re-join the main waymarked route from Monjardín.

For **route ❶** via Monjardín veer right> at option point (wooden signpost) down and over the N-111 to pilgrim-friendly:

0.7 km Irache *H***Lur Gorri** *Irache* €50+ © 948 558 286 *[Alt. route from Ayegui joins here]*. S/o between hotel and **camping** (chalet €28+) onto path through holm oak and pine forest crossing road **[1.6 km]** to plaza in Azqueta **[1.7 km]**.

3.4 km **Azqueta** quiet village bypassed by the N-111 with Church of San Pedro. *Alb.* **La Perla Negra** *Priv.[9÷3]*+ €27 incl. menú © 627 114 797 (Helena) c/Carrera,18 adj. *bar Azketako*. Veer right> down past farm buildings and steeply up towards Villamayor. Just before entering the village we pass the 13th C Fountain of the Moors *Fuente de Los Moros* with its distinctive Mozarabic double arch (see photo) to:

1.9 km **Villamayor de Monjardín** *Centro* XIIth C San Andrés Church and tower and splendid views of the surrounding countryside. The conical peak of Monjardín forms a distinctive backdrop with the ruins of St. Stephen's Castle *Castillo de San Esteban (tomb of Sanchez I)* atop. *Alb.* **❶ Villamayor** *Priv.[20÷3]*+ €15 incl. (+€40) © 677 660 586 adj. the church. Climb the steps to the Plaza mayor *Bar* and ♥ *Alb.* **❷ Hogar** *Asoc.[25÷5]* €5 (shared dinner €10) © 948 537 136 run by Dutch ecumenical group. **CR Montedeio** €35-50 © 948 551 521 c/ Mayor, 17. *[Next Albergue: Los Arcos – 11.5 km]*. The route now follows the access road down past Monjardín Bodega to turn right> onto a pathway parallel to the A-12 through vineyards to crossing where the alt. camino from Luquín joins by grove of trees.

3.4 km **Cruce** *alt. camino* pilgrims join and continue along remote farm tracks through mixed farmland and vineyards interspersed with olive trees, but with little shade. Gaudy signs count down the distance to a mobile cafe where Eduardo fills a need for the hungry and thirsty pilgrim (summer only) at:

2.7 km **Café Móvil** *Eduardo.* Continue s/o passing site of the ancient pilgrim hospital *Cugullo* and Fountain of the Well *Fuente del pozo de Baurín* (not drinkable) by río Caudiel **[3.1 km]** (dry) but with pleasant shade from the pine trees. Finally we take a gentle climb up through the Pass of the Goats *Portillo de las Cabras* before our descent to the outskirts of **Los Arcos** *[F.]* **Venta** **[2.5 km]**. We make our way down c/ Mayor passing: *Alb.* **❶ la Fuente** *Priv.[48÷6]*+ €8 + © 948 640 797 all facilities + patio. Continue down the main street to Plaza de la Fruta *Alb.* **❷ Casa de la Abuela** *Priv.[24÷2]*+ €9 (+€35) © 948 640 250 adj. Plaza Mayor **[0.5 km]**.

6.1 km **Centro** Plaza de Santa Maria and the splendid Church of St. Mary of the Arches **❶** *Iglesia de Santa María de los Arcos XIIth C.* The church was embellished in 16th, 17th and 18th centuries and in addition to the original Romanesque has Gothic, Baroque and Classical elements without affecting the overall harmony. The bell-tower and peaceful cloisters are particularly noteworthy and the sumptuous interior has a fine statue of Santiago Peregrino and the reredos has a black Virgin with pale blue eyes and the Latin inscription 'I am black but beautiful'. The balcony choir stalls also have a relief of both St. James *Maior* and *Menor*. Pilgrim mass each evening.

Continue via ❷ *Portal de Castilla* cross road *and* river turn right> by pilgrim fountain *Fuente de Peregrinos* to *Alb.* ❸ **Isaac Santiago** *Muni.[72÷8]* €6 ©️ 948 441 091 municipal hostel run by Flemish confraternity opp. the modern civic centre and library. All facilities incl. outside patio. Close by in c/ El Hortal *Alb.* ❹ **Casa Alberdi** *Priv.[24÷3]* €10 ©️ 948 640 764 enter via converted garage (mixed reports). ❏ **Other Lodging:** *P* **Mavi** €30 ©️ 948 640 081. c/del Medio 7 separate to bar/ restaurant Mavi at the

Portal de Castilla

central crossroads opp. *H*°° **Mónaco** ©️ 948 640 000 €40+ Plaza del Coso. *Hs* **Suetxe** €40 ©️ 948 441 175 in refurbished building on c/Karramendabia (far side of N-111) and further out on c/La Serna (on the road to Zarragoza) *Hs* **Ezequiel** €25-40 ©️ 948 640 296. Several shops and bars including the popular basement restaurant below *Gargantúa* opp. the church and useful adj. grocery *alimentación* (see town plan). *[Mués 5 km north of Los Arcos (free transport ©️ 948 441 152) H rural Latorrién de Ane €70-180 incl. c/ mayor 128.]*

LOS ARCOS crossroads town (pop. 1,200 declining) straddling the N-111 and connecting Estella with Logroño with regular bus service to both. It was and remains a classic pilgrim halt and has Roman origins. The eastern gate (no longer visible) into the old walled city was called Gate of the Shells *Portal de la Concha* which also provided access to the Jewish quarter in the town. A *Turismo* sometimes opens in either ❸ *Casa de la Villa del Coso* XVI^{th}C and its *Balcón de Toros* (a reference to the bullfights that were witnessed from here) or the town hall ❸ *Ayuntamiento* also from XVI^{th}C.

Santiago – Iglesia de Santa Maria

Wander around the narrow streets and soak up the tranquillity.

REFLECTIONS:

❏ **Your daily life is your temple and your religion.**
— *Kahlil Gibran*

07 **641.1** km (398.4 ml) – Santiago

LOS ARCOS (Navarra) – LOGROÑO (La Rioja)

....	--- ---	18.4	--- ---	66%
▬▬▬	--- ---	8.3	--- ---	30%
▬▬▬	--- ---	1.1	--- ---	4%
Total km		**27.8** km	(17.3 ml)	

▲ --- --- 29.3 km (^300m + 1.5 km)
Alto ▲ Ermita de N. Sra. del Poyo 570m (1,870 ft)
< Ⓐ Ⓗ > Sansol **6.8** km – Torres del Río **7.8** – Viana **18.4** km.

❏ **The Practical Path:** The majority of this stage is on natural paths through open arable farmland. Shade is limited to a few isolated pockets of pine and drinking fonts are few, so fill up the water bottle and protect against the sun. This is a long stage and there are some short but very steep sections into the rio Linares (Torres del Río) and Cornava river valleys so be particularly mindful when negotiating these steep paths. Just before entering Logroño we pass into the great wine-producing region of La Rioja, as witnessed by the many old stone 'beehive' wine observation huts *Guardaviñas* that we pass. *Note: If you don't want to stay in a busy city hostel or want more time to visit Logroño, consider staying in Viana where there are now several albergues. This would allow a longer stopover at Logroño the following day (9.4 km from Viana centre) to spend more time exploring this interesting city or visit the city on your way through to the next intermediate hostel at Navarrete (12.7 km) for a total of 22.1 km for this alternative 'next' day.*

❏ **The Mystical Path:** Will you stop and visit this holy temple built by the same Order of Knights that created the magnificent church at Eunate? Will you sense the similarity of form and look up and see the eight-sided star that forms this simple structure, symbol of the sacred and full of grace and mystery? The beautiful 13th century figure of Christ crucified hangs above the altar. If our life is a reflection of our temple, to whom have we dedicated it and what have we placed upon its altar?

❏ **Personal Reflections:** *"... The deepening lines on her aging face cannot hide her welcoming smile. Her name means happiness and she has welcomed pilgrims for decades giving her blessing and stamping credenciales. Some see her unofficial presence an intrusion, preferring to hurry by to avoid interaction. I sit beside her and observe myself judging them as they are judging her. A whole Order was condemned to die by those fearing a loss of control and wanting an exclusive right to bless. I realise in this moment that no one needs permission to offer love. We all have the right to bestow blessings – perhaps it is our beholden duty..."*

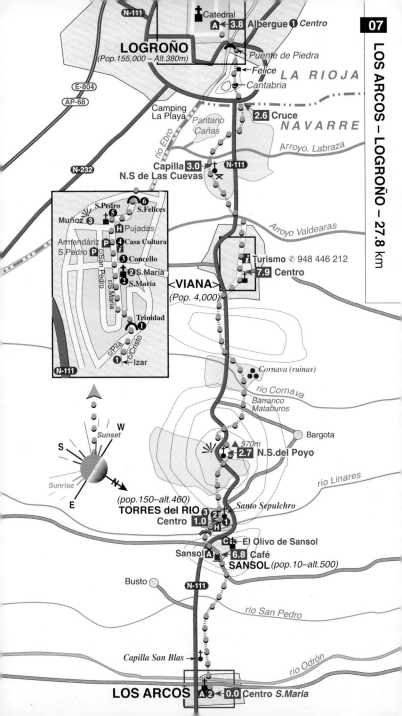

`0.0 km` **Los Arcos** *Centro* out ***Portal de Castilla*** and s/o up past the cemetery *[the inscription over its portal translates; 'you are what I once was, and will be what I am now'].* Flexing our physical and spiritual muscles we stride out along a wide earth track passing XIII[th]C Capilla de San Blas (left). We continue along a delightful level track through arable farmland over dry river bed and across ***río de San Pedro [5.4 km]*** and gently up to quiet country road turning <left into ***Sansol [1.4 km]***:

`6.8 km` **Sansol** *Café* (left). To visit the church turn up right> Iglesia de San Zoilo *(a Christian martyr who gives his name to this sleepy hamlet and the monastery in Carrión de los Condes). CR* **El Olivo de Sansol** €30+ incl. © 948 648 345 overlooking Torres de Río adj. the church. *Alb.* **Sansol** *Priv.[24÷1]* €10 / menú €8 © 948 648 473 (Arantxa) c/ Barrio Nuevo, 4 with courtyard & bar. The waymarked route crosses the N-111 down a short but steep ravine [!] to stone bridge over the río Linares *[F.]* (left - medieval *fuente* below) up steeply, passing café *Casa Lili* (left) and new hotel complete with *piscina H***San Andrés** €45+ © 948 648 472 into:

`1.0 km` **Torres del Río** *Centro Alb.* ❶ **Casa Mariela** *Priv.*[50÷5]* €7 © 948 648 251 all facilities with bar, restaurant & shop. ❷ **la Pata & Oca** *Priv.[32÷3]*+ €5-10 + priv. © 948 378 457 formerly *Via Láctea* + bar and menú c/ Mayor 5. Behind the parish church at the top of town in c/Casas Nuevas ❸ **Casa Mari** *Priv.*[26÷5]* €7 © 948 648 409 all facilities including patio with terrace overlooking the countryside.

TORRES DEL RÍO: Quintessential pilgrim village with its exquisite ***Iglesia de Santo Sepulcro*** XII[th]c linked to the Knights Templar and based on the octagonal church of the Holy Sepulchre in Jerusalem. The cross-ribbed cupola forming an 8 sided star, is emblematic of the Knights. The simple interior has a XIII[th]c crucifix and, like the church in Eunate, fine acoustics if you feel inclined to offer a song of prayer. If the church is closed ask for the custodian *guardián* who lives adj. €1). Continue up through the village past shop with patio out past cemetery on earth track and that undulates across open countryside crisscrossing N-111 at hairpin bends. Join the main road briefly to pass:

`2.7 km` **Ermita** *de Nuestra Señora del Poyo* Precariously situated on the road at its high point (*poyo* means raised platform or podium) from here we have a good view west over the flat plains with Viana and Logroño in the distance. We now cross the N-111 over a secondary road that leads to the village of Bargota (right). From here the path drops steeply down into a steep ravine [!] to cross the ***río Cornava*** (site of an ancient settlement) and up to the N-111 which we have to join for a 1 km stretch (Viana now clearly visible ahead).

`7.9 km` **Viana** cross N-111 into the suburbs passing *Alb.* ❶ **Izar** *Priv.[18÷1]*+ €8-12 © 948 090 002 with all facilities before climbing steeply up into the medieval heart of ***Viana Iglesia de Santa María*** XIII[th]C with fine recessed doorway in front of which is the tomb of the notorious Cesare Borgia who was killed nearby *(initially buried in the church but when his mausoleum was vandalised he was re-interred outside.)* The interior has an early statue of St. James. The parish has converted an adj. building to a pilgrim hostel *Alb.* ❷ **Santa Maria** *Par.[15÷4]* €-donativo ©

948 645 037 and shared meal with grace. Access is from the main square *Plaza de los Fueros* with its central fountain and collection of cafes and bars. The town hall has a fine carved façade with colonnades and houses the ***Turismo*** *Ⓒ* 948 446 302. Continue down the main street past the former XV[th]C pilgrim hospital (N°18 – now casa de Cultura) to the far end and turn sharp <left by the impressive ruins of San Pedro to the main hostel (400m from Santa María):

Alb. ❸ **Andrés Muñoz** *Mun.[54÷4]* €6 *Ⓒ* 948 645 530 c/San Pedro located in a quiet part of the old town with elevated terrace to the rear overlooking Logroño in the distance. 54 beds in several open sections in tiers of three! – all facilities including a baronial lounge-dining hall. Originally a monastery, it was acquired and transformed into a pilgrim hostel by one of the great *amigos* of the way, *Andrés Muñoz*. **Other Lodging:** *P[**]* **Casa Armendáriz** *Ⓒ* 948 645 078 c/Navarro Villoslada 19. *P[**]* **San Pedro** €30-40 *Ⓒ* 948 645 927 c/Medio S.Pedro13. At the top of town and price (opp. ruins of San Pedro) the restored palace *H[***]* **Palacio de Pujadas** (photo>) €60-80 *Ⓒ* 948 646 464 which also runs the adj. *cafetaria Portillo*. Beds also available at **Casa Asun** €25+ *Ⓒ* 948 645 149 c/La Rueda, 46 just off the camino as you leave town. There is a wide selection of shops bars and restaurants. *[Next accommodation: Logroño – 9.5 km]*

VIANA is a lively town with a resident population of 4,000. The camino passes through its historical centre, which is little changed since medieval pilgrims plodded through its ancient streets – its architectural heritage still largely intact. Back in the 15th century Viana was a major pilgrim halt with no less than 4 *hospitales de peregrinos* and it was during this period that Cesare Borgia became linked to the town. *[*Illegitimate son of Rodrigo Borgia, who was elected Pope Alexander VI in the pivotal year of 1492, Cesare was appointed commander of the Papal*

Portico Santa María

armies and patronised both Leonardo de Venci, who acted as his military architect, and Machiavelli who, no doubt, helped form some of his political ideology. When Pope Alexander VI died, his successor promptly banished Cesare to Spain where he was killed defending Viana in the siege of 1507. Colourful to the end, it has been suggested that Borgia's strong countenance may have been used by artists of the period, such as Leonardo, to model the popular image of Christ Jesus.] Owing to its border location the town has always been something of a hot spot and its defensive walls are well preserved on its western side (as you leave).

To stay or not to stay, that is a question. Whatever you decide, stay long enough to reflect on the ruins of the Church of St. Peter *San Pedro* and to soak up the atmosphere of this abandoned church and the terraced gardens that lead from it. Leave the town through the medieval stone arch *Portal San Felices* and drop down to the suburbs below following the path around the back of houses and over waste ground and abandoned factory buildings to cross over the N-111 onto a quiet road to:

`3.0 km` Ermita de la Trinidad de Cuevas *[F.]* peaceful picnic spot in grove of trees by tributary of the Ebro, site of an earlier pilgrim hospice of the Trinitarian Order of nuns. Veer right> at fork (to the left are the extensive lakes *Lagunas de Las Cañas* home to many species of waterfowl with bird observatory. [*The low-lying meadows in this area were notorious for the witches' covens that gathered here in the 16th century]. The Cantabrian 'Hill' is now visible ahead (with Logroño city behind). Watch carefully for the camino waymarks (other local walks around the lakes are also marked) and make your way back over the N-111 via *pasarela [1.6 km]* onto path through pine woods past Saicapack *factory [1.0 km]* over innocuous river to pass from Navarra into the famous wine-growing region of La Rioja:

`2.6 km` Cruce / La Rioja Here the autonomous region of La Rioja begins at the new city bypass. Make your way under the ring road on a new earth-*coloured* concrete track, a hard 'gift' from the local government and start the gradual (but long) climb up the northern flank of the Cantabrian hill *Cerro de Cantabria [*site of the prehistoric city of Cantabria – excavations of its Roman (and earlier) ruins are still in progress].* Shortly after we start our descent prepare to part with a few cents for good luck and in memory of Felisa, a legendary gatekeeper of the camino whose daughter now commands this welcoming border post and will stamp your credencial while you partake of figs, water and love *higos, agua y amor* (emblazoned on the stamp). Continue past the garden allotments *huerto urbanos* to the stone bridge ❶ *Puente de Piedra* (pilgrim information centre) cross the wide waters of the Ebro into the city of Logroño. The bridge, rebuilt in 1880, replaces the earlier medieval pilgrim bridge attributed to St. John Of the Nettles *San Juan de Ortega*. Once over the bridge turn right> across junction [!] into the cobbled c/Ruavieja (the original 'old' road) passing (right) ❷ *Ermita San Gregorio y Casa de la Danza* opposite ❸ *Iglesia y claustro Santa Maria del Palacio XIIthC* with its graceful octagonal tower (known locally as the needle) which is situated next to:

`3.8 km` Logroño *Albergue* ❶ Logroño *Asoc.[68÷3]* €7 ⓒ 941 248. 686 c/ Ruaviejo Nº32 the original hostel in the old quarter. 3 floors (in cubicles of 4 in large dormitories) all facilities and outside patio. Nearby at Nº42 is ❷ **Santiago Apóstol** *Priv.[68÷3]* €10 (+€30) ⓒ 941 256 976 modern facilities in this refurbished town house. ❸ **Santiago** *Par.[30+÷3+]* €-donativo (Jun-Sept) c/Barricocepo, 8. adj. Iglesia de Santiago. Basic facilities and beds miraculously made available 'as necessary' communal dinner and prayers. ❹ **Logroño** *Priv.[30÷6]+* €10 (+€30) ⓒ 941 254 226 c/Capitán Gallarza, 10. ❺ **Entresueños** *Priv.[92÷10]+* €10 c/ Portales, 12 adj. the cathedral ⓒ 941 271 334. ❻ **Check In Rioja** *Priv.[30÷1]* €11-€15 ⓒ 941 272 329 c/Los Baños, 2. ❼ *Albas* (*Puerta del Revellín*) *Priv.*[22÷1] €12 ⓒ 941 700 832 modern building in Plaza Martínez Flamarique, 4 (adj cafe *El Albero*) 700m east of Puente Piedra.

❏ *Turismo:* c/Portales,50 ⓒ 941 291 260. ❏ *Other Lodging Central:* H''' F&G €60+ ⓒ 941 008 900 Av. Viana. P' Redondela €30+ ⓒ 941 272 409 c/Portales,21. c/ San Juan P Daniel ⓒ 941 231 581 + P Sebastian ⓒ 665 974 651 + P San Juan ⓒ 941 231 581. H'''Marqués de Vallejo €50 ⓒ 941 248 333 c/Marqués de Vallejo,8. Hs'' La Numantina ⓒ 941 251 411 Sagasta, 4. P Villar ⓒ 941 220 228 plaza Matínez Zaporta (adj. Café Moderno). H''' Mayor €70+ ⓒ 941 232 368 boutique hotel c/Marqués. H''' Portales €80 ⓒ 941 502 794 c/ Portales, 85. ❏ *Suburbs:* H'''Murrieta €50 ⓒ 941 224 150 Marqués de Murrieta, 1. P Laurel Gonzalo de Berceo, 4. €37 ⓒ 941 225 154. P El Camino €25 ⓒ 618 65 50 00 c/ La Industria,2. ❏ *Planeta Agua* trekking shop Av. de Navarra,8 ⓒ 941-252 764. *Lavanderia S.Mateo* c/Doce,4 open 08:00-22:00.

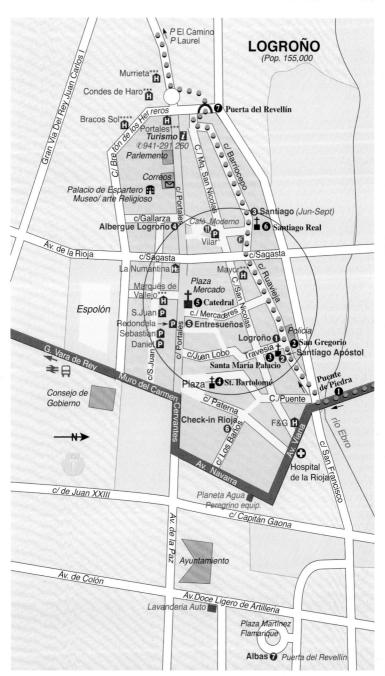

LOGROÑO
(Pop. 155,000)

Gran Via Del Rey Juan Carlos I

P El Camino
P Laurel

Murrieta***

Condes de Haro***

Bracos Sol****

C/ Bretón de los Herreros

Portales***
Turismo i
©941-291 260

Parlemento

Corréos

Palacio de Espartero
Museo/ arte Religioso

c/Gallarza

c/ Portales

c/ Mª San Nicolás

c/ Barriocepo

7 Puerta del Revellín

3 Santiago *(Jun-Sept)*

6 Santiago Real

Café Moderno

Albergue Logroño 4

Vilar

F

Av. de la Rioja

c/Sagasta

c/Sagasta

La Numantina

Marqués de
Vallejo***

S.Juan

Redondela →

Sebastián

Daniel

Mayor***

*Plaza
Mercado*

c/ San Nicolás

c/ Ruavieja

5 Catedral

c/ Mercaderes

5 Entresueños

c/ Portales

c/Juan Lobo

Logroño 1

Policia

2 San Gregorio

Santiago Apóstol

Travesía

Santa María Palacio

Espolón

G. Vara de Rey

Muro del Carmen

c/S.Juan

Plaza

4 St. Bartolomé

C./Puente

**Puente
de Piedra 1**

río Ebro

*Consejo de
Gobierno*

N→

c/ Paterna

**Check-in Rioja
6**

c/ Los Baños

F&G

c/ Viana

**Hospital
de la Rioja**

c/ San Francisco

c/ de Juan XXIII

Av. de la Paz

Av. Navarra

*Planeta Agua
Peregrino equip.*

c/ Capitán Gaona

Ayuntamiento

Av. de Colón

Av.Doce Ligero de Artillería

Lavandería Auto

*Plaza Martínez
Flamarique*

Albas 7 *Puerta del Revellín*

LOGROÑO: University City with rapidly growing population currently 155,000. Capital of La Rioja and a pleasant blend of medieval and modern. At the heart of the old town is the Gothic ❺ *Catedral de Santa María de la Redonda XIV*th*C* (built on an earlier Romanesque structure). Its impressive twin towers *Las Gemelas* (the twins) were a later addition and it adjoins the Plaza del Mercado lined with shops and cafés. The city is also capital of the famous wine-growing region of La Rioja and the festival of San Mateo heralds the harvest in a week-long frenzy of celebration at the end of September. There are a multitude of bars, restaurants and shops centred around

the pedestrian main street **c/ Portales** or try the popular •*Café Moderno* on plaza Matínez Zaporta. At the east end of c/ Portales close to the junction with the c/ Muro de Cervantes is Plaza Amós Salvador and ❹ *Iglesia San Bartolomé* with its exquisitely carved 13thc. porch. At the West end is the neocolonial edifice of the *Correos de Telégraphos* adj. the 18thc. Palacio del Espartero (museum) off which is c/Laurel, famous for its tapas bars. For other monuments along the waymarked Ruaviejo see *(next stage)*.

LA RIOJA One of the smallest and yet more diverse of the autonomous regions of Spain and justifiably renowned for its superlative wines. However, it is not only its grapes that will tempt you, for here you will meet a friendly people who have been welcoming pilgrims since medieval times. Indeed, kings and noblemen were promoting the camino through La Rioja as early as the 11th century as a means of exporting its famous wine and wares throughout Europe (and a way of attracting artists and stonemasons to build the great cathedrals, monasteries and monuments along the route). Sandwiched between the mountains of Navarra and the flat plains of the Meseta of Castilla y León, La Rioja is geographically split between High Rioja *Rioja Alta* to the northwest (the main wine growing region) and the lower *Rioja Baja* where market gardening is more prominent. The famous battle of Clavijo marks a turning point in the turbulent history of the provinces. With the defeat of the Moors came a great boost to Christianity and by extension, the Camino de Santiago. Logroño has good road and rail connections to all parts of Spain.

Detour: Clavijo is only 16 km south of Logroño. The sombre ruins of its castle stand sentinel over the fields where legend has it Santiago first appeared on his white charger to turn the tide of this historic battle in favour of the Spaniards over the occupying Moors in 844. It is, however, approached through a rather disappointing village landscape. Check transport details with the *Turismo*.

REFLECTIONS:

_____
_____
_____
_____
_____
_____
_____
_____
_____
_____
_____
_____
_____
_____
_____
_____
_____
_____
_____
_____
_____
_____

❏ **We are speeding up our lives and working harder,
in a futile attempt to slow down and enjoy it.** *Paul Hawken*

08 613.3 km (381.1 ml) – Santiago

LOGROÑO – NÁJERA (La Rioja)

٭٭٭٭٭٭٭٭٭٭	--- ---	23.1 --- ---	*80%*
▬▬▬▬▬	--- ---	3.8 --- ---	*13%*
▬▬▬▬▬	--- ---	<u>2.0</u> --- ---	*7%*
Total km		**28.9** km (18.0 ml)	

▲ 30.4 km (^300m + 1.5 km)
Alto ▲ Poyo Roldán 600m (1,968 ft)
< 🅰 Ⓗ > Navarrete **12.7** km – Ventosa **18.4** km *(opción + 1.4 km).*

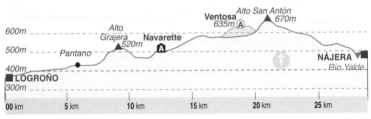

❏ **The Practical Path:** Waymarking out of Logroño now goes via Parque S. Miguel increasing pathways to 80%. However, we still have to contend with fast moving traffic out of the city and with ongoing road improvements, waymarking may be disturbed, so stay fully focused or you might lose your way – or your body. If nerves become frayed, you can always take refuge in the beautifully renovated intermediate albergues in Navarrete or Ventosa. The natural pathways now turn to the rich red clay soil of La Rioja – beautiful in the sun and a nightmare in the wet as it clings to footwear like a leech!

❏ **The Mystical Path:** Hundreds of pilgrims have taken time to make a cross and place it in this godforsaken hill above the roar of traffic on the motorway. Symbol of that greater mystery that lies beyond the business and suffering of this world, are you inclined to add yours? Will you stop awhile to admire the beautiful stone portal, gateway to another journey that awaits us? Will you ponder the monument to a pilgrim that went this way? Will you navigate direct to Nájera or venture to Ventosa?

❏ **Personal Reflections:** *"… I found him hanging up some pilgrim's washing. His smile said welcome; his refuge a veritable haven of peace. He suggested I stop and stay the night – we could share our stories over a meal. I declined his invitation and hurried onward anxious to reach the destination I had set myself. The next hostel was full and the hotel had no vacancy. I hurried on. It was getting late and I was tired. The next village was two hours away …"*

0.0 km **Logroño** From albergue ❶ we follow the brass scallop shells inlaid into the ancient c/Rúaviejo and c/Barriocepo past the pilgrim fountain *Fuente de los Peregrinos* decorated with Jacobean motifs, adjoining a square with mosaics setting out the 'Game of the Goose' *Juego del Oca*. Up ahead is the impressive façade of ❻ *Iglesia Santiago Real XVI*[th]*C* (right) with a statue of Santiago Matamoros high up

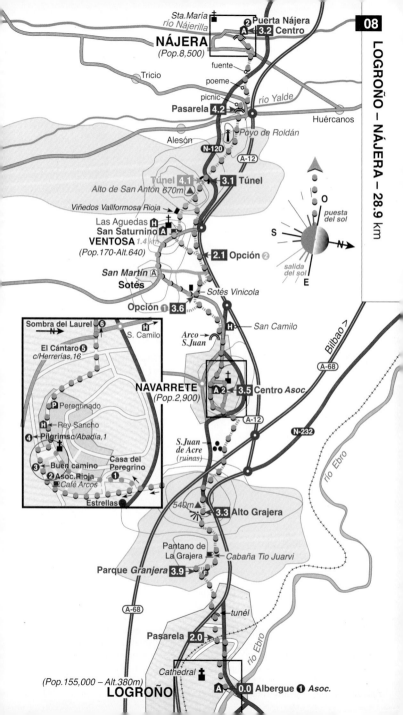

Sta.María
río Nájerilla
NÁJERA
(Pop.8,500)
Tricio

Puerta Nájera
3.2 Centro
fuente
poeme
picnic
Pasarela 4.2
río Yalde
Huércanos

Alesón
Poyo de Roldán
N-120 **A-12**

Túnel **4.1**
Alto de San Antón 670m
3.1 Túnel

Viñedos Vallformosa Rioja
Las Aguedas
San Saturnino
VENTOSA *1.4 km*
(Pop.170-Alt.640)

2.1 Opción ②

San Martín
Sotés
Sotés Vinicola

Opción ① **3.6**

puesta
del sol
O
S
N
salida
del sol
E

Sombra del Laurel ⑥
H S. Camilo
Arco S.Juan
H — *San Camilo*

El Cántaro ⑤
c/Herrerías,16

P Peregrinado

H Rey Sancho
④ Pilgrims *c/Abadía,1*
NAVARRETE
(Pop.2,900)
A ② **3.5** Centro *Asoc*
A-12
③ Buen camino
② Asoc.Rioja
Café Arcos
Casa del
Peregrino ①

Estrellas ●

Bilbao ➤
A-68

*S.Juan
de Acre*
(ruinas)

N-232

río Ebro

540m ▲ **3.3 Alto Grajera**

Pantano de
La Grajera
Cabaña Tio Juarvi
Parque *Granjera* **3.9**

A-68

tunél

Pasarela 2.0

río Ebro

Cathedral ✝
(Pop.155,000 – Alt.380m)
LOGROÑO
A **0.0 Albergue** ❶ *Asoc.*

above the south door (see photo right). The present building occupies the site of an earlier 9th century church erected to celebrate the defeat of the Moors at Clavijo. The interior also has several images of St. James. Adjoining the church is the parish pilgrim hostel. Continuing on through the narrow cobbled streets of the Old Town *Casco Antiguo* until it opens up into the paved Parliament Square *Plaza del Parlamento* with the impressive facade of the Parlamento de la Rioja whose building has been used for activities as diverse as a Carmelite convent and a tobacco factory! (*Turismo* to rear)

Leave the medieval quarter through the original pilgrim's gate ❼ *Puerta del Camino* [0.5 km] alternatively called Muralla del Revellín or Puerta Carlos V, the latter being a reference to the splendid armorial shields that adorn it. [!] Take a moment to collect your bearings – the next few kilometres are through the frenzied suburbs of Logroño. *[Waymarks are plentiful but have to compete with advertising signs, and are less obvious. With focus, you will make it to the peaceful lake shore café of La Grajera with relative ease].* Veer s/o <left at large roundabout past *Kutxabank* [0.5 km] on corner of Marqués de Murrieta (signposted Burgos N-120). At next roundabout turn <left into *c/ de los Duques de Nájera* [0.7 km] and turn off right> to newly waymarked route through *Parque de San Miguel* [0.3 km] *[F.]* :

2.0 km Pasarela *ferrocarril* through the linear park emerging into roadway to take the tunnel under the *A-12 Ruta Mural Jacobeo!* [1.5 km]. The next section is through open parkland along a newly paved track with concrete benches, somewhat hard underfoot (and buttocks) but now thankfully separated from the motorway bypass. This leads to a grove of pine trees visible ahead and beyond we arrive at Logroño's reservoir *pantano* wildlife reserve and **park [2.4 km]**:

3.9 km Parque de la Grajera *[F.]* turn right> along the reservoir wall, through pine forest and over a footbridge past the panoramic *Café Cabaña del Tio Juarvi* and picnic area with wonderful views of the lake. The route leads around the lake along gravel pathways passing Marcelino's *ermita del peregrino pasante* onto an asphalt track up towards the woodland on the horizon to:

3.3 km Alto de la Grajera High point with good view back over Logroño. The track runs alongside the highway where hundreds of crosses have been made out of strips of bark from the adj. sawmill and placed on the wire fence that separates us from the motorway: a timely reminder, perhaps, of the sacred nature of our journey and the tenuous boundary that separates us from a secular perspective. Along this stage we are told *there is no way to happiness – Happyness IS the Way!* We now join the hard shoulder of the N-120 [!] before crossing over onto an earth track through fields and vineyards over the autopista A-68 where, on the far side, we come to the ruins of the medieval monastery of the Order of San Juan de Acre founded in the 12th century to look after pilgrims. The splendidly carved entrance porch has been resited as the gate to the cemetery that we will pass on the far side of town. Continue through the vineyards of *Don Jacobo* up the steep steps to bypass & Option [!] **[a]** Carretera Burgos, 9 (left) albergue **El Camino de las Estrellas** *Priv.[40÷3]*+ €10 (+€40) ℰ 618 051 392. S/o over bypass into Navarrete and option **[b]** s/o along Calle la Cruz or **[c]** up right> into Calle Mayor Baja, both lead to the main square.

3.5 km Navarrete **[b]** *upper via c/ Mayor Baja Albergue* ❶ **Casa del Peregrino** *Priv. [18÷1]*+ €8 (+€25) ℰ 630 982 928. **[a]** *lower* s/o *via c/ Cruz.* ❷ **Navarrete Centro** *Asoc. [50÷4]* €7 ℰ 941 440 722 (see photo) adj. popular *café Los Arcos.* ❸ **Buen Camino** *Priv.[6÷1]*+ €9 ℰ 941 440 318 (rec.Hs Villa c/ Cruz). ❹ **Pilgrim's** *Priv.[32÷4]*+ €9-28 ℰ 491 440 707 *(Michael)* c/ Abadía,1. ❺ **El Cántaro** *Priv.[12÷1]*+ €10 (+€20) ℰ 941 441 180 mod. house in c/Herrerías. ❻ **A la Sombra del Laurel** *Priv.[16÷2]*+ €15 +€30 ℰ 639 861 110 Carretera de Burgos, 52. *[Next albergue: Ventosa – 7.1 km].* **Other Lodging:** *Central Hs*˙ **Villa de Navarrete** €30 ℰ 941 440 318 c/La Cruz. *H*˙˙˙ **Rey Sancho** €40 ℰ 941 441 378 c/Mayor Alta + *P*˙ **Peregrinando** €35 ℰ 941 441 324. *H*˙˙ **San Camilo** €50 ℰ 941 441 111 northern bypass.

NAVARRETE This historic town has been well maintained with the original period houses and handsomely carved family crests and armorial shields. The imposing 16th century Church of the Assumption occupies a commanding position overlooking the top square *[F.]* and below it is a Turismo ℰ 941-440 005 (summer only) and tapas *Bar Deportivo* with tables on the square. At the lower end of the town, on the noisy main road, is another square with a number of cafés and restaurants.

Leaving albergue centro pass along the arcaded street up to the church square into the c/Mayor Alta passing Hotel Rey Sancho and turning down into c/Arrabal which merges with the main road (c/San Roque) and continue s/o over rio de la Fuente and pass the town *cementerio* with its splendidly carved 13th century entrance gateway (relocated here from the ruins of the hospice of San Juan de Acre on the eastern outskirts). One of the capitals depicts the battle between Roldán and Ferragut (see *Poyo Roldán* which we pass later). Continue past the cemetery onto a track of bright red Riojan earth through vineyards to:

3.6 km Opción ❶ – ● ● ● ● *Sign to Sotés 1,3 km – in fact 2.1 km up steep asphalt road to albergue* **San Martín** *[8÷2]* €10 ℰ 650 962 625 c/ S.Miguel, 67]. Continue s/o past wine co-op down to A-12 and follows it to 2nd option to Ventosa:

2.1 km Opción ❷ – ● ● ● ● detour to Ventosa on *el camino original* turn <left (Ventosa visible ahead) to **road [1.2 km]** turn right> to bar and Nájera *or* s/o (left) along calle Mayor to **albergue [0.2 km]** *albergue* **San Saturnino ♥** *Priv.*[42÷6] €10 ℰ 941 441 899. Sensitively restored and well-maintained hostel with good facilities incl. rear patio. Also *H*˙˙ **Las Águedas** €45-65 ℰ 941 441 774 on Plaza S. Coloma, rooms from €45. Also *AT* **Loft & Garden** €30 ℰ 607 855 432. Re-join the main route up past the church, down past *Café Juanka* (free internet) and turn <left *Viñedos Vallformosa Rioja* to rejoin main route **[1.3 km].**

For the direct route continue by the A-12 past picnic site and s/o over road **[1.1 km]** continue on track. The alt. route from Ventosa joins **[0.5 km]** we now climb through an pass between two low hills with stone 'altars' painstakingly erected by individuals pausing to soak up the mystery of this mythical place. We crest the hill at *Alto de San Antón* [1.0 km] site of an early pilgrim hospital established by the Antonine Order *Convento de San Antón* (no longer discernible left) while on the right is Roldan's Hill *Poyo de Roldán.*

(Here we are led to believe Roldán slew the Muslim giant Ferragut with a well-aimed rock. Roland liberated the town (where Ferragut ruled) and freed the captive Christian knights of Charlemagne's army. This legend, reminiscent of David and Goliath, retains its powerful impact along the camino]. Continue through the pass (the high point of this stage at 610m) and head down towards Nájera passing under the N-120 tunnel [0.5 km]:

3.1 km **Túnel *N-120*** continue along a wide farm track through vineyards passing beehive hut (left) across minor road around the side of the gravel works to:

4.2 km **Pasarela *río Yalde*** turning right over footbridge and then left around picnic area beyond. We next pass the graffiti poem *Pilgrim Who Calls You?* And while contemplating the question we pass the blessing from *La Fuente de Paulino [F.]* Cross N-120 [!] to the modern outskirts of Nájera passing the sports centre *polideportivo* over main roundabout with *Albergue* ❶ **El Peregrino** *Priv.[20÷1]* €10 ✆ 640 072 753 c/ San Fernando 90. and follow the road as it narrows and descends towards the río Nájerilla passing ❶ *iglesias Santa Clara* and *Madre de Dios*. Cross over bridge ❷ (it replaced the medieval bridge erected by San Juan de Ortega).

3.2 km **Nájera *Puente*** Well located just over the bridge at the entrance of the 'old town' ❷ **Puerta de Nájera** *Priv.[34÷6]* €10-15 c/Carmen ✆ 941 362 317 nearby *off* c/Mayor. ❸ **Calle Mayor** *Priv.[9÷1]*+ €9 + €50 (double room) C/Dicarán,5 ✆ 941 360 407. Follow waymarks through the old town *or* take the river path direct to: ❹ **Nido de Cigüeña** *Priv.[19÷3]* €10-€15 + €35 (double room) ✆ 941 896 027 Calleja Cuarta San Miguel,4. ❺ **Nájera** *Asoc.[90÷1]* €-donativo ✆ Turismo – one room dorm adj. river. ❻ **Sancho III** *Priv.[10÷2]* €10 ✆ 941 361 138 reception at *La Judería* (menú €8). *(Alb. Alberone closed).* ❑ *Turismo* ✆ 941 360 041 Plaza San Miguel. **Other Lodging *old town*:** **Fonda el Moro** c/Martires, 21 ✆ 941-360 052. *Hs*** **Ciudad de Nájera** €45+ ✆ 941 360 660 calleja San Miguel, 14 (backing on to the cliffs) or the up-market *H**** **Duques de Nájera** €50+ ✆ 941 410 421 c/ Carmen, 7 by the bridge. On the other side of the river: *Hs** **Hispano** €30 ✆ 941 363 615 c/La Cepa,2. *(Hotel San Fernando closed). Bar Naxara* on c/Mayor (by bridge) opens at 06:30 for early breakfast. **NÁJERA:** Capital of the Kingdom of Navarre in the 11th and 12th centuries, with strong connections to the Camino, marking the beginning of stage V of the Codex Calixtinus. The waymarked route passes the tourist office in Plaza S.Miguel to pride of place ❸ *Monasterio Santa María de la Real* with its Royal Pantheon housing the burial place of many of the illustrious kings, Queens and knights of Navarre. Of singular beauty is the tomb of Doña Blanca de Castile y Navarre (1156). The Pantheon is part of this fine church, as is the cave, which gave rise to it. *[The church was built at this spot following the legend that the son of Sancho the Great, Don García,*

followed his hunting falcon into this cave and came upon a statue of the Virgin Mary – see photo above] The church also has interesting choir stalls bearing pilgrim motifs carved into the seat rests. The splendid Knights Cloister is accessed through the museum *Museo Najerillense* (Roman artefacts). Nájera has an expanding population of 8,500 and we enter through the modern eastern quarter with the old town sandwiched between the river Najerila and high rock face that acts as

a dramatic backdrop with its ancient ❹ *Castillo*. The narrow c/Mayor has a wide selection of shops, bars and cafés and leads to myriad side streets. At the far end of town, close to the municipal albergue, are Plazas de España and Navarra with a variety of bars serving pilgrim menus.

Local Detours: ● ● ● ● The tourist office has a pamphlet *a través sus sendas* showing various local walks. If you have time and energy a trip to **[1] Castillo** [1.2 km / 2.4 km round trip) has fine views of the town and the routes to Azofra and San Millán. *Directions*: From the church of S.Maria turn up the waymarked camino and turn left 300m by old football ground and *up* left again onto new woodland track that winds steeply up to the top of the hill with ruins of the castle 900m (total ascent 1.2 km). **[2] Cruz de Malpica** similar to [1] with access right off camino 400m from S.Maria. **[3] Pico Nájera** and **[4] Pasomalo** continue past football ground and turn off left after another 300m.

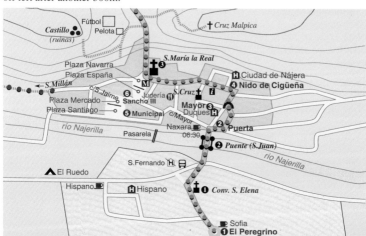

Detour: ● ● ● ● (18.0 km) **San Millán de la Cogolla and the monasteries of Suso and Yuso.** Declared a world heritage site by UNESCO in 1997 as testimony to its unique contribution to Christian monasticism from the 6th century. It was also here in the 10th century that the native Spanish language *Castellano* was first written down by an anonymous monk. Two centuries later it was further embellished in the verse of the poet monk Gonzalo Berceo. Suso (the smaller and higher of the two monasteries) is set on the hillside in this gloriously peaceful valley located just beyond the village of Berceo. It has Visigothic, Mozárabe and Romanesque characteristics while Yuso, built from 11th century onwards, is mainly Baroque and houses some fine artefacts including the famous library.

This is one of the more remote of the alternative routes and offers a special experience on that account, hence this new 'purple' category (main guidebook only). It bears the following warnings: 'proceed with caution' *pase con precaución* and 'danger of landslide' *peligro desprendimientos.* Local vineyard owner Alonso states with conviction: *'I have walked this path my entire life but was only ever in real danger while coming here along the main road; but they don't put warning signs there!'* Don't walk this route if you lack confidence or in wet weather as the earth track turns to mud and the river beyond Badarán can make the path impassable.

The Royal Way *Camino Real* is ideal for anyone seeking solitude and time for reflection away from the noise and bustle of the main camino. It is steeped in history and mysticism and provides an opportunity to walk the Landscape Temple in silence with the gentle sound of nature informing and enriching us. If you intend to walk with a colleague you can, perhaps, allow conversation to subside and return to speech only as you pass through Badarán, or while partaking of a picnic en route?

You will need a day to walk the path from Nájera to San Millán **18.0 km** and a day to walk back to rejoin the camino at **[1] Nájera [2] Azofra** via the Cistercian abbey of S.María **[3] Cireñuela** (See map next page). Or **[4] Return Nájera by bus.** Take a day pack to San Millán early in the morning; explore the monastery(s) and take the bus (Estollo–Nájera €1.70) 15:00 / 19:00 (mon-Fri) 19:45 only on Sat/Sun (check times) ...or return by taxi.

`0.0 km` Nájera The route is signposted 'bad way' *paso malo* for a good reason! It starts along a narrow path under the steep cliffs (see photo). The 'discreet' waymarks start in Plaza Mercado (adj. Plaza Santiago) via c/San Jaime onto a path under the sandstone cliffs with river down to our (left). Continue s/o at sign for blue route (right) *Ruta Collado Castillo* **[1.0** km]. Turn right at T-junction / **stream [0.9** km] (*not* track imm. over stream) and veer left onto next **track [0.1** km] and continue s/o through gently rolling vineyards all the way down into Badarán **[6.6** km].

8.6 km **Badarán** s/o main street *c/ Real* passing *Iglesia Expectación* and *Ayuntamiento* (right - with paleolithic finds from the area) + *CR* **Di Vino** €50+ c/ Ricardo Herreros, 8 ℂ 619 714 029. pass *Hs* **Comercio** (*Hs* **Ribera** ℂ 618 138 944 to the rear).  Turn <left down *c/Cuesta Molino Arriba* **[0.7 km]**. [*H***°°°Conde de Badarán** €50+ 200m s/o main road ℂ 941 367 055]. Continue over **río Cardeñas [0.3 km]** and turn right> **[0.2 km]** onto track (often wet) parallel to river. Follow waymarks along low lying tracks veering left at junction **[3.2 km]** and right at T-junction back towards river and past ruins of Convento de San Martin **[1.5 km]** (right) and at cross tracks *(before San Andrés visible ahead with Estollo beyond – take this route for the main road bridge)* veer right **[1.2 km]** cross over river and veer left onto *ruta de Gonzalo de Berceo* **[0.4 km]** part of the network of paths in the area known as *Los Pasos de San Millán (village of Berceo above)* up to main road in **San Millán de Cogolla [0.7 km]** *(bus stop up to our right)*. Continue s/o into the main street and at the far end we turn down to the entrance to the **monastery [1.0 km]**.

9.4 km **Monasterio de San Millán de Suso**. *H***°°°°Hosteria del Monasterio** ℂ 941-373 327 single from €50 (pilgrim discount). *Hs***°° La Posada / La Calera** ℂ 941-373 161. Good facilities and accommodation also in Berceo, & Badarán.

REFLECTIONS:

❏ **Yesterday is history, tomorrow a mystery and today a gift.**
That is why it is called the present. *Anon.*

09 **584.4** km (363.1 ml) – Santiago

NÁJERA – SANTO DOMINGO de la CALZADA

....	--- ---	15.1	--- ---	71%
————	--- ---	5.0	--- ---	23%
━━━━	--- ---	1.2	--- ---	6%
Total km		**21.3** km	(13.2 ml)	

▲ --- --- 22.8 km (^300m + 1.5 km)

Alto ▲ Cirueña 745m (2,444 ft)

< ▲ ⊞ > Azofra **6.2** km – Cirueña **15.3** *(+0.1 km).*

[Elevation profile]
700m — Campo de Golfe ⓖ ▲ Cirueña 745m ▲▲⊞ Ciriñuela
600m — SANTO DOMINGO ■
500m — Azofra ■▲ⓕ
■ NÁJERA   rio Tuerto
400m —
00 km   5 km   10 km   15 km   20 km

❏ **The Practical Path:** The majority of this stage (71%) is on wide country tracks passing through remote and gently undulating farmland with only the last·stretch into Santo Domingo alongside the main road. Beyond Azofra the camino crosses a secondary road (to Alesanco) where the new A-12 has been built and the waymarks now take the most direct route parallel to the motorway directly to Cirueña. There is little shade and few drinking fonts so take protection against the sun and fill up the water bottle as you pass Azofra and Cirueña (both have *fuentes*). See map for detours to San Millán de Cogolla and Cañas.

❏ **The Mystical Path:** Will you pause to admire the medieval stone column that marks an ancient border? What does symbolise it to you and where is the border between your ancient Homeland and the world you now inhabit? Will you rest awhile in the leafy shade of the cool glade beyond to ponder such mysteries? How many pilgrims in the past has this venerable oak grove sheltered from the noonday sun and how many will it shelter in the future? Will you accept its sombre gift in the passing moment, a present from the acorn past?

❏ **Personal Reflections:** *"... I was alone in the cool interior and made to leave but as the bells stopped the nuns began filing in to the chapel. I knelt in silence and lifted my head at the sound of approaching footsteps. The eyes I met beamed such unconditional love as she beckoned me to follow her to the choir stall. Tears streamed down my face as the nuns started their heavenly chanting... The love I felt overwhelmed me and I collapsed onto the pew. The nun in front turned and quietly laid her hand on mine. She produced a tissue from the sleeve of her habit and bent down and whispered gently, 'breathe.' I write these notes in the quiet of the convent, and am struck by the realisation that she could not have known where I was from and yet spoke the only word in English that was needed. In that moment she, or rather that which she represented, quite literally in-spired me.*

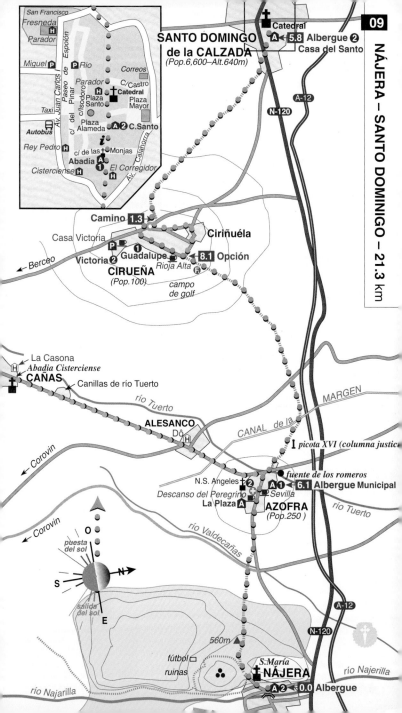

Inset map (Santo Domingo de la Calzada):

San Francisco
Fresneda
Parador
Miguel P
Río P
Paseo de Espolón
Av. Juan Carlos
Paseo del Pinar
Correos
Parador
C/Isodoro
C/Castro
Catedral
Plaza Santo
Plaza Mayor
Taxi
Plaza Alameda
A 2 C.Santo
Autobus
Rey Pedro H
c/ de las Monjas
Abadía A 1
Cistercience H
El Corregidor
Av. Calahorra

SANTO DOMINGO de la CALZADA
(Pop.6,600–Alt.640m)

Catedral
A 5.8 **Albergue** 2
Casa del Santo

A-12
N-120

Camino 1.3
Casa Victoria
Ciriñuéla
Berceo
P
Victoria 2
Guadalupe 1
8.1 Opción
CIRUEÑA
(Pop.100)
Rioja Alta
campo de golf

La Casona
Abadía Cistercience
CAÑAS
Canillas de río Tuerto
río Tuerto
MARGEN
ALESANCO
Dô
H
CANAL de la
Corovin
picota XVI *(columna justic*
fuente de los romeros
N.S. Ángeles 2
A 1 6.1 **Albergue** Municipal
Descanso del Peregrino
Sevilla
La Plaza A
AZOFRA
(Pop.250)
río Tuerto
Corovin
río Valdecañas

O
puesta del sol
N
S
salída del sol
E

560m ▲
fútbol
ruinas
S.María
NÁJERA
río Najerilla
A 2 0.0 **Albergue**
río Najarilla
A-12
N-120

0.0 km **Nájera** From albergue ❶ out under the arches in Plaza Estrella along c/ Carmen into c/S.Miguel and up right past the Church of Santa María Real into c/ Costanilla and up steeply past sports grounds (left) through the delightful *zona natural* between pine trees on a wide red earth track to the high point *alto* [**1.3** km] (560m). The track continues down over road and río Valdecañas to join quiet roads and tracks all the way into Azofra for the remaining [**4.8** km].

6.1 km **Azofra Centro** *Cafe Peregrino* (left) *Sevilla* (right) *Alb.* ❶ **Azofra** *Muni.[60÷30]* €7 ©
941 379 220 purpose built hostel in c/Las Parras, 200m (right) from the central fountain. Facilities incl. patio/cafe. ❷ **Herbert Simón** *Par.[26÷2]* © 607 383 811 parish hostel adj. the Church of Our Lady of the Angels *Nuestra Señora de los Ángeles* (statue of Santiago Peregrino and mass at 19:00) situated at the top end of town with small patio. Renovated by a German Confraternity (Herbert Simón) now operated by the council. The cool,  atmospheric surroundings compensate for the basic facilities (opens when main hostel is full). **Other Lodging:** *P* La Plaza €30-45 © 941 379 239 Pl. de España 7 & Exclusive hotel **Real Casona de las Amas** © 941 416 103 c/Mayor 5 €80-160. Note: former hostel *La Fuente* closed. *(Next albergue: Cirueña – 9.3 km).*

AZOFRA A tranquil village with a declining population of 250 owing much of its continuing existence to the camino. As you leave the village a small park *[F.]* (left) is dedicated to the patroness of La Rioja *Virgen de Valvanera* and on the other side of the road (50m off route) the ruins of the medieval pilgrim's fountain *Fuente de los Romeros* adjoining a lay-by with a modern monument. There are 2 inconspicuous shops (adjacent to the albergues) and several bars that compete to provide the pilgrim with sustenance. There were several pilgrim *hospitales* here in medieval times and a pilgrim cemetery from the 12th century. Azofra is another place from which to detour along the 'monasteries route' *ruta de los monasterios* and the birthplace of the Spanish language *la cuna del Castellano* in Yuso (see previous stage).

Detour Cañas ● ● ● ● [**5.1** km] – all by quiet country road via **Alesanco 1.8** km *H** Dô* © 941 379 110 and **Caniilas de Rio Tuerto 2.7** km (no facilities) and **Cañas 0.5** km home to the splendid Cistercian abbey *Abadía Cisterciense de Cañas* founded in 1170 for the order of nuns that still occupy it (10:30-13:30/ 16:00-19:00 closed Mondays). It is renowned for the natural light *luz* that pours into it through the original alabaster  windows that reach up to the vaulted roof. Off the adjoining garden courtyard is a small museum housing the early 13th century sarcophagus of Doña Urraca López de Haro founder of the abbey and, reputedly, one of the finest sarcophagi in Spain. The abbey is also celebrated for the visit of Saint Francis of Assisi who allegedly stayed here while journeying to Santiago. Cañas is the birthplace of Santo Domingo de Silos (not to be confused with Santo Domingo de Calzada) who restored the famous monastery that now bears his name and the home of Gregorian chant in Spain (see Burgos detours). *Hs* **La Casona** © 941-379 150 rooms from €24. *Hs* **La Posada del Santo** © 941-204 187.

From Azofra s/o crossroads (Alesanco left) park *[F.]* by rio Tuerto and onto track past the medieval marker *la picota* **[1.3** km] and shortly afterwards raised canal *Canal de la Margen* and then down towards A-12 over **road [1.8** km] and over river (usually dry) and up towards Cirueña and *Rioja Alta Golf Club* past rest area *Área de Descanso [F]* **[4.2** km] and s/o to option **[0.8** km]:

8.1 km Cirueña *Opción* competing arrows are one of many consequences* of the *crisis económico* evident in Cirueña. *(Turn right for alternative route to Ciriñuela where former albergue Virgen de las Candelas remains closed*)*. S/o for main route where the exclusive golf club now welcomes pilgrims to its bar* *Rioja Alta* s/o through soulless new suburbs with maze of empty apartment blocks* giving rise to the sobriquet *Sevende** (for sale!). Pass 2nd *Área de Descanso [F.]* to 3rd rest area *[F.]*
▼ *Albergue* ❶ **Virgen de Guadalupe** *Priv.***[23÷5]* €7 ✆ 638 924 069 (left 100m) c/ Barrio Alto. Also 100m s/o and turn left 250m: ❷ **Victoria** *Priv.***[12÷2]*+ €10–€40 ✆ 941 426 105 new build at end of the village c/S.Andres. Owners also run *P** **Casa Victoria** €35+ ✆ 941 426 105 adj. *Café/bar Jacobeo.*

▼ To continue cross main road turn down right to roundabout and <left onto wide track where alternative route from *Ciriñuela* joins at waymarked camino crossing:

1.3 km Cirueña *Camino* The camino now gently undulates over crop fields until we reach the outskirts of St. Dominic of the Roadway *Santo Domingo de la Calzada*. Here we pass behind industrial buildings before reaching the busy **N-120 [4.6** km] which we follow crossing over into the old town. If you lose the waymarks in the busy streets ahead follow the signpost for the *Parador* up the **c/Mayor [1.2** km] to:

5.8 km Santo Domingo de la Calzada *Alb.* ❶ **Abadía Cistercienses** *Conv.[33÷5]* €5 run by Cistercian nuns ✆ 941 340 700 on c/Mayor 29-31 (left) as you enter the old quarter (close to Tourist office and opp. hotel El Corregidor). Good facilities with shaded terrace and garden to the rear. Vespers *Vísperas* at 18.30. ❷ **Casa de la Cofradía del Santo** *Asoc.[140÷4]* €7 Spanish Confraternity ✆ 941 343 390 who also publish *El Peregrino*. Centrally situated in the old quarter on c/ Mayor, 44. All facilities incl. garden with chicken coop where the cocks and hens are kept for their pivotal part in the cathedral myth (See next page).

❒ *Turismo* ✆ 941 341 238 c/Mayor, 33 part of the *Centro de Interpretación del Camino* weekdays 10:00–14:00 / 16:00–19:00. **Other Lodging:** *Hs*** **Hospedería Cistercienses** *(Santa Teresita)* €40+ ✆ 941 340 700 modern hostel run by the Cistercian nuns c/Pinar, 2 (rear of albergue). *H**** **El Corregidor** €40+ ✆ 941 342 128 c/Mayor,14. *Hs** **Rey Pedro I** €45+ ✆ 941 341 160 c/S. Roque, 9 (the main road and tree-lined paseo). *Hs* **La Catedral** €40 c/ Isidoro Salas 651 948 260. *P** **Miguel** €25+ ✆ 941 343 252 c/ Juan Carlos I, 23. *[P** **Río** ✆ 941340 277 c/Etchegoyen, 2 currently closed]. *Hs** **El Molino de Floren** €40 ✆ 941 342 031 c/Margubete. For 4 star luxury in the original pilgrim hospital on Plaza del Santo (adj. the cathedral) *H***** **Parador de Santo Domingo** €85+ ✆ 941 340 300 or *H**** **Parador Bernardo de Fresneda** €90+ ✆ 941 341 150 located at the far end of town beside the pilgrim monument in the recently refurbished 16th century Convento de San Francisco.

Town Hall *Ayuntamiento*

SANTO DOMINGO de la CALZADA: The winding streets of this ancient town evoke a sense of history intimately linked with the camino. *Saint Dominic* dedicated his life to improving the route for pilgrims in the 11th century, building roads and bridges. A giant among men Domingo García was born in 1019 in humble surroundings in Viloria (see next stage). His effort to heed God's call to become a monk was thwarted by the monastery at San Millán who were not inclined to accept this illiterate son but the loss to the intelligentsia has been the gain of pilgrims for the past millennium. He built a pilgrim hospital, now the Parador and a church which evolved into the Cathedral. Both are situated in the historic town square *Plaza del Santo* and, like many other religious structures, renovated over many centuries and therefore combining different architectural styles. The original church was consecrated in the 12th century, although the independent tower was not added until the 18th century. The dark interior houses the tomb of Santo Domingo, the chapel of La Magdalena and a fine altarpiece. St.Dominic's spirit is as alive today as the cock in the cathedral coop, one of the more unlikely exhibits at the rear of the church containing a live cock and hen.

Embellished over the years it has become one of the more endearing stories along the Way of St. James. Legend has it that a pilgrim couple and their son stopped at an inn here on their way to Santiago. The pretty innkeeper's daughter had her eye on the handsome lad, but the devout young fellow thwarted her advances. Incensed by his refusal she hid a silver goblet in his backpack and reported him for stealing it. The innocent lad was caught and condemned to hang. Some accounts suggest the parents continued on their way, oblivious of the fate of their son and on their return from Santiago they found him still hanging on the gallows but miraculously still alive thanks to the intervention of Santo Domingo. They rushed to the sheriff's house and found his lordship about to tuck into dinner. Upon hearing the parents, he retorted that their son was no more alive than the cock he was about to eat, whereupon the fowl stood up on the dish and crowed loudly. The miracle was not lost on the sheriff who rushed back to the gallows and cut down the poor lad, who was given a full pardon. We are left to speculate on the fate of the foxy maiden. Indeed so many miracles were ascribed to the intervention of Santo Domingo that the town that came to carry his name was also referred to as the Compostela of Rioja.

A museum is attached to the cathedral and on the opp' side of the square is the original pilgrim hospital dating from 14th century, now a luxury Parador that still retains its medieval splendour. The town has a wide variety of restaurants, bars and shops along both the c/Mayor and the busy Paseo and the narrow interconnecting streets all serving the inflow of tourists, pilgrims and the local population of 6,600. The town and its network of medieval streets has been declared a site of historic interest and its main fiesta, in honour of the saint, takes place during the first 2 weeks in May.

REFLECTIONS:

❐ **When you meet anyone, remember it is a holy encounter.**
And as you see *them* you will see *yourself*.
——————————————————— *A Course In Miracles*

10 **563.1** km (349.9 ml) – Santiago

SANTO DOMINGO de la CALZADA – BELORADO
(La Rioja)   (Castilla y León)

▓▓▓▓▓▓	--- ---	16.2	--- ---	72%
▬▬▬	--- ---	5.4	--- ---	24%
▬▬▬	--- ---	0.8		4%
Total km		**22.4** km	(13.9 ml)	

▲ --- --- 23.9 km (^300m + 1.5 km)
Alto ▲ Vilamayor del Río 810m (2,657 ft)
< 🅰 🅷 > Grañón **6.7** km – Carrasquedo **7.9** km (+1.2 km) – Redecilla **10.5**
Castildelgado **12.2** km (+200m) – Viloria de la Rioja **14.1** km –
Villamayor del Río **17.5** km (+300m *off* route).

The Practical Path: It is no tribute to Saint Dominic who did so much to assist
the pilgrim that today we are forced by new roads to travel closer to the dangerous
N-120 more than at any other stage of our journey so far. New waymarks go directly
to Grañón alongside the A-12 but the old path still offers an alternative. Be prepared
for half today's walk to be parallel to the busy main road with little shelter and water,
apart from the villages you pass through.

❐ **The Mystical Path:** There is much to reflect on as you walk the road of the Saint.
Denied access to the seat of knowledge, yet endowed with wisdom. Which do you
seek? Which will provide you with real meaning? The burial place is on all the maps
but will you discover the place of birth? Will you stay awhile and soak up the light
of this tranquil place and drink the cool water from the well that nurtured the infant
child? The only monument to this extraordinary saint is a ruined house protecting,
perhaps, the peace of this place from the tour buses. A light-filled place providing
refreshment for the soul and space to contemplate our own renewal.

❐ **Personal Reflections:** *"… I resisted his advances and resented his intrusion.
He could see I was limping badly and persisted in his offer to help. My resistance
finally crumpled and he removed my boot and sock with tenderness. My foot was
an awful mess – it had gone way beyond what any reasonable person would have
asked of it. He fetched a basin of warm water and gently washed away the blood.
The broken skin was easily dressed and the remaining blisters drained. Afterwards
he took my torn boot to the nearby cobbler to have it stitched. He had healed my
foot and mended my boot but the real healing was happening inside of me. How
many times had I adversely judged my fellow travellers when each one is a Christ
in disguise …"*

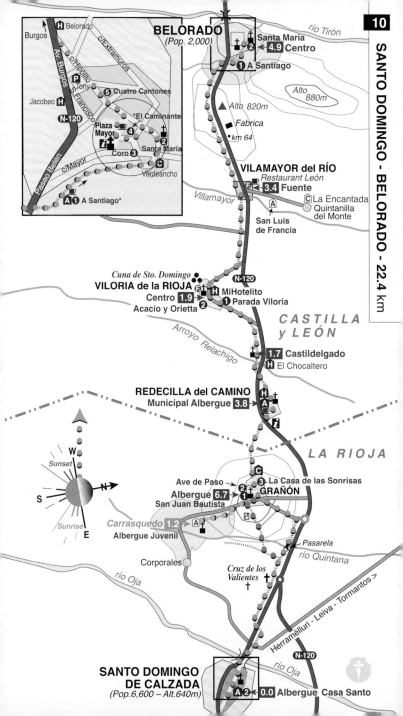

río Tirón

BELORADO
(Pop. 2,000)

☩ ☩ **Santa Maria**
■ **2** ◄ **4.9** **Centro**
1 **A Santiago**

Burgos

H Belorado

c/Extramuros

Av. Burgos

c/Hipolito

S. Francisco

Tony **P**

Jacobeo **H**

5 **Cuatro Cantones**

N-120

El Caminante

4

Plaza
Mayor ■

i

Coro **3** **Santa María** ■ **2**

c/Mayor

C

Verdeancho

Paseo Belen

A **1** **A Santiago***

▲ *Alto* 820m

■ *Fabrica*

• km 64

Alto 880m

VILAMAYOR del RÍO

F *Restaurant León*
■ **3.4** **Fuente**

Villamayor

A

**San Luis
de Francia**

C La Encantada
Quintanilla
del Monte

Cuna de Sto. Domingo ●
VILORIA de la RIOJA ☩
Centro **1.9** **H** **MiHotelito**
■ **2** **1** **Parada Viloria**
Acacio y Orietta

N-120

*CASTILLA
y LEÓN*

Arroyo Relachigo

☩ **1.7** **Castildelgado**
H El Chocaltero

REDECILLA del CAMINO
Municipal Albergue **3.8**

H ☩
A ■
i

LA RIOJA

W
Sunset
S ⊕ N
Sunrise
E

C

Ave de Paso
■ **2** **3** **La Casa de las Sonrisas**
Albergue **6.7** **GRAÑÓN**
■ **1**
San Juan Bautista

Carrasquedo **1.2**
A ■
Albergue Juvenil

Corporales

Pasarela

río Quintana

*Cruz de los
Valientes* ☩

río Oja

Herramelluri - Leiva - Tormantos ➤

N-120

río Oja

**SANTO DOMINGO
DE CALZADA**
(Pop.6,600 – Alt.640m)

☩
A **2** **0.0** **Albergue Casa Santo**

`0.0 km` **Santo Domingo** Leaving albergue ➋ **Casa Santos** pass cathedral down c/ Mayor cross main road out of town to small *ermita* on the bridge over the río Oja **[0.9** km]. *[Before the arrival of Dominic, medieval pilgrims had to veer off right along the river towards Leiva to follow the Río Tirón into Belorado].* Cross *Puente del Santo* onto track (right) s/o over road to Leiva and turn <left over **N-120 [1.0** km] along gravel path to **Cruz de los Valientes [1.7** km]. *[so called because of the combat between two locals, one from Santo Domingo and the other from Grañón, over disputed ownership of some nearby land. In medieval times, it was sometimes the custom to submit such matters to the Divine Judge on the basis that He would protect the innocent party – the valiant combatant from Grañón was favoured in this instance. A modern steel replacement overlooking the N-120 marks the spot.]* The gravel track continues down to **option [1.2** km]: ▼

Alternativo: ● ● ● ● away from the N-120 turn left (old waymarks Grañón visible on rise ahead) take the first track right over river (dry in summer) and s/o up (ignoring track and waymark down right) past cemetery and right on road (detour to Carrasquedo left) Pass the ruins of Ermita de los Judiós XIV[th]C and over crossroads by bus stop to the church ahead [2.6 km –versus– new route 2.2 km].

▼ For the new waymarked route continue s/o alongside N-120 and cross river over pasarela under the N-120 flyover and continue up to roundabout **[1.3** km] and take the access road down and then steeply up into Grañón. Climb the steps ahead *[F.]* (left) into the town centre **[2.2** km]:

`6.7 km` **Grañón** *Iglesia S. Juan Bautista* ♥*Alb.* **S. Juan Bautista ❶** *Par.[40÷2]* €-donativo © 941 420 818 upper floors of the annex to the Church of Saint John the Baptist (photo right) reserved for pilgrims who have travelled from further back than Santo Domingo. This atmospheric hostel offers a communal meal and prayers much treasured by pilgrims for the hospitality, cool interior and tranquil setting. A pilgrim mass (and, perhaps sacred chant) is offered by the welcoming priest. **GRAÑÓN** originally had 2 monasteries & pilgrim hospice, now a population of 290 occupy this tranquil Jacobean village. Also offering communal

dinners; ➋ **Ave de Paso** *Priv. [10÷2]* €6 © 666 801 051 (Manu Pérez) c/ El Caño 19. ➌ **La Casa de las Sonrisas** *Priv. [14÷2]* €-donativo c/Mayor Nº16. **Other Lodging:** €45+ *CR* **Jacobea** © 941 420 684 c/Mayor Nº32. *CR* **Cerro de Mirabel** Nº40 © 660 166 090. On main square: *Mercado Piedad* & •*Bar Teo*.

Detour ● ● ● ● **1.2 km Carrasquedo** (2.4 km round trip) to the Basilica of Nuestra Señora de Carrasquedo, the patroness of Grañón village, situated amidst a grove of trees on the outskirts of the town (1.3 km) on the road to Corporales along a delightful tree-lined pathway. You can stay in the youth hostel, a venerable period building adjoining the basilica *Albergue* **Carrasquedo** *[40]*+ €8 © 941 746 000 no kitchen but dinner (21:00) and breakfast (09:00) (phone in advance to check availability - mixed reports).

Leave along c/Mayor by viewpoint *[F.]* down onto tracks and cross stream and then <left up to a signboard heralding the fact that we have left modest La Rioja behind and stepped into the autonomous region of Castilla y León (province of Burgos) a fact they are keen to demonstrate **[2.0** km].

La Rioja   Castilla y León

CASTILLA Y LEÓN The largest autonomous region in Spain with an area of 95,000 km^2 (11 times the size of the region of Madrid) but a population of only 2.5 million (less than half that of Madrid). You will spend over 50% of your time travelling through 3 of its 9 separate provinces BURGOS, PALENCIA and LEÓN. It contains the incomparable *Meseta* the predominately flat table or plateau region that makes up a third of the Iberian peninsular and lies between 1,000 and 3,000 metres above sea level and follows the line of the Duero river basin. Cereal crops *cerales* hold sway here, mainly wheat but with oats on the poorer land and some sheep and goats grazing on the hillier parts. It is a sparsely populated arid region, primarily flat but with gently rolling hills. However, the seemingly endless horizons are broken up with delightful villages seemingly unaffected by the speed of modern life.

We start off through the Montes de Oca with the Sierra de la Demanda to our left (south) and the Cordillera Cantábrica to our right (north) with the occasional view of the snow covered Picos de Europa behind them – the highest peak is Peña Vieja 2,613m (8,500 feet). We then pass through the Montes de León which supports one of the enduring symbols of the *camino francés* the Iron Cross *Cruz de Ferro* at the high point of our route 1,505m (4,937 feet). Beyond this is the western arm of the Cordillera Cantábrica, which forms the boundary between Castilla y León and Galicia, which we enter through the Puerto de Pedrifita do Cebreiro at 1,110m (3,640 feet) but that is over 400 km away!

You will find many pamphlets (some in English) that detail the rich history of this vast region. Suffice to say that the ancient kingdom of Castile is well named for its many castles, which sought to protect and promote the kingdom. This promotion was nowhere more conspicuous than along the *Camino de Santiago*. It is well to recall that, up until the time the Saint's tomb was discovered, Spain was largely under the influence of the Moors. Fernando I established Castile in 1035 and the 1090's saw the legendary figure of El Cid turning the tide against the Moors from his base in Burgos. 200 years after its foundation Castile was united with León under Fernando III *El Santo*. It was an uneasy union and even today you will see many defaced signboards that bear the joint arms of the former separate jurisdictions, a separation that some would clearly like to see re-imposed.

Cross ¡N-120! into *Redecilla del Camino* with rest area *[F.]* and *Turismo* ✆ 947-588 080 (summer only). Proceed into the main street *c/Mayor* to the church dedicated to Our Lady of the Street *Nuestra Señora de la Calle* with beautiful baptismal font *XIVthC*, located directly opposite the pilgrim hostel and bar **[1.8 km]**.

3.8 km Redecilla del Camino *(Pop. 150) Alb.*❶ San Lázaro *Muni.[40÷4]* €5 ✆ 686 563 548 (Carmen) c/Mayor 24. *Alb.*❷ Essentia *Priv.[10÷2]* €7 ✆ 606 046 298 c/Mayor 34. built on the site of the medieval hospital of San Lázaro, now a busy bar, all facilities adjacent *H* Redecilla €50+ ✆ 947 585 256. Continue up c/Mayor and cross the ¡N-120! onto track which runs parallel to the road into:

1.7 km **Castildelgado** *(Pop. 80)* fine Romanesque *XIIᵗʰC Iglesia San Pedro* adjoins the ruins of the house of the Counts of Berberana and pilgrim hospice founded by Alfonso VII. Hospitality is now limited to *Hs* **El Chocalatero** € 25+ © 947 588 063 on the main road (+200m). Continue through the village down to main road over stream and turn <left onto country road into:

1.9 km **Viloria de la Rioja** *(Pop. 70)*

Peaceful village – birthplace *cuna* of Saint Dominic, but the Romanesque baptismal font that witnessed his Christening has been removed and, inconceivably, the adj. house where he was born demolished – a blessing perhaps, as tourist coaches (and some pilgrims) bypass this historic idyll. Pause awhile by the shaded rest area *[F.]* (there is a fresh spring just behind the church) and give thanks for the famous illiterate son of this quaint village who did so much to help pilgrims along the way... or stay?

Albergue ❶ **Parada Viloria** *Priv.[16÷3]* €5 menú €-donativo © Toni: 639 451 660 / Mariaje: 610 625 065 c/Bajera, 37 (at entrance) ❷ **Acacio & Orietta** *Priv.[10÷1]* V €5 © 947 585 220 (m: 679 941 123) c/ Nueva just below the church on a tranquil square in the centre of this delightful village. All facilities with shared dinner *donativo*. Acacio da Paz is a key figure in the Asociacion Jacobea *paso a paso* and helped instigate the network *red de albergues* that has worked tirelessly to improve pilgrim facilities along the camino. **MiHotelito** €70+ © 947 585 225 Plaza Mayor, 16. Proceed out of the village by quiet country road to re-join a track alongside the **N-120 [1.5 km]** over stream into the village square **[1.9 km]**:

3.4 km **Villamayor del Río** *(Pop. 50)* *[F.] área de descanso.* On the far side of the N-120 popular *Restaurante León* with shop selling quality products from the region incl. their renowned air-dried sausages *embutidos*, *morcillas* and *chorizo*. Nearby is: *Alb.* **San Luis de Francia** *Priv.*[26÷8]* €5 / menú €8 © 947 580 566 *off* route 300m (sign visible from the main road) dinner and breakfast available. 1 km beyond the albergue in Quintanilla del Monte is enchanting *CR* **La Encantada** €50 where Ana de la Cruz offers a warm pilgrim welcome and free transport © 947 580 484.

The camino continues // to main road all the way into Belorado. Just before entering the town we ¡cross! **N-120 [3.9 km]** and follow wide track into Belorado passing: *Alb.* ❶ **A Santiago** *Priv.*[98÷8]* €5-7 © 947 562 164. Facilities incl. café/ restaurant & small swimpool but pilgrims generally prefer the welcome found in the town centre. Continue along the earth track *[passing plaque to commemorate the fallen on the slopes of the castle (right) in the peninsular war]* to paved road by *CR* **Verdeancho** © 659 484 584 €50 + bar s/o to parish church **[1.0 km]**.

4.9 km **Belorado** *(Pop. 2,100)* ❷ **Santa María** *Par.[24÷4]* €-donativo © 947 580 085 original parish hostel adj' *Iglesia Santa María y San Pedro* in a quiet oasis 200m from the main square. The welcoming ambience and tranquil setting softens the minimalist furnishings. Behind the albergue are cliffs with ancient (and modern) cave dwellings and a path up to the castle ruins. **Other Albergues:** ❸ **El Corro** *Muni.[40÷4]* €8 © 947 581 419 c/ Mayor, 68 (c/ El Corro) menú €8 breakfast €3. ❹ **El Caminante** *Priv.*[22÷1]*+ €5+€35 © 947 580 231. ❺ **Cuatro Cantones** *Priv. [62÷5]* €8+ © 947 580 591 c/Hipólito Lopez Bernal, good facilities with outside patio area and small swimpool in summer. *[Next albergue – Tosantos 5.0 km].*

Other Lodging: *CR* **Waslala** ♥ (oasis of peace & harmony) €25 full board €45 ✆ 947 580 726 c/Mayor 57. *P* **Ojarre** P ✆ 947 580 223 c/Santiago, 16. *P* **Toni** €30-40 ✆ 947 580 525 c/Redecilla del Campo adj.*Correos*. *H* **Jacobeo** ✆ 947 580 010 €70 on the main road or at the end of town *H* **Belorado** ✆ 947 580 684 €25 with bath.

BELORADO: *Turismo centro Jacobea* (10:30-14:00 / 16:00-20:00) ✆ 941 341 238 Plaza Mayor. Historic town built in the steep valley of the río Tirón with its confluence with the río Verdeancho. The Church of Santa María *XIV^{th}C* has a fine altarpiece with images of *Santiago Matamoros y Peregrino* and is built up against the limestone cliffs. The ancient cave dwellings, once home to hermits, are still visible behind the Church (as well as an interesting modern  conversion!). San Capraiso was one of the hermits that sought refuge here, but inspired by the fearlessness of a young martyr, also gave himself to be martyred and subsequently became patron saint of the pilgrim route to Rome *Via Francigena*.

The castle ruins point to the town's defensive past straddling the old border of Castile and it has Roman origins. The area at its base known as *El Corro* was granted the first licence ever issued to operate a 'town market' a privilege accorded by Alfonso I in 1116. The hermitage of Our Lady of Bethlehem *N.S. de Belén* on the eastern outskirts is all that remains of the pilgrim hospital that used to adjoin it.

As we leave town on the western side we pass the Convento N.S. la Bretonera. The other church in town is dedicated to San Nicolás. Belorado has a delightful 'down at heel' feel where the residents conduct affairs at a leisurely pace. The spacious plaza Mayor has an interesting medieval arcade lined with shops, bars and restaurants and *Turismo* ✆ 947 580 226 adj' town hall with camino display *Promoción Jacobea* adj. the church of S. Pedro (see photo above).

REFLECTIONS:

❏ **Man cannot stand a meaningless life.**
— Carl Jung

11 **540.7** km (336.0 ml) – Santiago

BELORADO – SAN JUAN de ORTEGA

....	--- ---	22.5 --- ---	93%
▬▬▬	--- ---	1.5 --- ---	6%
▬▬▬	--- ---	0.2 --- ---	1%
Total km		**24.2** km (15.0 ml)	

26.7 km (^500m + 2.5 km)

Alto ▲ Montes de Oca: 1,150m (3,773 ft)

< Ⓐ Ⓗ > Tosantos **4.8** km – Villambistia **6.8** +200m – Epinosa del Camino **8.4** km – Villafranca **12.0** km. *[Agés 27.8 km]*

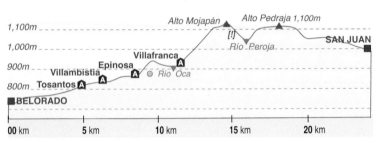

❏ **The Practical Path:** Today is one of much variation in terrain and a glorious 93% on paths and earth tracks. From the suburbs of Belorado the path continues parallel to the N-120 along level open countryside but with some shade provided by hedgerow and woodland. Half way along this stage, at *Villafranca Montes de Oca*, the path climbs through these 'mountains' (high point 1,150m) with its cover of oak and pine before dropping down to the remote pilgrim village of St. John of the Nettle *San Juan de Ortega* a disciple of Santo Domingo. Here, far from the distractions of the modern world we find a slower pace and time, perhaps, to contemplate the inner journey. Additional albergues in next tranquil village Agés a further 3.6 km.

❏ **The Mystical Path:** Here at the start of the 21st century our path takes us past the ruins of an ancient monastery whose foundations extend back to the 9th century. The rough masonry is softened by the horseshoe entrance, a symbol of its Mozarabic past. Where were we when the first stone was laid to this ancient memorial to God? Where will we be when the last stone falls to the ground and is lost to physical sight? Will we take time to find and fufil our purpose for this incarnation? 'It takes so many thousand years to wake, but will [we] wake for pity's sake.'

❏ **Personal Reflections:** *"... Finally I was able to pay my dues. The last time I stayed here I was indignant at its shabby interior and had left without offering a donation towards its upkeep. I never considered why the mop had been left there. I presumed it was for someone else to do the cleaning. How many times have I passed a mop and bucket with the expectation that someone else will clean up after me? Is this the pilgrim way? Before enlightenment: chop wood, carry water, clean floor. After enlightenment: chop wood, carry water, clean floor. In the trivia of life one finds the meaning of Life. That I will awaken is not in doubt, but when, oh when? ..."*

8.6 ◄ Albergue San Juan
San JUAN de ORTEGA
(Pop. 20 – Alt. 950m)

La Henera

N-120

Ermita Valdefuente

Puerto
Pedraja
1,095m

▲ **Alto**
1,120m

Embalse
de Alba

arroyo Peroja

3.6 Monumento *a los Caídos*

Fuente de Mojapán

Virgen de Oca

Pozo
S.Indalecio

N.S. de Alba

San Antón Abad
San Antón Abad ***
VILLAFRANCA MONTES DE OCA
(Pop. 200 – Alt. 950m)

Municipal Albergue 3.6 ◄ El Pajaro

río Oca   *río Oca*

San Felices
(ruinas)

La Campana
1.6 ESPINOSA *del CAMINO*
Epinosa

VILLAMBISTIA
Iglesia *San Roque* **2.0** ► San Roque

Ermita Virgen de la Peña

TOSANTOS
San Francisco de Asís Albergue **4.8** ► Los Arancones

N-120

San Miguel
de Podroso

río Tirón

BELORADO
(Pop. 2,000 – Alt. 770m)

Santa María
0.0 Albergue

`0.0 km` **Belorado** From albergue ❷ make your way via Plaza Mayor into the narrow c/Hipolito Lopez Bernal past albergue Cuatro Cantones, over ring road past Hotel Belorado (left) to cross the N-12 and over the rio Tirón via *pasarela* **[1.3 km]** (the road bridge replaces one originally built by Santo Domingo) onto gravel track // to the main road passing Repsol garage and picnic area outside **Tosantos [3.5 km].**

`4.8 km` **Tosantos** *(Pop. 60) Alb.* ❶ ♥ S. Francisco de Asís *Par.[30÷3]* €-donativo shared meal with prayers ✆ 947 580 371. The basic facilities are enhanced by the warm welcome and patio area. ❷ **Los Arancones** *Priv.[16÷1]* €10 ✆ 947 581 485 (Jessica) c/ de la Iglesia. *Bar El Castaño* on the main road adj. church. ▼
Detour: ● ● ● ● **0.9 km** (1.8 km round trip) on the far side of the main road is the unusual hermitage of Our Lady of the Crag *Ermita de la Virgen de la Peña (la Chiesa)* built into the side of the cliffs with a 12th century image of the Christ Child. It is usually locked and so the mystery of what lies within remains hidden. You can, however, see its white facade from the camino as you leave Tosantos (the hospitalero in the albergue may arrange a visit).
▼ Continue to the back of Tosantos on track all the way to:

`2.0 km` **Villambistia** *Iglesia San Roque* *(Pop. 50)* rest area by river *[F.] Alb.* **San Roque** *Muni.[14÷1]* €6 ✆ 680 501 887 (200m off route) good facilities and *bar menú* in the centre of this small hamlet.

`1.6 km` **Espinosa del Camino** *(Pop. 40) Bar menú*, opp' *Alb.* ❶ *Priv.* ✆ 630 104 922 ❷ **La Campana** *Priv.[10÷2]* ✆ 678 479 361 €17 incl. cena comunitaria (mixed reports). Continue out this sleepy hamlet onto earth track up a short rise at the top of which Villafranca becomes visible. Continue down passing the 9th century ruins of *Monasterio de San Félix de Oca* with its distinctive arch

[Count Diego Porcelos, founder of Burgos, was interred here – we pass his statue on the way into the city]. The track now takes a wide sweep away from the main road before joining it again onto a narrow path over the river Oca and into:

`3.6 km` **Villafranca de Montes de Oca** *(Pop. 200) Alb.*❶ **Villafranca** *Mun.[60÷4]* €5-7 ✆ 691 801 211 on the busy N-120 adj' farmacia & health centre with courtyard to the rear (back room quieter). ❷ **San Antón Abad** *Priv*.[26÷2]+ €5-10 +€60 ✆ 947 582 150 to the rear of the exclusive hotel (of which it is part). The owner has travelled the camino and the hostel fulfils his wish to 'give something back'. All modern facilities.

Other Lodging: *Hs*****San Antón Abad €60 ✆ 947 582 151. *CR* **La Alpargatería** €25 ✆ 686 040 884 adj' *Hs* El Pajaro €25 ✆ 947 582 029 rooms above the bar on noisy main road, popular with truckers and pilgrims (opens early for breakfast). Try adj. *Meson Alba* for home cooking and 'relative' quiet.

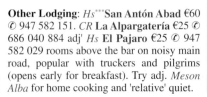

VILLAFRANCA de MONTES de OCA: The untidy approach, with its truck stop for vehicles using the Puerto de la Pedraja, belies the historic roots of this town that welcomed pilgrims as early as the 9th century. This is one of several *Villafrancas* along the way that became home to Franks arriving as pilgrims and returning as artisans thus giving these towns their familiar appellation which also alludes to 'free towns'. The Spanish translation for goose is *oca* giving a romantic notion of wild geese whereas the name may actually derive from an earlier settlement *Auca*. The village is located at the foot of the *Montes de Oca*, formerly a wild unpopulated area and notorious for the bandits that roamed its slopes preying on pilgrims.

The bandits in turn would doubtless pray for protection from the Saint himself in the safety of the Church of Santiago (rebuilt several times and housing an unusual shell baptismal font and several images of the Saint) or perhaps find shelter and succour from the pilgrim Hospice of Saint Anthony the Abbot *Hospital de San Antonio Abad* which has recently been restored. This handsome building was sometimes referred to as the Queen's Hospice, as witnessed by the royal coat of arms that adorn the entrance gate. Today, the town straddles the noisy N-120 which cuts its way through the Pedraja pass and runs broadly parallel to the camino until the latter strikes off to the remote village of San Juan de Ortega. This is the last chance to buy food and fill up with water until St. Juan (11.5 km).

Detour: Pozo de San Indalecio ● ● ● ● **2.3 km** (4.6 km round trip) at the far end of the village (signposted) we pass *ermita N.S[ra] de Alba (Santa María)* **[1.4** km] and s/o to the remote *ermita Virgen de Oca.* **[0.6** km] A local pilgrimage *romería* on 11th June each year, the feast day of San Indalecio, to commemorate his martyrdom. To the rear of the chapel cross the medieval bridge *puente viejo* to the fountain named in his memory *Pozo de San Indalecio* **[0.3** km]. If you are feeling adventurous a further 1 km up the rocky gorge ahead will bring you to the reservoir *Embalse de Alba* at the head of the rio Oca. Allow 2 hours for this detour, which is not recommended unless you plan to stay in Villafranca.

Turn up by Church of Santiago *XVIII[th]C* (left) *[F.]* and Hospital de San Antonio Abad *XIV[th]C* (right) and climb steeply up into beautiful oak woods to refresh yourself *Moisten Bread Fountain* **Fuente de Mojapán** **[1.4** km] *[one assumes the early pilgrims did just that but, alas, today the fountain is not certified drinkable]* Covered shelter, rest area and viewpoint overlooking the Sierra del San Millán (often covered in snow until early summer). From here until we reach San Juan de Ortega we have the shade of ancient oak woods and pine forest. Continue climbing to our high point (1,150m) a fitting memorial to the Fallen *los Caídos* **[2.2** km].

3.6 km Monumento de los Caídos Tragic symbol of Spain's unhealed memories of the civil war. This is not just a memorial; it marks the shallow graves of those who were summarily executed. Adj' rest area with tables in the shelter of the trees and a backdrop of wind turbines on the rise behind. From here we descend to a footbridge over the *arroyo Peroja* before a steep climb up the other side where the track widens out and we continue s/o through 'crossroads' *(ermita de la Valdefuentes* off *route left by the main road)* past wayside cross where the route begins its gentle descent towards the isolated hamlet of St Juan de Ortega.

8.6 km San Juan de Ortega *(Pop. 20) Alb.* San Juan *Par.[70÷3]* €7 *Ⓒ* 947 560 438 historic parish hostel one of the classic pilgrim halts for the medieval and modern *peregrino* alike. The basic facilities boast access to a 16th century courtyard patio. The peaceful setting and ancient buildings provide a monastic atmosphere and soften the lack of services and spartan maintenance. The traditional bread and garlic soup *sopa de ajo* instigated by the

former parish priest José María (died in 2008) continues to be offered to pilgrims after the pilgrim mass in the evening 18:00. *[Next albergue: Agés – 3.6 km].* The adj' *Bar Marcela* with menú. The owners also operate the only other lodging in the hamlet opp' the church *CR* **La Henera** €40 *Ⓒ* 947 409 935 m: 606 198 734. Also *H°° Sierra de Atapuerca* €40 *Ⓒ* 947 106 912 *Santovenia De Oca / N-120 (3.9 km off route).*

SAN JUAN was a disciple of Santo Domingo and like his mentor became known for his great works to serve the pilgrim to Santiago. He built bridges, hospitals, churches and hostels throughout this region. Here, in this wild and isolated place (*Ortiga* is Spanish for nettle) fraught with danger and difficulty for the medieval pilgrim, he founded an Augustinian monastery in 1150. The chapel is dedicated to **San Nicolás de Bari**, who allegedly saved San Juan from drowning on his way back from pilgrimage to the Holy Land and is constructed in such a way that at each equinox the rays of the setting sun strike the Virgin Mary in the scene of the annunciation (*this amazing phenomenon was only re-discovered in 1974).* A representation of this biennial miracle of celestial light, which is linked to San Juan's miraculous powers

in restoring fertility, is portrayed in the adjoining photograph. The barren Queen Isabel of Castile *la Católica* came here in 1477 and later conceived a child and in consequence greatly embellished the church. In the crypt there is a beautiful Romanesque sepulchre with fine tracery stonework bearing an effigy of the Saint. San Juan, however, is buried in the monastery church in a simpler stone sarcophagus depicting scenes from his life; a more down to earth resting place for this most practical of saints.

REFLECTIONS:

❏ I don't know what your destiny, but one thing I know; the only ones among you who will be truly happy are those who have found how to serve.

Albert Schweitzer

12 516.5 km (320.9 ml) – Santiago

SAN JUAN de ORTEGA – BURGOS

˙˙˙˙˙˙˙˙˙˙˙˙˙˙˙˙	--- ---	17.7	--- ---	68%
▬▬▬▬	--- ---	4.4	--- ---	*17%*
▬▬▬▬	--- ---	<u>4.0</u>	--- ---	*15%*
Total km		**26.1** km (16.2 ml)		

◣◢ --- --- 27.1 km (^200m + 1.0 km)
Alto ▲ Sierra Atapuerca 1,080m (3,543 ft)
< 🅰 🏠 > Agés **3.6** km – Atapuerca **6.1** km – *Olmos de Atapuerca alt. 8.5 km.*
Cardeñuela **12.4** km – Orbaneja **14.5** km – Castañares **19.1** km

Exma. Diputación Provincial de Burgos

Atapuerca
Yacimientos paleontológicos
Patrimonio de la humanidad
Unesco 30-11-2000

❏ **The Practical Path:** This stage starts along the río Vena valley before ascending the lonely Sierra Atapuerca. From here we descend to the bustle of Burgos. Familiarise yourself with the various options available (see map opposite) and prepare for the long hike into the city itself – after the relative tranquillity of the camino, city life can come as something of a shock.

The route into the city keeps changing but has improved since the new hostel opened next to the cathedral and the possibility of walking the riverside path ❸ (highly recommended). While not 'officially' waymarked, this delightful *parque fluvial* follows a path alongside the río Arlanzón into the heart of the city avoiding the industrial suburbs. It is shown as a continuation of recommended route ❶ via Castañares. Road route ❷ (Villafría) via N-1 is on asphalt and hard city pavements. From start option point X all routes are a similar distance (c.16 km).

❏ **The Mystical Path:** On each side of the Montes de Oca we find two ancient monasteries each one the final resting place of a noble personage from this area. One inherited his title the other earned it through service to God. Why is one in ruins while the other remains intact to offer shelter? Why does the spirit of *St John of the Nettles* live on to feed the souls of the hungry? How hungry are you and has your soul found nourishment here?

❏ **Personal Reflections:** *"... I met them in the Park. Their welcome was ecstatic even though Ramón was in much pain and was making arrangements to go home. The hospital had diagnosed a stress fracture. He had simply gone too far too fast. His disappointment and sense of failure was palpable. Above all he didn't want to leave the friends he had made along the way. We all have to leave the camino at some stage, but our friendships don't have to end. He looked reassured as I took my leave. I can still see his tears and his hand waving as I passed out of sight – but not out of mind Ramón; not out of mind ..."*

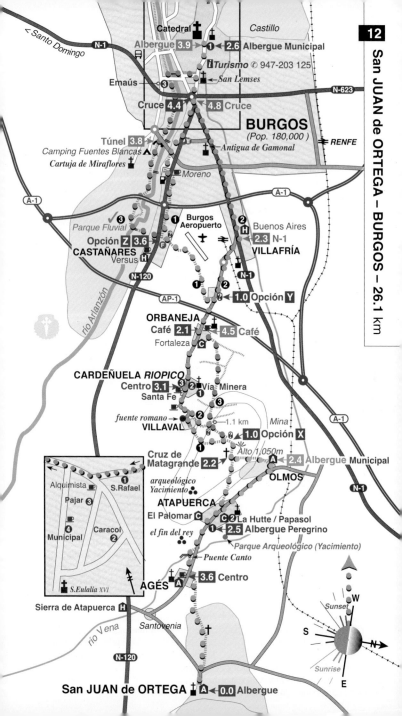

Catedral

Castillo

Albergue **3.9** **2.6** Albergue Municipal

i Turismo ℗ 947-203 125

San Lemses

Emaús

Cruce **4.4** **4.8** Cruce

BURGOS
(Pop. 180,000)

RENFE

Túnel **3.8**

Camping Fuentes Blancas

Cartuja de Miraflores

Antigua de Gamonal

Moreno

A-1

Parque Fluvial **3**

Opción **Z** **3.6**

CASTAÑARES

Versus

N-120

Burgos Aeropuerto **1**

2 Buenos Aires

2.3 N-1

VILLAFRÍA

AP-1

1.0 Opción **Y**

ORBANEJA

Café **2.1** **4.5** Café

Fortaleza

CARDEÑUELA *RIOPICO*

Centro **3.1**

Santa Fe

Vía Minera

fuente romano →

VILLAVAL

1.1 km *Mina*

1.0 Opción **X**

A-1

Cruz de Matagrande **2.2**

Alto 1,050m

2.4 Albergue Municipal

OLMOS

arqueológico Yacimiento

ATAPUERCA

El Palomar **C**

el fin del rey

La Hutte / Papasol

2.5 Albergue Peregrino

Parque Arqueológico (Yacimiento)

Puente Canto

AGÉS **3.6** Centro

S.Eulalia XVI

Sierra de Atapuerca **H**

río Vena

Santovenia

N-120

San JUAN de ORTEGA **0.0** Albergue

Alquimista **1** S.Rafael

Pajar **3**

4 Municipal Caracol **2**

W Sunset

S

N

Sunrise E

0.0 km **San Juan de Ortega** from the albergue s/o over access road (Santovenia and N-120 left) onto path through pine and scrubland levelling out onto open hill pasture. The occasional wooden cross provides some comfort that we're headed in the direction (it's likely to be dark or misty in the early morning mist that is frequently experienced at this altitude of 1,000m). The camino here is little changed from what the medieval pilgrim experienced as we enter the tiny village of:

3.6 km **Agés** *(Pop. 60)* at entrance *Alb.* ❶ **San Rafael** *Priv.[34÷6]+* €10 Ⓒ 947 430 392 bar/menú €10 *vegetariana* V. €12! if busy, try café *El Alquimista. [F.]* ❷ **Casa Caracol** *Priv.[9÷2]* Ⓒ 947 430 413. ❸ **El Pajar** *(the hay loft) Priv.*[32÷4]* €9 Ⓒ 947 400 629 *menú €10* also operate **La Casa Roja.** ❹ **Agés** *Muni.[36÷1]* €8-10 *Bar La Taverna menú* €10 *[Next albergue: Atapuerca – 2.6 km].*

[The parish church of S.Eulalia XVI[th]c rose to fame when the mortal remains of the Navarrese King Don García were interred here after he was slain by his brother, Fernando I of Castile, in the battle of Atapuerca in 1054 (see church window right). A stark stone memorial marks the lonely spot between here and Atapuerca. Don García's final resting place, you may recall, is back in the Royal Pantheon in the church of Santa María de Real in Nájera but his blood was spilled here!].

Beyond the village is the simple medieval stone bridge built by San Juan de Ortega over the río Vena (a tributary of the río Arlanzón) that we cross again as we enter Bugos. Picnic site and *[F.].* The peaceful surroundings of *Puente Canto* are a far cry from those in the Plaza San Lesmes in Burgos. The stretch of asphalt ahead is relieved by standing stones placed to commemorate the famous battle.

2.5 km **Atapuerca** *(Pop. 200) Alb.* ❶ **El Peregrino** *Priv.*[36÷6]+* €8+€35 Ⓒ 661 580 882 *centro turístico* at the entrance with good facilities incl. garden. ❷ **La Hutte** *Priv.[18÷1]* €5 Ⓒ 947 430 320 300m *off* route right (mixed reports) located just below the parish church of San Martin *XV[th]C* visible on the rise above and adj' *CR* **Papasol** €50 (also mixed reports). *CR* **El Palomar** €20-40 incl. Ⓒ 947 430 549 + popular *Restaurant* with terraza on c/ Revilla 22. A variety of bars and restaurants serve pilgrims and tourists who come to view the archeological sites.

Homo Antecessor: It's official, our earliest ancestors lived here! The prehistoric caves of Atapuerca were declared a UNESCO World Heritage site on account of their source as the earliest human remains ever discovered in Europe and provide an exceptional record of the way of life of the first human communities and, yes, it is confirmed that our ancestors were cannibals! The site is 3 km off route and was discovered while cutting a rail link to the nearby mines. The archaeological dig is on-going and the latest analysis points to human activity going back 1.2 million years, and counting. An information centre has been built just outside the village 500m (right). This includes a mock-up of an early settlement, which feels disappointingly artificial. You can visit the award-winning *Mueso de la Evolución Humana* in Burgos instead which has displays and an interpretation centre. Continue down the main street past *bar* and *[F.]* (right) where we have an option:

Detour: ● ● ● ● Alternative route to *Olmos de Atapuerca* 2.4 km with municipal hostel *Alb.* **Olmos** *Muni.[24÷2]* €7 © 633 586 876 located behind *Meson los Hidalgos menú* €10 who hold the keys. Renovated village house opposite the parish church in c/ La Iglesia. Basic facilities (accommodation shared with other tourists) patio to rear. This is a detour along a quiet country road with direct route out of Olmos to the Alto Cruz Matagrande (2.6 km). To re-join the main camino turn up at the back of the village onto track that winds its way up the sierra Atapuerca, through holm oak and scrubland – round trip 5.0 km.

For **main route** turn up <left by games field onto the Sierra Atapuerca. Shaded picnic site (right) alongside military site (left). The gradual climb becomes a steeper rocky path towards the summit and is rewarded with splendid views.

2.2 km **Cruz de Matagrande** *Punto de Vista*. High point at 1,080m (3,543 ft). To the west is our first sight of the city of Burgos (unless it is shrouded in the early morning mist that frequents this high sierra). Down below us to the left are the villages we will pass through to reach Burgos. Along the stony ridge to the right (north) are the scars of an open cast mine and radio masts. Continue down past viewpoint to fork in the path (the first of 3 options):

1.0 km **Opción [X] [?] [!] Stop! Focus! Choose!** ▼ Turn down <left ❶ *or*:

● ● ● ● For peaceful but remote alternative route ❸ (*entirely by earth tracks but waymarks not so obvious and it bypasses the facilities on the main route*. Continue s/o to **option** ❷ **[1.1 km]**. *If visibility is poor turn off left down steeply towards Villalval just before entering the village turn right and join the main route on asphalt road*. Otherwise s/o (up right) and turn <left **[0.2 km]** and veer <left again after **[0.9 km]** *off* main track (*old waymarks here also point s/o*) and follow the contour above the slope. Continue s/o at next cross tracks **[0.7 km]** down into Orbaneja now visible ahead to road and cafe where main route joins **[1.6 km]** at café.

▼ For main route ❶ turn down left to the village of **Villalval [1.4 km]** remote village at the top of a valley where the inhabitants appear reluctant to connect to the world beyond. Pass the dilapidated parish church (right) and the Roman well at the far end of the village (*still working after 2 millennia*) adj' picnic area *[F.]* (left). S/o to bend in road where route ❷ joins from our right. Continue by road past *Bocaderia Miguel* (run by Albergue Minerva) at start of **Cardeñuela Riopico [1.7 km]**

3.1 km **Cardeñuela Riopico** *Alb.* ❶ **Vía Minera** *Priv.[20÷1]+* €8 +€40 c/ La Iglesia © 634 407 091 off route up to the right adj. church *menú* €9. ❷ **Cardeñuela** *Muni.[16÷1]* €5 © 646 249 597 (Manolo) also runs the adj. *Bar La Parada*. ❸ **Santa Fe** *Priv. [10÷1]+* €8 +€35 © 947 560 722 m: 626 352 269 (Miryam) with popular bar & *menú* (*+Vegetarian V.*) opp. La Parada in the town centre. Take the asphalt road out of the village passing *un Alto en El Camino* and *CR* **La Cardeñuela** €50 © 947 210 479 and into **Orbaneja** to the far end by parish church of S.Millán Abad.

2.1 km **Orbaneja** *(Pop. 140)* Bar El Peregrino. Note: last opportunity to obtain a snack and fill water flasks before heading into the suburbs of Burgos. *CR* **Fortaleza** €50 © 678 116 570 c/Principal, 31. Proceed over A-1 to option point by new residential development *urbanización Riopoco*:

1.0 km **Opción [Y] [?] [!] Stop! Focus! Choose!** For main route ❶ turn down <left (not well signposted) *or* for road route ❷ via Villafría and N-1 continue s/o.

Alternative road route ❷ Villafría proceed s/o along road over roundabout and over **rail [1.8 km]** *(over to right is the bell tower of the parish church presiding over what remains of the old town of Villafría that was granted to the monastery of San Pedro de Cardeña in the 10th century)*. Continue to **N-1 [0.5 km]**:

2.3 km Villafría with several cheap hotels & eateries. *H*^{**} **Iruñako** €28 *Ⓒ* 947 484 126. *H*^{**} **Buenos Aires** €26 *Ⓒ* 947-483 770. *H*^{**} **Las Vegas** €30 *Ⓒ* 947 484 453. Villafría a modern industrial suburb with bus service into the centre of Burgos. Continue along the N-1 past the industrial complexes of Gamonal over the A-1 **[1.5 km]** into c/Vitoria where the city high-rise starts. You pass the impressive 13th century church dedicated to N.S. La Real y Antigua de Gamonal (left) **[2.4 km]** (with stone cross and image of Santiago Peregrino) and join the recommended route at the Telefonica roundabout **[0.9 km]**.

4.8 km Gruce *Glorieta de Logroño* Av. de la Constitución Española.
❖ For main route ❶ turn down sharp <left *off* the road (not well signposted) by *urbanización Riopoco* onto track around Burgos airport security fence to main road.

3.6 km Castañares N-120 Opción [Z] [?] *[F.]* ❖ Sleepy suburb straddling the N-120. Opp. the fountain (on far side of main road) is a small square with chapel and café/restaurante *El Descanso* with adj. bus stop to the city centre. *H*^{***} **Versus** €45 *Ⓒ* 947 474 977 pilgrim discount. *Note*: To avoid traffic take the scenic path ▼ ✓ alongside río Arlanzón. (if you haven't yet experienced one of these alternative routes, this is a good opportunity. Walk with a fellow pilgrim as this is a city park and can be lonely, especially during twilight hours (see green panel opp.)
 ❶ turn right on gravel track by the N-120, cross over airport access road and under the **A-1 [1.0 km]** over the rio Pico and Polígono Industrial Gamonal still on gravel track to next junction *c/del Alcade Martín Cobos*. S/o past Repsol garage (opp¹) and take the pedestrian crossing by *Café El Moreno*. **[0.9 km]** turning right into c/Mayor through **Villayuda** onto track and over new bypass **[1.4 km]** s/o and turn right up to the N-120 and the modern pilgrim fountain and <left to the next roundabout **[1.1 km]**.

4.4 km Cruce *Glorieta de Logroño* (alternative road route ❷ via Villafría joins here). Guardia Civil HQ and Militar Academia (opp. Telefonica building). *[An alternative here is to go s/o along c/Vitoria into the Paseo Espolón and the Arco Santa María leading to the cathedral and albergue – see city plan].*
 For the waymarked route cross over to the *Museo Militar* (right) into c/ San Roque and <left just before the shopping centre *Via de la Plata* **[0.4 km]** into c/Farmacéutico and over the busy Av. Cantabria [!] **[0.5 km]** into c/de las Calzadas into *Plaza San Lesmes* **[0.9 km]** (formerly plaza San Juan with the ruins of Antiguo Monasterio de San Juan (part of the Museo Marceliano) and Iglesia de San Lesmes. *[*San Lesmes is patron saint of Burgos. Formerly a French abbot called Adelhelm who was persuaded to stay in Burgos by the wife of Afonso VI].*
 Cross the río Vena (whose calm waters we heard back in Agés) under the **Arco de San Juan** *XIIIthC* into the medieval city itself. Continue via c/San Juan *[detour left into c/Santander to visit Casa del Cordón, 150m left with its outstanding 15thc facade, Columbus was royally received here on his return from the Americas]* or continue s/o past the hotel *Norte y Londres* €24 dormitory €44 private opp. Plaza Alonso Martínez with main tourist office (right). Continue into c/Avellanos and c/ San Gil veering <left into c/Fernán Gonzalez up the cobblestones to Nº. 28 **[0.8 km]**.

2.6 km **Burgos** *Centro Albergue* ❶ **La Casa del Cubo** *Lerma*

▼ ✓ Scenic route ❸ cross N-120 through the modern suburbs *Lugar del Barrio Castañares c/ O Bidus* past the sports ground (right) and Garcia gravel works (left) and over footbridge *pasarela* [0.5 km] continue s/o along concrete path through woodland and turn left down under the city bypass (Rubiera sign on bridge) by river **culvert** [0.7 km] up into the *Parque Fluvial (ecosistema de Ribera de rio Arlanzón)*. At this point there are many tracks through the extensive parkland but if you keep the river always immediately to your right you cannot lose your way! Continue past **bridge** [1.3 km] (right connects with alt. route) and camping ground *Fuentes Blancas* [0.3 km] (left - *Bungalows for 2 from €39).* Continue s/o to lake Fuente del Prior with sandy shoreline (time for a paddle? Note: *Cartuja de Miraflores is close by at this point - see details p.132)* s/o under new road bridge *túnel* [1.0 km]:

3.8 km | **Túnel** *[At this point the pedestrian bridge (right) connects to the 'official' waymarked route at the roundabout Glorieta de los Peregrinos on the N-120].* Continue s/o parallel to river (right) to roundabout and under city by-pass [1.7 km].

Detour: Albergue Emaús 0.5 km ● ● ● ● Directions: Cross c/ Cartuja Miraflores (N-120) through playground by the castellated stone wall (the hostel is in the grounds on the far side). S/o into c/ Maestro Ricardo and right into c/San Pedro de Cardeña. The albergue is on the right behind the imposing edifice of the Parroquia San José Obrero and Jesuit college. ❸ *Casa de Peregrinos Emaús Par.[20÷4]* C/ de San Pedro de Cardeña with 20 beds €5 shared meal *donativo* following the tradition of Emmaus with Christian prayer and blessing.

To continue along the scenic river route proceed to the next road bridge *Puente Gasset* [0.7 km] with statue of Diego Porcelos atop his steed (see photo right), founder of Burgos in 884 and whose burial site we passed yesterday at the Monasterio de San Félix de Oca. Take the next pedestrian bridge *pasarela* [0.2 km] over the river Arlanzón and s/o into calle Hotel Gran Teatro across c/ Vitoria into c/San Lesmes alongside the rio Vena to rejoin all routes in

Plaza San Lesmes [0.5 km]. Here we join the main waymarked route via Arco San Juan to the cathedral.

3.9 km | **Burgos** *Centro* Albergue ❶ La Casa del Cubo *Lerma* Asoc.*[150÷6]*

Albergue ❶ **La Casa del Cubo** *Lerma Asoc.[150÷6]* €5 ✆ 947 460 922 modern building behind handsome16[th]c facade with all facilites incl. lift to its 4 floors.

Close by in c/Laín Calvo, 10. ❷ **Divina Pastora** *Asoc.[16÷1]* €5 ✆ 947 207 952 central location above the chapel offering respite from the bustle of the city & daily mass. Popular hostel which fills early (photo right). ❏ *Turismo* Plaza Alonso,7 ✆ 947 203 125 also several tourist kiosks around the city. Burgos is always busy so find accommodation *before* setting out to explore. ❏ **Other Lodging** *under €55 low season: Sequentially from the entrance:* ■ *Off Plaza S. Lemses* (c/Cardenal Benlloch) *Hsr*[**] **Acacia** ✆ 947 205 134. *Hs*[**] **Monjes Magnos** ✆ 947 205 134. *Hs*[**] **Lar** €25 ✆ 947 209 655. *Hsr*[**] **Carrales** ✆ 947 263 547 c/ Puente Gasset,4. *Hsr*[**] **Manjón** ✆ 947 208 689 c/Gran Teatro adj. *H*[****] **Almirante Bonifaz** ✆ 947 206 943. ■ *Old town barrio antigua:* *H*[***] **La Puebla** ✆ 947 203 350 c/La Puebla Nº4 + Nº6 *Hr*[****] **Cordón** ✆ 947 265 000. *Hr*[*] **El Jacobeo** ✆ 947 260 102 c/San Juan *Hr*[****] **Centro Los Braseros** ✆ 947 252 958. *Hsr*[**] **Norte y Londres** ✆ 947 264 125. ■ *Near Plazas Libertad & Mayor: Hr*[*] **García** ✆ 947 205 553 c/Santander, 1. *Hsr*[*] **Hidalgo** ✆ 947 203 481 c/Almirante Bonifaz, 14. *H*[**] **España** ✆ 947 206 340 Paseo Espolón. ■ *Central c/Fernán Gonzaléz* €65+: *H*[***] **Palacio de los Blasones** ✆ 947 271 000 @Nº10 (*pilgrim discount*). *H*[****] **Mesón del Cid II** ✆ 947 208 715 @Nº62. *H*[*****] **Abba Burgos** ✆ 947 001 100 @ Nº72 (antiguo Seminario). ■ *Across river:* *Hr*[**] **Conde de Miranda** ✆ 947-265 267 c/Miranda, 4 (adj. estación de autobuses). *H*[***] **Via Gotica** ✆ 947 244 444 Plaza de Vega. *H*[****] **NH Palacio de la Merced** €75+ ✆ 947 479 900 c/Merced.

❏ **Monumentos históricos:** ❶ *San Lesmes XIV & Mo. S.Juan* (mueso Marceliano) ❷ *Arco S. Juan XIII* ❸ *Casa del Cordón XV* ❹ *San Gil XIV* ❺ *S. Esteban XIV* (mueso Retablo) ❻ *S. Nicolas de Barri XV* ❼ *Catedral de Santa María XIII* ❽ *Arco & Puente de Santa María XIV* ❾ *Solar del Cid* ❿ *Arco S.Martin XIII.* ●-11 *Santa María la Real de Las Huelgas XII* (museo). ●-12 *Hospital del Rey XII* (antiguo hospital del peregrino). ● *Cartuja de Miraflores XV (4 km south/east)* with mausoleum of King John II and Isabella of Portugal. Check *Turismo* for opening times.

Catedral de Santa María **XIII**[th]c. Among the most beautiful of Spain's many cathedrals and one of its largest (after the Giralda at Sevilla). Essentially Gothic, it nevertheless combines many different styles, having been embellished by the great master builders and architects down through the centuries. Soak in its magnificent edifice and inspirational spires and the bustle of the medieval streets that surround the cathedral – designated a World Heritage Site. Whatever condition

you are in, it is worthy of a visit to the interior. You are unlikely to find much peace in its crowded aisles but you will find a wealth of art treasures and artefacts to satisfy the most jaded of palates. The west door, off Santa María square, is the most striking but we enter by the equally evocative south door. Open daily 9:30-18:30

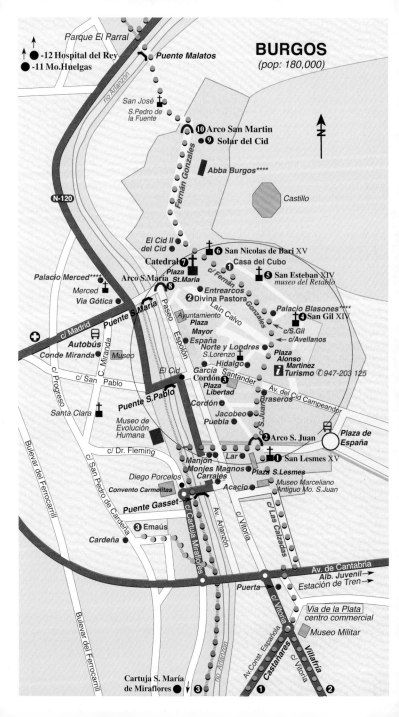

€7 (pilgrim with credencial €3.50) which includes a floor plan and pamphlet (in several languages) and access to the left luggage lockers *consigna*. Open throughout the day in high season. Amongst the many outstanding chapels (there are 21) are St. Thecla and St. James (off Plaza Santa María) and St. John & St. James behind the high altar with a statue of St. James the Moor-slayer *Santiago Matamoros*. The north door (closed) has the lovely Renaissance Golden Staircase *Escalera Dorada* designed by Diego de Siloe, while at the transept crossing, directly underneath the huge star lantern at the heart of the cathedral, lie El Cid and his wife Jimena. The 14th century Gothic cloisters have an array of sculptures. If you want to find somewhere cool and quiet try **Iglesia de San Nicolás** (12:00-13:30 / 17:00-19:00 €1.50) with its magnificent altarpiece, situated directly on the camino immediately above the cathedral (at the top of the steps). Its austere 15th century façade and the steep climb up from the cathedral square *plaza Santa María* acts as a deterrent to the crowds of tourists milling around the cathedral and so preserves the relative peace to be found here. Alternatively head out to the river through the impressive **Arco de Santa María** (Tues-Sat 11:00-13:50 / 17:00-21:00 free) the medieval entrance dating back to the 14th century to the Puente de Santa María, which joins the linear park that runs along the banks of the río Arlazón. Rest awhile under the shade of the trees or take a well-earned drink in one of the cafés that line the riverbank.

BURGOS CITY: *(pop: 180,000 – alt. 860m).* While warning of the vagaries of city life (stories of theft and overcharging) we must also emphasise the beauty of many of the city's buildings and their artefacts. Burgos is a veritable architectural jewel and full of monuments worthy of exploration and appreciation. The city marks the beginning of stage VI of the Codex Calixtinus. Sometimes referred to as the Gothic capital of Spain, it was also the seat of Franco's Government until 1938, an indication of its nationalist and establishment leanings. A burgeoning population seems unable to shake off its austere religious and political image. It is, after all, named after its heavy defensive town towers *burgos* and was home to the warlord El Cid. The week either side of 29th June is the city's main festival of *San Pedro y Pablo*. Accommodation at this time is doubly difficult to secure at twice the price. The new **Museo de la Evolución de Humana** on Paseo Sierra de Atapuerca is worth a visit (10:00-14:30 / 16:30-20:00 €6).

Count Rodrigo Díaz de Vivar the champion *campeador* was better known as *El Cid* a Muslim title of respect, and remains the great legendary son of Burgos. He was born here in 1040 and the camino passes the site of his house by Arco de San Martín. On the death of Ferdinand I the kingdom was divided between the monarchs 5 children. The eldest son, Sancho, felt he should have inherited the lot and so set about recovering it from his siblings and the Moors – enter El Cid who was appointed his commander-in-chief of the armed forces. All was going well for El Cid until Sancho was killed trying to recover the town of Zamora from his sister Urraca. Now enters Sancho's surviving brother Alfonso VI who both despised and feared El Cid and alternately exiled him (twice) and in between married him off to his niece Jimena. El Cid died in Valencia in 1099 having recovered the city from the Moors. His body, and that of his trusty horse *Babieca*, were eventually re-interred in the monastery of San Pedro de Cardena and then El Cid and his wife were re-re-interred in the cathedral!

On your way out the following day, suitably refreshed, you might be more inclined to explore the **Real Monasterio de Las Huelgas** (10:00-17:30 closed lunch) and the adjacent **Hospital del Rey** (now part of the university) both of which are within a few minutes walk off the camino near Parque El Parral in the westerly suburbs and well worth a visit. Las Huelgas was founded in 1187 by Alfonso VIII who, along with several other royal personages, was crowned and subsequently buried there. Founded as a Cistercian convent, primarily for aristocratic novitiates, it has a lovely cloister and is now a museum. Amongst its many fine treasures is the statue of St. James with a moving arm that was used by the Order of the Knights of Santiago to bestow knighthoods. Hospital del Rey was one of the largest and best-endowed pilgrim hospitals along the camino. The Pilgrim's Gate *Puerta de Romeros* is a plateresque jewel and now forms one of the entrances to the university (200m off the camino). Other more distant detours might be considered (check with tourist office): **Detour** [1] *Cartuja de Miraflores* 4 km. [2] *Monasterio de San Pedro de Cardeña* (9 km). [3] *Santo Domingo de Silos* (62 km) site of the world-renowned Gregorian chanting monks.

❏ **Travel**: Note the new railway station *Rosa de Lima* is 5 km outside the city off Av. Asturias - bus 25, 43 & 80 from Plaza España). RENFE central ticket office c/Moneda, 23 ✆ 947-209 131. Central bus station ✆ 947-288 855 or contact Alsa. The airport ✆ 947-478 588 now has daily flights to Barcelona.

REFLECTIONS:

❏ **Foxes have holes and the birds of the air have nests,**
  But the Son of Man has no place to lay his head. *Matthew 8.24*

13 **490.4** km (304.7 ml) – Santiago

BURGOS – HORNILLOS del CAMINO

....	--- ---	14.0 --- ---	*67%*
▬▬▬	--- ---	3.2 --- ---	*15%*
▬▬▬	--- ---	<u>3.8</u> --- ---	*18%*
Total km		**21.0** km (13.0 ml)	

▲▬ 21.7 km (^150m + 0.7 km)

Alto ▲ Meseta 950m (3,117 ft)

< 🅰 🄷 > N-120 Burgos **2.2** km – Tardajos **10.5** – Rabé de las Calzadas **13.0** km.

❏ **The Practical Path:** Today we leave behind the built environment and enter the relative wilderness of the sublime *Meseta*. Over half this stage is by way of earth track across the peace and quiet of the endless crop fields; wheat on the better ground and barley and oats on the higher and poorer soil. We might come across a shepherd and his flock or the occasional fox, otherwise you will have the birds to keep you company. There is little or no shade on the Meseta, so protect yourself from the sun. Hornillos provides a welcome respite from the conspicuous consumerism of the city.

Options: If you plan to stay at Hornillos; this stage is only 21 kilometres which provides an opportunity to visit the monastery at *Las Huelgas* and the ancient pilgrim *hospital de Rey* on the way out... and time to recover from the busy-ness of Burgos in the peaceful surroundings of one of the few medieval pilgrim villages still surviving. Many pilgrims continue to the popular pilgrim village of Hontanas (+10.8 km – 31.8 km in total). In this latter case you need to leave Burgos early as this would be a very long day. It does, however, allow you to get to Castrojeriz early the following day and take some time to relax and enjoy the interesting historical sites, museums, cafes and restaurants it has to offer.

❏ **The Mystical Path:** The forces of materialism are nowhere more evident than in city life. A wealthy professional, a man of the law, informed Jesus he would follow him wherever he went – prompting Christ's quotation (top) recorded in Matthew's gospel. Another man then came to Jesus and said he would follow him wherever he went but first he must go and bury his father. Christ's response, 'Follow me and let the dead bury their dead.' As we leave Burgos we pass a former pilgrim hospital converted at great expense to house a law school and the opulent monastery of Las Huelgas built to shelter the elite daughters of the aristocracy and as a royal pantheon to house the deceased monarchs of Castilla. Who will we follow today, God or Mammon? Christ or Ahriman?

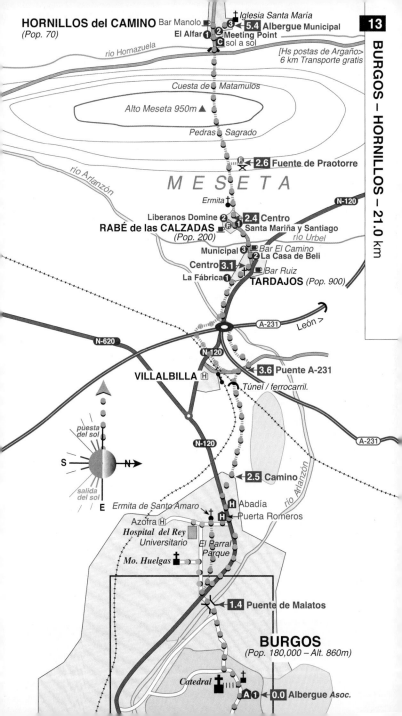

HORNILLOS del CAMINO
(Pop. 70)

Bar Manolo

† *Iglesia Santa María*
3 **5.4** **Albergue Municipal**
El Alfar 1 **2** Meeting Point
C sol a sol

[Hs postas de Argaño>
6 km Transporte gratis

río Hornazuela

Cuesta de Matamulos

Alto Meseta 950m ▲

Pedras Sagrado

2.6 Fuente de Praotorre

M E S E T A

Ermita †

Liberanos Domine **2** **1** **2.4 Centro**
RABÉ de las CALZADAS ■ Santa Mariña y Santiago
(Pop. 200) *río Urbel*

río Arlanzón

N-120

Municipal **3** ■ *Bar El Camino*
2 La Casa de Beli
Centro **3.1** † ■ *Bar Ruiz*
La Fábrica 1 **TARDAJOS** *(Pop. 900)*

N-620

A-231

León >

N 120

3.6 Puente A-231

VILLALBILLA Ⓗ

Túnel / ferrocarril.

A-231

N-120

2.5 Camino

río Arlanzón

puesta
del sol

S — N

salida
del sol

E

Ⓗ **Abadía**
Ermita de Santo Amaro † Ⓗ **Puerta Romeros**
Azofra Ⓗ
Hospital del Rey
Universitario *El Parral*
Parque
Mo. Huelgas ■ †

1.4 Puente de Malatos

BURGOS
(Pop. 180,000 – Alt. 860m)

Catedral ■ † ⫞⫞⫞ †
■ **A 1** **0.0 Albergue** *Asoc.*

❐ **Personal Reflections:** *"… The full moon slowly breaks the eastern horizon, an enormous orb of reflected silver light. It is awesome against the pale blue of the early evening sky. I am alone, lost in the deep peace of the empty Meseta. But I don't feel lost or lonely. I take out the small phial I have been carrying since leaving Findhorn. A gift of love from the sacred mountain of Kailash offered to the world and poured into the deep rich soil of the camino. The words of the Great Invocation linger in the cooling air before rippling out into the universe. Two deer break cover in the stillness. I was not alone after all …"*

0.0 km **Burgos** From albergue ❶ **La Casa del Cubo** continue along the cobbled c/Fernán González past the cathedral and church of San Nicolás (right) and luxury Hotel Abba Burgos to the twin obelisks of the ***Solar el Cid* [0.7 km]** which provides a simple monument to this notorious soldier of fortune and pugnacious son of Burgos who lived in a house on this spot. Just beyond we leave the medieval city through what remains of its fortified walls and the *Arco de San Martín.* We now head across the road and down into *c/Emperador* past the Jacobean church of **San Pedro de la Fuente [0.2** km] (left) and *Hostal Monasterio de San José.* Turn <left into *c/Benedictinas de San José* and *c/Villalon* to cross the *río Arlanzón* over the Bridge of Maladies ***Puente de Malatos* [0.5 km].**

1.4 km **Puente de Malatos / Opción:** The waymarked route continues either through the parkland *El Parral* ahead (recommended) or around the side of the park adjoining N-120. This is a good opportunity to visit the Royal Monastery *Monasterio de las Huelgas Reales* (

Detour: Monasterio de las Huelgas Reales ● ● ● ● 0.6 km. Take the road alongside the park *Paseo de los Comendadores* and turn <left [400m] into c/ de Bernardino Obregón to the monastery [200m]. Allow an hour for the group tour (in Spanish) to look around the copious buildings. The Chapel of St. James *Capilla de Santiago* contains the unusual statue of the saint with a moving arm. The *Sala Capitular* contains the royal standard *pendón* used in the battle of Las Navas de Tolosa (you may have seen the heavy chains, another trophy from this battle, back in Roncesvalles). Soak up the atmosphere in the spacious Romanesque cloisters with their elegant twin columns, reminiscent of the cloisters at San Pedro de la Rúa in Estella (coincidentally this suburb of Burgos was also called San Pedro) and the museum of medieval fabrics *Museo de Telas Medievales.*

For the waymarked route continue through *parque El Parral* (former pilgrim refuge left) and out the gate at the far end to the tiny chapel opp' dedicated to the humble pilgrim saint from France **San Amaro de peregrino [0.9** km] who, on his return from Santiago, settled here and dedicated his life to the welfare of other pilgrims, leaving a legacy of healing miracles. From here we can also admire another piece of pilgrim history – the beautiful Kings Gate *Puerta del Rey* (60m left) on Pilgrim street *calle de los Romeros.* The magnificent 12th century King's Hospital *Hospital del Rey* was formerly a pilgrims hospice and is now the law faculty of Burgos university. From San Amaro turn right> and join the N-620 and N-120 (to Palencia and Carrión respectively) by *H[··]* **Puerta Romeros** ℂ 947 460 738 on the corner and turn <left along the main road with pilgrim statue (see photo right) and the modern

university campus and continue past the *Hs*********Abadía Camino Santiago** ☏ 947 040 404 and *Hs*******Vía Láctea** ☏ 947 463 211 and leave the main road by car park **[0.8 km]** opp' Restaurant *Bellavista* (also has rooms). Follow the minor road past *Iglesia y Residencial N.S del Pilar* where the city effectively ends and the camino begins by the municipal nursery *Los Guindales forestal* **[0.8 km].**

2.5 km **Camino** continue along track with the watch towers of the state prison on the far side of the river and poplar plantation (right) up to road over the río Arlanzón **rest area [2.0 km]** *[F.]* s/o to track through tunnel under railway *túnel* **[0.9 km]** the track continues to a bridge over the new autopista **[0.7 km].**

3.6 km **Puente** *autopista [Note 1*: Ongoing road works here may necessitate a temporary camino diversion. Follow any detour signs to rejoin the original waymarked route. Note 2: Also at this point there is an option to detour (left) to* **Villalbilla** *a suburb of Burgos on the N-120 with several hotels].* If roadworks allow then turn right> over bridge and the track wends its way under the A-231 over the N-120 and río Arlanzón via *puente del Arzobispo* **[1.6 km]** *[*Temporary diversion joins here].* We now join a track alongside the N-120 to prominent roadside cross *Cruceiro* at the entrance to the village of **Tardajos [1.5 km]** *(pop. 900).*

3.1 km **Tardajos** *Cruceiro Alb.* ❶ **La Fábrica** *Priv.[14÷4]*+ €12 +€35 ☏ 646 000 908 renovated flour mill 300m down c/La Fábrica + *menú.* ❷ **La Casa de Beli** *Priv. [30÷3]*+ €10–€45+ ☏ 947 451 234 Av. Gen. Yagüe 16. *Bar Ruiz* & *P* **Mary** €15-20 ☏ 947 451 125 c/ Pozas N-120 + *menú.* S/o into c/Mediodía past town square to: ❸ **Tardajos** *Muni.[18÷3]* €-*donativo* ☏ 947 451 189 modern semi-detached building managed by Madrid asoc. No kitchen or lounge but small garden and *Bar El Camino* adj'. Continue on quiet asphalt road over río Urbel (formerly a marshy area, hence the suffix of the next town Rabé *causeway*) up into the village visible ahead:

2.4 km **Rabé de las Calzadas** *(pop. 200)* Pass road (right) to *Casa Museo. (Note: Hotel Deobrigula reamains closed).* At the entrance to town (left) is *Bar La Peña* who also run *Alb.* ❶ **Libéranos Dómine** *Priv. [24÷4]* €8 ☏ 695 116 901 + *menú* €8. The original hostel ❷ **Óspital Santa Marina y Santiago** *Priv.[8÷1]* €8 *menú donativo is* centrally located also on Plaza Francisco

Ribera off which is Iglesia de Santa Mariña *XIII*[th]*C* (see photo). *[F.]* This is the last chance to fill up with water. Continue out the village by the tiny *Ermita de Nuestra Señora de Monasterio* before heading up onto the incomparable *Meseta:*

2.6 km **Fuente de Praotorre** isolated rest area whose fountain may be dry and the young trees still struggling to provide shade. The camino continues up through the peaceful landscape temple with its sacred stones *piedras santos* and cereal fields stretching to the horizon to the high point on the Meseta before descending steeply down the aptly named Mule-Killer Slope *Cuesta Matamulas!* Cross a quiet road that runs alongside the río Hormazuela into:

5.4 km **Hornillos del Camino** *(Pop. 60)* c/Cantarranas / Rua Real *Albergue* ❶ **El Alfar** *Priv.[20÷3]* €9 (Pilar) ☏ 619 235 930 + *menú* € 8. Adj' shop *Area KM 469!* Opp.*CR* **de sol a sol** €35 ☏ 649 876 091 with rear garden. *Alb.* ❷ **Meeting Point**

138

Priv.[32÷3] €9 *(Omar)* © 608 113 599
purpose built hostel with all mod cons and
rear garden. Off the central square *Alb.* ❸
Hornillos *Muni.[32÷3]* €5 © 689 784
681 sensitively renovated building adj'
the church. Additional beds in the town
hall and overflow space also available on
mattresses *colchones* in the large sports
hall to the rear. The municipal albergue
is managed from the popular Bar on the

main square *Casa Manolo* © 947 411 050 with *menú*. **Other Lodging:** *CR* **La Casa
del Abuelo** €30+ © 661 869 618. *Note:* Free transport *transporte gratis* is offered
to: *CR* **Las Postas de Argaño** © 947 450 156 in Villanueva de Argaño 6 km away
close to the A-231. Also *CR* **El Molino** © 947 560 302 in Vilviestre de Muño. They
will also pick up and drop back the next morning. *[Next albergue: San Bol – 5.7 km]*.

Gothic Church of San Román Plaza de la Iglesia. The church occupies the dominant
position in this delightful medieval village and adjoins the picturesque Hen Fountain
Fuente del Gallo. Hornillos del Camino is a classic pilgrim village and important
medieval halt on the way to Santiago, little changed over the past centuries and a
good place in which to soak up some of the ancient atmosphere of the way.

The name Hornillos possibly derives from kiln or oven *horno* with the diminutive
illos suggesting a small stove. All along the Meseta we find this suffix – *illos*
appended to place names. It has been suggested that this might have arisen due to a
sense of the relative impermanence of man when experienced against the seemingly
endless horizon under the vast vault of the Meseta sky. We can likewise use this idea
to contemplate the relative insignificance of the physical body when compared with
the eternal nature of our spiritual identity. Apart from such musings there is little to
occupy the pilgrim here other than the priceless peace that pervades this village. A
small shop and bar further up the main street offers the possibility of a meal. Chill
out and try doing nothing *nada* – and experience beingness...

REFLECTIONS:

❏ **The holiest of all the spots on earth is where
an ancient hatred has become a present love**…
——————————— *A Course In Miracles*

14 **469.4** km (291.7 ml) – Santiago

HORNILLOS del CAMINO – CASTROJERIZ

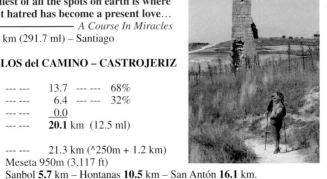

▩▩▩▩▩▩	--- ---	13.7	--- ---	68%
▬▬▬▬	--- ---	6.4	--- ---	32%
▬▬▬▬	--- ---	0.0		
Total km	--- ---	**20.1** km	(12.5 ml)	

◣◤ --- --- 21.3 km (^250m + 1.2 km)
Alto ▲ Meseta 950m (3,117 ft)
< Ⓐ Ⓗ > Sanbol **5.7** km – Hontanas **10.5** km – San Antón **16.1** km.

900m Alto Meseta **San Bol** **Alto (Meseta)** 940m
HORNILLOS ▲   Ⓐ▽   ▲   ℚ **Hontanas**   **Arco**   **CASTROJERIZ**
          Río Sanbol   Ⓐ   **San Antón** 800m
800m - Ⓐ - - - - -
700m _ _ _
00 km   **5 km**   **10 km**   **15 km**   **20**

❏ **The Practical Path:** Today we again travel the lonely Meseta with the sounds of
nature the only likely intrusion on the peace that pervades it. There is little shade and
so again we need to take care with the sun and carry plenty of water. Hontanas and
Castrojeriz are both classic pilgrim towns with good facilities

❏ **The Mystical Path:** … *Forget not that a shadow held between your brother and
yourself obscures the face of Christ and the memory of God. Your footprints lighten
up the world, for where you walk forgiveness gladly goes with you.* Will we walk
today with a forgiving heart or hold on to old hurts that keep us feeling separated
from our fellow pilgrims? Will you find the sacred symbol of healing used by knights
and monks, ancient and modern? Will you place your hand in the niche that offered
bread to passing strangers and leave a mark of love? will you break bread with a
stranger today? Will we compound the problem or become part of the solution?

❏ **Personal Reflections:** *"… She offered to stitch my torn shirt and began to sew. I
had not met her before and yet she seemed familiar. Santiago and his jovial friend
showed me how to make a real Spanish tortilla. We ate together with great merriment
despite our fatigue and difficulty with language. Such deep respect and joy amongst
strangers who were not strangers. Our laughter sent great vortexes of loving energy
out into the world. If only we would live our lives with this open heartedness – what
changes might we bring about to our war-torn world …"*

0.0 km **Hornillos de Camino** From the albergue / Bar Casa Manolo follow the
main street *c/Real*, part of the original camino and veer right at the far end past the
stand of poplars and start the gentle climb back up onto the Meseta. The track levels
out and continues in a westerly direction until we begin the steep descent to the
arroyo San Bol where the isolated refuge is clearly visible (left).

5.7 km **Cruce** *San Bol* Cross over the stream and continue s/o up *or* turn left

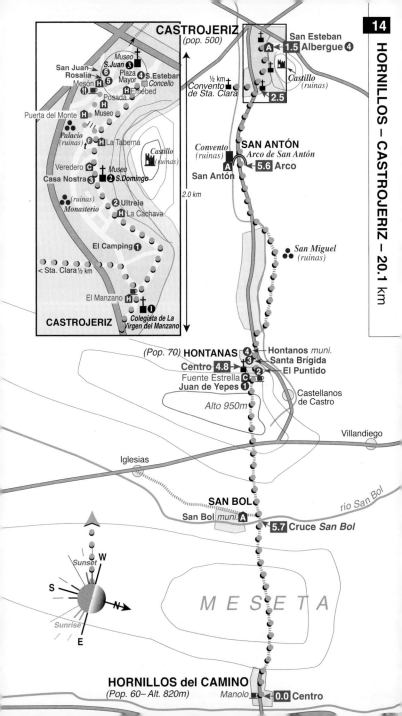

CASTROJERIZ
(pop. 500)

San Esteban
A **1.5** Albergue **4**

Castillo (ruinas)

2.5

½ km
Convento de Sta. Clara

Convento (ruinas)

SAN ANTÓN
Arco de San Antón

A **5.6** Arco

San Antón

San Miguel
(ruinas)

2.0 km

Castrojeriz (inset map)

Museo
S.Juan 3
San Juan → **Plaza Mayor**
Rosalía **6** **5** **4** S.Esteban
Mesón **H** **H** **Concello**
H Enébed
Posada
H

Puerta del Monte **H** Museo

Palacio (ruinas) **F**
H La Taberná
Castillo (ruinas)

Veredero **C** † Museo
Casa Nostra **3** **2** S.Domingo

(ruinas) Monasterio **2** Ultreia
H La Cachava

El Camping **1**

< Sta. Clara ½ km

El Manzano **H**
1
Colegiata de La Virgen del Manzano

CASTROJERIZ

(Pop. 70) **HONTANAS 4** ← Hontanos *muni.*
3
Centro **4.8** ■ Santa Brígida
Fuente Estrella **C** **2** El Puntido
Juan de Yepes **1**

Castellanos de Castro

Alto 950m

Villandiego

Iglesias

SAN BOL
San Bol *muni.* **A**
5.7 Cruce *San Bol*

río San Bol

W
Sunset
S
N
Sunrise
E

M E S E T A

HORNILLOS del CAMINO
(Pop. 60– Alt. 820m)
Manolo ■ **0.0** Centro

to visit San Bol 300m (left) *Albergue* **San Bol** *Muni.[12÷1]* €5 © 606 893 407 also provides breakfast and snacks to passing pilgrims. Basic hostel (new shower and w.c.!) with communal meal offered. Delightful location by grove of poplar trees offering shade by the river. The waters from the well are said to have healing properties and to cure aching feet – the peace of this isolated spot can heal more than feet. The nearest village *Iglesias* lies 4 km further off the camino along a dirt road. At one time a monastery dedicated to San Boal (or San Baudito) of the Antonine order served this area and gave it its name - now managed by Santa Brigida hostel in Hontanas. Climb up again out of the narrow Sanbol valley back onto the Meseta. Pass over a minor road (linking Iglesias and Olmillos de Sasamón) and spectacularly the Meseta suddenly falls away to reveal:

4.8 km **Hontanas** *Centro* *(pop. 70)* another classic pilgrim village tucked in a fold of the Meseta. Situated off a minor road into Castrojeriz and largely undiscovered except by pilgrims. As we enter pass the tiny chapel of Santa Brigida (right) and Fuente Puntido (left) adj' new *Albergue* ❶ **Juan de Yepes** *Priv.[54÷9]*+ €7 (communal dinner €9) © 638 938 546 (Amalia) c/ Real 1. The solid parish church of the Conception *XIV[th]C* (see photo) dominates the tiny village square and contributes to an air of quiet reverence that pervades this little Jacobean haven of the fountains *Fontanas* from which the name derives and a fine example *[F.]* spills out its refreshingly cool waters in the shade of the church, and: ❷ **El Puntido** *Priv.*[50÷4]*+ €5–€25 © 947 378 597 centrally located opp' the church (see photo right). Good facilities and popular bar and menú. Further down the main street. ❸ **Santa Brígida** *Priv.*[16÷3]* €7 © 628 927 317 also provides meals and runs the municipal albergue opp' ❹ **San Juan El Nuevo** *Muni.[55÷2]* €5 © 628 927 317 no patio but pilgrims hang out on the main street (+ their clothes!). The lounge is built over the

original medieval foundations (visible through the glazed floor) and the hostel won an architectural award for its imaginative reconstruction. When the hostel is full other municipal albergues *may* open as follows: **La Escuela** *Muni.[21÷1]* in the old schoolhouse and **El Viejo** *Muni.[14÷2]* located in the Town Hall. **Other Lodging:** Opp' El Puntido *Hs˚* **Fuente Estrella** €25+ © 947 377 261 and just below *CR* **El Descanso** €30+ © 947 377 035 also with bar and restaurant. *[Bar Vitorino is finally closed. One of the famous characters along the camino* Vitorino *could drink a litre of wine from the porrón (jug with spout) by pouring it onto his forehead and letting it flow into his mouth without drawing breath. A feat he accomplished frequently which lead to a wonderfully erratic menú del dia].*

Continue through the village past the municipal swimming pool with bar-café (open high summer only) and cross over the minor road shaded with trees (an alternative is to walk the quiet country road and use the shade). The waymarked path continues roughly parallel to the road passing the ruins of an old mill and the long abandoned village of San Miguel to re-join the road just before:

`5.6 km` **Arco San Antón** *Albergue* **San Antón** *Priv.[14÷1]* €-*donativo* (summer only) situated amongst the ruins of the ancient *convento de San Antón XIV[th]C* basic facilities (no electricity) with shared meal. Pass under St. Anthony's archway *Arco de San Antón* with recessed alcoves where bread was left for pilgrims of old *[the tradition continues with pilgrims leaving messages here instead. This*

was the ancient monastery and hospice of the Antonine Order founded in France in the 11th century and connected to the work of the hermit Saint Anthony of Egypt **San Antón Abad** *patron saint of animals and usually depicted with a pig at his feet. The Order's sacred symbol was the 'T' shaped cross known as the Tau – nineteenth letter of the Greek alphabet and symbolising divine protection against evil and sickness. Increasingly referred to and worn as the Pilgrim Cross* **Cruz del Peregrino**. *The Order was known for its ability to cure the medieval scourge known as St Anthony's fire (a fungal skin disease often turning gangrenous leading to death) essentially by using the power of the Tau (Love) in its healing practice].*

As we leave these splendid ruins behind, the **Convento de Santa Clara** (*Clarisas*) opens up to our left (½ km): founded in the 14th century where you can buy one of the wooden Tau crosses made by the nuns (open most days, closed lunch, mass 17:15) – or buy one in Castrojeriz which now opens to view in front of us. The prominent castle (ruins) stands sentinel over the town and surrounding countryside. Turn right off the main road at cross and signboard. **Note:** *The town straddles a long winding road – 2 kilometres from start to finish. A long way at the end of the day!*

`2.5 km` **Castrojeriz** *Iglesia Santa María* collegiate Church of Our Lady of the Apple ❶ *N.S Manzano XIV[th]C*. Its spacious interior wonderfully cool after the way. The fine rose window sheds light on some interesting treasures, including a statue of St. James in pilgrim regalia festooned with scallop shells and a fine statue of Our Lady. The church has been renovated as a museum of sacred art. Opp' the church is bar and hostal *Hs[*]* **El Manzano** ☎ 620 782 768. **Note:** Lodging is listed sequentially from this point: [300m <left] *Alb.* ❶ **Camino**

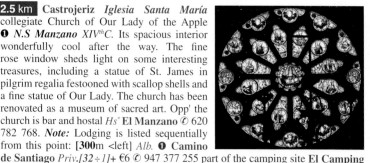

de Santiago *Priv.[32÷1]+* €6 ☎ 947 377 255 part of the camping site **El Camping** with *CR* **del Camping** €25. Facilities incl' terrace with a backdrop of trees, a shop, bar and restaurant. Continue along the upper street *c/Real Oriente* with a selection of chic *casa rurales* and *hoteles rurales* gently 'calling' with Gregorian chant: [300m N[o]83 right>] *Hs[**]* **La Cachava** ☎ 947 378 547 and just beyond at N[o]77 ❷ **Ultreia** *Priv.[40÷2]+* €9–€40 ☎ 947 378 640 the newest albergue with patio at rear and communal dinner. [100m N[o]72 <left] *CR* **El Veredero** €30+ ☎ 696 985 323 newly renovated with terrace. [100m N[o]54 <left] ❸ **Casa Nostra** *Priv.[26÷3]* €9 ☎ 947 377 493 another traditional town house with cool interior patio and good facilities. Opp' church of St. Dominic ❷ *Iglesia de Santo Domingo* (museum of sacred art) combining Gothic, Baroque and styles but lying 'hidden' in the narrow streetscape and barely noticeable. Keep your inner ear and eye open for another hidden gem at N[o]25 ♥*Hospital del Alma* where the soul is refreshed in this magical space dedicated to love and healing. [200m] small plaza with *CR* **Grevillea** ☎ 947 378 644 @ N[o]36 on

the corner and at N°43 right> *Hs* **La Taberna** © 947 377 120 with restaurant and tables on the square. Continue up to next square [**100**m] *Plaza Fuero restaurant El Fuero* on corner with viewpoint. ▼ **option [a]** *s/o up* to albergue in *Plaza Mayor* [**400**m]

1.5 km Castrojeriz *Plaza Mayor albergue* ❹ **San Esteban** *Muni.[30÷1]* €5 © 947 377 001 commanding position overlooking the square at the top end of town (gets the evening sun – see photo right). Municipal hostel on upper floor of restored civic building (*Casa Cultura*) one open dormitory with water heated from the roof solar panels. Attractive town square *Bazar El Peregrino* (ponchos etc), cafes. *Correos* and town hall also *Posada* **Emebed** €45+ © 616 802 473 all facilities and terrace on Plaza Mayor, 5.

▼ *Plaza Fuero* **option [b]** instead of heading up to plaza mayor this brings us down the steps (left) onto *paseo del Monte* passing the lower level entrance to *Posada* **Emebed** (see above) past the *museo etnografico* (summer only) opp' *H***``Puerta del Monte** *Iacobus* €35 © 947 378 647 (15 rooms) also bar and restaurant to the rear with large open patio and views of the surrounding countryside. Just before the central 'crossroads' *H***``**La Posada** €45 © 947 378 610 (12 rooms) and *H***`` **El Mesón** €30 © 947-378 610 on c/Cordón opp'. ❺ **Rosalía** *Priv.[32÷5]* €10 © 947 373 714 (Javier). Also restaurants *Mesón / El Cordón / El Lagar* and *Oliva* opp' which is the last of the albergues ❻ **Tradicional de San Juan** *Asoc.[28÷2]* €-donativo © 947 377 400 the traditional (original) pilgrim hostel with garden patio at the side. From here there is a connecting lane (up sharp right – not waymarked) to Plaza Mayor 200 metres. Pilgrims staying in this 'lower' part of town have a good selection of restaurants and bars and often bypass the Plaza Mayor (see town map) and vice-versa. Castrojeriz warrants exploration! [*Next albergue: Puente Itero – 9.1 km*].

Both routes join at the ❸ *Iglesia de San Juan XVI[th]C* largely Gothic but with a Renaissance baptismal font attributed to the 15th century master sculptor and architect Diego de Siloé whose outstanding work we have already come across in Burgos, his city of birth. There is also a fine cloister and the entire building has been renovated and now acts as a museum and art gallery.

CASTROJERIZ: Delightfully sleepy town with declining population of 500 who seem to be permanently occupied with siesta except during the garlic festival *fiesta del Ajo* in July which adds a bit of seasoning to life. It had a more active past evident in its ruined castles and monasteries. A historic fortified town *castrum* with Roman and Visigothic remains, and scene of much fighting. Castrojeriz rose to prominence during the *reconquista* and as a major stopping place on the medieval camino with no less than 8 pilgrim hospitals. If you have the energy, a walk to the hilltop castle *castillo* (established in the 9th century) will be rewarded with fine views over the town and countryside – otherwise a short walk to the sites already referred to will give you a flavour of this historic town. Local shops on main road adjacent the bus-stop include *Farmacia*. Alternatively, just hang out with a cool beer in one of the bars of this typical pilgrim town... or join the locals and take a siesta.

REFLECTIONS:

❐ **If you follow your bliss, you put yourself on a track that has always been there waiting for you. And the life you should be living is the life you are living.**

Joseph Campbell

---

15 **449.3** km (279.2 ml) – Santiago

CASTROJERIZ – FRÓMISTA

	(Burgos)	(Palencia)	
⸱⸱⸱⸱⸱⸱⸱⸱⸱⸱⸱⸱	--- ---	22.0 --- ---	88%
▬▬▬	--- ---	2.9 --- ---	12%
▬▬▬	--- ---	0.0	
Total km	--- ---	**24.9** km (15.5 ml)	

▲	--- ---	26.1 km (^250m + 1.2 km)
Alto ▲	Alto de Mostelares at 900m (2,952 ft)

< Ⓐ Ⓗ > Puente de Itero (S.Nicolas) **8.9** km – *Itero del Castillo 8.9 (+1.4 km off route)*. – Itero de la Vega **10.6** km – Boadilla **19.1** km.

❐ **The Practical Path:** A glance at the map of today's stage might give you a false impression. Look carefully and you will see that while the camino appears in a web of asphalt roads it seldom connects with them. A glorious 22 km (88%) is on earth tracks. Be prepared for the strenuous climb out of Castrojeriz onto the Meseta. The view back over the valley floor, coupled with the knowledge that what goes up must come down should be enough to revive any flagging spirit. Apart from the trees that line the río Pisuerga and the Canal de Castilla there is little shade and few water fonts, so take precautions.

❐ **The Mystical Path:** The track we start off on today was laid two thousand years ago. Tomorrow's track is the first stretch of the soulless modern *senda* with its harsh concrete bollards that flies over the new Frómista bypass and was built only a few years back. How many pilgrims have walked the old Roman road and how many will walk the modern senda? How many followed their bliss? How many have paid equal respect to the inner and outer path? Which path are you on? Is your life in tune with your purpose? What is your purpose? Life without an inner direction is fruitless and only leads down a cul-de-sac called despair with only disillusionment and death at the end. Bliss is found another way – along the inner pathways of soul.

❐ **Personal Reflections:** *"… I have seldom witnessed such dedication to a path of service – the whole family's unwavering hospitality to pilgrims on their way to Santiago. Every action is performed with such care and precision and made to feel right, not just look right. I am reminded how much my own life has been squandered in posturing. The pretence that comes from making something look right on the surface, while ignoring the underlying lack of integrity and the feeling of discontent that follows. Tamed man addicted to the approval of family and friends masking the wild man determined for the freedom that comes with living an authentic life painted on a larger canvas. Eduardo and his family are artists in more ways than one …"*

< Palencia **N-611**

A-67

5.8 Albergue Centro

S.Martín ❶ ✝ ❷ S.Martín S.Pedro
Garigolo Apóstol
Camino de Santiago
❷ H ❸ ✝Estrella

Canal de Castilla ❶ S.Pedro H ❹ Betania
H Doña Mayor
❸ S.Maria del Castillo
Leyenda del Camino

FRÓMISTA
(Pop. 840 - Alt. 790m)

W
Sunset
N
Sunrise
E

Santa María XV
columna justicia XV ✝ Titas
Plaza Iglesia **8.5** ❹
H ❸
En El Camino **BOADILLA del CAMINO**
Escuela ❷
Putzu ❶ F

T I E R R A d e C A M P O S

Canal de Castilla

Canal Pisuerga

Bodegas ◯

❸ Hogar del peregrino
Municipal ❹ ❷ La Mochila
ITERO de la VEGA **1.7** Centro
Puente de Itero ❶ Fitero

P A L E N C I A

A **1.5** Albergue *Muni.[7÷1]*

San Nicolás A
Albergue **1.5** **ITERO del CASTILLO**

B U R G O S R ✗ **3.9** Fuente del Piojo

río Pisuerga

▲ Alto 900m
✗ **3.5** Alto de Mostelares

río Odrilla

(Pop. 500 – Alt. 810m)
CASTROJERIZ ✝ St.Juan
■
A ◀ **0.0** Albergue ❹ *Centro*

0.0 km **Castrojeriz** *Centro* From either albergue ❹ On Plaza Mayor or ❺ on the lower road c/Cordón in the centre of Castrojeriz continue past the church of San Juan and cross over the main road to join a track that runs alongside the Roman causeway to a bridge over the río Odrilla (tributary of the río Pisuerga which we cross later). The slopes of Mostelares lie ahead as we start the steep climb to:

3.5 km **Alto de Mostelares** a covered rest area has been created to help us get our breath back but the real masterpiece is the landscape temple that surrounds us. Continue along the high Meseta dropping down steeply past pilgrim shrine (left) to option for alternative route to **Itero del Castillo [1.7 km]**. ▼

Detour: Itero del Castillo 3.7 km ● ● ● ● *a direct earth track veers right. The tower of the church in Itero del Castillo soon becomes apparent. Cross road [2.4 km] and make your way to c/Sol [1.3 km]. Albergue Mun.[12÷1]* €10 *incl. Menú* Ⓒ *642 213 560 (Toni) basic hostel adj. the town hall . The town name refers to its strategic position on this historic border point on the banks of the río Pisuerga. Rejoin main route at the bridge over río Pisuerga [1.5 km].*

▼ Continue s/o to **[2.2 km]** *[F.]* rest area with some shade and cool spring water and *Kiosco movíl* (summer).

3.9 km **Fuente del Piojo** We now join the minor road to San Nicolás.

1.5 km **Ermita de San Nicolás** *Albergue* **San Nicolás** *Asoc.[12÷1]* €*-donativo*. Directly on the camino just before the bridge. Popular hostel (June-Sept only) no electricity, phone or other mod-cons (excepting a shower and toilet in an extension to the rear) but a shared dinner and breakfast €*-donativo*. The 13th century buildings were restored by an Italian Confraternity who

retain candlelight as the source of illumination which adds to the healing atmosphere of this veritable haven where ritual 'washing of the feet' is offered. Space is limited so count your blessings if a bed is available. The original pilgrim hospice was founded in the 12th century and later a Cistercian monastery was added. Continue s/o to:

    Puente de Itero whose eleven arches carry us over the río Pisuerga and into the Provincia de Palencia. The river provided the natural historical boundary between the kingdoms of Castilla and León. *[Several place names around here start with Itero a derivation of Hito meaning landmark or boundary stone].*

    Provincia de PALENCIA *Tierra de Campos* extensive agricultural area well served with rivers and canals that irrigate its rich soils with cultivation mainly of wheat with some vegetable and wine production. It is a flat region lying between the rivers Pisuerga and Cea at Sahagún. There are few trees to offer shade from the relentless sun that dries the deep red earthen walls of many of the adobe villages we pass through. The absence of wood and stone made earth the natural building material – initially air-dried bricks and eventually kilns speeding up the process and stability but still lacking long-term durability. There is also increasing evidence of wine cellars *bodegas* whose Hobbit-like structures, built into the sides of hillocks, appear all over the countryside to store the local wine in the relative cool of their subterranean stores.

A shaded track follows the river past the *Ermita de la Piedad XIII*[th]*C* with picnic area *[F.]* and Jacobean motifs at the entrance of this sleepy village:

1.7 km **Itero de la Vega** *(Pop.190)* Hs+Alb.**❶ Puente Fitero** *Priv.[22÷2]+* €8 +€30-40 ℂ 979 151 822 c/ Santa María at the entrance with popular bar. *Alb.* **❷ La Mochila** *Priv.[22÷3]* €6-10 *Menú* ℂ 979 151 781 c/Santa Ana. **❸ Hogar del Peregrino** *Priv.[8÷4]* €12 + *Menú* ℂ 970 151 866 c/Santa Maria. **❹ Muni.** *[12÷1]* €5 ℂ 605 034 347 adj. *iglesia San Pedro XVI* Plaza Iglesia. *[Next albergue: Boadilla – 8.0 km]. Bar Tachu [to visit the Plaza Mayor with its attractive fountain of prancing ponies watched over by a handsome Gothic rollo veer right].* Continue via c/Santa Ana past *[F.]* (right) and s/o at T-junction onto wide farm track **[0.8 km]**.

The village of Bodegas (left) with wind farm on the ridge beyond. We next cross the **Canal Pisuerga [1.7 km]** *[The intensive farming here is the result of the building of a series of canals in the late 18*[th] *century].* The farm track continues all the way up a gentle incline and then down to a shaded river stretch with unusual wheel pump in the woodland glade *[F.]* (left) **[5.6 km]** on the outskirts of Boadilla. *Albergue* **❶ Putzu** *Priv.[16÷5]* €7 basic hostal at entrance (left). Cross the river to **❷ Escuela** *Muni.[12÷1]* ℂ 979 810 390 (Zoraida Cerrato) basic €5 in former school building on c/Escuelas where the run-down children's playground provides space for relaxation. S/o (left) to the church and *rollo* in the main square **Plaza Mayor [0.4 km]**

8.5 km **Boadilla del Camino** *(Pop.160)* **❸ En El Camino ♥** *Priv.*[48÷2]* €7 ℂ 979 810 284 m:619 105 168 popular hostal adj. church. Typical Castilian menu prepared by artist Begoña whose paintings adorn the walls and the whole family work tirelessly to offer the pilgrim a warm welcome In 2014 they opened the adj. *H*[+] **Rural en el Camino** with 16 en suite rooms from €35 (phone number above) with

separate bar / restaurant & basement swimming pool! Just before leaving the village we pass the newest hostel **❹ Titas** *Priv.[10÷1]* €10 ℂ 979 810 776 with bar and restaurant. *[Next albergue: Frómista – 6.4 km].*

    Boadilla del Camino: The original population of over 2,000 that once served the several pilgrim hospitals here continues to decline – a characteristic of many rural communities along the way. But the re-awakening of the camino is beginning to turn the tide. The parish Church of **Santa María XVI**[th]*C* contains an exceptional stone **baptismal font XIV**[th]*C* and there is an equally fine medieval jurisdictional column **Rollo** in the square complete with scallop shell motifs.

    Continue out the village onto another farm track through the *Tierra de Campos* to the **Canal de Castilla [1.7 km]** that flows all the way into Frómista along a peaceful tree-lined path. While the modern Canal Pisuerga was designed exclusively for irrigation purposes, this 18th century canal provided transportation of the cultivated crops as well as power to turn the corn mills. With the advent of motorways its use is now restricted to irrigation and leisure. There is a plan to restore the canal system with all its original 50 locks.

    Shaded canal-side walk to the lock gates (disused) *esclusa* **[3.2 km]** continue down to the main road to pass under the railway **[0.9 km]** *Alb.* **❶ Canal de Castilla** *Priv.[16÷1]+* €17 +€20-30 incl. menú ℂ 979 810 193 converted railway building at the station adj' *Mesón Bodega.* S/o up to the main crossroads **Turismo** ℂ 979-810 180 (summer only) in Paseo Central which we cross over veering right and then left into the **Plaza de San Martín [0.6 km]:**

5.8 km Frómista *(Pop. 800)* **Plaza de San Martín** *Alb.* ❷ Frómista *Muni.[56÷6]* €8 Ⓒ 979 811 089 / Carmel 686 579 702 all facilities incl' patio. Adj' *HR°* **San Martín** €40-50 Ⓒ 979 810 000 with popular bar and tables on the square also *P* **Marisa** Ⓒ 979 810 023. In the street to the rear of albergue 2 are: *CR* **Antonio y Marcelino** *y* **Serviarias** Ⓒ 626 959 079. **Other lodging** is spread out either side of the wide main road *Av. del Ejercito Español* as follows: *Hs°* **San Pedro** €35-45 Ⓒ 979 810 409. *Hs°* **El Apostol** €37 Ⓒ 979 810 255. *Hs°* **Camino de Santiago** €25+ Ⓒ 979 810 282 and to the rear (same ownership) ❸ **Estrella del Camino** *Priv.[34÷3]*+ €9 Ⓒ 979 810 399 with sheltered garden terrace. On the far side of the main road in N°26 ❹ **Betania** *Priv.[5÷3]* Ⓒ 638 846 043 €-donativo open during winter months.

Just off the main street on c/Francesa *H°°°* **Doña Mayor** Ⓒ 979 810 588 from €60. *P* **La Vía Láctea** €32+ Ⓒ 696 009 803 c/ Julio Senador 2. *[Next albergue: Población – 3.8 km].* There are a wide variety of bars and cafes but for an authentic Castillian meal in an historic pilgrim *hospital* try *Hostería Los Palmeros* Ⓒ 979 810 067 opp. the Church of San Pedro on Plaza San Telmo patron saint of sailors, who was born here in the 12th century and who died on the *camino Portugués* and is buried in Tui.

FRÓMISTA with a declining population of 840 is best known (and visited) for the beautiful **Iglesia de San Martín** *XI°C* (consecrated in 1066) and reputedly one of the finest examples of pure Romanesque in Spain. The church has exquisite proportions and is built with a lovely mellow stone with over 300 external corbels each carved with a different human, animal or mystical motif. It was de-consecrated, painstakingly restored and declared a national monument all in the same breath. Endless coach parties have turned it into a must-see tourist site and it appears to have lost something vital in the process. At the other end of town is the Gothic **Iglesia de San Pedro** *XV°C* that has a more prayerful atmosphere and a small museum of religious artwork and a statue of St. James. **Sta. Mª del Castillo** tucked away up a side street houses the Vestigia multimedia presentation *Leyenda del Camino.*

The importance of Frómista to the camino is evident in the fact that there were several pilgrim hospitals here in medieval times such as the Hostería Los Palmeros. *Palmeros* is a reference to pilgrims to the Holy Land whose symbol was a palm leaf as distinct from the scallop shell representing the pilgrimage to Santiago. Frómista is derived from the Latin word for cereal *frumentum* this area having provided copious supplies of wheat to the burgeoning Roman Empire and is also perhaps the reason why we find the unusual reference to pilgrims heading east to Jerusalem via Rome rather than west to Santiago. This marks the beginning of stage VII of the Codex Calixtinus.

REFLECTIONS:

_____

_____

_____

_____

_____

_____

_____

_____

_____

_____

_____

_____

_____

_____

_____

_____

_____

_____

_____

_____

_____

_____

_____

❏ **So I began to have an idea of my life… as the gradual discovery and growth of a purpose that I had not known.** *Joanna Field*

---

16 **424.4** km (263.7 ml) – Santiago

FRÓMISTA – CARRIÓN DE LOS CONDES

··············	--- ---	16.1	--- ---	83%
▬▬▬	--- ---	3.2	--- ---	17%
▬▬▬	--- ---	0.0		
Total km	--- ---	**19.3** km	(12.0 ml)	

◣◢ --- --- 19.5 km (^50m + 0.2 km)
Alto ▲ Carrión 830m (2,725 ft)
< 🅰 🅷 > Población **3.4** km – Villarmentero **9.3**
Villalcázar de Sirga **13.6** km.

❏ **The Practical Path:** Today we have our first taste of the somewhat soulless *sendas** (*pilgrim autopistas*) that run alongside the main roads. In today's stage we can increase the natural paths by leaving out the senda from Poblacíon to Villalcázar and taking the recommended scenic path via Villovieco. This scenic route follows a tree-lined riverside path offering both shade and silence away from the traffic (*excepting the last 1.7 km into Villalcázar by local road. Note also this alternative road route is 0.9 km longer*). Both routes join in Villalcázar with its beautiful Templar church. Make time to visit the interior with its Retablo of the life of St. James.

❏ **The Mystical Path:** Today we will take 21,000 steps and we can choose to make each one a prayer for peace as we walk through the 21st century. Humanity is coming of age and we hold the key to a new era. The choice is ours as to which way we turn it, but we have only two real choices. We can add to the problems humanity currently faces or become part of the solution. The choice we make will imbue this millennia with either love or fear. It is time to reawaken to the purpose of our life, time for the long walk to freedom in the footsteps of Mandiba. The Maitreya is known by many names, Messiah, Imam Mahdi, Mahatma… the rebirth of Christ Consciousness.

❏ **Personal Reflections:** *"… I sit on the balcony and look out to the soft evening colours changing from delicate blue to pink and now turning to a deepening red. It is strange how we experience the sun sinking whereas in reality the light is fixed and the earth and I are merely turning away from it into the shadow. The Inquisition offered Galileo the opportunity to recant on his challenge to the orthodox view or face a painful death. The possibility that the earth was not the centre of the universe was simply too threatening to the established authority. As I, too, begin to challenge the consensus reality around me, I ask for the courage to stay open to truth as it is revealed in each changing moment and not to seek the protection afforded by the popularly held perspective. My purpose becomes clearer with each passing day …"*

Real Monasterio H****
H *San Zoilo* ❹

Río Carrión

**CARRIÓN
DE LOS
CONDES**

(Pop. 2,200)

❷ *S.Maria*
❷ ◄**0.5** Albergue S.Maria
N-120
A-231

S.Clara ❶ ◄**5.2** Albergue

Albe **H** Belén
❹
Pz. Generalísimo
✝❸*Santiago*
H Santiago
→El Resbalon
Pz.S.María.
Pz.Santillana

Espíritu
Santo ❸

San Juan

La Corte **H**
La Abuela
✝❷ *S. María*
i

centro salud
Museo ❶
S. Clara ❶

VILLALCÁZAR DE SIRGA
A Casa Aurea
← *Santa María la Blanca XIII*
Municipal
Alb. **4.3** ►◄**A**◄**1.7** Albergue
🏠 Palomar

río Ucieza

✝ *Ermita de la
Virgen del río*
◄**4.8** Puente

Arconada

VILLARMENTERO DE CAMPOS
Casona Doña Petra **C**
S.Martín de Tours→✝ **Amanecer**
Albergue **2.1** ►◄**A**+*Tipis*.

✝ **VILLOVIECO**
◄**4.1** Puente

REVENGA DE CAMPOS
Centro 3.3►

❶ ❷ ✓

Puente / Opción **0.5** ► **Amanecer**
H
Ermita de San Miguel →✝ ◄**A**◄**3.4** Albergue Escuela

río Ucieza

A-67
N-620

0.0 Albergue
✝ *S.Martín* **A**❷ *S.Pedro* **A**❸
FRÓMISTA

← *Palencia*

O
*puesta
del sol*
S
*salida
del sol* E

0.0 km **Frómista** From albergue ❷ return to the crossroads *bar Garigolo* and head out along the P-980 signposted Carrión de Los Condes over the Frómista bypass N-611 and the new A-67 roundabout onto the pilgrim gravel track *senda*. *[On the outskirts of Población (left) is the Romanesque Ermita St. Miguel XIII[th]C in a shaded glade on the opposite side of road]*. Turn right> down the concrete path to:

3.4 km **Población de Campos** *(Pop. 150)* *Alb.* **Escuela** *Muni.[18÷1]* €4 basic hostel in former school building as you enter the village with playground. Keys held at adj. *Hs˚*Amanecer ♥ *(dawn)* © 979 811 099 with rooms from €30 and pilgrim menú €9. *Bar Arrabal* adj. the Casa Consistorial. The parish church *XVI[th]C* is dedicated to Mary Magdalene. Continue past the diminutive *Ermita de la Virgen del Socorro XIII[th]C* (left) to the stone bridge over the río Ucieza and option.

0.5 km **Puente / Opción [?]** ▼

For tranquil **river route** ❷ ✓ ● ● ● ● (adds 0.9 km to the main route) do *not* cross the bridge but s/o right> (sign Ermita del Socorro) along road (becomes track) and turn off <left parallel to the tree-lined río Ucieza (left) to Villovieco bridge.

4.1 km **Villovieco** *(Pop. 100)* parish Church of St. Mary with Santiago artefacts. Leave the village by the bridge *Parque* with •*Bar [F.]* and turn immediately right> along the rio Ucieza for a delightful shaded path to join the quiet road into:

4.8 km **Puente** *Ermita de la Virgen del Río* Hermitage of Our Lady of the River housing an image of Santiago. Turn <left, continue along road past *Café y museo Palomar Del Camino* © 653 916 600 into:

1.7 km **Villalcázar de Sirga** where the main route joins from the left.

▼ For the main route cross the bridge and rejoin the senda into:

3.3 km **Revenga de Campos** village with pilgrim statue & church of San Lorenzo *XII*. Pick up the *senda* again as you exit with picnic halt and *[F.]* right s/o into:

2.1 km **Villarmentero de Campos** *Albergue* **Amanecer** *Priv.[18÷2]* €6 bunkbeds or tipi also hammocks €3! © 629 178 543 All facilities incl. snack bar and communal dinner €8. Church of San Martín de Tours on opp' side of road, adj' to *CR* **Casona de Doña Petra** €35 © 979 065 978 also offers dinner. Continue through the town – shaded picnic tables *[F.]* (right) at far end back onto the *senda* s/o into:

4.3 km **Villalcázar de Sirga** *(Pop. 200)* *[F.]* s/o into the square *Alb.*❶ **Villalcázar** *Muni.[20÷2]* €-donativo © 979 888 041 with access off Plaza del Peregrino (photo right). Basic facilities in this traditional hostel overlooking the main square and church of Santa María la Blanca. At the far end of town c/Real,23 *Alb.* ❷ **Tasca Don Camino** *Priv.[28÷4]+* €7-15 © 979 888 053 part of *CR* **Aurea** with menú. **Other Lodging**: *HsR˚* **Infanta Doña Leonor** €35 © 927 888 015 & on the main square opp' the church is popular bar & *CR* **Las Cántigas** €30 © 979 888 027. *[Next albergue: Carrión de los Condes – 5.2 km]*.

VILLALCÁZAR DE SIRGA (VILLASIRGA – town of the canal towpath) is well known for its hospitality having welcomed pilgrims here since the 12th century when it became a commandery of the Knights Templar. There is a popular *Café-Bar* opp' the church and fine fare in the well-preserved medieval inn *Mesón Villalcázar*. The town is home to the magnificent Templar church of **Santa María** *la Virgen Blanca XIIIthC* housing the tombs of nobles and royalty and now declared a national monument. The porch with its sculptured south door is particularly noteworthy as is the rose window. If visiting churches along the way is not your 'thing' make an exception for this one: open 10:00–13:00 and 16:00–20:00 and light up the retablo (coin operated) with its splendid panel depicting the life of St. James; his meeting with Jesus to martyrdom and transference to Galicia. In another side chapel is the statue of Santa María La Blanca, to whom is ascribed many miracles. Also the tombs of Infante Don Felipe (son of Fernando III and brother of Alfonso X the wise *el Sabio*) and Felipe's wife Doña Leonor.

We make our way back to the main road and pick up the gravel *senda* that runs parallel to it all the way to the outskirts of Carrión de los Condes.

5.2 km Carrion de los Condes *Entrada*
Cross road, past ermita N.S. de la Piedad to *Albergue* ❶ **Santa Clara** *Conv.[30÷6]+* €5–€22 ☏ 979 880 837 Located (left) at the entrance to the town. Hostal run by the *Madres Clarisas* off a tranquil courtyard that also provides access to ❶ *Museo y Real Monasterio y Ermita de La Piedad XIIIthC*. St. Francis of Assisi allegedly stayed here.

The town centre and parish hostel are now only 500m further on – continue up to the main road and cross over by *Turismo* ☏ 979 880 932 (summer only) site of the *Puerta de Santa María* that provided the entrance to the old walled city and the 12th century Romanesque church of St. Mary of the Way *Santa María del Camino*. Unusual buttresses form the main entrance which depicts the miracle wrought by the Church's namesake, when the notorious annual 'tribute' of the 100 maidens *doncellas* imposed by the Moors on the Christian population was finally broken. Turn right> immediately after the church into square (market every Thursday) and:

0.5 km Carrión de los Condes ❷ **Santa María** ♥ *Par.[52÷3]* €5 ☏ 979 880 768 centrally located behind the church on the corner of plaza Santa María. Volunteer

Augustinian Sisters (summer) provide a warm Christian welcome with ritual and song 18:00, pilgrim blessing in adj. church 20.00 and shared dinner 21.00. ❸ **Espíritu Santo** *Conv.[90÷7]* €5 run by *Hijas de San Vicente de Paul ©* 979 880 052 Plaza San Juan near the health centre with common prayers at 17:30. ❹ **Casa de espíritualidad N.S de Belén** *Conv.[52÷52!+40÷20]* €22 (€28 incl. dinner) © 979 880 031 adj. church at the top end of town run by the Philipine Brothers *R.R Filipenses.* *[Next albergue: Calzadilla de la Cueza – 17.2 km].* **Other Lodging:** *Hs˚* **La Corte** €45 © 979 880 138 c/Santa María, 34 (opp. the church) rooms off a rear courtyard and popular restaurant. *HsR˚* **Santiago** €35 © 979 881 052 Plaza de los Regentes (central). *CR* **La Abuela Me** adj' *café Yadira* on main road (Plaza Conde Garay). *P˚* **El Resbalon** © 979 880 433 c/Fernan Gomez, 19 above the restaurant of the same name. *Hs* **Albe** €30 © 699 094 185 Esteban Colantes,2. On the other side of the river the luxurious but pilgrim hesitant *H˚˚˚˚***Real Monasterio San Zoilo** €60+ © 979 880 050. *Bar España* by bus stop at the town entrance gets the crowds. *Bar Carmen* in Plaza G.Franco gets the evening sun.

CARRIÓN DE LOS CONDES occupied a strategic position in this volatile border area and at the height of its influence had a population in excess of 10,000; now reduced to some 2,200 (and declining). This interesting town retains a medieval atmosphere within its meandering side streets and was home to no less than 14 pilgrim *hospitals.* It was effectively the capital of much of the *tierra de campos* area and ruled by the Leónese Beni-Gómez family, the Counts of Carrión, several of whom met a premature death at the hands of the equally pugnacious El Cid, after they reputedly, and very unwisely, mistreated his daughters. Mistreatment here was endemic further attested to by the frieze in the ❷ *Iglesia de Santa María del Camino XII[th]C* which depicts the frightful annual 'tribute' of 100 maidens demanded by the conquering Moors. These intrigues and disputes were not limited to this medieval period. The main square still proudly bears the plaque Plaza del Generalisimo Franco, a name generally erased from public display because of its fascist past. Here we find the Church of

Santiago ❸ *Iglesia de Santiago XII[th]C* which was itself destroyed during the War of Independence (1809) but thankfully leaving the magnificent facade and frieze intact (Christ in majesty) as a national monument and the church itself has been adapted as museum (€1) where the image of *Santiago Matamoros* continues the theme of death and retribution. San Roque (pictured above) appears in his familiar guise of pilgrim. **SAN ZOILO Real Monasterio** *XIth–XVI[th]C* connected with the Order of Cluny and dating from 11th century with Romanesque elements but largely influenced by the Renaissance period including the splendid platueresque cloisters. We pass San Zoilo on the way out of town. It is now a national monument and has been restored as a private hotel similar to a Parador. Here you can rest your weary limbs and stroll at leisure around the cloisters and 'meet' the Counts of Carrión whose murdered remains are laid to rest more permanently in its hallowed halls.

REFLECTIONS:

"If we could read the secret history of our enemies, we should find in each person's life – sorrow and suffering enough to disarm all hostility." Longfellow

❐ **An eye for an eye only ends up leaving the whole world blind.**
————————————— *Mahatma Gandhi*

17   **405.1** km (251.7 ml) – Santiago

CARRIÓN de los CONDES – TERRADILLOS de los TEMPLARIOS

┅┅┅┅┅┅	--- ---	18.7	--- --- 70%
▬▬▬▬	--- ---	8.1	--- --- 30%
▬▬▬	--- ---	0.0	
Total km		**26.8** km (16.7 ml)	

◣◣◣ --- --- 27.3 km (^100m + 0.5 km)
Alto ▲ Ledigos alto 900m (2,950 ft)
< Ⓐ Ⓗ > Calzadilla de la Cueza **17.3** km – Ledigos **23.4** km.

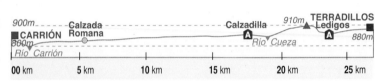

❐ **The Practical Path:** We pass through a flat and somewhat featureless landscape with little or no shade. 70% is on gravel paths, most of which overlay the old paved Roman road *Via Aquitana* that connected with Astorga. Anticipate *no* facilites between Carrión and Calzadilla (17.2 km) with no water and no toilets *(there is a mobile cafe in the summer at 10.1 km)*. Ensure your water flasks are full and have breakfast before you leave or bring something to eat with you.

❐ **The Mystical Path:** Today we leave a fortified town that has witnessed countless battles, conquests, re-conquests, shameful violations, betrayals and revenge killings. We pass the murdered relics of the Counts of Carrión and the martyred San Zoilo. But what of our own sense of justified retribution and how often have we wished someone ill? When did we last send healing thoughts of love and peace to our supposéd enemy? Mahatma means Great Soul and it takes one to incarnate in a Hindu body to re-interpret the Christian scriptural teaching (above) to remind us of the futility of revenge. Will we find the courage today to open our hearts and offer love instead of fear whenever we feel attacked?

❐ **Personal reflections:** *"... I only saw him after I had collapsed onto the rickety metal chair. He just sat there looking at me with those intense black eyes framed by jet-black curls of hair that fell down over his shoulders. Spread across his face was a half smile that disappeared into his thick beard. I think he had intended to scare me. He reminded me of a picture I once saw of Rasputin ... I returned from the village, thankful that he was nowhere to be seen. My sense of relief quickly faded when I opened the door to the bunk room. Behind it stood his evil looking staff, festooned with black feathers and other symbols of his craft. It was strange how I felt his presence before I actually saw him ..."*

0.0 km   **Carrión** from the central *albergue* ❷ continue through the old town down c/Santa María turning right> past the main square with Church of Santiago (right) into the narrow c/Esteban Collantes turn <left into c/Pina Blanco and over the main bridge to the poplar-lined path and causeway to:

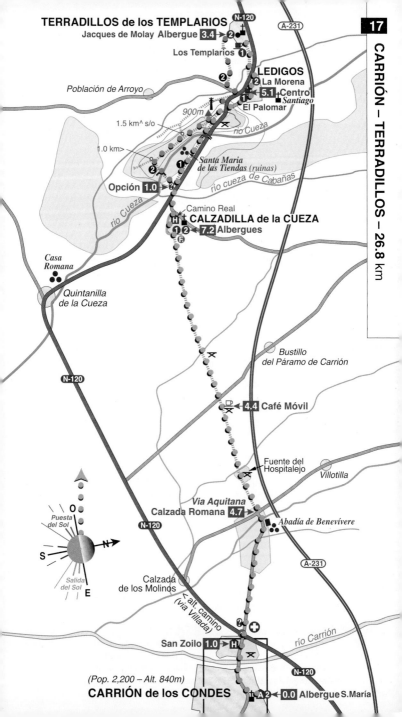

TERRADILLOS de los TEMPLARIOS
N-120
A-231

Jacques de Molay **Albergue** `3.4` ❷

Los Templarios ❶

❷

LEDIGOS
❷ La Morena
`5.1` **Centro**
❶ **Santiago**
El Palomar

Población de Arroyo

900m

río Cueza

1.5 km^ s/o

1.0 km>

❷ ❶ *Santa María
de las Tiendas* (ruinas)

río cueza de Cabañas

Opción `1.0` ❷

río Cueza

Camino Real

H † **CALZADILLA de la CUEZA**
❶ ❷ `7.2` **Albergues**
F

*Casa
Romana*

*Quintanilla
de la Cueza*

N-120

*Bustillo
del Páramo de Carrión*

`4.4` ◄ **Café Móvil**

*Fuente del
Hospitalejo*

Villotilla

Vía Aquitana
Calzada Romana `4.7`

Abadía de Benevívere

A-231

N-120

O
*Puesta
del Sol*
S

N

*Salida
del Sol*
E

*Calzada
de los Molinos*
< alt. camino
(vía Villada)

río Carrión

San Zoilo `1.0` ► H

N-120

(Pop. 2,200 – Alt. 840m)
CARRIÓN de los CONDES
† A ❷ `0.0` **Albergue** S.María

1.0 km **San Zoilo** former monastery, now a luxury hotel and just beyond it we cross the Carrión by-pass [!] *[Note: an alternative route* **Antiguo camino francés** *along the N-120 to Sahagún via Villada (Albergue Ⓒ 979 844 005) turns left here].* We head s/o along a quiet country road passing the *Cruz Rioja* building and just before crossing the second of 2 streams we find the ruins of the once illustrious 12ᵗʰ century Franciscan Abbey *Abadía Santa María de Benevívere* known for its 'good living' *bene vivere* (right). Shortly afterwards we cross the river and at a T-Junction we head s/o onto the roman road.

4.7 km **Calzada Romana / Via Aquitana / Cañada Real Leonesa**. *[We now join a stretch of the original Roman road still intact after 2,000 years of use – save for a new gravel covering! What is more remarkable is the fact that this section goes through an area of wetland devoid of any stone for its construction. It is estimated that 100,000 tons of rock was needed just for the substrata to raise the surface above the winter flood levels and every ton had to be transported from elsewhere. No wonder Roman villas and other remains have been found in the area – most notably at Quintanilla de la Cueza 5 km South of Calzadilla on the N-120].*
We next pass an area of remaining wetland and the *Fuente del Hospitalejo* in a small poplar grove (right). The fuente no longer offers hospitality but this is provided shortly afterwards at:

4.4 km **Area de Descanso** *rest area* Café Oasis / bar improvisado / cafe móvil needing no translation but open summer only *¡sólo en verano!* Imm' beyond we cross the road to Bustillo and pass a wayside shelter with map of the *Cañada Real Leon. [one of Spain's long-distance drove routes that crisscross the Iberian peninsular and used by pastoralists to move cattle and sheep to new grazing; linking this area to the south via the Cañada de Madrid].* We cross several small streams *arroyos* before finally descending into:

7.2 km **Calzadilla de la Cueza** *[F.]* (right) at entrance. *Albergue* ❶ **Calzadilla Muni.*[34÷2]** €5 Ⓒ 670 558 954 adj.' ❷ **Camino Real** *Priv.*[80÷2]* €7 Ⓒ 616 483 517 no kitchen but pilgrim *menú* €10 in *Hs* **Hostal Camino Real** €30 Ⓒ 979 883 187 waymarks point to this popular bar and restaurant behind the albergue (the owner  César Acero, a seasoned pilgrim, owns both). CALZADILLA *(Pop. 60)* typical camino village with a central main street that forms the way itself. The parish Church of San Martín has an altarpiece installed when the nearby *monasterio de Santa María de las Tiendas* was de-consecrated. We leave the village by rest area and *[F.]* and continue over the bridge and the N-120 to option:

1.0 km **Opción** [?] Here a map carved into a stone block shows 4 optional routes. Essentially we have 2 choices: ❶ s/o via roadside senda or ❷ turn <left for quiet woodland path (500m longer more remote and few waymarks). ▼

● ● ● ● Option ❷ *[3.7 km -v- 3.2 km]* turn left over bridge onto woodland path that climbs gently and veer right **[1.0 km]** to continue along the top of an escarpment (radio mast visible ahead). Continue s/o at junction **[1.5 km]** (track to the left provides an alternative 'loop' but with no waymarks). We now begin a gentle descent to re-join the main route **[1.2 km]**. Both routes continue down towards Ledigos.

▼ The main route takes the gravel senda s/o alongside the road past *monasterio de Santa María de las Tiendas* (left) *[the ruins a distant memory of its illustrious past as the Hospice of the Great Knight, a reference to its 12th century existence as a grand hospice administered by the Knights of St. James].* The path crosses the rio Cueza up to the top of the rise where the other route joins from the left **[3.2 km]**. Shortly after we pass a rest area on the far side of the road and we reach the high point of todays stage Alto (910m) after which we take a short loop and descend to main road. *[Option ❷ continues s/o].* To access Ledigos cross main road [!] into Ledigos **[1.9 km]**.

5.1 km Ledigos *Alb.* ❶ El Palomar *Priv.*[52÷7]* €6-8 ✆ 979 883 614 and the newly renovated ❷ La Morena *Priv.[37÷8]* €8-€15 ✆ 979 065 052 c/ Carretera 3 with all mod cons. Small shop and bar and the XIIIthC Parish church of Santiago with image of the saint.

●●●● Option ❷ *[2.8 km -v- 3.4 km]* a quieter and 600m shorter alternative but it bypasses albergue [1] in Terradillos: Take the road opp. the albergue in Ledigos signposted Población del Arroyo. (typically arrows here have been blacked out but recommence later). Turn right by dovecote **[0.3 km]** onto farm track veer left at fork **[0.5 km]** s/o into the 'back of' Terradillos and albergue **[2.0 km]**.

From Ledigos continue past rest area *[F.]* and cross the N-120 [!] **[0.7 km]** onto gravel senda and just before entering Terradillos **[2.1 km]** *Albergue* ❶ Los Templarios *Priv.[34÷6]*+ €7+€28 ✆ 667 252 279 good modern facilities including laundry room. No kitchen but bar and menú. Continue along senda and turn <left into the village to the original albergue **[0.5 km]**.

3.4 km Terradillos de los Templarios *Albergue* ❷ Jacques de Molay *Priv.*[49÷9]* €8-10 ✆ 979 883 679 in the centre of this hamlet. No kitchen but the resident family offer wholesome home cooking (dinner and breakfast) and small private garden. *[Next albergue: Moratinos– 3.2 km].*

TERRADILLOS DE LOS TEMPLARIOS *(Pop. 80)* After the relative luxury of Carrión we now experience rural simplicity, thankfully bypassed by the N-120. Formerly a stronghold of the Knights Templar nothing, on a physical level, remains of this noble Order but its spirit lives on in the place name and that of the stream *arroyo de Templarios* that separates it from the next village that, like Villalcázar de Sirga, also had historical links with the Templars. Jacques de Molay was the last Grand master of the Order. The simple red brick parish church is dedicated to San Pedro and houses an unusual 13th century crucifix. This year (June–Sept.) the Cathedral Chaplaincy will welcome pilgrims during the day followed by Pilgrims' Mass in the evening (also in Maratinos). Terradillos de los Templarios approximates to the halfway point between St. Jean de Pied de Port and Santiago de Compostela.

❏ **Something opens our wings. Something makes boredom and hurt disappear. Someone fills the cup in front of us. We taste only sacredness.** *Rumi*

18   **378.3** km (235.1 ml) – Santiago de Compostela

TERRADILLOS de los Templarios *(Palencia)* **via SAHAGÚN** *(León)*
❶ **BERCIANOS del Real Camino** ❷ **CALZADILLA de los Hermanillos**

⋅⋅⋅⋅⋅⋅⋅⋅⋅⋅⋅	--- ---	19.6	--- ---	83%
▬▬▬	--- ---	3.7	--- ---	16%
▬▬▬	--- ---	0.2	--- ---	01%
Total km		23.5	km	(14.6 ml)

◣   --- ---   23.5 km (+ 0 m)
Alto ◣   Terradillos 880m (2,890 ft)
< Ⓐ 🅷 >   Moratinos **3.2** km – San Nicolás **6.0** km – Sahagún **13.0** km – Calzada del Coto **18.2** km.

❏ **The Practical Path:** Many pilgrims stopover in Sahagún, a town full of ancient monuments. If you stay the night the next logical step is to El Burgo Ranero (a further 17.9 km) – both towns have a wide choice of accommodation. The alternative is to visit Sahagún and possibly stop for lunch on your way to Calzadilla de los Hermanillos. ❶ *Real Camino Frances 23.5 km* the most popular route by gravel path *senda* now with shade alongside quiet road parallel to the autopista. Option ❷ *Via Romana 26.7 km* almost the entire is by wide earth tracks across remote bush country so take water, especially for the section from Calzada de Coto.

❏ **The Mystical Path:** Yesterday we sought to forgive another and to see past any apparent attack...to the cry for help that it disguised. Perhaps when we look past error we will witness our own innocence. Will we look for mundanity or divinity in our fellow traveller? What will fill our cup today? Will we drink the pure waters that flow from the scallop shell at the pilgrim fountain and taste only sacredness?

❏ **Personal Reflections:** *"... The evening light was painting the countryside pure pink. I stopped to rest awhile and to absorb the warmth of the colours. It was not until I slaked my thirst from the pilgrim fountain that I noticed him. He stood 100 metres from me and yet I could see every facet of his wrinkled face. He wore a smile of such unconditional love that I became enraptured by the embrace. Surrounded by his flock of quietly grazing sheep, this shepherd held the focal point of a biblical picture of such sublime proportions and colours, that I was momentarily transported to an overwhelming sense of pure bliss... While leaning on his crook, he raised his hand slowly to greet and bless me. Tears rolled down my cheeks in a flood of joy. No words passed between us and none are able to convey the sense of total love and acceptance I felt from this stranger who yet seemed so familiar. My heart began to ache with the unfamiliar intensity of this greeting. My hands spontaneously went to my longing heart. Namasté, I whispered, 'When the God in me greets the God in you, in that, we are One'..."*

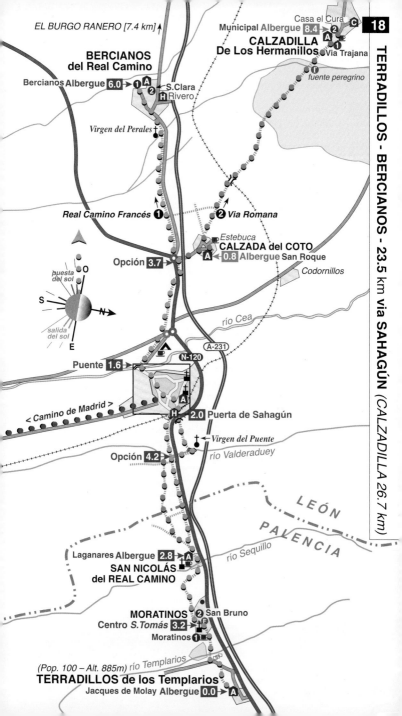

18

EL BURGO RANERO [7.4 km] ↑

Casa el Cura

Municipal **Albergue** 8.4

CALZADILLA
De Los Hermanillos • Vía Trajana

BERCIANOS
del Real Camino

Bercianos **Albergue** 6.0

S.Clara
Rivero

fuente peregrino

Virgen del Perales †

Real Camino Francés ❶

❷ *Vía Romana*

Estebuca
CALZADA del COTO

Opción 3.7

0.8 **Albergue** San Roque

Codornillos

puesta
del sol O

S

N

salida
del sol E

río Cea

Puente 1.6

(A-231)

(N-120)

< Camino de Madrid >

H 2.0 **Puerta de Sahagún**

† ← *Virgen del Puente*

Opción 4.2

río Valderaduey

L E Ó N

P A L E N C I A

río Sequillo

Laganares **Albergue** 2.8

SAN NICOLÁS
del REAL CAMINO

MORATINOS ❷ San Bruno

Centro *S.Tomás* 3.2

Moratinos ❶

(Pop. 100 – Alt. 885m) río Templarios
TERRADILLOS de los Templarios
Jacques de Molay **Albergue** 0.0

`0.0 km` **Terradillos de Los Templarios** from albergue ➋ **Jacques de Molay** proceed out of the village onto earth track and continue over the arroyo Templarios <left on country road (by solar panels) and right> onto track with a line of poplar trees passing shaded rest area (site of the medieval village of Villaoreja) into:

`3.2 km` **Moratinos** *(Pop.30) Alb.*➊ **Moratinos** *Priv.[10÷2]+* €10 ⓒ 979 061 466 c/ Real at entrance. S/o past the parish church dedicated to St. Thomas with shaded porch and pilgrim mass (summer). *[F.]* and *Alb.* ➋ **San Bruno** *Asoc.[16÷2]+* €7-9 ⓒ 979 061 465 c/ Ontanón with large garden and menú. Also *Bodegas El Castillo* with menú. Continue onto pleasant gravel track (away from the N-120) all the way into:

`2.8 km` **San Nicolás del Real Camino** restaurante *Casa Barrunta* (right 100m) *Alb.* **Laganares** *Priv.*[20÷4]+* €9–€30 ⓒ 979 188 142 network* hostel adj. the church in the village square with bar and restaurant. Refurbished using the traditional local mud and straw method in this peaceful village linked to the Templar Order. The parish church *Iglesia de San Nicolás Obispo* (its humble exterior also serving as a pelota court!) disguises a fine Baroque altarpiece. At the far end of the village is a shaded picnic spot and water font *[F.]* The route now turns right to follow a gravel senda alongside the N-120. *[An old route* ● ● ● ● *(now faded waymarks) veers up left and winds it way back to the N-120 at option point].*

PROVINCIA DE LEÓN: A population of 495,000 (515,000 a decade ago) part of the Autonomous region of Castille y León and offering the most varied terrain on the camino. We start off with a continuation of the now familiar *Tierra de Campos* with its flat and well-irrigated agricultural land. The adobe walls of the villages, bright red in the intense Leónese sun, rise up to greet us out of the flat plains. Then we enter the busy and sophisticated style of the capital of León itself. Artisans, museums, restaurants, hotels and shops all compete for our attention. León is famous for its pork products – cured hams, chorizos and morcilla and the local cheese and quince jelly *queso con membrillo.*

Later on we enter the *Maragatería* and the *Montes de León* (between Astorga and Molinaseca) where we experience the remnants of Maragato culture in the distinctive dress and cuisine of this mountainous region. The pastries *mantecadas* are worth sampling and the hills provide game with trout from the streams. The obscure origins of the Maragatos may date back to the 7th century when King Mauregato and his followers became isolated in this remote area during the Arab invasions. Today the isolationism continues in the abandoned villages of the mountains, such as Foncebadón. Beyond Ponferrada we enter the magic of the Bierzo with its gently rolling hills and vineyards. In the spring, you can see the white of the cherry blossom, in the autumn the bright red of its fruit and, in between, every shade of green. Eat of its sun ripened fruits and drink of its wines and the friendliness of its people. Windswept Galicia lies beyond.

4.2 km Rio Valderaduey *[● ● ● ● option to continue along the main road by senda directly into Sahagún].* For the recommended route cross the N-120 [!] along
the river to the tranquil (excepting April
25th when a local pilgrimage *romería*
takes place here) hermitage of Our Lady
of the Bridge *Ermita Virgen del Puente
XIIthC* an unpretentious sanctuary with
Romanesque foundations but the original
pilgrim hospice has long gone. The tiny
Mudéjar-style chapel occupies a cool and
shady poplar grove by the river. Past the
grandiose gateway *centro geográfico del*

camino (dependiendo!) up to Sahagún under the N-120 past the grain silos to:

2.0 km Sahagún *entrada Hs***Puerto de Sahagún* pilgrim price €25 and menú.
[Note: It is 1.6 km to the town exit]. Continue over road. *(right 200m to): Alb.* ❶
Domus Viatoris *Priv.*[50÷1]+ €7+€30 © 987 780 975 Travesía del Arco with all
facilities. S/o past bullring and over railway bridge (station left) and turn right> to:
❷ **Cluny** *Muni.[64÷1]* €5 © 987 782 117 central hostel with 64 bunks in cubicles
of 6 on the upper floor of the *iglesia de la Trinidad* with tourist office and exhibition
space on the ground floor - pilgrim statue at entrance. At the other end of town
(on the way out) is: ❸ **Monasterio de Santa Cruz** *(Madres Benedictinas) Conv.
[16÷4]*+ €8 single occupancy from €25. © 987 781 139 c/ Nicolas, 40. Immaculate
rooms maintained by the voluntary hospitaleras from the Madrid association.
Facilities incl. kitchenette and use of courtyard with an air of tranquillity. Dinner
available. *[Next alb.: Calzada del Coto – 5.2 km].*

SAHAGÚN: *(pop: 2,800 – alt. 820m)*
seat of great ecclesiastical power, largely
courtesy of the influence of Alfonso VI
who, along with his various wives, is
buried in the Benedictine *convento de
Santa Cruz.* Owing to the lack of stone
for building purposes many of the grand
edifices were constructed with brick and,
accordingly, many have disappeared.

Little remains of the famous abbey of San Benito founded in the 10th century
and rose to become one of the most important Benedictine monasteries in Spain.
Charlemagne was also linked with the town which, from these earliest times, has
given shelter to the pilgrims on their way to Santiago de Compostela; so we follow
illustrious footsteps. Monasteries, churches and pilgrim hospices abounded. The
foundations of the town however extend much further back to its Roman past. It
was here that Saint Facundo was martyred which gave rise to a monastery bearing
his name as early as the 9th century. Despite Arab invasions and counter attacks that
destroyed the monastery on several occasions, it was ultimately the loss of interest
in things religious that finally reduced it to the rubble that now lies to the west of
the town. However, the martyr lives on in the name Sahagún itself, a derivation
of Sanctum Facundum, whose remains lie buried in the church of St. John along
with fellow martyr Primitivo. Despite decaying edifices you will not be at a loss for
religious buildings and art to admire. If you follow the *blue* detour route shown on
the town map you will pass the following:

❶ *Iglesia de la Trinidad XIII–XVII[th]C* (municipal albergue + Turismo). ❷ *Iglesia San Juan XVII[th]C* (tombs of San Facundo y Primitivo) Baroque Church just past albergue [2] with a sculpture of the town's patron saint *San Facundo*. Continuing down c/del Arco into Plaza San Lorenzo and its outstanding ❸ *Iglesia San Lorenzo XII[th]C* a fine example of the brick Mudejar style and whose prominent tower is a good landmark. From here it is a short walk to the Plaza Mayor where you can refresh yourself in its array of cafés and bars and admire its handsome Town Hall *Ayuntamiento*.

Exit via c/Flora Florez (the narrow street behind the bandstand) and turn sharp right> down c/San Benito into Plaza Lesmes Franco and turn <left to Plaza de San Tirso where the distinctive 12th century tower of Iglesia de San Tirso leads to the first church to use brick in its construction and credited with starting the craze for the Mudejar style in the area ❹ *Iglesia San Tirso (Mudejar – ruins)*. Adjoining is Parque San Benito and the ruins of the monastery of that name which  became one of the most powerful in Spain leading, inevitably, to its downfall. We now have an opportunity to walk under its impressive ❺ *Arco San Benito* adj. *Monasterio y Museo de Santa Cruz* (Madres Benedictinas) with tomb of Alphonso VI and *museo* which houses the beautiful statue of the Virgin dressed as a pilgrim which originally adorned the church of the *Monasterio de la Peregrina* whose crumbling brick walls and Moorish arches are situated on the outskirts of town ❻ *Iglesia Señora La Peregrina XV[th]C* formerly a Franciscan convent (past Escolar Fray Bernardino c/San Francisco on the rise ahead).

❏ *Turismo:* Iglesia de la Trinidad C/ del Arco ✆ 987 782 117. *Hoteles: Hs[**] La Cordoniz* €40 ✆ 987 780 276 c/ del Arco opp. Turismo. *Hs[*] La Bastide Du Chemin* €28 ✆ 987 781 183 c/ del Arco, 66. *Hs[**]Alfonso VI* €30 ✆ 987 781 144 c/Nicolás, 4. *P La Asturiana* ✆ 987 780 073 Plaza de Lemses Franco, 2. *Hs Don Pacho* ✆ 987 780 775 Av. Constitución, 84. *Hs[*] El Ruedo II* ✆ 987 781 834 Plaza Mayor, 1. *Hs[*] Escarcha* ✆ 987 781 856 c/Regina Franco, 12. *P Los Balcones del Camino* €30 ✆ 676 838 242 c/ Juan Guaza 2 (Av. Constitución 53).

Note [1]: If you want to view the interior of *all* the above sites you will need to stay the night. Otherwise, allow extra time to walk around them but don't leave Sahagún at such a late hour that you end up, unintentionally, short of your planned destination. **[2]:** If you are continuing on the **alternative scenic route** (less travelled but little shade) to Calzadilla de los Hermanillos it is advisable to have a meal in Sahagún or buy supplies for the journey ahead. **[3]:** Not particularly recommended (unless you have specific interest) are 2 detours on the camino from Madrid that joins here in Sahagún. **Detour [a]** (5 km south of Sahagún on the LE-941) is a gem of a national monument, the Romanesque monastery of *San Pedro de las Dueñas* where the Benedictine Mothers operate another hospedería adjacent to the 12th century church with its impressive crucifix. **Detour [b]** 8 km south on the C-611 are the sweeping walls of the monumental castle and palace at *Grajal de Campos* birthplace of legendary knights and scene of epic battles.

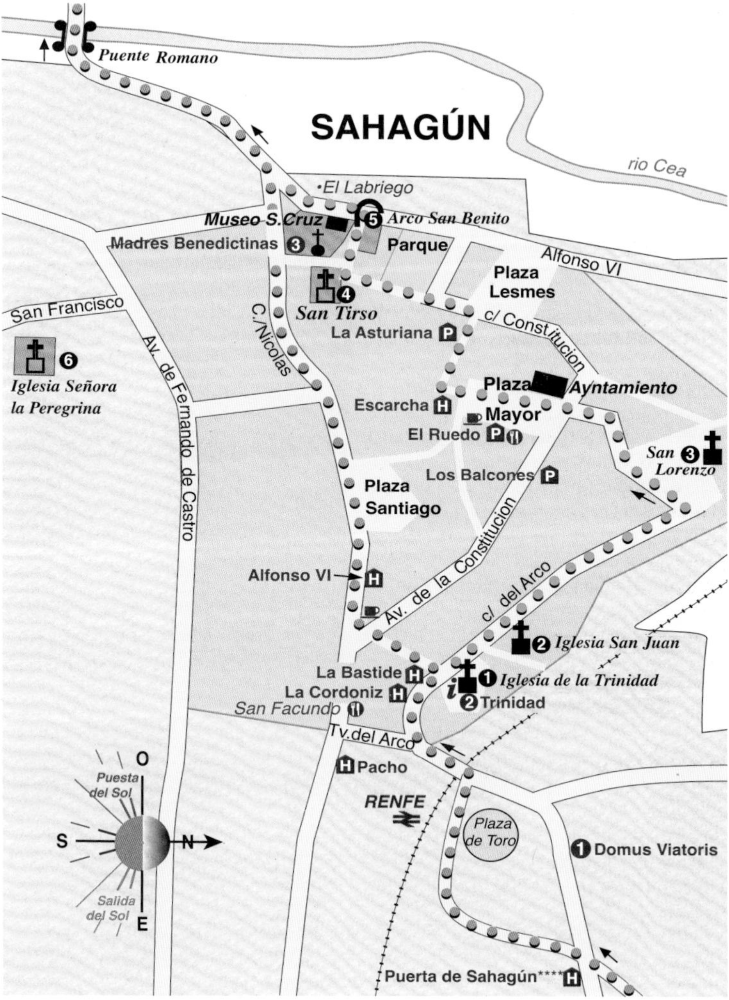
Puente Romano
SAHAGÚN
rio Cea
El Labriego
Museo S.Cruz
5 Arco San Benito
Madres Benedictinas 3
Parque
Alfonso VI
Plaza Lesmes
4 San Tirso
c/ Constitucion
San Francisco
C/Nicolas
La Asturiana
6 Iglesia Señora la Peregrina
Av. de Fernando de Castro
Plaza Ayntamiento Mayor
Escarcha
El Ruedo
San 3 Lorenzo
Los Balcones
Plaza Santiago
Av. de la Constitucion
c/ del Arco
Alfonso VI
2 Iglesia San Juan
La Bastide
La Cordoniz
1 Iglesia de la Trinidad
2 Trinidad
San Facundo
Tv.del Arco
Pacho
O
Puesta del Sol
RENFE
S
N
Plaza de Toro
1 Domus Viatoris
Salida del Sol
E
Puerta de Sahagún****

For the waymarked route through town head into c/Antonio Nicolas at junction by *Café Asturcon* down into the unimpressive Plaza de Santiago to the next crossroads by *El Labriego* and down to:

1.6 km **Puente Canto** (1.6 km from Sahagún entrance) historic stone bridge (originally Roman but reconstructed in the 11th and 16th centuries) its five strong arches have stood the test of time and the powerful waters of the river Cea. Continue on senda with shade from the poplar grove otherwise known as *The copse of Charlemagne's lances* where legend has it that the lances of his troops turned into saplings after they had been planted in the earth here; an ominous sign to the forthcoming battle with the Moors which was to litter the area with corpses.

Continue out past *Camping Pedro Ponce / café* and municipal sports grounds s/o on past first roundabout to cross over [!] N-120 to 2nd rounabout and option:

3.7 km Opción [?] junction of N-120 and A-231. **For main route ❶** ● ● ● ● the Royal French Way **Real Camino Francés** stay on this (left) side of the bridge and continue down to the gravel senda alongside a quiet country road now with shade parallel to the autopista. Under **bridge [2.8 km]** past the simple brick hermitage of Our Lady of the Pears *Ermita de Nuestra de Perales XI[th]C* **[1.2 km]** *[which formed part of the Hospital of O Cebreiro and is scene of an annual pilgrimage on 8th September]*. The *senda* continues past *[F.]* into Bercianos crossroads **[1.4 km]**. Here on the right **[a]** *Hs* **Rivero** €28 © 987 744 287 with bar and restaurant. **[b]** s/o up c/ Mayor for *Alb* ❷ **Santa Clara** *Priv.[10÷2]*+ €10+ €35 Rosa Fures © 605 839 993 located down side street towards the village exit c/ Iglesia, 3 near Plaza Mesón. Or **[c]** turn left into c/S. Roque and up into c/San Salvador to:

6.0 km Bercianos *del Real Camino Alb.* ❶ **Bercianos** ♥ *Par.[46÷6]* €-donativo © 987 784 008 (photo right) communal meal and inclusive evening prayers are offered in the quiet room set aside for contemplation. There is an inconspicuous shop near to the hostel. *[Next albergue El Burgo Raneros – 7.4 km]*.

Bercianos del Real Camino (Pop. 200 – Alt. 860m) derives its name from the settlement of the town with citizens from the Bierzo in 955.

For the remote **alternative scenic route ❷** ● ● ● ● via the original Roman road *Via Romana (Trajana)* proceed right> over the motorway into Calzada de Coto.

0.8 km Calzada del Coto *Albergue* **San Roque** *Muni.[36÷2]* €-donativo © 674 587 001 on c/Real down right of the entrance past the pelota court and children's play area. The town has few facilities but *bar Estebuca* welcomes thirsty pilgrims and is tucked away behind the church and town hall (+200m).

Continue through the town via c/Mayor, past the parish church of San Esteban and out onto the *Via Romana* on the western outskirts of the town **[0.5 km]** where you pick up the earth track *[it is possible here to rejoin the camino francés by taking the left hand track – signposted]*. Waymarks are few but you head s/o for the railway bridge on the horizon and cross over **[1.8 km]**. Continue on the earth track that winds its way though scrubland in the area of the remote farm *Dehesa de Valdelocajos* **[3.1 km]**. There is nothing to disturb the wilderness except the occasional shepherd grazing his flock and a few sporadic metal camino signposts with their inane cartoon character. Even the game hunters appear to have taken offence at these signs, as evidenced by the lead shot that has been fired at them. We pass a remote country lodge (right) to arrive at a shallow valley with the village of Hermanillos in the distance and *[F.]* pilgrim fountain *fuente del peregrino* **[1.1 km]** in a shaded rest area in a poplar grove by an old riverbed. Continue for the final leg **[1.9 km]** into:

8.4 km Calzadilla de los Hermanillos *Albergue* ❶ **Via Trajana** *Priv.[20÷5]*+ €15–€35 © 987 337 610 on c/Mayor (right) with popular restaurant and bar *menú* *peregrino*. 100m beyond (left) *Alb.* ❷ **Calzadilla** *Muni.[22÷2]* €-donativo Ⓒ 987 330 023 in former school building (part of the El Burgo Ranero municipality). **Other Lodging:** Welcoming *HR***°**Casa El Cura** €38-80 Ⓒ 987 337 647 c/La Carratera 13 on the northern outskirts with variety of rooms and restaurant and welcoming owners, English spoken. *[Next albergues on route* ❶ *El Burgo Ranero 6.5 km from Calzada (3.1 km off route) Reliegos 17.4 km (1.0 km off route)].*

In days long gone by the monks *Little Brothers of the Road / Calzadilla de los Hermanillos* welcomed pilgrims here but the hospitality is still felt especially in *Comedor Via Trajana* and *El Cura* that cater for weary pilgrims. There is a small inconspicuous shop behind the pelota court and a health clinic off the main street. 2 smokey bars make up the other facilities. The parish church is dedicated to St. Bartholomew where there is an impressive statue of him overpowering the devil. The chapel of Our Lady of Sorrows *Ermita Nuestra Señora de los Dolores* is located on the main street and is much venerated in the area.

REFLECTIONS:

_____
_____
_____
_____
_____
_____
_____
_____
_____
_____
_____
_____
_____
_____
_____
_____
_____
_____
_____
_____

Real Camino ❶
Francés

Via Romana ❷

❒ **Silence is golden.**

19 354.8 km (220.5 ml) – Santiago

BERCIANOS — MANSILLA
del Real Camino   de las Mulas

⅏⅏⅏⅏	--- ---	23.1	--- ---	87%
────	--- ---	3.6	--- ---	13%
────	--- ---	0.0	--- ---	0%
Total km		**26.7** km	(16.7 ml)	

▰▰	--- ---	26.7 km (+ 0 m)

Alto ▲ El Burgo Ranero 880m
< Ⓐ ⒣ > El Burgo Ranero **7.4** km – Reliegos **20.5** km.

BERCIANOS 850m   El Burgo Ranero
900m   ▪Calzadilla   Reliegos
800m - - - - - - - - - - - - - - - - río Valdecasa - MANSILLA
                                             río Valdearco
00 km   5 km   10 km   15 km   20 km   25 km

❒ **The Practical Path:** The *Real Camino Francés* ❶ ● ● ● ● has mellowed with age and the trees alongside the senda have matured and provide some shade. The monotony is relieved by several small streams, mostly dry in summer. Pilgrims on the *Calzada Romana* ❷ ● ● ● ● will encounter no asphalt, no sendas, no houses but also no water and little shade apart from the few rivers that crisscross this tranquil landscape – so bring food and water to fortify you along this remote path. Classified as the longest extant stretch of Roman road left in Spain today, we follow in the footsteps of Emperor Augustus himself! *[Note: A good option is to access facilities in Reliegos and continue into Mansilla on the main from there].*

❒ **The Mystical Path:** Only the weeds and wild flowers have changed in the two millennia since this path was laid. While Roman artefacts lie behind glass cages in dislocated museums, here we walk on the original foundations. The muted silence of museums, broken by the giggles of tour parties, are nothing to match the original setting and the golden silence of the wide prairie. Here the call of the occasional bird of prey or buzz of a bee only seems to emphasise the silence and adds to the tranquillity. The bee transforms the pollen to golden nectar. Will the alchemist in you extract the purest gold from this day?

❒ **Personal Reflections:** *"… In my exhaustion I missed the hostel on the way into the village. A group of children appeared and started to dance around me shouting and waving. They evidently did not know of my need for quiet at the end of a long day. What an unreasonable expectation of mine. A few minutes later I saw their enthusiasm in a different light, as an excuse to access the albergue and empty the donation box, which they did with alacrity. Why did I assume it would go into their pockets and not to the hospitalero or parish priest? I am still so quick to judge and condemn others. Perhaps it is a reflection of my own dishonesty. But it takes only an instant to change an unloving thought to a loving one – What, then, is this process? Is it just intention? Can it be that I simply see what I choose to see? What did the shepherd see in me? What did Christ see in the thief crucified alongside him? …"*

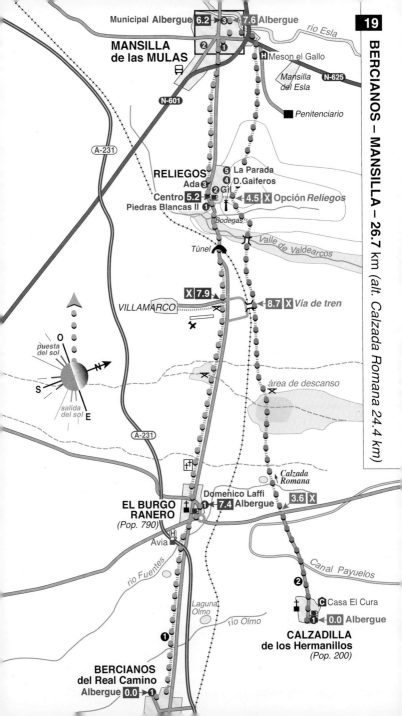

río Esla

Municipal Albergue **6.2** → **3** **7.6** Albergue

**MANSILLA
de las MULAS**

2 **1**

H Meson el Gallo

Mansilla
del Esla

N-625

N-601

A-231

Penitenciario

RELIEGOS
Ada **3**

5 La Parada
4 D.Gaiferos

Centro **5.2**
Piedras Blancas II **1**

2 Gil

4.5 X Opción *Reliegos*

Bodegas

Valle de Valdearcos

Túnel

X 7.9

VILLAMARCO

8.7 X Vía de tren

O
*puesta
del sol*

S

E
*salida
del sol*

A-231

área de descanso

*Calzada
Romana*

Domenico Laffi
1 ← **7.4** Albergue

3.6 X

**EL BURGO
RANERO**
(Pop. 790)

Avia H

río Fuentes

Canal Payuelos

2

C Casa El Cura

*Laguna
Olmo*

río Olmo

1

1 **0.0** Albergue

**CALZADILLA
de los Hermanillos**
(Pop. 200)

1

**BERCIANOS
del Real Camino**
Albergue **0.0** → **1**

0.0 km Bercianos from *Albergue* ❶ pick up the *senda* on the western edge of the village passing wetland reserve Laguna Olmo (right) out under autopista to pick up the asphalt road into El Burgo Raneros. Head **[a]** s/o down c/Real or **[b]** veer right *[The road to the right off the roundabout leads to the Via Romana – 3.1 km]* to:

7.4 km **El Burgo Ranero** *(Pop. 250) Alb.* ❶
Domenico Laffi *Asoc.[28÷4]* €-*donativo* ℰ 987
330 023 municipal hostel dedicated to the 17[th]c.
Italian pilgrim and located at the edge of the town
on c/Fray Pedro. Good facilities and attractive
hostel built in the adobe style of the area using
mud and straw. Opposite is: ❷ **El Nogal** *Asoc.*
[30÷8] €7-10 ℰ 627 229 331 and 100m further
out: ❸ **La Laguna** *Priv.[18÷1]+* €9-25 ℰ 987
330 094 c/La Laguna part of *Piedras Blancas.*
[Next albergue: Reliegos – 11.4 km.]Other lodging: Hs **el Peregrino** €30 ℰ 987
330 069 with cafe and the adj. Hs **Piedras Blancas** €30 ℰ 987 330 094. Try *Cafe*
El Camino (Paella!) ℰ 674 58 39 47 c/ Real 53. *[½ km south is Avia motorway*
services with restaurant and H **Castillo El Burgo** ℰ 987 330 403 *rooms from €35].*
From El Burgo Ranero continue out onto the *senda* passing the town cemetery and
several picnic sites amongst trees by the rivulets *arroyos* (dry in the summer) past
the aerodrome at crossroads:

7.9 km **Cruce** *Villarmarco* Villarmarco (left) railway / *Calzada Romana (right).*
A display of agricultural equipment lines the path into Villarmarco but otherwise no
facilities. Continue along senda under railway tunnel over river with picnic site and
up to high point before descending past a series of *bodegas* built into the surrounding
hillocks into:

5.2 km **Reliegos** *(Pop. 200 – Alt. 830m) on* main road *Alb.* ❶ Piedras Blancas II
Priv.[8÷2]+ €9–€45 ℰ 607 163 982. Veer right for*Bar Gil II* and village centre for
trendy *Bar Elvis / La Torre (Sinín) [F.]* adj. ❷ **Gil** *Priv.[12÷2]* ℰ 987 317 804 with bar.
On the main street is newly renovated ❸ **Ada** ♥ *V. Priv.[20÷2]+* €7 Vegetarian menú
€8 ℰ 691 153 010 (Pedro) + *Sala de meditación* c/ Real 42. Further back +400m ❹
D.Gaiferos *Muni.[45÷2]* €5 ℰ 987 317 801 former school building on c/Escuela adj.
❺ **La Parada** *Priv.[36÷7]+* €7 €30 ℰ 987 317 880 with bar and restaurant.

Continue down c/ Real and pick up the *senda* at pelota court *[F.]* passing rest area
by **factory [3.8 km]** (shade no water) s/o over **N-601 [1.3 km]** and over canal to the
main crossroads in **Mansilla de las Mulas cruce [0.7 km]**. *Albergue* ❶ **El Jardín del
Camino** *Priv.[32÷2]+* €8–€10 +Priv ℰ 987 310 232 c/Camino de Santiago 1. Good
facilities and cafe with pilgrim menú. The latest albergue is now up to the left off the
main road to Valladolid: ❷ **Gaia** ♥ *Priv.[18÷2]* €5 ℰ 987 310 308 m: 699 911 311
(Carols y Marisa) Av. Constitución 28.

Cross the main road and enter the town through the medieval gate *Puerta Castillo*
(only the walls remain) up c/Santa María (where the alternative route from Calzadilla
joins from the right) *Plaza del Pozo* (left). Continue s/o into c/del Puente to **[0.4 km]**:

6.2 km **Mansilla de las Mulas** *Centro Alb.* ❸ **Centro** *Muni.[76÷8]* €5 ℰ 661 977
305 centrally located on c/del Puente, 5 where *Laura* and a team of volunteers has
been welcoming pilgrims for many years. The hostel is actually several buildings
grouped together around a central patio where pilgrims eat, drink or just hang out.

❶: Original Roman road *Via Romana (Via Trajana).* ● ● ● ●

`0.0 km` Calzadilla de los Hermanillos From the albergue(s) proceed out the village onto a flat plateau of wheat and cereal crops to cross over irrigation canal to:

`3.6 km` Cruce (El Burgo Ranero left on alternative route 3.1 km). We now leave the asphalt s/o along the *Calzada Romana* for 19.4 km of uninterrupted (but uneven) track although the last section has recently been covered with gravel suggesting future 'improvements.'

[This stretch of Roman road is part of the east/west highway built to link the gold mines of Gallaecia to Rome via Astorga *Asturica Augusta and used by Ceasar Augustus in his campaigns against the Cantabrians; also referred to as Via Trajana being the spur that connected the route to Bordeaux. It was subsequently used by the armies of Islam and Christianity including Charlemagne in their battles for supremacy over the Iberian peninsular. After the re-conquest it became known as Calzada de los Peregrinos; known and loved today as the Camino de Santiago].*

On our right (northern) horizon are the Cordillera Cantábrica, an extension of the Pyrenees, and just visible beyond (on a clear day) are the Picos de Europa with the highest peak at 2,648m (8,687 feet). The track leads to wetlands around the meandering *arroyo Solana* where a plantation of pine struggles to establish itself in the bleak landscape and a covered rest area *área de descanso* (right). The track now takes a wide curve towards the railway line and remote crossing and halt (disused):

`8.7 km` Cruce *Via de tren / Paso de Villarmarco* level crossing to the village of Villarmarco just visible on the horizon. Stay this side of the tracks and continue over several shallow riverbeds and we encounter a more pronounced river valley with a grove of poplars offering shade if a rest or picnic is needed. A new concrete bridge over the *arroyo Valle de Valdearcos* has removed the need for pilgrims to ford the river and the path now climbs gently through scrubland past information board on the construction of *Calzada Romana.* We cross a new canal cutting up to the high point of this day's stage and option:

`4.5 km` Cruce *Opción* (Alto 920m): At this point we can continue s/o past the radio mast and join the alternative route in Reliegos which is now only 1 kilometre and which has several bars and albergues (see alternative route for details) or [2] turn right> and start the long descent into the río Esla valley towards Mansilla de las Mulas just visible on the horizon. Continue down the wide gravel track passing road (right) to prison compound *Cárcel de León / Penitenciario)* to junction with N-625 and *Hs* El Gallo ✆ 987 310 359 (right).

Cross over N-625 and continue <left on path on far side past football ground and bordello *Bahillo* down under the town bypass into Paseo del Esla past the water tower and town cemetery through the only remaining medieval city gate still in existence **Arco de Santa María [1.3** km] s/o up c/de la Concepción passing the *Hs* **Alberguería del Camino** (left) and parish church of Santa María (with pilgrim statue) to turn right> into Plaza del Pozo with town hall and into c/del Puente and on our (left) **[0.4** km]:

`7.6 km` Mansilla de las Mulas *Albergue Centro.*

MANSILLA DE LAS MULAS: *(pop: 1,900 – alt. 805 m)*. An important pilgrim halt today, no less than in its illustrious medieval past, which sheltered pilgrims in 3 separate pilgrim *hospitales* (long disappeared). This was and remains the meeting place for the two converging routes, the *Real Camino Francés* which enters the old quarter via the east gate *Puerta de Castillo* (only the wall remains) and the *Calzada Romana* that enters via the north gate *Arco de S. María*.

The name of this interesting town is derived from *Mano en Silla* (hand on the saddle) that also defines the town's coat of arms. The addition of *de las mulas* (of the mules) most likely refers to the town's earlier prominence as a livestock market. Whatever about its agricultural roots, the medieval wall (12th century) still protects the town from the encroachment of modernity. The best preserved section is by the bridge. Take time to wander the meandering streets and admire the architectural layout and buildings around Plazas del Grano and Leña or just watch the trout jumping for the evening fly as the sun sets over the río Esla… or join them and take a swim from the sandy shore accessed by a footbridge towards *el camping*.

❏ *Turismo* © 987 310 012 Plaza del Pozo (summer). **Hostales (centro):** *Hs*° **El Puente** €35 © 987 310 075 with restaurant and access on main street c/Mesones. *Hs*°°°**Alberguería del Camino** €38+ © 987 311 193 c/Concepción 12. *(Outside walls):* *P*° **Blanca** €25-€65 © 626 003 177 Av. Picos de Europa 4 (behind Café Fábrica). *Hs*° **San Martín** €20+ © 987 310 094 Av. Picos de Europa 32 (near bypass). The town has a range of shops and variety of bars and restaurants (most offer a pilgrim menu). For a special atmosphere try *bar/restaurante La Curiosa* near Plaza del Grano or the lively *café Alonso* on plaza del Pozo.

A museum *Museo Etnográfico* is located on c/ Agustín in the finely restored Convento de San Agustín (photo right) 10:00-14:00/16:00-19:00. Several detours are available from here (only advised if you have special interest) as follows: **Detour [1]** Over the bridge (first turning left 1.1 km) takes you through Mansilla Mayor and on to Vilaverde de Sandoval and the Romanesque *Monastery of Santa María de Sandoval XII*°*C*, an important Cistercian

monastery in its day but now de-consecrated – 8 km round trip (or continue on to León). **Detour [2]** Over the bridge (first turning right 1.4 km) takes you via Vilafalé to *Monastery of San Miguel de Escalada XII*°*C* designated a national monument on account of its exceptional Mozarabic architecture – 25 km round trip (share a taxi?).

Forward planning for León: While it is only 18 km into León we have been on remote paths over the past few days so prepare for the slog into the city centre along the busy N-601. There is the possibility to avoid the busy (and dangerous) main road into (and out of) León by taking the bus from Mansilla direct to the city centre (€1.65). Both the route into León alongside the N-601 and out along N-120 can be wearisome. The bus depot is ½ km on the outskirts of Mansilla on the Valladolid

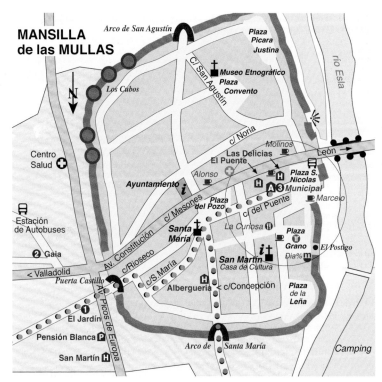

MANSILLA de las MULLAS

Arco de San Agustín

Plaza Picara Justina

río Esla

C/ San Agustín

† *Museo Etnográfico*
Plaza Convento

Los Cúbos

c/ Noria

Molinos

Centro Salud ✚

Las Delicias
El Puente

León →

Alonso

Ayuntamiento *i*

Plaza S. Nicolas
A 3 *Municipal*

Plaza del Pozo

c/ del Puente

Marcelo

La Curiosa

Estación de Autobuses

Santa María †

c/ Mesones

Plaza Grano

② Gaia

Av. Constitución

San Martín
Casa de Cultura

i†

El Postigo
Día%

< *Valladolid*

c/Rioseco

c/S María

Albergueria < *c/Concepción*

Plaza de la Leña

Puerta Castillo

❶

Picos de Europa

El Jardín

Pensión Blanca P

San Martín H

Arco de *Santa María*

Camping

road. Several bus companies vie for this lucrative route and leave every half hour or so from about 07:00. This would enable you to explore the city at leisure, stay overnight and bus it to La Virgen del Camino early again the following morning. Refreshed from your break you could pick up the recommended route via Villar de Mazarife and make it to Hospital de Órbigo (29.1 km) a pleasant town with 4 good albergues and several restaurants. *Tempted?* The majority of pilgrims will have committed to travel the whole route by foot, which is highly commendable but others have different physical and time constraints. If the idea of taking transport seems like heresy it might be useful to ask ourselves – why not? We could more than make up the distance by walking to Finisterre! The ego and its obsessive behavioural patterns can be just as limiting as a *laissez faire* attitude and indifference. What is our motivation for this journey, the intention we set out with? How does our decision to walk the entire route serve that purpose? Do you judge other pilgrims who take the bus as 'pilgrim cheats' and dishonest in some way? Can we know all the circumstances to be able to judge the actions and motivations of others? Ask yourself this question, 'is this my business, their business or God's business?' Let us walk today without judgement but with love in our hearts and an open mind... making every step a prayer for peace and acceptance.

"How would your life be different if you stopped making negative judgmental assumptions about people you encounter? Let today be the day you look for the good in everyone you meet and respect their journey." Steve Maraboli, *Life, the Truth, and Being Free.*

❏ **Here inside of me is a force that makes its own weather, winning through thickest clouds to the shining sun.** '*J.B.' His Life and Works*

20 **328.1** km (203.9 ml) – Santiago

MANSILLA de las MULAS ❸ – LEÓN ❷

▪▪▪▪▪▪▪▪▪▪▪	--- ---	10.2	--- ---	56%
━━━━━	--- ---	3.5	--- ---	20%
▬▬▬▬▬	--- ---	4.4	--- ---	24%
Total km		**18.1** km	(11.2 ml)	

◣◣◣ --- --- 18.6 km (+ 0.5 km)

Alto ▲ Alto del Portillo 890m (2,920 ft)

< 🅰 🄷 > Villarente **6.1** km – Arcahueja **10.6** km – Puente Castro **15.6** km.

900m - Alto del Portillo ▲ - - - **Puente** - *820m*
MANSILLA   **Vilarente**   **Arcahueja** 🅰   Valdelafuente ○   **Castro**   **LEÓN**
▪*800m*   🅰   🅰   ▪
           río Porma   *río Torio*

00 km   **5 km**   **10 km**   **15 km**

❏ **The Practical Path:** Apart from a brief respite along a dedicated pilgrim track around Arcahueja this stage is mostly road or *senda* that runs parallel to the busy N-601. Tourism and industrial activity, with their requirement for rapid transport, are decidedly *de rigeur*. A walking pilgrim requires nothing more than a simple path and respect for the ancient camino; both are in short supply around León. From this point you need to stay focused so as not to miss the waymarks amongst the busyness of the suburbs. The reward is the sheer magnificence of the historic heart of León city centre. An extra day would allow you time to explore its many treasures.

❏ **The Mystical Path:** What route does your heart follow today? Never mind about the outer path, what awareness is there of the inner journey – is it flat or mountainous? Never mind about the outer weather, are you aware of the inner conditions – is there sunshine or cloud? The outer is fixed, only the inner can be changed at will. "*It is not what life does to you that is important – but what you do with what life does to you that really matters.*"

❏ **Personal Reflections:** "*… The rain was heavy and persistent, drenching my papers every time I tried to take notes. I followed the sign by the consultorio and shortly afterwards realised the only way forward was across a deep trench. Too lazy to return and not realising the depth of the ditch I slithered down the steep bank and found myself waist deep in cold, grey water. I started to curse out loud, the offending expletives borne away on an unusually stiff wind. Old regretting patterns started to emerge and by grace, not will, I came to the sudden realisation that I created my own weather. I started to smile, cleansing my dark thoughts in the ripples of laughter that bubbled up from somewhere deep inside …*"

0.0 km **Mansilla de las Mulas** from albergue ❸ proceed out over the río Esla and onto the *senda* that runs parallel to the main road passing turn-off (right) Vilafalé-**San Miguel** and Mansilla Mayor / **Sandoval** (left) **[1.5 km]**. Pass café/petrol station **Agip [1.8** km] on far side or road behind which is the ancient hill fortress of Lancia.

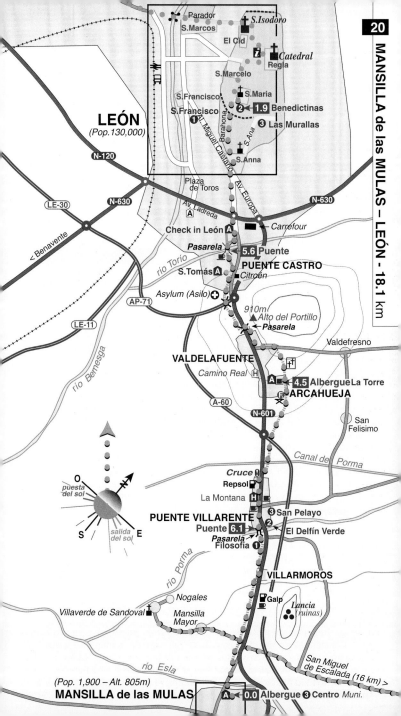

Parador
S.Marcos
† S.Isodoro
El Cid
Catedral
Regla

S.Marcelo
■ S.Maria
LEÓN
(Pop.130,000)
S.Francisco
2 **1.9** Benedictinas
S.Francisco **1**
3 Las Murallas
S.Ana
S.Anna

N-120

LE-30
N-630

< Benavente

Plaza de Toros
Av. Ladreda
Check in León A
■ *Carrefour*
N-630

Pasarela
5.6 Puente
PUENTE CASTRO
río Torío
S.Tomás A
■ *Citroën*

AP-71
Asylum (Asilo) ✚
☆
910m
▲ Alto del Portillo
Pasarela

LE-11
Valdefresno
VALDELAFUENTE
Camino Real **H**
A ■ **4.5** Albergue La Torre
río Bernesga
ARCAHUEJA

A-60
San Felisimo
N-601

Canal del Porma

Cruce
Repsol ■
La Montana **H** ■
3 San Pelayo
PUENTE VILLARENTE
2
Puente **6.1**
El Delfín Verde
Pasarela
Filosofía **1**

O
puesta del sol
S
salida del sol
E

VILLARMOROS

río Porma
■ *Galp*
Lancia (ruinas)
Nogales
Villaverde de Sandoval †
Mansilla Mayor

río Esla
San Miguel de Escalada (16 km) >

(Pop. 1,900 – Alt. 805m)
MANSILLA de las MULAS
A ■ **0.0** Albergue **3** Centro *Muni.*

[Here the indigenous Asturians, despite their heroic defence, met their demise at the hands of the Roman legions. Artefacts have also been recovered from the Neolithic period and excavations are on-going and compete with excavations for the motorway]. Continue over the río Moro into **Villarmoros** [**1.1** km] on the N-601 [!]. with Iglesia de San Esteban. Continue back onto senda passing *Alb.* **Filosofía** *Priv. [10÷1]*+ €8 +€15 ✆ 602 073 335 (formerly Casa Blanca).and just before the road bridge over the río Porma a new *pasarela* [**1.5** km] provides some respite from the traffic and gives a view of the 'Giant' bridge *Puente Ingente* so called on account of its 20-arch span. Continue up into **Villarente** [**0.2** km]:

6.1 km **Villarente** shaded rest area down by the river. *[The first building (left) was a medieval pilgrim hospital which operated a donkey ambulance for sick pilgrims into León]* while (right) *Alb.* ❶ **El Delfín Verde** *Priv.[30]* ✆ 987 312 065 visible with gaudy signage. Continue on main road and turn off right 50m into c/El Romero and follow signs to the popular and quieter *Alb.* ❷ **San Pelayo** *Priv.*[56÷4]*+ €8 ✆ 987 312 677 (photo right). Good facilities and all meals available (continue to end of track and turn left back to main road). Several cafés compete for the pilgrim trade along the busy N-601 also *Hs** **La Montaña** ✆ 987 312 161. Continue through this modern satellite town past the *Centro de Salud* and *gasolinera Repsol* services and cross over [!] onto dedicated pilgrim track [**1.3** km] and continue past **canal del Porma** [**0.5** km] under A-60 [**1.7** km] climbing up the gravel track past rest area *[F.]* to the top of the rise in Arcahueja [**1.0** km]:

4.5 km **Arcahueja** *[F.]* This is the last chance to take a rest in the relative quiet before we hit the city traffic. 150 metres off route (left) is the welcoming bar and *Albergue* **La Torre** *Priv.[26÷3]*+ €8 +€25 ✆ 987 205 896. No kitchen but all meals available in the bar. Continue up past *cementerio Baja* and *cementerio Alto* down to industrial park and turn left to the **Valdelafuente** [**2.5** km]. Various bars and showrooms spread along this busy section of the N-601, one of the main arterial roads into León, also modern *Hs*** **Camino Real** ✆ 987 218 134. We skirt up briefly around the side of *Alto del Portillo* before taking the new pilgrim footbridge *pasarela* over dual carriageway onto narrow path above the road to cross another *pasarela* over motorway ring road past mental asylum *Hospital Santa Isabel* back to the main road by *Caja España* on Av. Madrid and opp. bus stop by **Citroën** [**2.6** km]. 200m left on Av. de La Lastra (rear of first modern building right) *Albergue* **Santo Tomás de Canterbury** *Priv.[60÷8]* €8 ✆ 987 392 626. All facilities with bar and meals (free bike hire to visit the city or take bus 6 by Citroën to centre €1.20).

Continue past Citroën garage and veer <left off main street into c/ Victoriano Martinez (opp. Iglesia San Pedro right). Down to rest area *[F.]* and cafes in *Puente Castro* [**0.5** km].

5.6 km **Puente Castro** *[The modern buildings here disguise the fact that this was an influential Jewish district in the 12th century and site of a former Roman settlement]*. Continue via the stone footbridge over the río Torio with part of the original Roman wall (right). We now make our way up to the wide main road Alcalde Miguel Castaño and at Nº88 is: **Check in León** *Priv.[40÷2]* €10 ✆ 987 498 793. Continue to roundabout *glorieta (Tourist info.)*. Proceed over the roundabout (pedestrian crossing) merging into Av. Del Europa which we cross at a fountain into *Plaza de Santa Ana* [**1.4** km] small shaded park and Iglesia de Santa Ana (with statue of Santiago). Here we can calm frayed nerves and take stock ▲. For the **main route** along the historic camino into the old city with hotels and *central* albergue ❷ Continue s/o into c/Barahona through Money Gate *Puerta Moneda* [0.3 km] one of the original gateways to the medieval city (note the vast city walls as you pass) and just *before* Iglesia N. S. del Mercado (lions guarding the entrance) turn right> (easily missed!) into *c/Escurial* [0.1 km] to albergue entrance [0.1 km]:

1.9 km Centro *Albergue* ❷ S.María de Carbajal *Conv.[132÷4]* €5 ℂ 987 252 866 situated in the old city on the tranquil *Plaza Grano / Santa María del Camino*. Wonderful location and good basic facilities run by the Benedictine nuns who issue *credenciales* and maintain a degree of peace in this otherwise busy city area (excepting when the adj. school is open). Sung Vespers (19:00) and pilgrim benediction (21:30) in the convent chapel which can provide a powerful sense of the sacred and reminder of the true nature of all our journeying.

Other City Hostels: ▲ Plaza Santa Ana continue left on Av. Alcalde Miguel Castaños where at Nº4 adj. gardens *Jardin San Franciso* (opp. post office *Correos*). ❶ San Francisco de Asís *Residencia Fundación Ademar Asoc.[166÷47]* €10-18 ℂ 637 439 848 drab building owned by the Capuchin Brothers run as student and pilgrim lodging by Ademar *(handball club)*. ▲ Or proceed right into c/ Santa Ana into c/Tarifa at Nº5: ❸ Muralla Leonesa *Priv.[70÷20]* €10-€35 ℂ 987 177 873 c/ Tarifa 5. Closer to the cathedral are: ❹ *Hs* Urban Rio Cea *Priv.[8÷2]*+ €15-18+€50+ ℂ 636 946 294 c/ Legión VII, 6/ 2º (behind the old Town Hall *Ayuntamiento Viejo*). ❺ LeonHostel *Priv.[20÷6]* €12-15 ℂ 987 079 907 c/ Ancha 8 close to the Catedral. ❻ Unamuno *Priv.[86÷16]* €10-20 c/ San Pelayo, 15 ℂ 987 233 010 *residencia Universitaria Unamuno* available to pilgrims on Plaza San Pelayo (From the cathedral take c/Pablo Floréz and turn left into c/S.Pelayo).

Before turning in for the night you might visit the adjacent and atmospheric *Barrio Húmedo* ('wet quarter' as in alcohol – on account of the variety of bars that abound here!) centred around the beautiful and intimate city squares surrounding Plaza Mayor with the original 17th century Baroque Town hall or lose yourself in the maze of narrow streets that connect them. Or simply hang out in the lovely *Plaza Santa María del Camino* watched over by the cherubs who play in the central neo-classical fountain symbolising the two rivers that embrace this magical city (see photo above). Also in this square we find the 10th century Church of Our Lady of the Market *Iglesia Nuestra Señora del Mercado* (with the lions). Here you can see a statue of the Virgin, Patroness of León (some say of the camino itself). Indeed the church was formerly called Iglesia Virgen del Camino until that honour was bestowed on the sanctuary on the western suburbs, which, along with the route through the city and the main sites, is described in the next stage (p.188).

❏ *Turismo:* Plaza Regla (Cathedral Square) ✆ 987 237 082 + *Turistica Info.* Plaza S.Marcelo *Ayuntamiento Viejo*. Credencial from *Asociación de Amigos del Camino* Av. Independencia, 5º (take lift to 5th floor) ✆ 987 260 530 / 677 430 200.
❏ *Pilgrim equipment & guides: Armería Castro* c/La Rúa 7 ✆ 987 257 020.
❏ *Hotels Central €30-60:* (old quarter sequentially between albergue and cathedral): *P*˙*Sandoval*˙✆ 987 212 041 c/Hospicio, 11-2º. *H**** *Monástica Pax* ✆ 987 344 493 Plaza Grano, 11 (adj. alb.1). *H**** *Toral* ✆ 987 207 738 Cuesta de las Carbajalas. *H*˙ *Rincón del Conde* ✆ 987 849 021 Conde Rebolledo. *Hr*****La Posada Regia I & II* ✆ 987 213 173 c/Regidores, 9. *H**** *París* ✆ 987 238 600 c/Ancha, 18. *HsR*˙*Albany* ✆ 987 264 600 La Paloma,13. *H**** *Le Petit Leon* ✆ 987 075 508 c/ Del Pozo, 2. *H***** *NH Plaza Mayor* ✆ 987 344 357 Plaza Mayor,15. *P*˙ *Puerta Sol* P ✆ 987 211 966 c/Puerta Sol,1. ❏ *Rear of cathedral: H**** *QH* ✆ 987 875 580 Av.Los Cubos,6. *Hs***Fernando I ✆ 987 220 601 Av.Los Cubos,32. *Hs*** *Casco Antiguo* ✆ 987 074 000 c/Cardenal Landázuri,11. ❏ *Rear of tourist office / route out*: *HsR*˙ *Guzmán el Bueno* ✆ 987 236 412 c/López Castrillón, 6. *HsR*˙ *San Martín* ✆ 987 875 187 Plaza Torres de Omaña, 1. *Hs***Boccalino ✆ 987 223 060 plaza S. Isodoro, 9. *HsR*** *Boccalino II* ✆ 987 220 017 Plaza S. Isodoro, 1. *H**** *Casa de Espiritualidad* **(S.Idodoro)** ✆ 987 875 088 Plaza Santo Martino (*not* Plaza San Martin). ❏ *Other options:* (modern quarter between Plazas Ana & San Marcos): *Hr*˙ *Reina* ✆ 987 205 212 c/Puerta de la Reina, 2. *HsR*˙*Alvarez* ✆ 987 072 520 c/Burgo Nuevo, 3. *H****Alfonso V Sercotel ✆ 987-220 900 Av. Padre Isla, 1. *HsR*˙ *Padre Isla II* budget hostel ✆ 987 228 097 Av.Padre Isla, 8. *HsR*˙ *Padre Isla* ✆ 987 092 298 Joaquín Costa,2. *H*** *La Torre S. Isidoro* c/Torre, 3, ✆ 987 225 594. ❏ *Near Bus & Rail: H*** *Orejas* ✆ 987 252 909 c/Villafranca, 8. *P*˙ *Blanca* ✆ 987 2521 991 c/Villafranca, 2. *H*˙ *Londres* ✆ 987-222 274 Av. Roma, 1. *HsR*** *Don Suero* ✆ 987 230 600 Av. Suero de Quiñones, 15. Finally 5 star luxury in the original pilgrim hospital *H****** **Parador San Marcos** ✆ 987 237 300 from €100 or just beyond on Av. Quevedo *Hs***Quevedo ✆ 987 242 975 from €29!

LEÓN CITY *(pop: 130,000)*: Roman military garrison and base for its VIIth Legion, hence the name – León, from *Legion*. Later it became the capital of the old kingdoms of Asturias and León. Conquered by Visigoth, Moor and finally Christian forces. Ancient and modern straddle the banks of the río Bernesga. The city, like the river, flows naturally along its tributaries, absorbing all in its eclectic embrace. Here every period and style is seamlessly accommodated: from Roman remains which support the medieval walls to the exquisite Romanesque Royal Basilica of St. Isodoro *Real Basílica de San Isodoro*, the Gothic splendour of León Cathedral *Pulchra Leonina*, the magnificent intricacy of Renaissance *San Marcos* with its plateresque façade, the controversial austerity of the neo-Gothic in Gaudi's *Casa de Botines*, to the modern edifice of León's superb museum (upper floor dedicated to the camino).

  You could spend days here and not see the half especially if you arrive during any one of the festivals that take place throughout the year. Particular highlights include: *San Juan and San Pedro* (21st–30th June) with its giant displays and running of the bulls during the day and concerts and fireworks at night. *San Froilán* runs (5th–12th October) with more parades and a local pilgrimage *romería* to the Virgin of the Way *Virgin del Camino*. If you are just passing through, the waymarked camino passes the prime sites in the medieval quarter, described in detail in the next stage.

❏ **Historical Monuments: ❶ *Puerta Moneda*** (*muralla romana*) **❷ *Iglesia de S. María del camino*** (Mercado) *XII*[th] **❸ *Iglesia S.Marcelo*** *XII*[th] - *XVII*[th] **❹ *Casa Botines*** (Gaudí). **❺ *Palacio Guzmanes*** *XVI*[th] (+patio). **❻ *Catedral*** *XIII*[th] (museo + claustro). **❼ *Basilica de San Isidoro*** *XII*[th] (Misa del peregrino 19:30 diario). **❽ *Panteón*** *XI*[th] **❾ *San Marcos*** (*Museo / Parador / Claustro XII*[th]*– XVI*[th]).

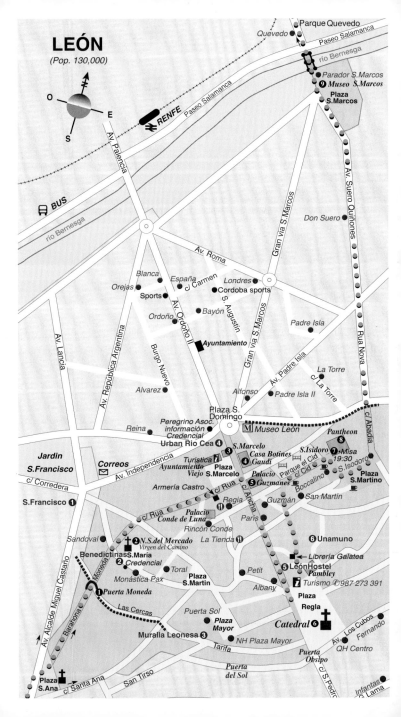

❶ Palacio de los Guzmanes *Diputación* / Casa Botines *Gaudí*
❷ Santa María de León Catedral *Pulchra Leonina*
❸ Catedral *puerta de entrada*
❹ Real Colegiata de San Isidoro
❺ Plaza de San Isidoro *Museo Panteón Basilica (misa del peregrino)*
❻ Parador de San Marcos *puerta de entrada*

REFLECTIONS:

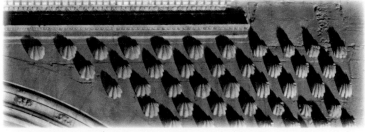

❑ **Solitude shows us what we should be; society shows us what we are.**

Lord Cecil

21 **310.0** km (192.6 ml) – Santiago

LEÓN – VILLADANGOS del PÁRAMO
Alt. VILLAR DE MAZARIFE

....	--- --- 9.8	--- ---	46%
	--- --- 5.4	--- ---	25%
	--- --- <u>6.1</u>	--- ---	29%
Total km	**21.3** km	(13.2 ml)	

21.9 km (^250m +0.6 km)

Alto ▲ Páramo 901m (2,956 ft)

< **Ⓐ Ⓗ** > Virgen del Camino **8.5** km – Valverde – **11.9** km

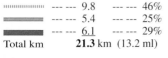

❑ **The Practical Path:** The route described below follows the waymarked circuit past the cathedral and out of the city via San Marcos but you need to have pencil sharp eyes to see the discreet shells in the pavement that compete with the many distractions in the busy streets. The scenic route via mazarife is recommended on account of the open *páramo*. The main route is more direct but runs parallel to the N-120 the entire way. Once you leave Virgen del Camino there are few facilities particularly along the relatively isolated stretch to Mazarife, so take a break and stock up with fruit or snacks in Virgen del Camino for the latter part of this stage.

❑ **The Mystical Path:** To what small group of pilgrim friends do we owe the gratitude for discovering an alternative way to the intrusive main road? In one stroke it has changed a frenetic experience into another, more peaceful, world. *'Never doubt that a small group of thoughtful people can change the world, indeed it's the only thing that ever has.'* And what of the ultimate peace, that passes all understanding? Where will that be found? What needs to change in us to discover what was never lost, only hidden behind some imagined veil?

❑ **Personal Reflections:** "… For me, the city has too many distractions, too much sensual and intellectual stimulation. I become isolated from my Self amongst the shops, the museums and churches. I become intoxicated with the glamour of the sense-perceptible world and the reality of the super-sensible becomes obscured. It is in the solitude of the camino that I seem to reach some altered state and find a deep peace. It is easier, for me, to see the Christ in the lone shepherd than in the shop assistant. Each mirrors a different aspect of my self; in one I find peaceful serenity, the other pretentious servility masking bored indifference. My prejudice persists.

0.0 km **León** from albergue ❷ in Plaza de Santa María at ❷ *Iglesia Virgen del Camino* pick up the brass waymarks in calle Rua into Plaza de San Marcelo presided over by the splendid *Ayuntamiento Viejo* and the 12th century ❸*Iglesia San Marcelo* (left). Here we have a good view of Gaudi's architectural masterpiece,

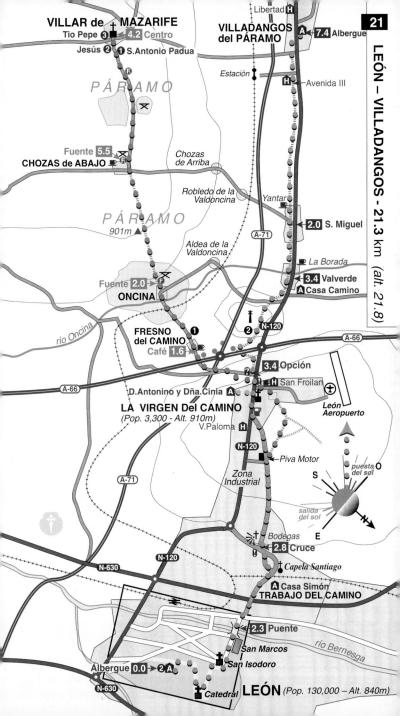

Libertad **H**

VILLAR de MAZARIFE
Tío Pepe ❸ ■ **4.2** Centro
Jesús ❷ ❶ S.Antonio Padua

**VILLADANGOS
del PÁRAMO**

A ▶ **7.4** Albergue

P Á R A M O

Estación

H — Avenida III

Fuente **5.5**
CHOZAS de ABAJO

*Chozas
de Arriba*

*Robledo de la
Valdoncina*

Yantar

2.0 S. Miguel

P Á R A M O

901m ▲

*Aldea de la
Valdoncina*

A-71

La Borada

3.4 Valverde
A Casa Camino

Fuente **2.0**
ONCINA

**FRESNO
del CAMINO**
Café **1.6**

❶

río Oncina

N-120

A-66

❷

3.4 Opción

H San Froilan

A-66

D.Antonino y Dña.Cinia **A**

LA VIRGEN Del CAMINO
(Pop. 3,300 - Alt. 910m)
V.Paloma **H**

*León
Aeropuerto*

N-120

▶ Piva Motor

A-71

*Zona
Industrial*

*puesta
del sol*

S

O

*salida
del sol*

E

Bodegas

2.8 Cruce

N-630

N-120

† *Capela Santiago*

A Casa Simón
TRABAJO DEL CAMINO

2.3 Puente

San Marcos

río Bernesga

Albergue 0.0 ▶ ❷ **A**

San Isodoro

N-630

■ † *Catedral* **LEÓN** *(Pop. 130,000 – Alt. 840m)*

the neo-Gothic palace ❹ *Casa de Botines*. *[This structure marks an historical and artistic turning point – it is one of the first monumental buildings constructed with private funds as a secular, middle class statement. Heretofore, buildings of this magnitude were funded by religious institutions or the aristocracy. While built on the back of a new wave of industrial endeavour Gaudí still follows a medieval expression with the slender towers and the*

image of St. George slaying the dragon above the main door]. Adjoining it (right) is the equally magnificent 16th century ❺ *Palacio de los Guzmanes* now the council offices and worth visiting to have a look at the marvellous inner courtyard. We now pass up the shopping mecca *c/Ancha* to:

❻ **Catedral [0.7 km]** *Pulchra Leonina* taking up the whole east side of Plaza Regal, opposite the Turismo where you can obtain more detailed information on the cathedral and other sites. Enter the late 13th century Gothic Cathedral via the west door with the Virgin *Nuestra Señora la Blanca* adorning the central column (see photo) and *Santiago Peregrino* to the right – now well worn by the hands of devout pilgrims. The cathedral is renowned for its magnificent 125 stained glass windows set high in the walls that shed such a lightness of touch to the interior. H. V. Morton described it as, *"… a conservatory that instead of keeping out the light, as most Spanish churches do, actually invites it in, showering this mosaic of colour all over it to become the gayest church in Spain."* He goes on to remind us, *"one of the chief functions of the medieval church was to instruct the illiterate and to give them pictures they could understand, to show them the story of the Gospels and the legends of the Saints – the novels of the medieval world. What more glorious picture book could there be than this church, whose illustrations are illuminated by God's own light."*

One consequence of this lightness is that the structural integrity of the building has been compromised and part of the nave caved-in during the 19th century following an earlier collapse in the 17th century! The cloisters off the north side and the cathedral museum *Catedral Museo* are also worth a visit. Next make your way back down the side of the tourist office to the tiny plaza Torres de Omaña where myriad narrow medieval streets branch out in all directions, head down c/ Fernandez Regueral (Hostal San Martín left) into Plaza San Isidoro, and:

❼ San Isidoro [0.5 km] the fountain in the square was built to commemorate the VIIth Roman Legion. Here, bedded into the Roman foundations and the medieval city wall, is this wonderful 11th century Basilica Church. The remains of San Isidoro were brought here from Sevilla to be buried in Christian Spain as the south was still under Moorish influence at that time. Admire the Door of Forgiveness *Puerta del Perdón* (right) through which medieval pilgrims, too ill to travel on to Santiago, could still receive the same indulgences. The exquisite sculptural work is from the hands of Maestro Estaban who also created the justly famous Puerta de las Platerías in Santiago cathedral. A pilgrim blessing *bendición a los peregrinos* takes place after evening mass at 19:30.

Take time to visit the fascinating *Museo* that provides access to the cloisters *claustros* and the royal burial vaults **❽ *Pantheón Real***. The Pantheón is the only part of the original 11th century building remaining and the final resting place of no less than 11 Kings, 12 Queens and 23 Princes. Look at the beautiful frescoes, still vivid 800 years after they were first painted, and because of which it has been called Spain's *Romanesque Sistine Chapel*. If you now need fresh air and refreshment try the cafés opposite the entrance in c/El Cid that also has a delightful small park – or continue into c/Sacramento and turn left at the rear of the basilica and cross directly over the busy Av. de Ramón y Cajal into c/Renueva, crossing Av. del Padre Isla into Av. de Suero de Quinoñes to:

❾ Plaza San Marcos [1.1 km] Admire the Renaissance craftsmanship that built and adorned the stunning plateresque edifice of this ancient monastery dedicated to St. Mark. Originally a more modest pilgrim hospital built by Doña Sancha in the 12th century it became the headquarters of the Knights of the Order of Santiago which was formed to protect the pilgrim way. Later still it was acquired and further embellished by King Ferdinand. The façade is a storybook in itself with many pilgrim motifs including the sword of Santiago entwined with the lion of San Marcos. A profusion of scallop shells cover the pediment of the church (and museum) entrance. Less evident are the interesting copper medallions all along the front (just behind the dwarf hedge - see photo below) with scenes from the pilgrim cities and towns we have passed through. You may also notice the medieval pilgrim sitting at the base of the stone cross, admiring the stately surroundings while resting his weary feet.

Take a peek inside the magnificent courtyard of the Parador (its cloistered galleries a museum in themselves) or perhaps treat yourself to a night in these sumptuous surroundings. You will find many fellow pilgrims checking out in the morning! Visit the Museo next door and admire the tantalising 11th century ivory crucifix *Cristo de Carrizo* (many of the artefacts are in the process of being moved to the mueso de Leon). All reminders of the influence and the gifts of the Way of St. James on León which, in times past, had no less than 17 such pilgrim *hospitales*. Take your leave of the central city and San Marcos Square, over:

2.3 km **Puente *río Bernesga*** 16th century stone bridge over the river Bernesga. We now make our way through the busy suburbs of León until we reach the open countryside of the *páramo*. The first 2.7 km are between the N-120 (signposted Astorga) and railway line before branching off uphill through an industrial area to re-join the N-120 again in La Virgen del Camino.

Continue past the Parque de Quevedo (right) *[named after the great 17th century Spanish poet whose writings so challenged the nobility that he was incarcerated in San Marcos during its spell as a prison!]* until we reach a pilgrim cross and pedestrian bridge (tourist kiosk) **[1.6 km]**. *[Option (back 100m) into c/de Guzmán El Bueno where at Nº52 we find Alb.* **Casa Simón** *Priv.[32÷2]+ €16 B&B +25 © 987 807 552]*. To continue take an elevated walkway over the railway line and re-join the main road again in *Trobajo del Camino*. This area has many links with the original camino as evidenced by the small chapel dedicated to St. James *Ermita Santiago* **[0.5 km]** (right) and just beyond the waymarked route takes a short detour (left) into *Plaza Sira San Pedro* back up to the main road **[0.7 km]** to:

2.8 km **Cruce [!]** cross main road and s/o steeply uphill (3t sign). [!] *Many pilgrims, heads bent low against the incline, miss this turning and keep on along the busy main road.* We now pass a series of underground wine cellars *bodegas* up c/Camino de la Cruz to crest the hill. A stone pedestal (30m left) a reminder we are on the 'way of the cross' on the historic camino. A good vantage point from which to look back over the sprawling expanse of León below. Continue past turning right to N-120 and ***Piva Motor*** **[1.3 km]** and option right 80m.

● ● ● ● **Alt. path 2.2 km** (adds 0.5 km. on remote paths *no* waymarks). Take the track opp. the end of Piva Motor factory directly towards the modern airport building visible on horizon. Pass ruins **[0.3 km]** s/o **[0.3 km]** (main track veers right) and s/o (left) at cross-tracks **[0.6 km]** onto asphalt road c/ Emigrante and s/o c/Tras Casa and s/o over town park and turn left in c/Dom Antonino y Doña Cinia and turn right on N-120 to rejoin main route at S.Froilan **[1.0 km]**.

For waymarked route continue s/o veering left to join **N-120 [0.4 km]** past Repsol gasolinera for some respite at 'square' *Cafe Acapulco* opp. *H*[***] **VillaPaloma** €35 © 987 300 990. Pass c/Cervantes (right) *Hs* **Julio Cesar** €25 © 987 302 044 to church of ***San Froilán*** **[1.3 km]** the modern sanctuary of the Virgen **La Virgen del Camino**. The huge bronze statues of the 12 Apostles stand above the west door with St. James looking out towards Santiago and the Virgin floating above them all. *[built on the site where a shepherd, in the early 16ᵗʰ century, saw a vision of the Virgin who told him to throw a stone and then build a church on the spot where it landed. The place became a pilgrimage in its own right on account of the miracles performed here].* This marks the last of the suburban sprawl and opp. to take refreshment at café *El Peregrino* adj. *Hs* **San Froilán** €30 ℂ 987 302 019 / *Hs*** **Plaza** €27 on c/Peregrino. Cross over [!] the N-120 to camino information board showing the alternative routes available. Up left *Hs* **Central** €25 ℂ 987 302 041 and behind it in c/Camino de Villacedré *Alb.* **D.Antonino y Dña.Cinia** *Muni.[40÷1]* €5 ℂ 615 217 335 part of

the adj. Seminary on Av. Padre Eustoquio in peaceful gardens at the edge of town with excellent modern facilities very well maintained. From the pilgrim information board on the N-120 proceed down parallel side road past pilgrim fountain to the low point where the routes diverge [?] marked by unsightly (and unseemly) paint sprawled across the asphalt road as Mazarife and Villadangos compete for your soul and wallet! **[0.4 km]**

3.4 km **Option** Recommended scenic route ❶ via Mazarife over remote páramo (13.3 km) or main route ❷ to Villadangos by *senda* parallel to the N-120 (12.8 km).

❷ At the hand-painted sign (Mazarife left) keep s/o up along the road past the cemetery (left) and s/o parallel to the N-120 down onto track that winds its way around the maze of roadways ahead through tunnel under the A-71 **[1.6 km]** (a track from the left connects with the route to Mazarife) and turn right up past radio mast and water tower and s/o down through industrial area back to the N-120 at Valverde to pick up the parallel track *senda.*

3.4 km **Valverde de la Virgen** *Alb.* **La Casa del Camino** *Priv.[32÷1]* €8 ℂ 669 874 750 (Alejandra) c/ El Jano, 2. Continue s/o into:

2.0 km **San Miguel del Camino**. *Café El Yantar del Peregrino.* The camino continues by *senda* parallel to the N-120 all the way into Villadangos passing *Hr*** **Avenida III** ℂ 987 390 311 into:

7.4 km **Villadangos del Páramo** *Alb.* **Villadangos** *Asoc.[54÷7]* €5 ℂ 987 102 910 on main road as you enter town with additional floor space available in this converted former schoolhouse. ***Other Lodging:*** *Hs*** **Libertad** €35 ℂ 987 390 123. Also several shops, bars and restaurant. *[Visit Iglesia de Santiago with its statue*

of Santiago Matamoros above the main altar that, unusually, shows him leaping out towards us (rather than in profile). This old town of Roman origins sits uneasily astride the main road. In the past it supported a pilgrim hospital and legend has it that in the numerological significant year of 1111 a battle was waged here between the forces of Doña Urraca of León and those of her former spouse Alfonso of Aragón].

❶ Scenic route **via Mazarife**. At option veer <left away from the N-120 on rough gravel track. (Don't be put off by the attempt to obliterate the waymarks at this point – clear signage reappears shortly) as we make our way over the A-71 intersection and then under the A-66 over river into:

1.6 km Fresno del Camino *Bar* (track under the motorway (right) connects with the route into Viladangos). Continue s/o over railway into:

2.0 km Oncina de la Valdocina *Fuente* peaceful hamlet with parish church of San Bartolomé. Turn right and immediately left to picnic area and *[F.]*.
We now head up the track out of the valley onto the glorious open countryside of the *páramo*. The rich red earth provides nourishment for crops and wild flowers in equal proportion. This wonderful natural path continues all the way to:

5.5 km Chozas de Abajo another peaceful village with rest area and *[F.]* (bar and shop in Plaza San Martin 300m off route). Continue s/o along a quiet country road passing rest area and *[F.]* just before entering the next village:

4.2 km Villar de Mazarife *Centro* on the outskirts we pass *Albergue* ❶ **San Antonio de Pádua** *Priv.[50÷1]*+ €8-10 + cena comunitaria ✆ 987 390 192. All facilities incl. physiotherapy. Opp: colourful ❷ **Casa de Jesús** *Priv.[50÷10]* €5 ✆ 686 053 390 with outside patio and courtyard. In the centre of the village adj. church ❸ **Tio Pepe** *Priv.[22÷4]*+ €9-€40 (€20 dinner, bed and breakfast) ✆ 987-390 517 bar provides meals and has a patio and garden. *[Next albergue: Hospital del Órbigo – 14.4 km].*

VILLAR DE MAZARIFE a decidedly pilgrim-friendly village where even the grocery store is called *Frutas de Camino de Santiago* and the church is also dedicated to St. James with several images of the saint inside. Several bars and restaurants, a gift shop, museum and art gallery make up some of the facilities of this peaceful hamlet. The local artist *Monseñor* a neo-Romanesque painter *Pintor Románico* specialised in religious works of art.

REFLECTIONS:

❐ **To dry one's eyes and laugh at a fall,**
And, baffled, get up and begin again.
— *Robert Browning*

22 **288.7** km (179.4 ml) – Santiago

VILLADANGOS – ASTORGA
Alt. MAZARIFE – PUENTE DE ÓRBIGO

▥▥▥▥▥	--- ---	22.2	--- ---	78%
▬▬▬	--- ---	5.8	--- ---	20%
▬▬▬	--- ---	0.5	--- ---	02%
Total km		**28.5** km	(17.7 ml)	

◣◣ --- --- 29.7 (^250m+1.2 km)
Alto ▲ Santo Toribio 905m (2,970 ft).
< Ⓐ Ⓗ > San Martín **4.7** km – Hospital de Órbigo **11.3** km – Villares **14.4** km
Santibáñez **16.9** km – San Justo **24.9** km. *(Alt. route [1] from Mazarife via the Páramo – Villavante 9.9 km).*

❐ **The Practical Path:** The majority of this stage is relatively solitary so bring food and water (there are few villages on the way) however there are attractive sections with trees and other shade in which to rest out of the sun. The first part to Hospital de Órbigo is relatively flat and easily covered. If you are planning to continue to Astorga (+16.8 km) the total distance is over 30 km on either route so leave early and allow some time to savour Órbigo (you could lunch here, it's around halfway). Note the last section beyond Órbigo has some (gentle) hills.

❐ **The Mystical Path:** What of our own inner battles, the jousting tournaments of the soul? How easily do we fall and how quickly do we get up again? Many knights, even an exiled bishop, fell to the earth on this very spot and rose again, dusted themselves down, and began afresh. True greatness is not in never falling, but picking ourselves up every time we do.

❐ **Personal Reflections:** *"… I sit in the shade of a grove of orange trees and sketch a stork patiently waiting by the pond to pluck a fish from its cool waters. I wonder why I don't take more time to observe and draw the beauty of life around me. I am so often caught up in my mental world of worries and responsibilities that I miss the wonder of the present moment. More tears begin to flow as I write this. Are they tears of sadness at lost opportunities or of gratitude at the peace that surrounds and holds me in its tranquil embrace?"*

0.0 km **Villadangos del Camino Main route ❷ via N-120 from Villadangos del Páramo:** Leave albergue and continue through the old town onto a tree-lined path that comes out on to the N-120 at a camping site. A senda runs parallel to the N-120 for most of the way into:

4.7 km **San Martín del Camino** *Centro* all hostals are directly on the N-120:

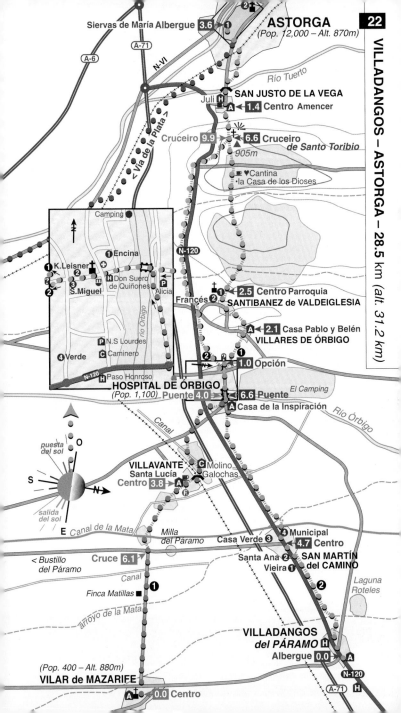

Siervas de María Albergue **3.6** ❶

ASTORGA
(Pop. 12,000 – Alt. 870m)

A-6

A-71

N-VI

Río Tuerto

< Vía de la Plata >

SAN JUSTO DE LA VEGA

Juli ⓗ
Ⓐ ◀ **1.4** Centro Amencer

Cruceiro **9.9** ◀ ◀ **6.6** Cruceiro
de Santo Toribio
905m

☕♥Cantina
·la Casa de los Dioses

Camping ●

❶ Encina

❶ K.Leisner ❷
❷ S.Miguel
❷ ⓗ Don Suero
de Quiñones
Ⓟ Alicia

Río Órbigo

N-120

❹ Verde
Ⓟ N.S Lourdes
Ⓒ Caminero
Francés ❷

❶ ◀ **2.5** Centro Parroquia
SANTIBANEZ de VALDEIGLESIA

Ⓐ ◀ **2.1** Casa Pablo y Belén
VILLARES DE ÓRBIGO

❶ ◀ **1.0** Opción

ⓗ Paso Honroso

HOSPITAL DE ÓRBIGO
(Pop. 1,100)
Puente **4.0** ◀ ◀ **6.6** Puente
Ⓐ Casa de la Inspiración

El Camping

Río Órbigo

Canal

puesta
del sol

O

S

N

salida
del sol

E Canal de la Mata

VILLAVANTE
Santa Lucía
Centro **3.8** ◀ Ⓐ

Ⓒ Molino
Galochas

Ⓕ

Milla
del Páramo

Casa Verde ❸

❹ Municipal
◀ **4.7** Centro

< Bustillo
del Páramo

Cruce **6.1** ◀

Canal

Santa Ana ❷
Vieira ❶

**SAN MARTÍN
del CAMINO**

❷

Finca Matillas ■

❶

arroyo de la Mata

Laguna
Roteles

(Pop. 400 – Alt. 880m)
VILAR de MAZARIFE

**VILLADANGOS
del PÁRAMO** ⓗ
Albergue **0.0**

Ⓐ

N-120

A-71

ⓗ

Ⓐ ☩ **0.0** Centro

Alb. ❶ **Vieira** *Priv.[40÷8]* €7 ⓒ 987 378 565 small swimpool and *V. comida vegetariana.* ❷ **Santa Ana** *Priv.[64÷3]*+ €6+20 987 039 322 (Patri & Xavi). Garden with swim pool + all facilities. ❸ **La Casa Verde** *Priv.[8÷1]* €10 ⓒ 646 879 437 (Beatriz Puente) Travesía de La Estación 8 (quieter location). ❹ **San Martín** *Muni.[68÷2]* €5 ⓒ 616 354 331 At the far end of town under water-tower. Continue through town and imm. past the Canal del Páramo turn off right> onto a shaded path lined with poplars that essentially runs parallel to the main road before turning right towards the distinctive water tower where the scenic route joins from the left and we proceed over the acequia de Castañón via calle el Paso Honroso into c/ Constitución down the cobbled street to:

6.6 km **Puente de Órbigo** this side of the bridge. **La Casa de la Inspiración** *Asoc.[12÷2]* €5 ⓒ 622 636 856 (Felipe y Verónica) c/ Paso Honroso 10 (Asociación de Amigos de la Meditación Zen). *P* **Fonda Alicia** ⓒ 987 388 349 and *P* **Lar la Puente** ⓒ 987 361 100. Parish church of Santa María. The significance of this village diminished in the 12th century when the Knights Hospitaller of St. John built a hospital on the far side of the river. One of the longest and best preserved medieval bridges in Spain dating from the 13th century and built over an earlier Roman bridge which formed one of the great historical landmarks on the camino. Its myriad arches carry you across the Río Órbigo via the passage of honour *Paso Honroso* so called because of the famous jousting tournament that took place here in the Holy Year 1434. *A noble knight from León, Don Suero de Quiñones, scorned by a beautiful lady, threw down the gauntlet to any knight who dared to pass as he undertook to defend the bridge (and presumably his honour) against all comers. Knights from all over Europe took up the challenge. Don Suero successfully defended the bridge for a month until the required 300 lances had been broken. Together with his trusted comrades he then proceeded to Santiago to offer thanks for his freedom from the bonds of love and for his honour, now restored! Or, in the words of Rupert Brooke:*

> Honour has come back, as a king, to earth
> And paid his subjects with a royal wage;
> And Nobleness walks in our ways again;
> And we have come into our heritage.

Apart from its link to such chivalrous acts, which may have been an inspiration for Cervantes *Don Quixote*, it also witnessed the battle in 452 when the Visigoths slaughtered the Swabians and subsequently provided the scene of confrontation between Christian forces under Alfonso III and the Moors. More productively it has facilitated trade since Roman times including the passage of livestock as part of the cattle trail *camino de la cañada* not to mention sweaty pilgrims like you and I!

0.0 km **Villar de Mazarife** from the centre of town head down past rest area and *[F.]*, over secondary road (linking Villadangos on the alternative route with Santa María del Páramo) out onto a quiet country lane that heads in a straight level line somewhat monotonously over river and canal through the open *páramo* over *rio de la Mata* past *Finca las Matillas (exploración Gandera)* **[4.5** km**]** over canal and s/o at crossroads **[1.6** km**]**:

6.1 km Cruce *Camino* s/o onto earthen track turn <left and s/o over canal de la Mata to follow earth track (// power lines) passing *[F.]* and right> into the village (other path s/o bypasses village facilities).

3.8 km Villavante pass picnic site to *Iglesia de la Virgen de Candelas (candles) XVIIᵗʰC*. Venue every August of a major bell ringing festival. *[The village also tells the quaint legend, reminiscent of Don Suero de Quiñones (see previous page) of a young suitor who feel in love with the beautiful Arab princess Zaida whose father lived here in the 11th century. He agreed to the marriage of his daughter but 'only' on condition that the waters of the Órbigo river flowed past his house. The young suitor set about constructing a dam Presa Cerrajera to divert the waters. His ingenuity won him Zaida and future generations the wonderful irrigation system of the Paramo!].* Alb. **Santa Lucía** *Priv.[24÷1]*+ €8–€28 ✆ 692 107 693 c/ Doctor Vélez. Continue out over **rail bridge [0.5** km**]** turning <left onto a track alongside to renovated mill by the river *CR* **Molino Galochas** ✆ 987 388 546 **[0.4** km**]**. Turn right> onto asphalt road and then take the track up over the **A-71 [1.3** km**]** and either **[a]** continue s/o across N-120 to join main route by water tower or **[b]** turn imm. <left onto track around factory building to cross [!] N-120 into c/ Constitución veering <left onto cobbled path in the village of **Puente de Órbigo [1.8** km**]** where the other route now joins from the right:

4.0 km Puente de Órbigo The village on the far side is Hospital de Órbigo.

Pass over the bridge to the equally delightful village which, on the far side, becomes Hospital de Órbigo and a Knights Commandery of the ancient Order of St. John *Caballeros Hospitalarios de San Juan* who maintained a pilgrim hospital here. *Alb.* ❶ **La Encina** *Priv.[16÷4]*+ €9-36 ✆ 987 361 087 Av. de Suero de Quiñones (right at end of bridge and a short detour further) ● *camping municipal*. *Hs**`* **Don Suero de Quiñones** ✆ 987 388 238 great position on the bridge but you pay for the position! Continue past hostal to town square (shops) & parish church of John the Baptist *Iglesia de San Juan Bautista* s/o up the main street *Álvarez Vega* to:

Hospital de Órbigo [0.5 km**]** ❷ **Karl Leisner** *Par.[90÷10]* €5 ✆ 987 388 444 (photo right). All facilities in traditional building renovated by a German Confraternity and built around a central courtyard that provides a convivial place to congregate. ❸ **San Miguel** *Asoc.*[40÷2]* €7 ✆ 987 388 285 good facilities in refurbished building maintaing a tranquil atmosphere that also acts as an exhibition space for Jacobean art.

◆ **Crossroads** turn left into Av. Fueros de León to far end (+500m) near the N-120 for ❹ **Verde** ♥ *V. Priv.[26÷2]* €9 ℭ 689 927 926. Hostel with vegetarian menu and yoga. *Other Lodging:* At church crossroads turn left into c/Sierra Pambley *CR* **N.S. de Lourdes** €20-40 ℭ 987 388 253 / 639 001 024 @Nº40 (+300m). All facilities incl. meals and well-kept garden and just beyond (+100m) at Nº56 *CR* **El Caminero** €50+ ℭ 987 389 020 and +100m further on N-120 adj. gasolinera Cepsa *H* **El Paso Honroso** €35 ℭ 987 361 010.

◆ Continue s/o over the crossroads (by albergue San Miguel) into c/ Camino de Jacobeo and up to the next crossroads **[0.5 km]**

1.0 km Opción [?] For **recommended route** ❶ turn right> at the last house (with artesian well) and continue on a track over canal into:

2.1 km **Villares de Órbigo** *Alb.* **Villares Casa de Pablo y Belén** ♥ *Priv.[26÷5]*+ €7–€20 ℭ 947 132 935 Good facilities with library and communal dinner. Adj. bar and parish church dedicated to St. James & image of *Santiago Matamoros*. We now enter a pleasant pathway that climbs gently passing rest area *[F.]* **[0.6 km]** to high point to join an asphalt road down across a small stream turning up right **[1.9 km]** to:

2.5 km **Santibáñez de Valdeiglesia** *Alb.* ❶ **Santibáñez** *Par.[20÷4]* €5 ℭ 626 362 159 communal dinner available. Adj. *bar Centro Social* basic facilities with peaceful orchard to the rear. ❷ **Camino Francés** *Priv.[12÷2]* ℭ 987 361 014 c/ Real newly opened with welcoming *bar-cafetería*. The church of the Holy Trinity *Iglesia de la Trinidad* has images of San Roque peregrino and Santiago Matamoros.

Continue *up* through farmyard and out of the village onto one of the more serene and naturally beautiful pathways of the camino. We pass the viewpoint and rest area *Cruz del Valle* up and down over 3 (dry) river valleys through woodland (mostly holm oak) before ascending to the high place and the Abode of the God's *la Casa de los Dioses* ♥ *Cantina* where *Davíd* will welcome you to his humble home and, if he remains in residence and you make time, you might receive the

key to your essential nature! Shortly afterwards we cross an asphalt road and the alternative route joins from our left as we come to the prominent:

6.6 km **Cruceiro Santo Toribio** stone cross commemorating the 5th century Bishop Toribio of Astorga who supposedly fell to his knees here in a final farewell having been banished from the town. It is Astorga's *Monte Gozo* where we have a wonderful view over the town. Behind the city stand the Montes de León that we cross in the days ahead through the highest part of the whole journey at 1,515m (4,970 feet). Over to the left (southwest) is El Teleno a mountain sacred to the Roman god Mars at 2,185m (7,170 feet) while due north stands Peña Ubiña at 2,417m (7,930 feet) marking the eastern flank of the Cordilera Cantábrica – and behind (not visible) lie the Picos de Europa and Santo Toribio de Liébana where the good bishop is buried along with a fragment of the True Cross which he brought back from Jerusalem and a place of pilgrimage (not to be confused with Santo Toribio Alfonso Mogrovejo, a 15th century bishop also from this area who was an early missionary to South America). Just below the cross is a viewpoint with orientation map.

Alternative route ❷ via N-120: at the option point by the last house in Hospital de Órbigo – continue s/o and veer left to the N-120 [**1.5 km**] from here a track runs parallel to the main road which undulates up and down the rolling countryside before turning off right> at the top of a rise [**7.4 km**] here we follow the track to cruceiro and viewpoint [**1.0 km**]:

9.9 km | **Cruceiro Santo Toribio** recommended route [1] joins from the right.

When you have taken in the scale of the horizon, focus carefully on the ground immediately ahead as the path now drops steeply to pick up the asphalt road into:

1.4 km | **San Justo de la Vega** *(Pop. 2,100)* an expanding residential satellite of Astorga with several bars, restaurants and on the main street c/ Real 61 **Amanecer** *Plgrim House Priv. [11÷3] donativo* ℂ 622 566 468 cena comunitaria. Opp: *HsR*° **Juli** ℂ 987 617 632. From San Justo de la Vega we continue out over the bridge and the *río Tuerto* and turn off right> [**0.8 km**] to take a pleasant track that runs along the river valley past the side of a factory crossing the Roman footbridge *Puente de la Moldería* [**1.5 km**] up to the main road and over railway *pasarela* into the outer suburbs of Astorga over town bypass *(albergue Camino y Via now closed).*Continue s/o left at the roundabout [!] before climbing up steeply (Via de la Plata route joins from left) through the *Puerta del Sol* [**0.7 km**] into:

3.6 km | **Astorga** *Plaza San Francisco Alb.* ❶ **Siervas de María** *Asoc.[164÷20]* €5 ℂ 987 616 034 prominently situated on Plaza San Francisco with excellent modern facilities. The original municipal hostel diagonally opposite adjoining the town park *Jardín de Sinagoga* provides additional accommodation when necessary. The other main hostel is situated at the other end of town close to the cathedral. ❷ **San Javier** *Asoc.*[95÷5] €9 ℂ 987 618 532 network* hostel associated with the Via de la Plata which joins here in Astorga. Conveniently located close to the cathedral in c/Portería, 6. All facilities with extensive dining and lounge areas and small open yard. This is a lovely conversion of one of the historic buildings in the old quarter close to the main sites in the town incl. hotel Gaudí with which it is also connected.

❏ *Other lodging (from entrance €45-65):* *H*°° **La Peseta** ℂ 987 617 275 also *Maragatería* restaurant on Plaza San Bartolomé, adj. *H*°°°° **Vía De La Plata** c/Padres Redentoristas, 5 €100 ℂ 987 619 000 sister hotel to *H*°°° **Astvr Plaza** ℂ 987 617 665 on Plaza Mayor (España). *H*°°° **Casa de Tepa** ℂ 987 603 299 c/Santiago,2. *H*°°° **Ciudad De Astorga Spa** ℂ 987 603 001 c/ los Sitios,7. *H* **El Descanso de Wendy** ℂ 987 617 854 c/ Matadero Viejo, 11. *H*°°° **Gaudí** ℂ 987 615 654 opp. Gaudí palace. ❏ *Outskirts*: *Hr*°° **Gallego** ℂ 987 615 450 Av. Ponferrada and *H* **Coruña** ℂ 987-615 009.

❏ There are a variety of restaurants, bars and cafés – try some of the local cuisine *cocido maragato* which starts with a hearty meat stew, usually pork *and* black pudding with beans and cabbage followed by vegetables and finished off with a bowl of broth!

❏ *Turismo:* ℂ 987 618 222 Glorieta Eduardo Castro, 5 near the cathedral which provides a map showing the pilgrim route *Ruta Peregrino* and Roman route *Ruta Romana*. If you are just passing through the town and want to visit the main sites *or* for the most direct route to albergue San Javier take the following 'tour' that takes in the main sites (see town plan) starting where we entered at the southern entrance *Puerta del Sol*.

❶ **Plaza San Francisco** with pilgrim hostels and lovely public gardens (fine views over the mountains), the Church of St. Francis of Assisi *Convento de San Francisco* (St. Francis allegedly came here on his pilgrimage to Santiago in 1212) and the adjoining Roman foundations (under a glass covering).

❷ **Plaza Bartolomé** where we find the *Iglesia San Bartolomé* and the *Ergástula* a Roman construction used down the ages as access tunnel, slave enclave, gaol and now a museum that also provides a short video (in Spanish) of life in Astorga during its Roman period.

❸ **Plaza Mayor** *España* and the graceful 17th century Baroque facade of the *Ayuntamiento* that houses one of the flags from the battle of Clavijo. Take a break in the square so that you can watch its ornate clock strike the hour as two mechanical figures (a man and a woman dressed in Maragato costume) strike the central bell. Before leaving this end of town there are a number of other Roman sites of interest. To the rear of the municipal library *biblioteca municipal*, situated off Synagogue Garden, are substantial remains of the original Roman walls and drains *murallas y cloachas Romanas* and the Roman baths *termas Romanos*.

❹ **Plaza Santocildes** identified by the handsome lion monument *monumento a los Sitios* in memory of the siege of Astorga during the Peninsular War. Continue out the far side of the square and on the left is c/Jose María where we find the *Museo del Chocolate*. Astorga was a main centre for the production of chocolate and the curator is a friend of the way and has been president of the local association.

❺ **Plaza Obispo Alcolea** here we find another of the original entrances to the walled city – the King's Gate *Puerta de Rey* no longer visible but to one side of which we can admire the façade of the Casa Granell. We now head towards the jewels in Astorga's crown:

❻ **Plaza Catedral** where the sensational Gaudí building known as the Bishop's Palace *Palacio Episcopal* greets us, its neo-Gothic turrets soaring heavenwards. It houses no bishops but the splendid museum of the Ways *Museo de los Caminos* with historical notes and artefacts on the many Roman roads that converged on this city and provided the main trade, military and pilgrim routes through northern Spain. Don't miss the section on the *Caminos de Santiago* and the original Iron Cross *Cruz de Ferro* that once stood atop Monte Irago. Also in this area is the cell which allegedly housed the city's 'fallen' or those of ill repute *Celda de las Emparedadas*. The Turismo and the Iglesia de Santa Marta behind which is the splendid 15th century Gothic Cathedral standing majestically over the square, a wonderful blend of Romanesque, Gothic and later styles of architecture and a Renaissance altarpiece with a Romanesque statue of the Virgen de la Majestad after whom the cathedral is dedicated. Behind the cathedral are the Puerta Romana and a well-preserved stretch of the original Roman walls that acts as an open-air museum in its own right.

Try and make time to visit the adjoining diocesan museum *Museo de Catedral* (a joint ticket will provide access to this and the Palacio Episcopal). This museum has a magnificent 15th century painting of the burial of St. James entitled 'The bridge of Life and Queen Lupa' *El puente de la Vida y la Reina Lupa* it shows the bulls pulling the sarcophagus of St. James and the bridge caving in by divine intervention, thus preventing the Roman soldiers from seizing the Apostle's disciples and their sacred cargo. There are many other depictions of pilgrimage and sacred art and artefacts sensitively displayed.

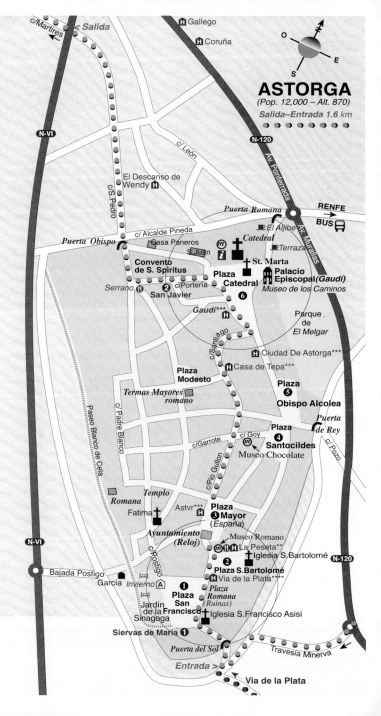

Adjoining the cathedral museum is the ancient Hospital de San Juan in which St. Francis reputedly stayed on his way to Santiago and further on the extensive monastery buildings of the Holy Spirit *Convento de Sancti Spiritus*. If you are heading on towards Rabanal turn right> and make your way out through Bishop's Gate *Puerta Obispo* into c/San Pedro and over the busy N-VI Madrid to La Coruña road. Alternatively, if you are staying the night then head towards your preferred hostel or the bars and restaurants around the many lively *plazas*.

ASTORGA *Asturica Augusta (pop: 12,000 – alt. 870 m)*. An attractive city (more akin to a lively market town) set atop a steep ridge with a wide range of shops and general facilities and an interesting array of historic buildings all tightly packed within its medieval walls. Originally a powerful Asturian community it became an equally important Roman city on account of its prominent position at the junction of several major routes. This is where the French Way *Camino Francés* (part of the Via Trajana linking this area with Bordeaux) and the Roman Road *Calzada Romana* (otherwise known as the Via Aquitana) joined the Roman *Vía de La Plata* from Sevilla and the south. This convergence of routes gave rise to over 20 pilgrim hospitals in medieval times. George Borrow, visiting Astorga in 1840, wrote 'Almost the entire commerce of nearly one-half of Spain passes through the hands of The Maragato whose fidelity to their trust is such that no one accustomed to employ them would hesitate to confide to them the transport of a ton of treasure from the sea of Biscay to Madrid'. As if this wasn't enough activity Astorga also acted as a crossroads for the royal drove roads *Cañadas Reales* that herded livestock up and down the Iberian peninsular. This European-wide system of nomadic grazing is known as transhumance and can still be witnessed on various caminos and is celebrated in Astorga (along with many other towns) in the festival *Fiesta de Transhumancia* when sheep are driven through the town.

Next we enter the *Maragatería* and the *montes de León*. Here, between Astorga and Molinaseca, we experience the remnants of Maragato culture in the distinctive dress and cuisine of this mountainous region. The cakes and pastries *mantecadas* are worth sampling and the hills provide game and trout from the streams. The obscure origins of the Maragatos may date back to the 7th century when King Mauregato and the Visigoths became isolated in this remote area during the Arab invasions. Today the isolationism continues in the abandoned villages of the mountains, such as Foncebadón.

Astorga is also sometimes referred to as the 'capital' of the Maragatería but the Maragatos themselves defy classification. Some suggest they are descended from the Berber tribes who came to Spain as part of the Moorish invasion in the 8th century becoming 'misplaced' in this remote mountainous region. Others link them to the Visigoths and their king Mauregato. The name may derive from captive Moors *Mauri captus* forced to work the mines in the area. Most agree they were muleteers and their number has dwindled to 4,000 spread around 40 villages in the area. Martin Martinez, president of the Maragato Cultural Society, in a recent Telegraph interview stated simply, 'We are trying to recuperate some of our traditions before it is too late. By celebrating our traditional games and weddings in our way we hope to keep it alive.' It is the same story we will hear in the Bierzo and Galicia. The mystery of the Maragatos may never be penetrated but we can experience the hospitality found amongst the villages that line the path ahead.

REFLECTIONS:

❏ **Distrust yourself and sleep before you fight. T'is not too late tomorrow to be brave.** *John Armstrong*

23 **260.2** km (161.7 ml) – Santiago

ASTORGA – RABANAL del CAMINO

....	--- ---	14.1	--- --- 68%
▬▬▬▬	--- ---	6.5	--- --- 32%
▬▬▬	--- ---	0.0	--- ---
Total km		**20.6 km** (12.8 ml)	

▲▲ --- --- 22.6 km (^400m+2.0)

Alto ▲ Rabanal 1,150m (3,770 ft)

< **Ⓐ Ⓗ** > *from albergue* ❶*:* Murias de Rechivaldo **5.1** km *[Castrillo Polvazares 7.3 km* off *route]* – Santa Catalina **9.4** km – El Ganso **13.7** km.

❏ **The Practical Path:** Today we head towards the mountains and tomorrow we climb to the highest point of the entire route. Rabanal can feed you, but it won't clothe you for the mountain weather, which can be unpredictable at the best of times. Astorga is the last opportunity to kit-out before the ascent. However, there are several small villages on today's stretch where you can buy food and refreshments, many bearing the suffix *somoza* from the Latin *sub montia* or *under the mountain*. This should be a relatively gentle day and the promise of a good nights rest in Rabanal to prepare you for the climb the following day.

❏ **The Mystical Path:** Where are the mountains of the soul? How high do we need to climb to reach the top and what will we find there? How well are we equipped and what do we need to take and, perhaps more importantly, leave behind? Tomorrow is time enough to climb towards another peak in our journey. What gift will you deposit at the top so that you can continue on, unburdened by the dross in your life?

❏ **Personal Reflections:** *"… The wind howled against the window as I warmed myself by the log fire. It was the constant squeaking of the bookcase that eventually roused me to quieten it and an old and faded document fell out from behind. It appeared to have been hidden and was entitled* The Third Secret of Fátima – The Collapse of the Roman Catholic Church. *The more I read, the deeper I became aware of the awesome impact that this document, true or false, would have on the future of the Church. Recent press revelations of scandals reaching at the very heart of the hierarchy made its predictions utterly clear. The irrational fear I felt was compounded when I read that the person who had professed to having seen the original letter had died in mysterious circumstances. I hid the document back where I found it, pondering on both the risk of collapse and the opportunities for renewal that the fulfilment of such a prophesy would entail…"*

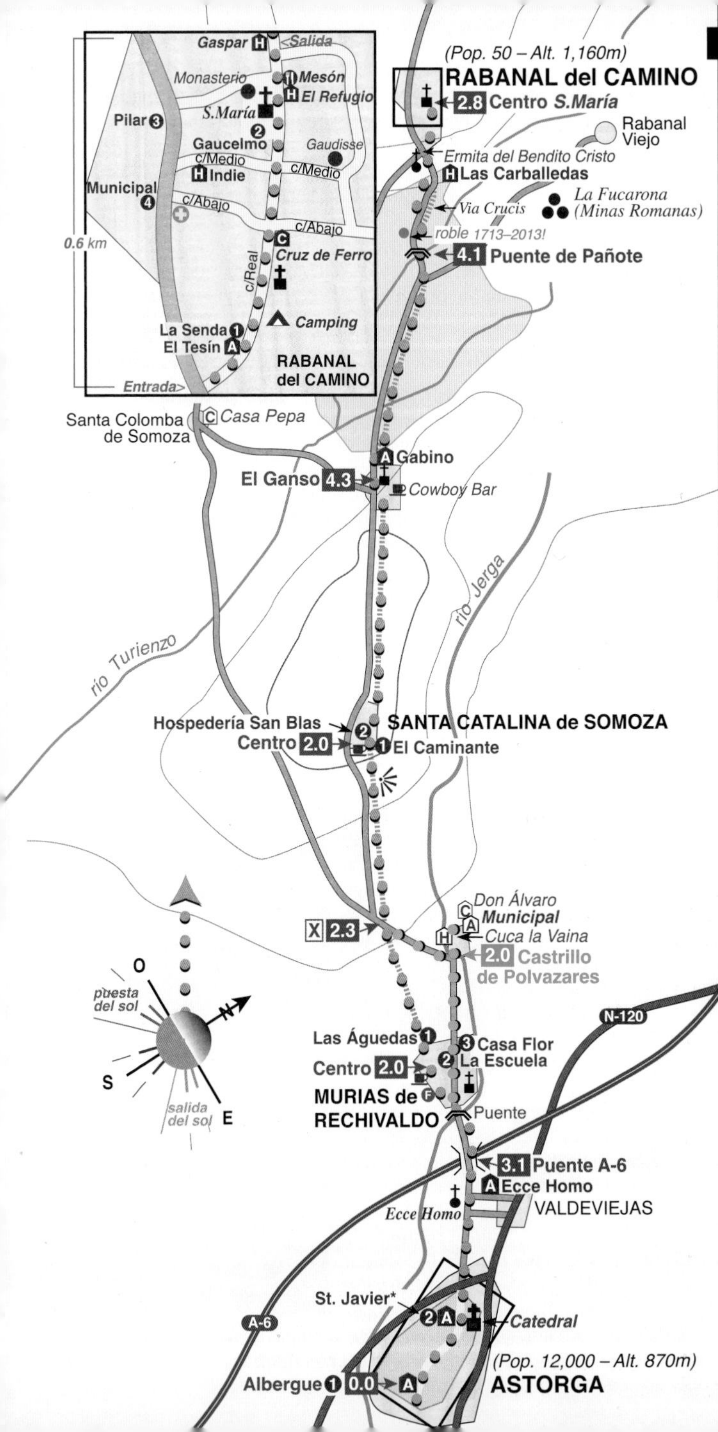

(Pop. 50 – Alt. 1,160m)
RABANAL del CAMINO
✝ **2.8** Centro *S.María*

○ Rabanal Viejo

Ermita del Bendito Cristo
Ⓗ **Las Carballedas**

La Fucarona
●● *(Minas Romanas)*

← *Via Crucis*
roble 1713–2013!
〰 **4.1** **Puente de Pañote**

Inset map (Rabanal del Camino):

Gaspar Ⓗ ― *Salida*
Monasterio
Ⓗ **Mesón**
Ⓗ **El Refugio**
✝ *S.María*
Pilar ❸
② *Gaudisse*
Gaucelmo
c/Medio
Ⓗ **Indie** c/Medio
Municipal ❹
c/Abajo
c/Abajo
0.6 km
Ⓒ
✝ **Cruz de Ferro**
c/Real
▲ *Camping*
La Senda ❶
El Tesín Ⓐ
RABANAL del CAMINO
Entrada>

Santa Colomba de Somoza Ⓒ *Casa Pepa*

Ⓐ **Gabino**
El Ganso **4.3**
Cowboy Bar

río Jerga

río Turienzo

Hospedería San Blas → ② **SANTA CATALINA de SOMOZA**
Centro **2.0** → ❶ *El Caminante*

🧭 O / puesta del sol / S / E / salida del sol

Don Álvaro
Ⓒ Ⓐ *Municipal*
Ⓗ ― *Cuca la Vaina*
2.0 Castrillo de Polvazares

Ⓧ **2.3** ←

Las Águedas ❶
❸ **Casa Flor**
Centro **2.0** → ② **La Escuela**
✝
MURIAS de RECHIVALDO Ⓕ
〰 *Puente*

3.1 **Puente A-6**
Ⓐ **Ecce Homo**
✝ *Ecce Homo* **VALDEVIEJAS**

A-6

N-120

A-6

*St. Javier**
② Ⓐ ✝ *Catedral*

(Pop. 12,000 – Alt. 870m)
Albergue ❶ **0.0** Ⓐ
ASTORGA

0.0 km **Astorga** from albergue ❶ in Plaza San Francisco follow the waymarks past the **cathedral [0.8 km]** and turn <left opposite the west door and out through the Puerta Obispo into Barrio de Rectiva thence c/San Pedro and past the modern church of the same name across the N-VI (Madrid – A Coruña) at busy crossroads (shops and cafés) signposted to Santa Colomba de Somoza straight ahead.

Note: Astorga was not only a major crossroads since Roman times but the connecting point for the route from Sevilla and the south usually referred to as the Silver Route *Via de la Plata* although scholars suggest 'plata' is a corruption of the Arabic word for wide *not* silver. Semantics aside, we travel the next few days over mountain terrain that produced gold, silver and other valuable ores from the mines between here and Ponferrada (*Las Médulas*). Here also medieval pilgrims would have to choose between the shorter but steeper route through Rabanal and Puerto Irago (1,505m) or the more circuitous but less steep Puerto Manzanal (1,225m) which today is where the N-VI and A-6 autopista and rail line cut through the Montes de León to connect Ponferrada and Astorga. The medieval writer König von Vach stated, "I advise that you avoid Rabanal at all costs." Today we can ignore such advice as Rabanal has since earned the reputation as one of the most authentic and welcoming villages along the entire camino. So we continue confidently but cautiously (several pilgrims have been killed on these roads in recent years – a cross on our right marks one such spot) to the medieval hermitage *Ecce Homo* **[2.0 km]** remnant of a former pilgrim hospice. Opposite the chapel is the road to Valdeviejas and *Alb.* **Ecce Homo** *Muni. [10÷2]* €5 ✆ 620 960 060. Continue s/o to **A-6 [0.3 km]**:

3.1 km **Autopista** *flyover* onto dedicated pilgrim track parallel to the road to cross the **río Jerga [1.2 km]** and pick up a grass track <left to Crossroads in **Murias de Rechivaldo [0.6 km]**. Parish Church (right). Continue s/o past *Meson Café El Llar* to albergue **[0.2 km]**.

2.0 km **Murias de Rechivaldo** *Alb.* ❶ **Casa las Águedas** *Priv.[40÷3]*+ €9 +€45 ✆ 636 067 840 last building (right) centred around a delightful courtyard in this traditional village house; all meals available. ❷ **La Escuela** *Muni. [14÷1]* €5 ✆ 987 691 150 on the main road adj. picnic site. basic facilities in a former school building. Opp. side of road: ❸ **Casa Flor** *Priv. [15÷3]*+ €10 (€20 dinner +B&B) ✆ 609 478 323. *Other Lodging:* La Valeta ✆ 616 598 133 Plaza Mayor in the centre. *[Next albergue: Santa Catalina – 5.7 km].*

Albergue ❶ *Las Águedas (top)*
Albergue ❷ *Municipal (below)*

 Murias de Rechivaldo is a typical Maragato village with interesting rustic parish Church of St. Stephen *San Esteban* and several bars, restaurant, shop and *[F.]*.

Options [?] [1] directly to **Santa Catalina** via earth track (4.3 km) or take the LE-142 detour [2] to the classic Maragato village of **Castrillo de Polvazares** (national monument) and thence join the main route (5.7 km). *[If you need space 'off the camino' a further option [3] visit Santa Colomba de Somoza CR* **Casa Pepa** *€80 double ✆ 987 631 041 Laura (will collect by car also from El Ganso 4 km or Rabanal 6 km)].*

For alternative route [2] pick up the minor road by albergue [2] and turn <left (LE-142 to Santa Columba) straight to the village visible ahead:

2.0 km Castrillo de Polvazares Maragato village with cobblestone main street lined with traditional stone buildings providing expensive tourist rooms, bars and restaurants. Rebuilt by local artisans it lacks the authentic ambience found in the crumbling villages spread along the camino itself. At least the tourist buses are kept at the entrance car park. The village was brought to life by the novelist Concha Espina who depicted life in Castrillo in her novel The Maragato Sphinx *La Esfinge Maragata*. *Alb.* ❶

Municipal.[8÷2] €5 © 655 803 706 c/ del Jardín (mixed reports). *Hs* **Don Álvaro** © 987 053 990 c/ La Magdalena. *Hs* **Cuca La Vaina** €45 © 987-691 034 c/del Jardin. *CR* **Casa Coscolo** €45 c/El rincon (Plaza de la iglesia). Proceed through the village veering left at the central cross to pick up a poorly marked camino over small stream that climbs up to re-join the asphalt road above you or return to the start of the village and take the road up to rejoin the main route into Santa Catalina

For recommended route [1] Continue past *[F.]* and café (left) and albergue ❶ (right) onto wide track that runs in a straight line alongside the overhead power cables to:

2.3 km Cruce cross the minor road (Castrillo de Polvazares right) and pick up the pilgrim track that runs parallel to the old asphalt road to enter:

2.0 km Santa Catalina *Alb.* ❶ **El Caminante** *Priv.*[16÷2]+ €5 © 987 691 098 plus café/bar and patio. *Alb.* ❷ **Hospedería San Blas** *Priv.*[20÷2]+ €5-€35 © 987 691 411 plus café/bar also with menú peregrino. Continue down the main street past *bar Camino Real* and opening (left) in the stone wall to **Albergue ❸** basic facilities on c/ La Escuela currently closed. *[Next albergue: El Ganso – 4.5 km].*

Santa Catalina is another village typical of the region in both its layout and population now reduced to a mere 50 persons – in bygone days it supported a pilgrim hospital. The parish church houses a relic of San Blas after whom the church and albergue are named. Continue through the village and back out onto the minor road and a track parallel that brings us into:

4.3 km El Ganso a hauntingly crumbling village, evoking a sense of loss or, perhaps, a reminder of a less hurried time. In the 12th century it boasted a monastery and a pilgrim hospital. El Ganso is the first of several semi-abandoned Maragato villages that we pass through in the relatively solitary mountains. However, amidst the collapsing thatch cottages are some signs of new life, such as the *Cowboy Bar* (see photo) adding to the incongruity of the modern *sendas* by which you arrive and

leave this enchanting piece of history. There is a Parish church dedicated to St. James with a statue of Santiago Peregrino and the Capilla de Cristo de los Peregrinos. If the opportunity arises to meet the locals, don't pass it by! (with side entrance to Bar la Barraca) and *Alb.* *Priv.* [30÷3] €8 © 660 912 823 private hostel on c/ Real just beyond the church at the exit. *[Next albergue: Rabanal – 6.9 km].*

From here all the way to the top at the Cruz de Ferro true 'Friends of the Way' have forged tracks either side of the LE-142 that snakes its way up valley. The road is heavily undulating with many blind spots so take every opportunity to use the natural pathways on either side. Here again we find many pilgrims, heads bent to the incline, staying on the narrow asphalt road. Accidents have been reported in recent years so don't let fatigue rob you of focus. Ignore signs to Rabanal Viejo and the Gold route *Ruta de Oro* (unless you want to visit the *site* of the original Roman gold mines *Minas de La Fucarona* 1.5 km up to the right*)*. Continue s/o to:

4.1 km **Puente de Pañote** a modest bridge over arroyo Rabanal de Viejo and a good place to refresh ourselves in its cool mountain waters before continuing the steeper ascent through mixed native woodland, holm oak *encina*, oak *roble* and pine *pino* past the site of the specimen 300 year old 'pilgrim oak' sadly felled during a recent winter storm. And onto the self-styled *Via Crucis* with crosses woven into the fence alongside the path. Just before Rabanal we pass *Apartamentos* **Las Carballedas** €60 © 686 705 595 (right) and *Ermita del Bendito Cristo de la Vera Cruz XVIII[th]C* (left) and veer right> off the road into c/Real the typical paved main street of Rabanal del Camino with *Alb.* ❶ **La Senda** *Priv.[34÷4]* €5–€7 © 696 819 060 adj. **El Tesín** €36-56 © 635 527 522 with *café/bar* also campsite opp. Continue up steeply past *Capilla de San José XVIII[th]C* (right) with entrance porch enabling viewing of the ornate retablo with image of Santiago Peregrino and up past shop with lodging above *CR* **A Cruz de Ferro** €30-40 © 627 147 115 (Miriam & Manuel who also manage the municipal albergue) and up into main square:

2.8 km **Rabanal del Camino** *Centro* Iglesia Santa María *XII[th]C* Romanesque parish church occupying the tiny central plaza with popular *Alb.* ❷ **Gaucelmo** *Asoc.[40÷3]* €-voluntary 987 631 647 run by the London based Confraternity of St. James and the Bierzo association (pilgrims with back-up support *not* admitted). Courtyard and orchard where camping is possible. Sensitively restored and well maintained with 'afternoon tea' on arrival and breakfast on departure. ❸ **N.S del Pilar** *Priv.[32÷2]+* €5 +35 © 987 631 621 located down on the main road in plaza Gerónimo Morán Alonso with lively bar around central courtyard. Adj. also on the main road ❹ *Muni.[34÷2]* €4 © 987 631 687 + picnic area. ● **Benedictine Monastery** *San Salvador del Monte Irago* © 987 631 528 retreat house *La Casa de Acogida* adj. the Church of Santa María for up to 10 pilgrims who wish to stay for 2+ nights of silent retreat. *Donation* basis. *The Gaudisse Asoc. hostal supports children with cancer. [Next albergue: Foncebadón 5.8 km].* **Other Lodging:** *H* **Casa Indie** €40-60 © Javier 635 527 522 / Alba 625 470 392 c/Medio 4a (El Tesín same owner). *Hs* **El Refugio** €35-50 © 987 631 592 adj. the church with popular bar and restaurant (pilgrim menu). *H**La Posada de Gaspar* €55+ © 987 631 629 top end of the village (and price bracket) by the exit in renovated 17th century former pilgrim hospital.

Rabanal del Camino continues a centuries old tradition of caring for the pilgrims before they take the steep path up and over Monte Irago. This was the IXth stage of Aymeric Picaud's classic itinerary and the Knights Templar are thought to have had a presence here as early as the 12th century ensuring the safe passage of pilgrims over this remote mountain terrain – the parish Church of Santa María was reputedly built by them. Today an order of monks originating from Bavaria have again (following earlier local concerns) taken up residence in a building on the square and the church, now restored, is once again resounding to the sound of Gregorian chant with Vespers at 19:00 and Compline 21:30 (daily incl. Sundays) and pilgrim blessing offered by the Benedictine missionary monks of the monastery of *San Salvador del Monte Irago* established here in 2001 and affiliated to the Abbey church of St. Ottilien.

REFLECTIONS:

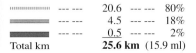

❏ **On all the peaks lies peace.** *Goethe*

24 **239.6** km (148.9 ml) – Santiago

RABANAL del CAMINO – MOLINASECA

▦▦▦▦▦	--- ---	20.6	--- ---	80%
▭▭▭▭	--- ---	4.5	--- ---	18%
▬▬▬	--- ---	0.5	--- ---	2%
Total km		**25.6 km** (15.9 ml)		

▰▰▰ --- --- 28.6 km (^600m + 3.0 km)

Alto ▲ La Cruz de Ferro 1,505m (4,940 ft)

< Ⓐ Ⓗ > Foncebadón **5.8** km – Manjarín **9.7** km – El Acebo **16.5** km – Riego de Ambros **19.9** km.

❏ **The Practical Path:** Today we head up through to the highest point of our journey. While the ascent is steep in places and will require determination remember that far most injuries (sprains and strains) are experienced going *down*hill. Use the new track that runs roughly parallel to the road effectively making the majority of this stage (80%) a safer natural pathway. When pausing to rest or meditate, remember that body sweat will turn cold quickly at this altitude as soon as physical exertion stops – so find a sheltered spot out of the mountain breeze and dress warmly. There are several drinking fonts *[F.]* along the way and the mountain villages are coming to life again supporting pilgrims with hostels and cafés but it is sensible to take some snacks and we need to fill our water bottles before leaving Rabanal.

❏ **The Mystical Path:** For many, today is a peak experience. How allusive to the rational mind is that peace that passes all understanding. What does an altered state mean to you? Words cannot convey the experience of a unified perspective, beyond the duality offered by the physical eyes. How long yet will we allow the sense-perceptible world to limit our perception and keep us imprisoned in our separate state? Will we allow our Self soar to new heights today and sense the super-sensible?

❏ **Personal Reflections:** *"... How my spirit soars in high places, connecting me to that place within me that touches God. My perspective shifts and I get an expanded sense of Self. This giant chestnut supports my back as I write these notes, shading me from the afternoon sun. I feel safe in its giant embrace and welcomed through the connection from previous visits and blessed by its unyielding yet undemanding presence. Strong yet silent but for the gentle rustle of your leaves ..."*

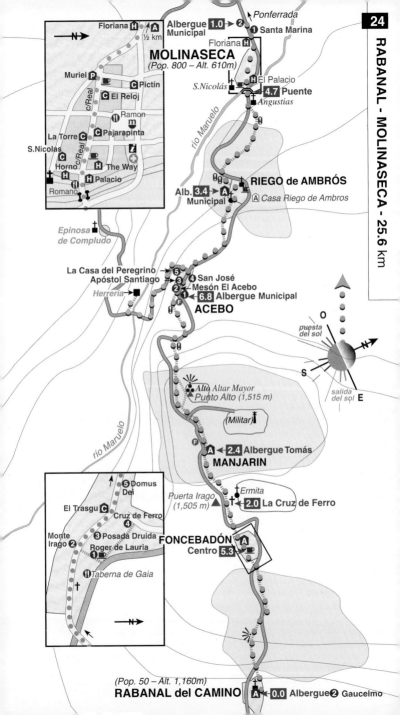

Ponferrada

Albergue **1.0** ➋ ➊ Santa Marina
Municipal

Floriana **H**

MOLINASECA
(Pop. 800 – Alt. 610m)

H El Palacio

S.Nicolás

4.7 Puente
Angustias

Floriana **H** **A**
½ km

Muriel **P**
C Pictín

C El Reloj

Ramon
Pajarapinta
C

La Torre **C**

S.Nicolas

río Maruelo

Horno **H**
H The Way

H Palacio

Romano

*Epinosa
de Compludo*

RIEGO de AMBRÓS

Alb. **3.4** ➤ **A**
Municipal

A *Casa Riego de Ambros*

La Casa del Peregrino
Apóstol Santiago

➎
➌
➋

➍ San José

Mesón El Acebo

1 **6.8** Albergue Municipal

ACEBO

Herreria

*puesta
del sol*

O

N

S

*salida
del sol*

E

*Alto Altar Mayor
Punto Alto (1,515 m)*

(Militar)

A **2.4** Albergue Tomás

MANJARIN

río Maruelo

*Puerta Irago
(1,505 m)*

Ermita

2.0 La Cruz de Ferro

➎ Domus
Dei

El Trasgu **C**

Cruz de Ferro
➍

Monte
Irago ➋

➌ Posada Druida

➊ Roger de Lauria

FONCEBADÓN
Centro **5.3**

A

Taberna de Gaia

A

(Pop. 50 – Alt. 1,160m)
RABANAL del CAMINO **A** **0.0** Albergue➋ Gaucelmo

0.0 km **Rabanal** *Centro Gaucelmo* proceed up through the village onto rough track that criss-crosses the asphalt road with spectacular views across the río Turienzo valley towards Monte El Teleno. Passing **pilgrim shelter [2.6 km]** *[F.]* up to camino signboard into **Foncebadón [2.7 km]** to:

5.3 km **Foncebadón** *Alb.* ❶ **Roger de Lauria** *(prev. Convento de Foncebadón) Priv.[20÷2]* €7 © 625 313 425 (Jessica & Marcos) popular bar & menú peregrino. ❷ **Monte Irago** *Priv.[22÷3]* €5 © 695 452 950 basic facilities. ❸ **Domus Dei** *Par. [18÷1]* €-*donativo* Basic parish hostel with mattresses *colchonetas* in renovated church with communal meal and prayers. ❹ **La Posada del Druida** *Priv.[20÷3]* €7 © 696 820 136 with sheltered courtyard. Top of the village: ❺ **La Cruz de Fierro** *Priv.[36÷2]* €7 © 669 752 144. *P* **El Trasgu** €25-35 © 987 053 877 & shop.

Home of the 12th century hermit Gaucelmo who built a church and simple pilgrim hospital here. A stark wooden cross adds a haunting beauty to this isolated mountain hamlet now stirring back to life with the reawakening of the camino. During the last few years several of the abandoned houses have been undergoing renovation together with its 'main' street incl. useful *mini-market/café* and *La Taberna de Gaia* with *palloza* on the main road. We continue out the top end of the village onto a muddy track to re-join the road and make our way up through the heather to this *doorway through the mountain* and its memorable cross that opens up to guide us, as it has for countless millions of other pilgrims over many centuries.

2.0 km **Puerto Irago** *Cruz de Ferro* such a humble monument marks this noble gateway. This majestic spot stands 1,504m (4,934) above sea level and a simple iron cross stands atop its weathered pole that has become one of the abiding symbols of the pilgrim way of St. James. Take time to reconnect with the purpose of your journey before adding your stone or other token of love and blessing to the great pile that witnesses to our collective journeying. A modern stone chapel *Ermita de Santiago* built to commemorate an earlier Holy Year, remains locked but a grander chapel surrounds us that will remain forever open and welcoming. A track continues parallel to the road to:

2.4 km **Manjarín** *Alb.* **Manjarín** *Priv.[35]* €-*donativo* 35 mattresses. The basic facilities incl. an outside toilet and water from a well with a solar panel providing (some) hot water while an open fire provides the smoky space heater. A simple communal meal is offered for those staying the night in this mountain sanctuary. *[Next albergue: Acebo – 6.8 km].* This is another 'abandoned' village brought vividly to life by the modern knight *hospitalero Tomás* who now gives the village an official resident population of – 1! (a pilgrim's hospital existed here as early as the 12th century linking it to the Knights Templar). You may have arrived in time for the Temple ritual and Gregorian chant (from a well-worn tape recorder) and maybe the inviting aroma of coffee is your cue to visit this little mountain refuge. The atmospheric surroundings are enhanced by a virtually constant mountain mist. Continue by road below the communication mast and military base that watches our every step. A threatening image to some and to others an encouraging sign of habitation and potential support in the lonely mountains. Cross road leading to miltary post **[2.2 km]** and continue to **optional track [0.9 km].**

● ● ● ● **Alto** *Altar Mayor* (up right) to the high point on the path at 1,515m (4,920). *[200m detour for a peak experience by taking the wide track (right) to climb to the cairn at 1,535m (5,036 feet!) and soak in the Landscape Temple (weather permitting) and taste the sacredness. Respect the silence of the surroundings and when you feel complete continue s/o down the track to join the waymarked route below].*

The sprawling suburbs of Ponferrada are still an insignificant blot on the landscape ahead on the western horizon. The path now descends sharply [!]. Don't miss the path through the narrow gorge s/o right> (it relieves some of the road work and a hairpin bend) shortly afterwards you cross the road and descend (very sharply) [!] to the *Fuente de la Trucha [F.]* before entering:

6.8 km **El Acebo** *Alb.* ❶ **Elisardo Panizo** *Muni.[10÷1]* basic hostel in first building (right) as we enter the village – key with next albergue. ❷ **Mesón El Acebo** *Priv. [18÷1]*+ €7-24 ✆ 987 695 074 (left) on main street *c/Real* with bar, menú and open terrace to the rear. When full they open ❸ **Taberna de José** *Priv.[7÷2]* at the lower end of the village (right) with basic facilities. ❹ **Apóstol Santiago** *Par.[23÷1]* €-donativo adj. to the parish church (left off the main

street) with communal meals and evening prayers (see photo above). ❺ **La Casa del Peregrino** *[96÷8]*+ €10-50 ✆ 987 057 793 new build at end of the village above c/Compludo with fine views and extensive modern facilities incl. swimpool. *[Next albergue: Riego de Ambrós– 3.4 km].*

Acebo is a typical mountain village of the region with one principal street running down the middle and an open surface drain as a token gesture to channel the rain that frequently overflows it. The parish Church of San Miguel has a statue of Santiago Peregrino and is located at the far end (left). **Other Lodging** (€40+)*:* from entrance: *CR* **La Rosa del Agua** *La Tienda* ✆ 616 849 738. *CR* **La Casa del Peregrino** ✆ 987 057 875. *CR* **La Casa Monte Irago** ✆ 639 721 242. *Hs* **Mesón El Acebo**. Opp. Junta Vecinal *(La Escuela viejo)* is c/Cruz and *CR*

La Trucha ✆ 987 695 548 leading to c/Peña and the parish albergue and small shop and bar *Tienda Casa Josefina* good picnic spot and parish Church.

On the way out of the village we pass a modern sculpture of a bicycle outside the village cemetery **cementerio** [0.5 km] memorial to another pilgrim killed on the roads here and an opportunity for several detours by quiet country roads (signposted but not waymarked) as follows:

Detour [1] Herrería ● ● ● ● ● immediately beyond the cemetery turn off (left)for the medieval iron foundry of Herrería **[2.0 km]** 'hidden' in the steep valley floor. One of the oldest forges still in use with a millrace providing the power. A delightful and peaceful tree-lined glade alongside the river brings you to this historic site. Note: The 4 km round trip is equivalent to twice that on account of the very steep descent and ascent – only contemplate it if you plan staying in El Acebo or the next village.

Detour [2] Compludo [3.5 km] (2 km *beyond* Herrería) birthplace of monasticism in this region with the founding of a monastery here in the 7th century by San Fructuoso. This is a strenuous 7 km round trip by quiet road from El Acebo. This was one of the routes followed by pilgrims to the Valley of Silence and was protected by the Knights Templars and the Monastery of Compludo (no longer evident). There are a number of *casa rurales* in Espinoso de Compludo **Las Cuatro Estaciones** ✆ 987 970 092 from €50 single. The beautiful *Valle del Silencio* and Peñalba de Santiago is a further 19 km beyond Compludo *uphill* by asphalt road. You need to be fit and in need of space and silence to contemplate this detour to the hilltop monastic settlement founded by San Genadio in the 10th century on these white crags *peñalba,* which are often covered in snow. Only the church with its Mozarabic double horseshoe arch remains (a national monument) but the legacy is the mountain scenery and silence now under threat by tourism coming from Ponferrada 27 km and the easiest access route by taxi or bus.

From Acebo continue down along asphalt road veering off <left **[1.8 km]** onto a path that winds down for **[1.1 km]** into:

3.4 km **Riego de Ambros** *Albergue* **Riego de Ambros** *Muni.[30÷2]* €5 ✆ 987 695 190 basic facilities and small patio adj. the chapel of San Sebastián as we enter this pretty village. Another attractive mountain village with the traditional overhanging balconies. Due to the relative proximity of Ponferrada and a distinctly warmer climate at this lower altitude, almost all the previously abandoned houses have been renovated for residential use (including, unfortunately, the former bar in the delightful village centre). However, bar and restaurant *Ruta de Santiago* ✆ 987 418 151 200m *off* route with pilgrim menu can be found on the main road up right from the centre of the village adj. the parish Church of Santa María Magdalena (see photo) which has a beautiful early 18th century altarpiece. Up on the main road is *P* **Riego de Ambros** €20-35 ✆ 987

695 188. Make your way down the main street veering left in the centre (restaurant s/o) and veer off right down a steep rock defile [!] (caution; very slippery when wet) which leads onto a beautiful path past a magical grove of giant sweet chestnut trees *castañas* some of which have been torched.

> Up the airy mountain,
> Down the rushy glen,
> We daren't go a hunting,
> For fear of little men.
>
> *William Allingham*

We now make our way over road **[1.6 km]** *Mesón el Jardín* to continue down this breathtakingly beautiful valley to re-join the road just above Molinaseca at *Iglesia de las Angustias* built into the rockface to cross bridge **[3.1 km]:**

4.7 km Molinaseca *Puente de Peregrinos* a medieval bridge carries us over the río Meruelo into the historical village of Molinaseca. The 17th century Church of San Nicolás (with statue of San Roque) stands atop a rise to the left while the original camino continues along c/Real. The house at the junction of c/Torre is reputedly that of Doña Urraca, later Queen of Castilla y León, which provides some idea of the exclusivity attached to this genteel area that today provides a range of bars and restaurants to suit all tastes and pockets. **Other Lodging:** *(Note several* casa rurales *to let in entirety only).* Others available with overnight rooms vie for the lucrative pilgrim trade in this tranquil quarter as follows: *(€25-55):* HsR** **El Palacio** ✆ 987 453 094 on the bridge. Adj. *Hs* **The Way** ✆ 637 941 017 c/El Palacio. *Hs* **El Horno** ✆ 987 453 203 m: 627 554 260 c/El Rañadero 3 (left) also *CR* **San Nicolas** €30-45 ✆ 645 652 008 C/ La iglesia 43. Further along c/Real; *CR* **Torre de Babel** c/ Real 987 453 064 (also let as entire). *CR* **El Reloj** ✆ 987 453 124 (often closed). *CR* **Pajarapinta** ✆ 987 453 040 and at far end of town: *Hs* **Posada de Muriel** ✆ 987 453 201 Plaza del Cristo. *Alb.* **Casa Pichín** €10 dormitory ✆ 655 469 017 Travesia Manuel Fraga,17 (right of c/Real). On the main road Av. Fraga Ibibarne, ultra modern *H*** **Floriana** €55 (shared rooms from €8 – depending on season) ✆ 987 453 146 and ½ km further out:

1.0 km Molinaseca *Alb.* ❶ **Santa Marina** *Priv.*[56÷5]* €7 ✆ 987 453 077 good modern facilities (no kitchen) but communal dinner and early breakfast available (see photo right). ❷ **San Roque** *Mun.[26÷1]* €5 with adj. field for camping in the summer. Imaginative conversion of the former chapel of San Roque and while on the main road, passing traffic is minimal. *[Next albergue: Ponferrada – 6.9 km].*

REFLECTIONS:

_____

_____

_____

_____

_____

❏ **In hoc signo vinces** *In this sign thou shall conquer.* Knights Templar

25 **214.0** km (133.0 ml) – Santiago

MOLINASECA – VILLAFRANCA DEL BIERZO
(via PONFERRADA)

	--- ---	10.0	--- ---	33%
	--- ---	16.5	--- ---	54%
	--- ---	4.1	--- ---	13%
Total km		**30.6 km** (19.0 ml)		

31.6 km (^200m +1.0 km)
Alto Alto Villafranca 550m (1,805 ft)
< 🅰 🏠 > Ponferrada **5.3** km – Camponarya **16.6** – Cacabelos **22.0** – Pieros **24.9** – Valtuille **26.3** km.

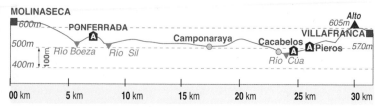

❏ **The Practical Path:** There are several options to avoid the worst of the busy road network around Ponferrada. And while this stage involves some road walking as we pass through the city, there are many cafés and bars to refresh us along the way. Remember also that waymarks through the city and its suburbs have to compete with the consumer culture and its advertising signs so extra vigilance is required. And we also have the beautiful *Bierzo* to anticipate with its sheltered microclimate and vineyards. In order to make sense of the road layout into and out of Ponferrada, this stage has been shown from Molinaseca to Villafranca. If you decide to stay in Ponferrada there is much to do and see and several interesting detours that you can take from there. Alternatively, you can visit the main sites (all of which are directly along the camino) and still make your way relatively easily to the albergue in Cacabelos (22.7 km) or with greater effort to Villafranca del Bierzo (30.6 km) by evening. But in this latter case, you must leave Molinaseca early in the morning.

❏ **The Mystical Path:** Out of the ruins of the Templar Castle and the fire that consumed its inhabitants, arises the phoenix and the tau, ageless symbols of change and growth that reveal the Divine behind the manifested form. Behind the symbols is the reality of Love that informs them. Will we allow the flames to burn up our old outworn beliefs and allow the new to reveal itself? Are we ready for a leap of faith?

❏ **Personal Reflections:** "*... Somewhere I passed an old man pushing a wheelbarrow. His toothless smile touched me so deeply that I had a momentary impression that he was my father: representing The Father. I am left speechless ... my reality is shifting ... why is it that I cannot recall the last few hours? This altered perception and emotional surge is overwhelming me. My heart feels so open my chest is aching. I seem to break in and out of conscious awareness, one instant of complete clarity, the next only haziness. I resolve in this moment to continue my pilgrimage in total silence. I don't know for how long; I know only that something is seeking to reveal*

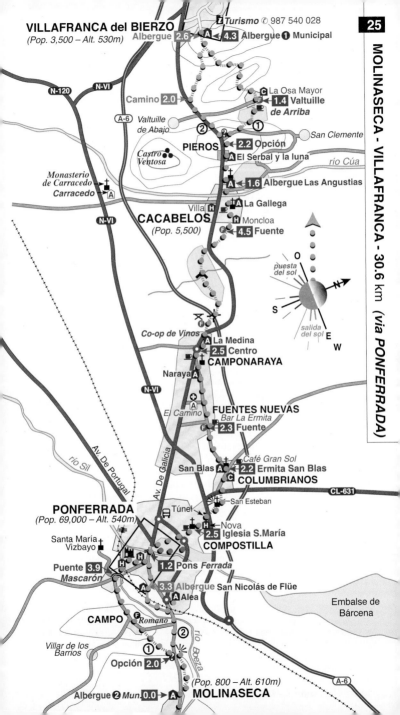

VILLAFRANCA del BIERZO
(Pop. 3,500 – Alt. 530m)

🛈 *Turismo* © 987 540 028

Albergue **2.6** ◀ 🅰 ◀ **4.3** Albergue ❶ Municipal

Camino **2.0** →

🅰-6 *Valtuille de Abajo*

◉②

PIEROS

🅲 La Osa Mayor
🅰 🅵 **1.4** ▶ **Valtuille de Arriba**
①

○ *San Clemente*

🅰 **2.2** Opción

🅰 El Serbal y la luna

río Cúa

N-120   N-VI

Monasterio de Carracedo ✝
Carracedo 🅰

N-VI

🅰 **1.6** Albergue Las Angustias

CACABELOS
(Pop. 5,500)

Villa 🅷 🅰 La Gallega
🅷 Moncloa
🅵 ◀ **4.5** Fuente

Castro Ventosa

🔺

puesta del sol

O

S

salida del sol

E

W

Co-op de Vinos

🅰 La Medina
🅰 **2.5** Centro
CAMPONARAYA

Naraya 🅰

N-VI

✚
El Camino

FUENTES NUEVAS

Bar La Ermita
🅵 **2.3** Fuente

río Sil

Av. De Portugal

Café Gran Sol
San Blas 🅰 ◀ **2.2** Ermita San Blas
🅲 **COLUMBRIANOS**

CL-631

✝ San Esteban

PONFERRADA
(Pop. 69,000 – Alt. 540m)

Túnel

🅷 Nova
🅰 **2.5** Iglesia S.María
COMPOSTILLA

Santa María Vizbayo ✝

🅷 🅷

Puente **3.9**
Mascarón

1.2 Pons *Ferrada*

🅰 **3.3** Albergue San Nicolás de Flüe

🅰 Alea

CAMPO

🅵 *Romano*

②

Villar de los Barrios

①

Opción **2.0**

río Boeza

Embalse de Bárcena

🅰-6

Albérgue ❷ *Mun.* **0.0** → 🅰 **MOLINASECA**
(Pop. 800 – Alt. 610m)

itself that can only be heard in the quiet. Amidst these uncontrollable tears I write this simple message to hang around my neck. I trust others will understand what I can't articulate and barely comprehend myself. I don't even know if it makes sense in Spanish, 'Saludos. Yo peregrino a pie, caminante en silencio. Paz.'

0.0 km **Molinaseca** from albergue ❷ continue down the main road *(or just beyond the tennis court turn off right to track alongside fruit orchards parallel to the road)* to top of a rise with Ponferrada visible ahead:

2.0 km **Opción** [?] viewpoint with the towers of the basilica, occupying the high point in the old town, now visible in the middle distance.

The alternative route ② **into Ponferrada** 0.9 km shorter to the Templar castle via main road with direct access to 2 albergues. S/o (right) along main road down to Puente río Boeza [**1.5 km**] *[formerly this entry into Ponferrada was known as the Passage of the Boat Paso de la Barca as the deep river could only be crossed with the help of the ferryman].* After [**0.4 km**] ❖[a] For albergue ❶ veer left off the main road by factories onto a path through waste ground veering up right [**0.8 km**] and right again to cross railway line [**0.4 km**] veering left to albergue [**0.2 km**]:

3.3 km Albergue ❶ San Nicolás de Flüe *Par.*
[174÷10] €-donativo Ⓒ 987 413 381 situated in the grounds of the convento del Carmen on c/de la Loma (off Av. del Castillo) purpose-built hostel (mixed reports) with patio and garden area. Evening prayers offered. *[Next albergue: Cacabelos – 17.5 km].* To continue to the Templar Castle and the camino turn left on Av. del Castillo and shortly after veer right at a tourist information board into Av. del Castillo to re-join the recommended route at **Castillo de los Templarios [0.6 km].** Alternatively, go s/o Av. del Castillo into c/Esteban de la Puente and into the main square *Plaza Ayuntamiento* where most of the shops and restaurants are situated and the relocated Tourist office. ❖[b] For alb. ❷ keep s/o along main road (LE 142) to its junction with calle de Castillo and turn up right and right again into Calle Teleno. *Albergue* ❷ *Alea Priv.[18÷4]* €10 Communal dinner €8 *V.option* Ⓒ 987 404 133 m: 660 416 251 c/Teleno, 33 with small patio garden, part of the modern suburbs.

For the **recommended** route ① veer <left onto wide gravel track down past pilgrim memorial (right) and up steeply and down again to *Campo* [**1.2 km**]. Interesting Roman water cistern *Fuente Romano* still functioning and worth the 150m detour (to the right as you enter the village). Campo is an historic pueblo with well preserved buildings emblazoned with coats of arms and the 17th century Church of St. Blase in a grove of olive trees (off route left). Continue down c/La Francesa past *Motor bar* over stream to open ground and **option** [**0.7 km**] to walk off road above the banks of the río Boeza to re-join road 1 km later via model aircraft park *Campo Municipal de Aeromodelismo* (passage prohibited when flying in progress). The waymarked route follows the asphalt road to enter *Los Barrios*, a modern suburb of Ponferrada passing *Bar El Cruce* to cross the pedestrian bridge over the río Boeza [**2.0 km**].

3.9 km **Puente Mascarón** *Opción* [a] If you intend staying the night in Ponferrada at the albergue then keep s/o on over the bridge then over the railway (Santiago-León) and up onto the busy Av. del Castillo [**0.4 km**] were the hostel is visible over to the right **[0.3** km]. **[b] Detour [1]** (see other detours later) *Iglesia de Santa María de Vizbayo* (national asset). Just before the bridge turn up the *camino de Otero* that snakes uphill for 0.7 km [1.4 km round trip] to this delightful 11th century Romanesque church with a fine view back over the city from its wooded site.

Note: the following waymarked route [1.2 km] takes us through the medieval city and past the main historic sites (see town plan):

Veer <left over the medieval bridge up the camino Bajo de San Andres under the railway bridge and turn right> into c/del Hospital past Hospital de la Reina into Av. del Castillo opp. the Baroque Church ❶ *Iglesia San Andrés XVIIᵗʰC* (with its statue *Cristo del Castillo* linking it to the Templars). On our right @N°112 *Alb.* ❸ **Guiana** *Priv.[90÷18]* €12 © 987 409 327 (Ana) and on the left ❷ *Castillo de los Templarios*.

The magnificent 12th century Templar castle has been declared a national monument and recently reopened after extensive renovations so we are able to explore its interior and revel in its romantic past. An incongruous modern exhibition centre has been added which currently displays replicas of Templar and other religious texts in the *Templum Libri* accessed by a lift! Ponferrada came under the protectorate of the Templar Order by decree of King Fernando II in 1178. Their official presence here was short lived as the Order was outlawed in 1312 and disbanded by a Church fearful of their increasing power and esoteric traditions. The modern town is on the other (western) side of the río Sil, visible from the castle entrance. If you don't want to pay the entrance fee there is a delightful walk riverside of the castle. Several cafés in the area serve pilgrim menus (and breakfast if you have come from Molinaseca) and adjoining the castle walls is a helpful tourist office.

From the Templar Castle (you can head back to the pilgrim hostel via c/ Pregoneros) or continue up c/ Gil y Carrasco (Fitzroy's outdoor clothing and equipment left) into the attractive Plaza Virgen de la Encina with more cafés and ❸ *Basílica de la Encina XVIᵗʰC*. *[In bygone days this whole region was covered with evergreen holm oak* encina *and in one such tree a vision of the Virgen appeared elevating this church to Basilica status and the Virgin to patroness of the Bierzo region].* The waymarked route directs pilgrims down past *La Galeria* via c/ Del Rañadero towards the exit. The following 'historic' detour adds only 200m! Take the c/del Reloj and just before the clock tower that gives the street its name is the Royal Prison *Cárcel Real* (right) ❹ *XVIᵗʰC* worth a visit just for the beautifully restored building now the *Museo del Bierzo* displaying artefacts from the Palaeolithic, Roman and modern eras. Continue under the Clock Tower ❺ *La Torre del Reloj XVIᵗʰC* into the Plaza Mayor with its impressive town hall *Ayuntamiento*. This covers the main highlights of the old city. If you plan to go on to Villafranca del Bierzo then you won't have time for any further exploring and should proceed <left down the winding steps (beside the modern kiosk) turning <left again into c/Calzada where the waymarked route joins from the left (c/ Del Rañadero) to cross the río Sil at:

1.2 km Pons Ferrada *Iron Bridge* ❖ (1.2 km from Puente Mascarón).

PONFERRADA: modern metropolis with an expanding population of 69,000 and capital of El Bierzo with its unique micro climate that produces the respected Bierzo wines worth sampling along with the thick pork sausages *botillo* locally marinated and served with boiled potatoes and vegetables *cachelos*. Most of the historic sites are neatly condensed into the old medieval city that occupies the high ground around the castle. The camino winds its way past these sites and so they can be explored on the way through (see previous page) between *Puente Mascarón* (entry) and Iron Bridge *Pons Ferrata* (exit). This latter bridge gives the city its name and is the reason for the sprawling modern suburbs that support a strong industrial base built on the back of the coal and iron reserves that have been mined in this area from medieval times. The original bridge was reinforced with iron as far back as the 11th century. There are a number of earlier Roman and Mozarabic sites in the area that include:

Detour ● ● ● ● ● **[1] Iglesia de Santa María de Vizbayo** (described above from Puente Mascarón). It is one of the oldest churches in the area and has a splendid view over the city from its quiet hillside site. **Detour [2] Iglesia de Santo Tomás de las Ollas** in the northern suburbs (2 km north of the Plaza Mayor, past the Parque del Planto) we find this magnificent Mozarabic 10th century church with the distinctive horseshoe arches. The original pilgrim road into the city used to go by here. It is little visited by pilgrims but well worth the trip if you are staying in Ponferrada. Further afield – by bus or share a taxi are: **Detour [3] Santiago de Peñalba** another 10th century Mozarabic Church located in its magnificent mountain hideaway in the Valley of Silence *Valle del Silencio* 25 km out of Ponferrada (referred to under Acebo detours) and usually visited along with **Detour [4] Las Médulas** – the Roman gold mines on the slopes of the Montes Aquilianos 23 km away off the road to Peñalba.

❏ *Turismo:* ✆ 987 424 236 c/ Gil y carrasco, 4. ❏ *Albergues* ❶ ❷ *(previous page)*. ❏ *Hoteles Centro:* Av del Castillo Nº84 ❸ *Hs*** **Rabel** €38 ✆ 987 417 176 / Nº115 ❹ *H**** **El Castillo** €45+ ✆ 987 456 227. ❺ *Hs*** **Virgen de la Encina** €35 ✆ 987 409 632 c/Comendador (opp. Turismo). ❻ *Hs*** **Los Templarios** €35 ✆ 987 411 484 c/Flores Osorio. ❼ *H**** **Aroi Bierzo Plaza** €55+ ✆ 987 409 001 Plaza del Ayuntamiento. *Other side of rio Sil:* ● *Hs*** **Río Selmo** €35 ✆ 987 402 665 c/Río Selmo,22. ● *H**** **Madrid** ✆ 987 411 550 Av. Puebla,44. ● *Hs* **San Miguel II** ✆ 987 426 700 c/Juan de Lama,18. ● *Hs* **San Miguel I** ✆ 987 411 047 c/Luciana Fernández,2. ❏ *Restaurantes:* wide selection includes: *La Fortaleza* c/ Gil y carrasco (by the castle). *Galeria* plaza Virgen del Encina. *La Fonda* plaza Mayor (first floor).

Pons Ferrada Cross the bridge and turn imm. right> into Pasaje de Telefonica c/Río Urdiales where the waymarks direct us diagonally <left over the large carpark ❖.

● ● ● ● ● *There is an opportunity here to take a path through* Parque de la Concordia *alongside río Sil turning left at the next bridge* Puente de Hierro *into c/ del Reino de Léon or to continue under the next bridge [0.6 km] past sports ground before veering up left on one of the paths by new road bridge* Av. de América *(earthworks here may require a degree of flexibility) to re-join the waymarked route into Av. Segunda.*

❖ From the carpark the waymarked route turns right along Av de las Huertas del Sacramento s/o at roundabout *La Máquina [monument to the pepper growers]*. Cross c/del Reino de Léon and right at next roundabout into Av. de la Libertad to next major roundabout *Glorieta* **[1.5 km]** (Av. de América / bridge). Here at the outskirts of the city we cross over onto our first dedicated pilgrim track (opp. derelict power station now *Museo Energia* past coal slag-heaps and <left into *Av. Segunda* and the neatly ordered suburb of Compostilla. The route here is well waymarked with concrete bollards past the Red Cross *Cruz Roja* and *Café-bar Compostilla / Casa Lola* through *archway* **[1.0 km]** to:

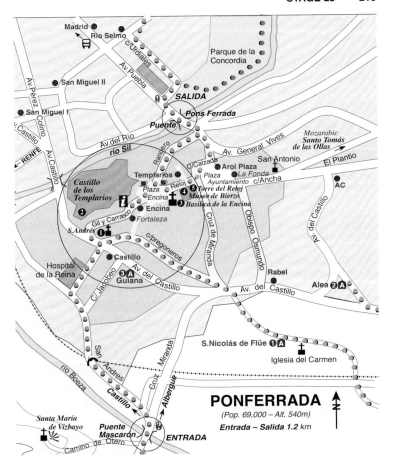

PONFERRADA
(Pop. 69,000 – Alt. 540m)
Entrada – Salida 1.2 km

2.5 km **Compostilla** *Iglesia Santa María* decorative murals around the covered portico and memorial to Santiago Peregrino. Turn right> down the side of the sports club passing a pilgrim cross and another mural on the gable end of a small chapel onto a track and under pylons to skirt the end of the suburbs at c/Cubo de Finisterre. The camino now heads out past *H*******Novo** © 987 424 441 through tunnel under the N-VI *ring road* [**1.0** km] past vineyards and the *Iglesia San Esteban [F.]* with delightful views from its arcaded *rear* porch. Cross main road [!] into the village of Columbrianos, a busy suburb of Ponferrada with *CR* **Almendro De María** €50+ © 633 481 100 c/ Real 56. Veer <left by ermita [**1.2** km].

2.2 km **Columbrianos** *Ermita San Blas* small chapel with pilgrim mural, site of original pilgrim hospice and **San Blas** *Priv.[18÷3]+* €8 +€30 © 611 614 149 (Jesús y Rosa Mari) c/ San Blas 5 (XVII). *Café Gran Sol* main road (right). Follow sign to Felix Castro along minor road through market gardens past rest area *[F.]* to:
2.3 km **Fuentes Nuevas** *Bar La Ermita* opp. tiny chapel *ermita del Divino Cristo* with pilgrim fountain *[F.]*. Proceed down main street of this sleepy town past *Taberna Mateo* junction of **c/La Iglesia [0.4** km] [*Detour 500m to El Camino*

© *672 057 061 c/ Médicos sin Fronteras, 8].* Continue s/o past *La Casona* into **Camponaraya** **[1.4** km] and *Albergue* ❶ **Naraya** *Priv.[26÷5]* €8 © 987 459 159 on Av. de Galicia, 506 just as we enter the straggling industrial suburb with the busy N-120 running through it with various cafes (waymarks impressed in the pavement slabs). Pass small park with shade and fountain *[F.]* adj. the modern parish Church of San Ildefonso. Proceed over the río Naraya to the town 'centre' **[0.7 km].**

2.5 km **Camponaraya** *Centro Meson El Reloj* and *La Guitarra* offer some respite from the traffic and the 'new' hostal (built in 1786!) ❷ **La Medina** *Priv.[20÷2]* €10 © 987 463 962 m: 667 348 551 Av. Camino de Santiago, 87. Continue along the main road to the wine cooperative *Cooperativa Viñas del Bierzo* **[0.9** km] with shop *tienda* offering a sample of wine and pincho for €1.50! or imm. beyond free *agua* and rest area *zona de descanso*. Continue over the A-6 onto track through vineyards over arroyo Magaz **[1.6** km] and continue through woodland to cross over the N-120 **[1.2** km] [!] and continue to pilgrim rest area at the start of Cacabelos **[0.8** km].

4.5 km **Fuente Cacabelos** *[F.]* opposite modern wine bodega. *Note municipal albergue is the far side of Cacabelos (1.6 km away).*

CACABELOS with a population of 5,500 was an important medieval pilgrim halt with 5 hospices founded for the care of pilgrims. Today we encounter a like number of hotels and pensions to care for us. The town has an archaeological museum displaying artefacts found at the nearby Roman settlements and a wine museum celebrating the increasingly popular wine from the area and the history of its production.

We enter the village via c/de los Peregrinos with wine store *Prado del Tope* built on the site of the former 17th century pilgrim hospital in Plaza San Lázaro which also offers us the exclusive *H*** **Moncloa de San Lázaro** €75 © 987 546 101 and restaurant *(try the first floor café – part of the original hostel accessed via staircase in the yard).* Continue past a variety of bars and restaurants to the church of **Santa María** *XVI.* The original 10th century apse safeguards a Baroque statue of the Virgin. Detour 100m (left) to the tree-lined *Plaza Mayor* with colonnaded houses and cafés and **Turismo** © 987 546 011 (summer only) and just beyond, on the main road, the pilgrim friendly *H**** **Villa** €36 © 987 548 148. **Other Lodging** in the central area directly on the camino in *c/Santa Maria* include: *Hs*** **Santa María** © 987 549 588 @Nº20. *Hs* **El Molino** © 987 546 829 @Nº10 and *Alb. Hs** **La Gallega** *Priv.[30÷7]* €10 © 987 549 476 m: 680 917 109 @Nº23 with adj. cyber bar and café.

There are several detours to sites of historical interest in the area: **[1]** ● ● ● ● 10thc **Monasterio de San Salvador de Carrecedo** *Albergue* **Monasterio** *Priv.[20÷1]*+ €10-30 © 608 888 211 (Begatur). 3 kilometres south (left) of the route in beautiful and peaceful landscape. Interesting monastic complex with royal palace including the exquisite Queen's balcony and museum on monastic life. **[2]** ● ● ● ● **Castro Ventosa**-Bergidum Flavium birthplace of El Bierzo with pre-Roman and Roman settlements. Situated on an elevated site 1 km south (left) of the camino, easily accessed from Pieros.

Continue past the church to join the N-120 and cross the bridge over the río Cua past the ancient olive press and weir to:

1.6 km Las Angustias far end of town (right) *Alb.* **Cacabelos** *Muni.[70÷35]* ℂ 987 547 167 on Plaza del Santuario. 70 beds in chalet style rooms with 2 beds in each arranged in a semi circle patio around the church *Capilla de Las Angustia XVIII* occupying site of an earlier chapel and pilgrim hospice. *[Next albergue: Pieros – 1.7 km].*

Continue along N-120 on gravel track up past simple wooden cross (left). *[The entire hill behind was the site of the Asturian city of Castrum Bergidum, which was later conquered and occupied by the Romans].* We now enter the small village of **Pieros [1.7** km] with 11th century parish church and *[F.]* on the main road and in c/ El Pozo (right on entry) *Albergue* **El Serbal y la Luna** *Priv.*[20÷3]* V. ℂ 639 888 924 communal vegetarian meal also library/quiet room & physiotherapy. *CR* **Castro Ventosa** ℂ 670 508 530 San Roque. Continue past *Bar tapas* to option at top of rise **[0.5** km]:

2.2 km Opción [?] ❖

For the alternative road route ② keep s/o over rio Valtuilles *Mesón Venta del Jubileo* Stay on the N-120 and watch out for the arrows that will take you off the main road to a pleasant track (right) past *Estudio de Escultura*:

2.0 km Camino turn right up onto a track that winds its way up through vineyards to rejoin the recommended route [1.4 km] into Villafranca [1.2 km].

2.6 km Villafranca del Bierzo Albergue ❶ see below for details.

❖ For the **recommended** old road *c/Viejo* ① turn right> onto a short stretch of asphalt and veer off <left **[0.3** km] onto a wide track that winds its way through vineyards onto a shaded lane down past *Café Escuela* continue along c/Camino de Santiago to the centre of this delightful sleepy hamlet **[1.1** km]:

1.4 km Valtuille de Arriba main square Plaza Miguel Ochoa *Cantina Estrella [F.]* La Osa Mayor *CR* ℂ 987 562 185. *[unfazed by the constant flow of pilgrims the villagers appear to have retained their deep respect for the Way of Santiago].* Continue through Plaza del Fondo del Lugar and head up the farm track into the stunning beauty of the El Bierzo landscape. Proceed up (and down) through the rolling hills covered with vineyards towards a whitewashed house between two pines on the horizon before our final descent past casa Burbia down to:

4.3 km Villafranca del Bierzo

Albergue ❶ **Municipal** *[62÷3]* €6 ℭ 987 542 356 located below the path (first building right) overlooking the town. Attic floor *buhardilla* (hot in summer) purpose-built municipal hostel *(overflow on colchones in Colegio Divina Pastora adj. Turismo).* Next we come to the beautiful 12th century Romanesque Church of Santiago with its north entrance 'Door of Forgiveness' *Puerta del Perdón [here medieval pilgrims unable*  *to continue to Santiago received absolution and a compostela. On this account Villafranca was sometimes referred to as 'little Santiago'].* In these contemporary times an 'alternative' physical and spiritual healing may be available in the adjoining legendary ❷ **Ave Fenix** *Asoc.[80÷5]* €5 ℭ 987 540 229 with communal supper €7 followed, perhaps, by a mystical *Queimada*. An additional service offered by the Jato family is transport of backpacks *mochilas* up to O'Cebreiro to await arrival at the albergue. (These services are available whether staying at this hostel or not). The Phoenix *Fenix* rises, literally, from the ashes. The previous hostel was destroyed by fire and rebuilt by volunteers and international donations, although many will recall the interim encampment, a veritable haven of hospitality. Recent feedback has not been so fulsome but the pilgrim accepts with equanimity the changing standards found along the way. As founding father Jesús Jato states, *'El Camino es tiempo de meditación interior, no itinerario turístico.'*

Other albergues: ❸ **El Castillo** *Priv.[22÷4]* €10 ℭ 987 540 344 (Marta y Javi) c/ El Castillo 8. ❹ **Hospedería San Nicolás El Real** *Priv.[75÷4]*+ €5-30 ℭ 696 978 653 c/Travesía de San Nicolás adj. Plaza Mayor. ❺ **Leo** *Priv.[32÷7]* €10 ℭ 987 542 658 m: 658 049 244 c/Ribadeo (c/ del Agua), 10. ❻ **de la Piedra ♥** *Priv.*[16 ÷2]*+ €8-24 ℭ 987 540 260 welcoming network* hostel c/Espíritu Santo,14 (one of the last houses as you leave town). *(albergue Viña Fermita on c/Calvo Sotelo remains closed following a fire).* [Next albergue: Pereje – 4.8 km].

Villafranca is a popular tourist venue as well as a pilgrim halt, so there is a wide range of lodging. At the top end of the town and price bracket *H***** **Parador** €85+ ℭ 987 540 175 a soulless rebuild on Av. Calvo Sotelo. **La Puerta del Perdón** €50 ℭ 987-540 614 Plaza Prim,4. *Central adj. Plaza Mayor* €45-55: *Hs* **Ultreia** ℭ 987 540 391 corner of Puentecillo. *H******Posada Plaza Mayor** ℭ 987 540 620. *H** **San Francisco** ℭ 987 540 465. *CR* **La Llave** ℭ 987 542 739 c/del Agua,37 and *H**** **Las Doñas del Portazgo** ℭ 987 542 742 boutique hotel (former toll house) adj. bridge. *Hs*** **Burbia** ℭ 987 542 667 Fuente Cubero, 13. *Hs*** **Tres Campanas** ℭ 670 359 692 Av. Paradaseca 27 (+500m). *Over rio Burbia: Hs*** **Casa Méndez** ℭ 987 540 055 c/Espiritu Santo 1. *Hs** **El Cruce** ℭ 987 542 469 c/San Salvador 37. *P** **Venecia** ℭ 987 540 468 on main road N-VI. *N.B: wherever you stay make sure you get a good nights sleep to fortify yourself for the strenuous but stupendous hike the next day. Tomorrow brings us up and over the pass into O'Cebreiro and Galicia.*

VILLAFRANCA DEL BIERZO with a population of 3,500 has a full range of restaurants and shops including *La Casita del Espejo* on c/del Agua which offers gifts for the pilgrim including Reiki massage and Tarot with Paula. A helpful *Turismo* ℭ 987 540 028 on Av. Bernardo Díez Olebar is located beyond the main square and overlooking the park. This delightful town began to develop in this idyllic spot along the *camino francés* in the 11th century. A tour of the main historic sites includes:

❶ **Church of Santiago** *XIthC* a Romanesque jewel with its fine *Puerta de Perdón* and handsome statue of St. James in full pilgrim regalia inside. ❷ **Castillo Palacio de los Marqueses** *XVthC* (just below albergue 2) with its distinctive turrets, several of which were destroyed during the Peninsular War of 1808 and, further down in town **Plaza Mayor** with Ayuntamiento and cafés tables spilling out onto the square. Up to the right along c/San Geronimo we come to ❸ **Monasterio de San Francisco** founded at the request of Doña Urraca in the 13th century (some say by Saint Francis himself). *[Note: if you continue past this church a footpath will bring you back to the albergues on the opposite side of the valley.]* Beyond Plaza Mayor we arrive at the austere ❹ **Iglesia San Nicolás** *XVIIthC* further on we pass the *Turismo* and adjacent ❺ **Convento Divina Pastora** (formerly one of the 5 pilgrim hospices that attended the large numbers of medieval pilgrims that passed this way). A walk through the public gardens *Jardin Municipal Alameda* brings us to ❻ **Iglesia Colegiata** formerly the Iglesia Nuestra Señora de Cluniaco (the monks from Cluny were amongst the first arrivals here from France). We can end this circular route by continuing out and up towards O'Cebreiro or return to the albergues via the medieval Water street *calle Agua* with its noble houses bearing their armorial shields. The famous Spanish novelist Gil y Carrasco was born here and we also pass ❼ **Convento y Iglesia de San José** founded in the 17th century by the canon of Santiago Cathedral and finally into c/Rua Nueva to ❽ **Convento de la Anunciada** where the Marqueses from the Palacio above are buried.

❐ **This is the way of peace; overcome hatred with love.** *Peace Pilgrim*

26 183.4 km (114.0 ml) – Santiago

VILLAFRANCA del BIERZO – O'CEBREIRO
Main route ❶ via Pereje.

▒▒▒▒▒▒	--- ---	15.3	--- ---	53%
▬▬▬	--- ---	11.4	--- ---	39%
▬▬▬	--- ---	<u>2.2</u>	--- ---	8%
Total km		**28.9 km**	(18.0 ml)	

◣◣	--- ---	33.4 km (^900m + 4.5 km)
Alto ▲	O Cebreiro 1,310m (4,297 ft)	

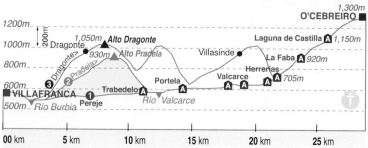

❐ **The Practical Path:** A strenuous stage, particularly at the end, but wide choice of hostels en route. 3 options on leaving Villafranca – determined by: **[a]** prevailing weather conditions **[b]** personal level of fitness and **[c]** the kind of experience you want to create. All routes are likely to prove demanding. This stage represents one of the steepest of the whole pilgrimage but the climb is rewarded with stunning views along the Valcarce valley that will keep spirits high. The least taxing option is the noisy N-VI route and while the completion of the A-6 motorway has greatly reduced traffic using it, there are several dangerous bends, so stay alert.

Intermediate accommodation: on **main route ❶** *distances from albergue* **❶**: Pereje **5.8** km – Trabadelo – **10.2** km – Portela Valcarce **14.1** km – Ambasmestas **15.5** km – Vega de Valcarce **16.5** km – Ruitelán **19.3** km – Herrerías **20.7** km – La Faba **24.1** km – Laguna **26.4** km. *Note*: first hostel on **scenic route ❷** is Trabadelo – **11.4** km and on **remote route ❸** Herrerías – **26.3** km! The valley is steep sided (*Vallis Carceras* = narrow valley) and heavily wooded with mostly pine and chestnut, so all options provide shade. There are shops, bars, hotels and pilgrim hostels all along the valley floor in the villages we pass through, but make sure you have water and some snacks for the Pradela route before leaving Villafranca and full provisions for the remote and poorly waymarked Dragonte route (seasoned walkers only).

❐ **The Mystical Path:** We cannot give peace unless we first create peace in our own hearts and minds. By giving Peace we extend It and thereby reverse the laws of this world for Peace, like Love increases the more we give it away. How much can we find to give away today? When we are able to respond lovingly to all our interactions we send an expansion of loving energy into our fear-filled world.

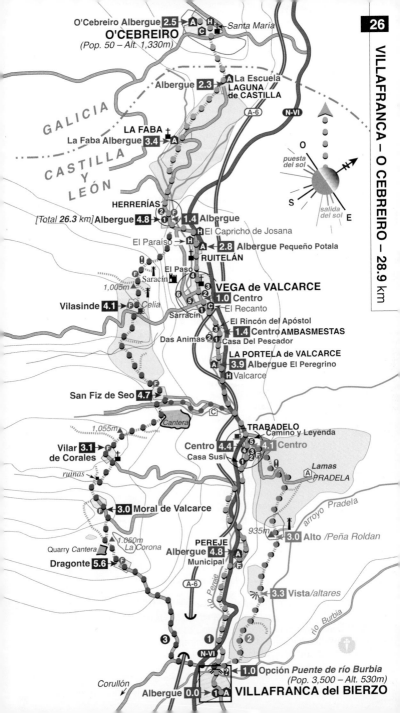

O'Cebreiro Albergue **2.5** → A H *Santa Maria*
O'CEBREIRO G
(Pop. 50 – Alt. 1,330m)

GALICIA

Albergue **2.3** A La Escuela
LAGUNA
de CASTILLA
A-6   N-VI

*puesta
del sol*

LA FABA †
La Faba Albergue **3.4** → A

CASTILLA
Y
LEÓN

O
S   E
*salida
del sol*

HERRERÍAS
[Total 26.3 km] Albergue **4.8** → F **1.4** Albergue
H El Capricho de Josana
El Paraiso → H
A **2.8** Albergue *Pequeño Potala*
El Paso   **RUITELÁN**
Saracin
1,005m

Vilasinde 4.1 → F
Celia
Sarracín

A **1.0** Centro
G
El Recanto

El Rincón del Apóstol
1.4 Centro **AMBASMESTAS**
Das Animas   Casa Del Pescador

LA PORTELA de VALCARCE
A **3.9** Albergue *El Peregrino*
H *Valcarce*

San Fiz de Seo **4.7** →
F

Cantera   C

1,055m

TRABADELO
Camino y Leyenda
Vilar 3.1 →   Centro **4.4** **4.1** Centro
de Corales   †   Casa Susi

A *Lamas*
PRADELA

ruinas

3.0 Moral de Valcarce
F

arroyo Pradela

935m **3.0 Alto** */Peña Roldan*

Quarry *Cantera*   *1,060m*
La Corona
Dragonte 5.6 → F

PEREJE
Albergue **4.8** A
Municipal
A-6

3.3 Vista/*altares*

río Burbia

③   ①   ②

N-VI   **1.0 Opción** *Puente de río Burbia*
(Pop. 3,500 – Alt. 530m)

Corullón
Albergue **0.0** → A **VILLAFRANCA del BIERZO**

❐ **Personal Journal:** *"…Sleeping under the stars has deepened my experience but today my muscles ache and my heart feels heavy. I don't understand what is happening but I will continue to walk in silence and trust that everything will reveal itself in time; 'when the student is ready the teacher appears.' The weariness I felt was intensified by a busload of raucous pilgrims who completely surrounded the bar. It seemed an age before I could get the owner to read my note so I chose, unwittingly, to extend resentment instead of love. They were my teachers, the lesson; If I am dependent on the behaviour of others I will never find peace within …"*

---

❶ **Ruta Carretera N-VI [28.9** km] ● ● ● ● (adjusted for climb 33.4 km – total ascent 900m). The road route is the shortest with several villages providing shops and bars along the way. However, it is dangerous where you have to cross the N-VI so stay focussed and walk inside the crash barriers wherever provided.

❷ **Ruta Pradela** ● ● ● ● **[30.1** km] (adjusted for climb 36.1 km – total ascent 1,200m). This scenic route is very beautiful and makes the most of the early morning sun which doesn't penetrate into the lower Valcarce valley until later in the day. The steep climb up (400m) is rewarded with wonderful views back over Villafranca, but you will need to allow an extra hour or two for this longer route with the extra the ascent *and* steep descent it involves. Its use is, inexplicably, discouraged by locals.

❸ **Camino Dragonte [34.5** km] ● ● ● ● (adjusted for climb 44.0 km /ascent – 1,950m). ***Note: For experienced walkers only. Plan to stay at Herrerias 26.3** km* **(32.5 adjusted).** Don't walk this route if you lack confidence or in poor weather as the mountain passes are remote and exposed. This is the longest and most arduous route and, accordingly, the most spectacular. You need to be fit and take food and water with you as the only bar is often closed! Waymarking is poor so you need a good sense of direction and reserve energy to retrace your steps should you get lost. The extensive woodland offers protection from rain or sun but mountain weather is unpredictable at any time of year so stick to the other routes if in any doubt.

0.0 km **Villafranca del Bierzo** from albergue ❶ make your way down into c/del Agua (c/Ribadeo) and at the far end turn <left (by hotel Las Doñas) up the steps by pilgrim statue and over río Burbia to option point.

1.0 km **Opción** – *Puente Burbia café Burbia* (right) first option point **[a]** 50m [!] *not* well indicated. If you intend to take the scenic Pradela route ❷ you *must* leave the asphalt road here up the steep cobbled street right> [!] (see photo right). For main N-VI route ❶ to Pereje continue s/o for 150m to option point **[b]** by Casa Mendez. *(left for Dragonte route ❸ see later).* For main route turn right> and continue along the río Valcarce on the old N-VI. The route follows

the river valley parallel to the main road which has been realigned many times and the traffic is now much reduced on account of the new autopista. It has also been improved with the addition of crash barriers that now separate pilgrims from the traffic but care is still needed when crossing over. Continue all the way into:

4.8 km **Pereje** *[F.]* **Alb. Pereje** *Muni.[56÷2]* €5 © 987 540 138 with outside terrace. **CR Las Corinas** © 987 540 138. The main street is called *Camino Santiago* witnessing to its pilgrim past. *[The administration of Pereje was the cause of a dispute between O'Cebreiro and Villafranca taking both monarchy and papacy to resolve. This seems to mirror the tension between the culture of the lowlands and highlands and between the provinces of León and Galicia. The atmosphere, topography and weather all appear to change in this valley].* Re-join the N-VI into:

4.4 km Trabadelo *[F.]* Alb. ❶ Casa Susi *Priv.[12÷2]* €-donativo © 675 242 114 (Eng.) / © 602 616 968 (Esp.) with communal dinner and riverside location. ❷ Crispeta *Priv.[34÷5]+* €6–€25 © 620 329 386. All facilities incl. sauna & outside terrace. ❸ Parroquial *[22÷4]* €5 © 630 628 130 c/La Iglesia. ❹ Municipal *[36÷6]* €6 © 687 827 987 adj. bar. ❺ Camino y Leyenda *Priv.[16÷6]+* €8–€28 © 628 921 776 (see photo >). *Other Lodging: CR* El Puente Peregrino €38 © 987 566 500 with vegetarian menu *V. CR* Os Arroxos (same family run Crispeta). *CR* Casa Ramón © 665 610 028. *CR* Pilar Frade © 649 844 307. *Hs* Nova Ruta €50 © 987 566 431 on

the main road. **Trabadelo** wide range of facilities. From as early as the 9th century the church here was under the possession of the cathedral in Santiago and an uneasy peace existed with other centres of administration. The castle of Auctares and the hills above Trabadelo were a base for outlaws to exact their own 'tolls' on innocent pilgrims. We now join the pilgrims who have taken the top Pradela route. *Note: alternative route [3] via Dragonte is described after Herrerías.*

For **scenic route** ❶ **Camino de Pradela** turn up right> into c/Pradela and, if the warning signs for fitness worry you, remember that if you have made it this far you should encounter no undue problems. Indeed, the lower route along the main N-VI may carry greater risk of injury and, depending on the time of day and year, the sun will not penetrate the valley floor in the morning. Many pilgrims use the road route because they are unaware of a choice or miss the narrow turning up into Pradela as signposts may have been defaced. Continue up the steep incline onto earth path that skirts smallholdings and vineyards on our left and pine forest above until we reach a **rock outcrop [1.0** km]. The path now climbs less steeply and levels out at sign for local walk (right) *Ruta Circular* **[1.7** km] we head s/o along the ridge and take the 2nd (higher) path towards the trees on the horizon ahead **[0.6** km].

3.3 km Vista / *altares* stunning views have inspired the creation of personal 'altars' to the journey of life. Continue above the tree line to the high point at:

3.0 km Alto / *Peña Roldan* we now enter a delightful stretch through chestnut woods *castaño*. *[Alb.* Lamas *Priv.[10÷1]* €5 / menú €10 Ana y Miguel © 677 569 764 off route 1 km in Pradela 4x4 available].* Several paths converge in the woods & waymarks are poor but head s/o (westerly) to emerge off route onto asphalt road (to Pradela) **[1.6** km] and cross over onto path that winds down steeply **[!]** on a new pilgrim track (cutting out the gentler but longer road bends) to re-join the main road **[2.6** km] at *[F.]*:

4.1 km Trabadelo *[F.]*. Main path joins.

Continue parallel to the main N-VI re-joining it briefly before reaching Portela *H*°°° Valcarce €25 ℂ 987 543 180. Take the detour left off the N-VI into:

3.9 km **La Portela de Valcarce** *[F.] Hs*°+ *Alb*. ❶ **El Peregrino** *Priv.[28÷8]*+ €9–€25 ℂ 987 543 197 + bar & menú. Pass church (left, *sello*) through Portela to *Hs*+ *Alb* ❷ **Camynos** *Priv.[10÷1]*+ €10–€35 ℂ 609 381 412 (Gerardo) + bar & menú. Continue and turn off for Ambasmestas (signposted Vega de Valcarce). *[At this point we leave the N-VI and have 4 days walking before we rejoin the national network again, the N-547, at Palas de Rei].* Continue into the traditional village of:

1.4 km **Ambasmestas** here the ríos Balboa and Valcarce join to give the village its name *aguas mestas*. A rural idyll somewhat spoilt by the A-6 flyover that serves as the backdrop. At the central crossroads hotel/ bar *H* **Ambasmestas** ℂ 987 233 768 rooms €35+. Also *Alb*. ❶ **Casa Del Pescador** *Priv.[10÷2]* €10-12 +€45 ℂ 603 515 868 riverside chalet and ❷ **Das Animas** *Priv.[18÷1]* €5 ℂ 619 048 626 c/Campo Bajo (100m off route on the far side of river). ❸ **El Rincón del Apóstol** *Priv.[8÷1]*+ €19 +€40 ℂ 987 543 099. Continue along the valley under A-6 flyover into:

1.0 km **Vega de Valcarce** *Entrada: (1 km from start to end)* CR **El Recanto** ℂ 987 543 202 at entrance (right). **Panadería** rooms (left) & *Alb*. ❶ **Sarracin** *Priv.[14÷1]* €10 ℂ 696 982 672 adj. river + menú. *Centro:* ❷ **Santa María Magdalena** *Priv.[8÷1]*+ €8 +€26 ℂ 987 543 230 (Matthew) adj. CR **Meson Las Rocas** ℂ 987 543 208. ❸

Municipal. *[92÷7]* €5 ℂ 722 786 186 c/Pandelo (below A-6 flyover). CR **Pandelo** ℂ 987 543 033. ❹ **ISANA** *Vegetariano* *Priv.[12÷4]*+ €5 ℂ 617 056 179 Menú *macrobiotica* €9. ❺ **El Paso** *Priv.[28÷6]*+ €10 ℂ 628 104 309 (Lalo) adj. church. *Over río:* ❻ *P* **Fernández** €15+ ℂ 987 543 027 Plaza del Ayuntamiento. ❼ **Virgen de la Encina** *Par.[26÷5]* €-donativo ℂ 649 133 272. Pleasant town founded in the IX[th]c by Count Sarraceno from Astorga (not a Sarracin). Built along the río Valcarce with variety of shops and restaurants, marred somewhat by the A-6 above. On the way out we pass *supermercado* and adj. parish church (recently renovated). Continue along road (outline of the XIV[th]C *Castillo de Sarracín* visible up to our left) into:

2.8 km **Ruitelán** *Albergue* **Pequeño Potala** *Priv.[34÷3]*+ *V.* €5–€30 ℂ 987 561 322 Shiatsu, massage and vegetarian menú make up some of the facilities of this popular haunt. Small shop and bar adjacent. Continue out of the village past the ancient church of St. John the Baptist (left) *sello*. The motorway is now out of sight thus preserving the tranquil setting of this quaint hamlet where San Froilán had a hermitage: Pass *posada* CR **El Paraíso del Bierzo** €40 ℂ 987 684 137 & turn off <left past CR **El Capricho de Josana** €32 ℂ 987 119 300 with bar/restaurant. Cross the Roman bridge over río Valcarce into the village ahead.

1.4 km **Las Herrerías** *Alb.*❶ **Las Herrerías** *Priv.[17÷2]* *V.* ℂ 654 353 940 up left at the start of this delightful village. *Alb.*❷ **Casa Lixa** *Priv.[15÷2]*+ €12+€45/59 ℂ 987 134 915. CR **A Casa do Ferreiro** ℂ 987 684 903 / 679 478 150 + bar with gluten free menú. CR **Polín** €30 ℂ 987-543 039 also with bar adj. local taxi José López Barreiro (Pepe) ℂ 649 647 504. This ancient hamlet stretches lazily along the river, its name derived from the iron foundry whose furnaces have long since disappeared. This is the point where the old Dragonte route (described next) re-joins the other routes from Villafranca.

Alternative route ❸ via Dragonte. Remote route used by pilgrims of yore to traverse the Valcarce Valley. It is longer, with 3 deep river valleys to cross, and is poorly waymarked as part of the GR-11 and variously referred to as *Camino de los Franceses* or *Camino Dragonte* with the more discreet green and white circular walking plaques or the red and white blaise predominating although the yellow arrow pops up occasionally. There are few facilities along the way and no accommodation until you reach Herrerías although you can take any of the roads down into the main valley and re-join the main route with its plentiful accommodation.

It is the 'road less travelled' and on this account will appeal to those seeking a more contemplative way and wishing to travel in the 'silence' of nature. It is not suitable for groups but individual pilgrims might sensibly join with another for added security in the mountains. It is very beautiful and, as yet, unspoiled. The distance from albergue [1] in Villafranca to Herreías, via Dragonte, is 26.3 km with an extra 8.2 km up to O'Cebreiro (total 34.5 km) in addition there is a total height climbed in the day of 1,900m (6,230 feet) so best plan to stay in or around Herrerías. *Waymarking is obscure* and the paths beyond Dragonte are frequently overgrown by scrub vegetation, particularly the last stretch down into Herreíras, so only contemplate this route if you are fit, have a good sense of orientation and an instinctive nature when faced with unexpected options. Don't expect to get lost but allow some additional time in case you do! Leave early in the morning and don't tackle it in the winter months when daylight hours are restricted or if the weather is bad or set to deteriorate. *"Ten hours after setting out, we emerged from the woodlands at the base of the slope into the village of Las Herrerias. It had been a very hard day, with over 30km of walking (including our unintended detours), but the rewards were magnificent mountain scenery and walking a path that few pilgrims tread. In the end, it was the day which gave us the greatest sense of achievement of our camino experience."* Pilgrim couple from Australia.

1.0 km Option point [b] by Casa Mendez veer left and the old N-VI [0.6 km] by the A-6 tunnel (signposted Corullón) and turn up sharp right> [0.4 km] signposted Dragonte by a walkers notice board and map. This first section into Dragonte is all by steep asphalt road (Taxi to Dragonte?) [4.6 km] but rewarded with splendid views back over Villafranca. Head up into:

5.6 km Dragonte *[F.]* (right) a welcome pilgrim fountain has been installed here. The path continues up (less steeply now) onto wide track keep s/o maintaining the contour as the track curves between quarry (left) and hill *La Corona* (right) to a high point on the track of 1,050m (3,445 feet) where, opp. a grove of trees (left) we turn off right> (easily missed) [!] at **GR-11 sign [2.0** km] onto narrow path through scrubland following a ditch around to our left up to high point and down to asphalt **road [0.7** km] into [0.3 km]:

3.0 km Moral de Valcarce village *[F.]* (no other facilities). S/o steeply down main path through wooded valley to **stream [1.5** km] which you have to wade and must turn right> [!] by derelict stone mill to regain dry path <left in 30m the path now winds its way up (keep to larger of several indistinct tracks through the woods) to emerge by **church [1.2** km] (formerly monastery and pilgrim hospice of San Fructuoso, viewpoint to rear) pass access road (right) and up [0.4 km] into:

3.1 km Vilar de Corrales *[F.]* isolated hamlet with *fuente* at far end but no other facilities (make sure water bottles are full before proceeding). Continue up right along the *Camino de los Franceses* and turn up right *off* **main path** [0.3 km] [!] to high plateau and keep s/o (several tracks branch off at this point at the brow of a wide mountain shoulder and our high point (1055m) [0.2 km].

We now begin the descent into the second of the 3 valleys we have to cross. Turn left [0.8 km] on main track and left [0.6 km] (*not* old track s/o) and follow it past an old quarry where it descends toward the main opencast stone quarry below. The descent is steep and the narrow paths are confusing as the waymarks here may have been obliterated by the quarrying activity but our destination, the valley road, is obvious so zigzag down as best you can. San Fiz de

Seo is visible across the valley. For general orientation keep to tracks on the left of the ridge, which eventually swing right towards the main quarry face. To add spice to an already exhilarating ride note that this is a blasting area *Zona de Voladuras!* Console yourself with the fact that many have passed this way before you and there will be others following! You finally join wide quarry road [1.1 km] and make your way through the quarry itself (watch out for trucks). Turn left down quarry access road. The dirt road now crosses the river onto the public road [1.0 km] with signs for the GR-1 *Ruta Wolfram* and *Ruta Verde (be careful not to confuse the various local walking paths in this area)*. Turn right> along the asphalt road and take the next turning <left [0.3 km] up steeply to the village church square [0.5 km]:

4.7 km San Fiz do Seo *[F.]* Church dedicated to Virgen de los Dolores (right). *Option: at this point it is a long climb up and down into Herrerías (allow 3+ hours for 'end of day' pace). An alternative is to take the main road (or parallel high road) to accommodation along N-VI [3.0 km] Hotel Valcarce [1.4 km].* Turn up left by small cantina (often closed) and make your way up through the village *[F.]* right at exit (make sure you have water for this next section before proceeding). The path now levels out – essentially we maintain the contour around the base of the hill on our right (ignoring tracks that turn up right towards it) continuing gently down at fork [1.1 km] passing beehives (right) all the way to the valley floor and over stream [0.8 km] before beginning our ascent up steeply towards Villasinde ignoring path down to the left Ruta Verde GR-1 to cross asphalt road for [2.2 km] into:

4.1 km Villasinde *[F.] Bar Celia* ♥ © 987 561 326 down right – If the door is closed knock (loudly) and it may be opened! Celia awaits and will prepare something to eat from her chickens and adjoining garden. *[Note: from here it is possible to take the road to the albergues at Vega de Valcarce – 4 km all on asphalt].* If you are still feeling adventurous and there is sufficient light left

in the day then head up and out of the village passing *[F.]* and parish church before veering right uphill following GR11 signposts towards the radio mast visible on the horizon (photo right). Continue up to crest the hill and join track **[1.6 km]** *(radio mast right)* and turn <left on this track (Alto 1,002m) and keep this contour as it swings around to the right (ignore path signposted Ruta S. Julián up to the left). Shortly afterwards pass *[F.]* and another radio mast appears on the

peak in front and at old **signpost [1.0 km]** turn off <left to start our descent into the valley floor with the A-6 viaduct and Herrerías now coming into view in the middle distance. The path down to the valley floor has recently been widened (allowing access for forestry work). We continue down steeply onto wet section of path **[1.4 km]** and turn right over mountain stream **[0.6 km]** into the village and turn left on road to **pilgrim hostel [0.2 km]**:

4.8 km **Herrerías** We now finally join the pilgrims coming up Valcarce for the climb into O'Cebreiro – another demanding stage of 8.4 km and an ascent of 620m (2,035 feet). This will have been a very full day so secure a bed here or Ruitelán (1.1 km further back) or try one of the several casa rurales in the area.

From **Herrerías Bridge** we wind our way through this quaint riverside village with its simple stone architecture. Fountain *Fuente de Quinoñes* links it with the chivalrous knight who defended the Puente de Órbigo. We pass the old forge *A Casa do Ferreiro* and the adj. **Al Paso** stables where you can *ride* into Galicia (2 hours ± €20) Victor Echevarria (photo right) © 638 041 823 will guide you up the hill. No previous riding experience necessary (the horses are on remote control!). At the far (western) end of the village we pass *Hospital Inglés*, a reference to the medieval English pilgrims who passed this way (a pilgrim chapel and cemetery were known to have existed here though the buildings are

no longer discernible). Fill up the water flask and gird your loins for the final assault on the mountain ahead. Continue along the quiet asphalt road before turning off <left onto **path [2.0 km]** that drops down briefly to the valley floor where we start our steep ascent through dense woodland, mostly chestnut *castaños* on a rocky path (slippery in wet) for **[1.4 km]** up into the pretty hillside village of:

3.4 km **La Faba** *Fab bar* (right). *Alb.* **La Faba** *Asoc.[66÷3]* €5 © 630 836 865 – 100m track (right) in parish house renovated by a German Confraternity in shaded parkland setting adj. the church *Iglesia San André*. This delightful hamlet has a small shop, bar and alternative hostel **Refugio** *Vegetariano V.* offering tea, yoga and massage (and possibly a bed if you're spaced out after a massage). The path continues up and out of the village along a path lined with Spanish chestnut trees and splendid views back over the Valcarce valley to reach:

2.3 km **Laguna de Castilla** *Alb.* **La Escuela** *Priv.*[20÷3]* €9-€35 © 987 684 786 and *menú peregrino* in *Café/bar*. This tiny hamlet may represent the last outpost in Castille but it houses a wonderful example of a functional Galician *palloza* in the farmyard just behind the fountain *[F.]*. These traditional structures built in the round with straw roofs can be visited in O'Cebreiro. Just above Laguna we pass the first concrete marker post *K.152.5 OS Santos.* These markers will accompany us all the way to Santiago (the route has been changed since they were originally surveyed so distances are no

longer accurate but they provide reassuring waymarks) and we arrive at the Galicia Frontera **[1.1 km]** a substantial marker records the fact that we are finally leaving the autonomous region of Castilla y León (provincia León) to enter Galicia (provincia de Lugo). The path continues through gorse and scrubland to skirt the stone wall that brings us the remaining **[1.2 km]** to:

2.3 km O'Cebreiro *Iglesia de Santa Maria Real* dating from the 9th century and the oldest extant church associated directly with the pilgrim way. This year (June–Sept.) the Cathedral Chaplaincy Outreach will welcome pilgrims (in English) during the day followed by an international Pilgrims' Mass in the evening. O'Cebreiro (Pron: *Oh-thay-bray-**air**-oh*) another significant gateway on the camino has ministered to pilgrims

since the twilight of the first millennium. ***Santa María la Real*** is patroness of the area and her 12th century statue is prominently displayed along with the chalice and paten connected with the miracle of O'Cebreiro *Santo Milagro* in which, 'a haughty celebrant' of the mass, dismissive of a devout and humble peasant, saw the bread and wine turn into the body and blood of Christ as he offered them to the supplicant who had risked life and limb to attend mass in a terrible snowstorm. The statue itself was also said to have inclined its head at the miraculous event.'

The church also marks the final resting place of ***Don Elias Valiña Sampedro*** (1929–1989) the parish priest who did so much during his lifetime to restore and preserve the integrity of the camino. It was his idea to mark the route with the familiar yellow arrow ➡ and it was largely as a result of his efforts that we walk the route today. It was also here that the caminoguides was born. His bust presides over the church square and many confraternities have placed their names on the plinth as a mark of their deep respect

for his life and efforts on behalf of the modern pilgrim. He was also responsible for the restoration of the adjoining Hostal *San Giraldo de Aurillac* that is now run by members of the family. These handsome stone buildings originally formed part of the monastic settlement dating back to the 11th century when King Alfonso VI assigned their care to the monks of the Abbé de Saint Giraldo from France. Queen Isabella stayed here in 1486 on her pilgrimage to Santiago. Opp. the church is a museum in a renovated Palloza. A 200m walk past the bars, shops and restaurants to: *Albergue* **O'Cebreiro** *Xunta. [104÷3]* €6 ℂ 660 396 809 on the western (far) end of the village on an exposed and elevated site above the main road. Purpose built

hostel with all facilities. *[Next albergue Hospital de la Condesa 5.5 km.].*

Note on Galician Albergues: the regional government *Xunta de Galicia* has constructed modern purpose-built pilgrim hostels or converted former school buildings all along the route from here to Finisterre. This is one of the better examples of a rather uninspiring uniform design. These hostels can generally be identified by the stark white walls and the blue Telefonica kiosk outside. They all have reasonable facilities, such as hot showers and toilets, but kitchens are frequently out of commission. The cynical might hint at exploitation by local restaurants but forewarned is forearmed and everyone needs to make a living. There is usually a restaurant close by, often run by the hospitalera. Uniform charge of €6 per night.

Other accommodation. *H* **O Cebreiro** hotel rustico ℂ 982 367 182 adj. church with restaurant bar & souvenir shop, also operates adj. **San Giraldo de Aurillac** ℂ 982 367 125. *CR* **Casa Carolo** ℂ 982 367 168 (mixed reports). *CR* **Venta Celta** with popular restaurante ℂ 667 553 006. *CR* **Casa valiña** ℂ 982 367 182. *CR* **Casa Frade** ℂ 982 367 104. O'Cebreiro is a popular tourist venue as well as pilgrim halt – demand for beds can outstrip supply in the summer which can, in some cases, lead to high prices and low standards. Find a bed before celebrating your arrival and note that Additional lodging can be found in Pedrafita O Cebreiro 4.5 km. *off* route.

GALICIA: The Valcarce valley and O'Cebreiro provide a wonderful foretaste of the distinctive Galician culture that now awaits. The mountains of Galicia are the first object in 5,000 km that the westerly winds across the Atlantic hit so you can expect an immediate change in weather with frequent rain showers and thunderstorms *chubascos y tormentas* and thick mountain fog *niebla (see photo)* all feed a maze of mountain streams and deep river valleys. The countryside is

reminiscent of other Celtic lands with its small, intimate fields and lush pastures grazed by cattle with sheep, pigs, geese and chickens all foraging amongst the poorer ground. Thick hot soups *caldo gallego* and rich vegetable and meat stews provide inner warmth from the damp. Local red wines with their coarser characters accompany most meals and help to fuel the inner glow. Nearer the coast, fish dishes such as steamed octopus dusted with paprika *pulpo a la galega* and shellfish *mariscos* will dominate. To accompany scallops *vieiras* try the white Ribeiros or the incomparable Albariño. Round off your meal with local cheese and quince jelly *queso y membrillo* or the famous almond tart *tarta de Santiago*. If you are still feeling cold, try the distilled grape skin *orujo* or its marginally less alcoholic and more refined cousin *hierbas* mixed with local herbs. Stone granaries *hórreos* are everywhere storing the local harvest, primarily maize *maíz* out of reach of rat and rain.

Galicia also shares many historical similarities with other Celtic regions like the west of Ireland. Too poor to provide much employment for its large family structures, emigration (particularly of the younger men) has cast its spectre across the region. Here, women drive the tractors or herd the oxen and seem to find time to do the cooking and tend the bars as well. Surprisingly you may find locals who speak good English on account of having spent time working abroad (or while visiting children working in the UK or USA). If any doubt remains as to its Celtic past then the strident whirl of its bagpipes *gaita* should dispel them. The language *Galega* is still spoken by a substantial minority and understood by the majority while poets such as Rosalia de Castro have helped preserve it more robustly than Irish or Scottish Gaelic. The most visible difference is in the spelling of place names and signposts where, for example, X now replaces J as in Xunta or Xardín. *Céad míle fáilte!*

Galicia's material poverty has left her with an abundance of spiritual wealth and the region is generally at peace with itself and its traditions largely intact. While a strong Catholic faith overlays its earthy spirituality, its pagan past never totally faded. Deep respect for, even veneration of, the natural elements remains as evident as the elements themselves. *Finis terra* was, after all, the end of the ancient world – west of Finisterre was the 'Land of Eternal Youth' *Tir-na-nog* where the sun never set. Long before the tomb of St. James was discovered and before Christianity spread to these shores, pilgrims from all over the known world came here to witness the sun sink in the west – and to open to some transcendental reality that emphasised the temporal aspects of this earthly life.

The countryside ahead is full of the dolmens and *mamoas* of these earlier settlers who were deeply reverent in character and who handed down this earthy respect for the natural world. The wayside *cruceiros* add an air of solemnity to the path and are a reminder of the deep spirituality of Galicia that seems to have survived the consumer culture and materialism that has swept over much of the rest of Europe. Santiago is the capital of the autonomous region of Galicia that is divided into the 4 provinces of A Coruña, Lugo, Ourense and Pontevedra. See *A Pilgrim's Guide to Finisterre* for a detailed account of the history and legends of this fascinating corner of Galicia – and try and make time to walk the route out to the end of the way and the world.

In 2016 the government *Xunta* started replacing the concrete bollards *monjón* with *historico* (main camino) and *alternativo* (routes to 'historical' sites not directly on the camino!). Adding to the confusion they are updating the original distances which had become seriously out of date. However, the route is constantly changing so it is best to use these bollards for directional purposes only.

REFLECTIONS:

_____
_____
_____
_____
_____
_____
_____
_____
_____
_____
_____
_____
_____
_____
_____
_____
_____
_____
_____
_____
_____

❏ **If you want the rainbow, you've gotta put up with the rain.** *Dolly Parton*

27 **154.5** km (96.0 ml) – Santiago

O'CEBREIRO – TRIACASTELA

░░░░░░░░	--- ---	19.7	--- ---	95%
━━━━━━	--- ---	1.0	--- ---	05%
▬	--- ---	0.0		
Total km		**20.7 km** (12.9 ml)		

▰▰▰	--- ---	21.7 km (+1.0 km)
Alto ▲	Alto do Poio 1,335m (4,380 ft)	

<▲ Ⓗ> Liñares **3.1** km – Hospital **5.6** km – Alto do Poio **8.6** km – Fonfría **11.9** km – Biduedo **14.3** km – Filloval **17.4** km.

❏ **The Practical Path:** While this stage is only 20.7 kms and mostly downhill, remember most injuries are sustained going down (not up) so extra care is needed. There are several villages and drinking fonts along the way and splendid views in every direction (weather permitting). Early morning mists can give rise to the most astounding ethereal *floating islands* where hilltops appear above the clouds. These exotic experiences generally give way to clearer skies, as the sun burns the swirling mists away. Whatever time of year, be prepared for *any* weather, as the mountains, and particularly Galicia, can be very unpredictable.

❏ **The Mystical Path:** High places help lift us towards Higher Mind. At such heights, a wider perspective opens up to both the physical and the inner eye. What do you see, feel and hear from this elevated space? Do the angels incline their heads to listen to your prayers? Does the silence and peace in your heart allow the inner voice to be heard? Are you open to receiving a miracle and to seeing the inner rainbow – symbol of God's Covenant?

❏ **Personal Reflections:** *"… The deluge continues and not a break to be seen in the clouds in any direction. I ask myself was it serendipity that sent the brief shaft of light through the tiny church window bathing me in its warm rich glow; its light so strong I was momentarily dazed by it. I sense again that altered state, devoid of ego, and all the pain of yesterday has gone. I feel inspired to write a pilgrim guidebook and Don Elias Valiña Sampedro appears to have given me his authority and blessing and so I commit to the Call of the Camino; right here and now …"*

0.0 km O Cebreiro *Albergue* A delightful forest track starts just above the albergue and winds around the hill before dropping down into Linares, thus avoiding the main road. *[!] Many pilgrims miss this track and take the asphalt road in error.*

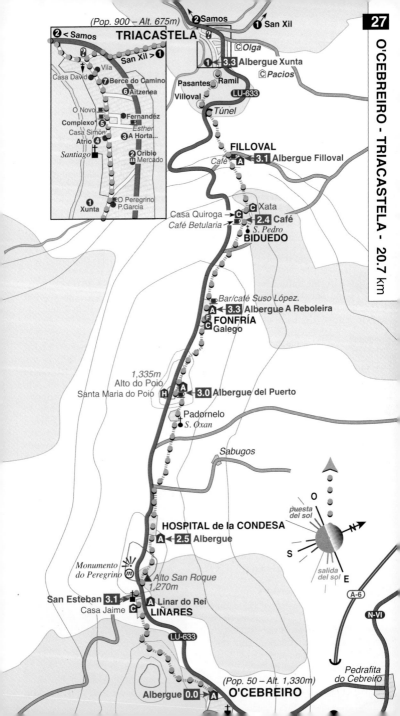

(Pop. 900 – Alt. 675m)

② < Samos **② Samos** **① San Xil**

TRIACASTELA

ⓒ *Olga*

① **3.3** **Albergue Xunta**

ⓒ *Pacios*

Pasantes **Ramil**

Villoval

LU-633

Túnel

FILLOVAL

Café Ⓐ **3.1** **Albergue Filloval**

ⓒ **Xata**

Casa Quiroga Ⓒ

2.4 **Café**

Café Betularia S. Pedro

BIDUEDO

Bar/café Suso López.

Ⓐ **3.3** **Albergue A Reboleira**

Ⓕ **FONFRÍA**

ⓒ **Galego**

1,335m
Alto do Poio
Santa Maria do Poio Ⓗ Ⓐ **3.0** **Albergue del Puerto**

Padornelo
S. Oxan

Sabugos

HOSPITAL de la CONDESA

Ⓐ **2.5** **Albergue**

puesta del sol

O

S

N

salida del sol

E

Monumento do Peregrino ⓜ

Alto San Roque
1,270m

San Esteban **3.1**

Ⓐ Linar do Rei

Casa Jaime Ⓒ

LIÑARES

LU-633

A-6

N-VI

(Pop. 50 – Alt. 1,330m)

Albergue **0.0** Ⓐ **O'CEBREIRO**

Pedrafita do Cebreiro

Inset map (top left): TRIACASTELA

② < Samos

San Xil > ①

Vila

Casa David

⑦ Berce do Camino

⑥ Aitzenea

O Novo

Fernández

Complexo ⑤

Esther

Casa Simón

③ A Horta...

Atrio **④**

Santiago

② Oribio ⓜ Mercado

O Peregrino
P.García

① Xunta

3.1 km Liñares small hamlet that once grew flax *lino (Linares)* for the linen trade. **Linar do Rei** *Priv.[22÷4]+* €10+ €40 *©* 616 464 831 (Erica). **CR Casa Jaime** *©* 982 367 166 + *bar*. The passes the ancient parish church of San Esteban VIII[th]c. Shortly afterwards we cross the road onto track up to *Alto de San Roque* **[1.0 km]** where an imposing statue of a medieval pilgrim looks out over the vast expanse of Galicia and its deep valleys. A path continues parallel to the road for **[1.5 km]** into:

2.5 km Hospital de la Condesa *Alb.* **Xunta.***[20÷1]* €6 *©* 660 396 810 located above the road (right) as we enter the village. **CR O Tear** *©* 982 367 183 with bar/restaurant & rooms. The village once boasted a pilgrim hospital (hence its name) and was reputed to have been one of the earliest ever built for Christian pilgrims on the way to Santiago. Take time to visit the pre-Romanesque *Iglesia St Juan XI[th]C* (also dedicated to San Roque) with delightful interior and unusual stone roofed belfry and cross of Santiago aloft. The track continues parallel to the main road turning off right> **[1.2 km]** down a minor road (signposted Sarbugos) for **[0.3 km]** before picking up a path into Padornelo **[1.0 km]** with the restored chapel *ermita San Oxan* connecting this area with the Order of St. John. A short but steep climb brings us to the highest spot on the camino in Galicia 1,335m. (4,380 feet) **[0.5 km]**:

3.0 km Alto do Poio *Alb.* del Puerto *Priv.[16÷1]* €6 *©* 982 367 172. Basic facilities adj. Bar Puerto caters for meals and a brisk breakfast trade with pilgrims from O'Cebreiro. On the opp. side of the road *Hs* **Santa María de Poio** *©* 982 367 167. Join track parallel to the road and turn right> onto path into:

3.3 km Fonfría typical Galician village *CR* **Núñez** *©* 982 161 335 bar & rest. *CR* **Galego** €25-35 *©* 982 161 461. Fill your flask from the cool waters of the *fons fría [F.]* after which the hamlet is named. At the far end of the village is *Alb.* **A Reboleira** *Priv.*[64÷3]+* €8 *©* 982 181 271 mod. building with adj. palloza. Menú €9. Adj. *Bar/café Suso López*. Continue on track parallel to main road and turn right> into:

2.4 km Biduedo rural idyll *capilla de San Pedro Meson Betularia* adj. *CR* **Quiroga** €30 *©* 982 187 299 (Celia). Also *CR* **Xata** €24-36 *©* 982 189 808 m:620 457 597. The path now begins to descend steeply with wonderful views over the countryside to the west. Next we arrive at crossroads and rest area:

3.1 km Filloval *Alb.* Filloval *Priv.[18÷2]+* €9–€30 *©* 666 826 414. *Casa Olga / café Aire do Camino*. S/o over country lane onto path down steeply across main road (muddy underpass) through *As Pasantes* **[1.4 km]** and *Ramil* **[1.7 km]** on the ancient camino worn down with the feet of countless pilgrims and local livestock, a classic stretch of *corredoira* (narrow lane walled-in with granite). Soak up the peace as you meander above the wooded valley of the arroyo Roxino that flows down from Monte Oribio. This primitive way is guarded by a venerable oak and chestnut trees offering shade into Triacastela **[0.2 km]**:

3.3 km Triacastela *Alb.* **❶** Xunta.*[56÷14]* €6 green-field site to left of the camino at the start of the village overlooking the river. Imaginatively restored stone buildings with modern extension. Lounge and outdoor recreation area. Opp. popular *O Peregrino* café-bar-restaurant (last of the evening sun) and adj. *P˙* **García** *©* 982 548 024. The ramp up at the side of bar ❖ connects to: *Alb*

❷ **Oribio** *Priv.[27÷2]* €8 ✆ 982 548 085 mod. building on the main road with all facilities. ❖ Continuing down c/del Peregrino (*right – access also off main road*) ❸ **A Horta de Abel** *Priv.[14÷2]+* €9–€40 ✆ 608 080 556. Adj. *P˚* **Fernandez** ✆ 982 548 148. *P˚* **Casa Simón** on corner (*left*) *Igrexa de Santiago* to rear adj. ❹ **Atrio** *Priv.[20÷4]+* €9 +€40-50 ✆ 982 548 488 (Juan José). ❺ **Complexo Xacobeo** *Priv*. [36÷3]+* €9–€40 ✆ 982 548 037 modern ext. to the rear with all facilities, adj. *Bar-restaurant Xacobeo* (same ownership). This marks the

central 'hub' of town. *Hs* **O'Novo** ✆ 982 548 105. Further on (*right*) slip road to ❻ **Aitzenea** *Priv.[38÷4]+* €8 ✆ 982 548 076. Sympathetic conversion of traditional stone house by a Basque architect (*aitzenea is Basque for stone-house*). At the end of town (700m from entrance) we find: ❼ **Berce do Camiño** *Priv.[27÷6]* €8 ✆ 982 548 127 all facilities in modernised terraced house adj. Caixa Galicia opp. *P˚˚* **Casa David** ✆ 982 548 105 and *Hs* **Mesón Vilasante** €30-40 ✆ 982 548 116. *CR* **Olga** €16+ p.p ✆ 982 548 134 c/ Castro 2 (+0.5 km). *CR* **Pacios** €35+ ✆ 982 548 455 Vilavella (+ 2.0 km) free transporte from *Café Esther* off rúa Peregrino.

■ *Note: Santiago city is now only a week away and pilgrim numbers increase exponentially and lodging is often full. [Next albergue: Route ❶ A Balsa (1.6 km) Route ❷ Lusio (4.5 km [400m off route]). If it is late in the day and all hostals are full you may need to consider [sharing] a taxi to other options. See next stage.*

TRIACASTELA town of the *three castles* none of which survive and an important stop for medieval pilgrims coming down off the mountain with several hospices and an extensive monastery. XI stage in the Codex Calixtinus. It is no less an attractive stop today with a wide selection of bars, restaurants and hostels serving the increasing number of pilgrims passing through. The parish church is dedicated to

Santiago and has an unusual 18th century tower on which is carved a relief of the three castles (see photo). Pilgrim mass daily for *every*one at 18:00 with the delightful Fr. Augusto. Nearby are the quarries that provided the limestone used in the building of Santiago Cathedral. Medieval pilgrims would carry as much as they were able to the lime kilns in Casteñeda (through which we pass during stage 31) and the pilgrim monument in the lower town square recognises this ancient tradition while acknowledging the rebirth of the camino – paying equal respect to both.

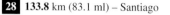

❐ **Happiness is a mystery, like religion, and should never be rationalised.**

——————————————————— *G.K. Chesterton*

28 | **133.8** km (83.1 ml) – Santiago

TRIACASTELA – SARRIA (via San Xil)

▩▩▩▩▩▩	--- ---	**11.2**	--- ---	*60%*
━━━━	--- ---	**7.5**	--- ---	*40%*
▅▅▅	--- ---	0.0		
Total km		**18.7 km** (11.6 ml)		

▲ --- --- 20.1 km (+ 1.4 km)
Alto ▲ Alto do Riocabo 905m (2,970 ft)
< 🅐 🅗 > ❶ *San Xil:* A Balsa **1.6** km –
Pintín **12.1** km– Calvor **13.4** km
San Mamed **14.8** km – Vigo de Sarria **17.7** km.
❷ *Samos:* Lusío **5.1** km (+ 0.4) – Samos **10.5** km –San Mamed **21.4** km

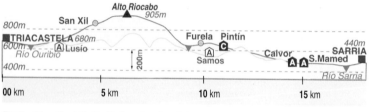

❐ **The Practical Path:** Before leaving Triacastela decide whether to take northern **direct route** ❶ *via San Xil* or the southern **detour route** ❷ *via Samos*. Recent improvements to the San Xil route (new woodland paths) have increased the natural pathways to 60%. The road route to Samos has sections along the busy LU-633 which can be dangerous. *(The criterion used in this guide is to always favour natural pathways)*. The San Xil route is shorter by 6.4 km and has the steep climb up to alto do Riocabo with splendid views. The Benedictine monastery of Samos is one of the oldest and largest in Spain and draws large tourist numbers. Both routes are attractive and offer good alternative accommodation:

❐ **The Mystical Path:** Will the winding river reveal her natural weir to you? The man-made example, which diverts water to the village mill, is no match for the beauty of this one. Will you rest awhile in the tiny Hobbit-like shelter whose entrance is shielded by the branches from the adjacent *castaño*? The unadorned beauty of this path remains largely undiscovered by officialdom. How long will it remain in its pristine state uncluttered by the trappings of man?

❐ **Personal Reflections** *"... The deepening silence coupled with a rare break in the downpour mingle with the glorious Landscape Temple to create an overwhelming sense of wellbeing. I am entirely alone and yet I feel more connected to a larger Way than at any other time in my life. The outer weather fades into insignificance as I open to an inner reality that seems more alive than anything on the level of form. My body is wet and cold for the umpteenth day in a row and yet I glow with an inner warmth as I sit under a dripping chestnut tree and contemplate the irrationality of it all. I am beginning to turn the conventional world on its head and everything suddenly becomes clearer. I feel at last I am turning toward Home ..."*

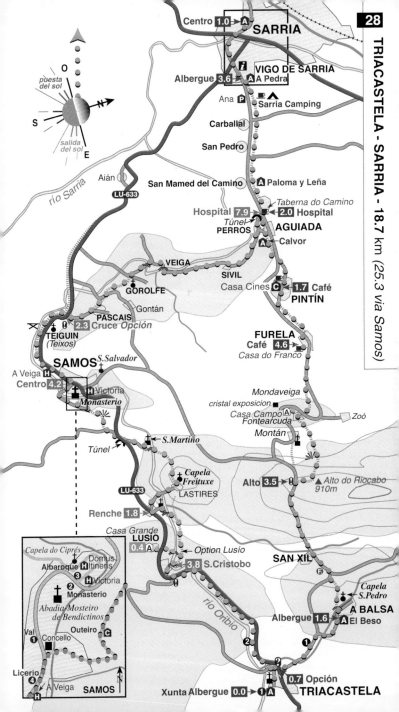

Centro **1.0** A SARRIA

i VIGO DE SARRIA

Albergue **3.6** A A Pedra

Ana P Sarria Camping

Carballal

San Pedro

San Mamed del Camino

A Paloma y Leña

O *puesta del sol*

N

S

salida del sol

E

río Sarria

Aián

LU-633

Taberna do Camino

Hospital **7.9** **2.0** Hospital

Túnel

PERROS AGUIADA

A Calvor

VEIGA

SIVIL

GOROLFE

Gontán

Casa Cines C **1.7** Café

PINTÍN

PASCAIS

TEIGUIN **2.3** Cruce *Opción*

(Teixos)

FURELA

Café **4.6**

Casa do Franco

S.Salvador

SAMOS

A Veiga H

Centro **4.2**

H Victoria

Monasterio

Mondaveiga

cristal exposicion

Casa Campo A

Fontearcuda

Zoó

Montán

Túnel

S.Martiño

Capela Freituxe

LASTIRES

Alto **3.5** Alto do Riocabo

910m

LU-633

Renche **1.8**

Casa Grande

LUSIO **0.4** A

Option Lusió

3.8 S.Cristobo

SAN XIL

F

Capela S.Pedro

río Oribio

Albergue **1.6**

A El Beso

A BALSA

Capela do Ciprés

Albaroque H

Domus H Itineris

Victoria H

Monasterio

Abadia Mosteiro de Bendictinos

Outeiro C

Val

Concello

Liceiro

A Veiga

SAMOS

H

Xunta Albergue **0.0** A

0.7 Opción

TRIACASTELA

`0.0 km` Triacastela from albergue ❶ proceed to the far end of town and option:

`0.7 km` Opción [?] For **route ❶ via San Xil** turn down right> and s/o over main road [!] (*not* left to Samos) onto secondary road and where it veers up left, we turn down right> **[1.0 km]** into **A Balsa [0.6 km]**. At the start of the hamlet (right)

`1.6 km` A Balsa *Alb.* **El Beso** *Priv.[12÷1]* *V.* €8 ℂ 633 550 558 with communal vegetarian menú *V.* €9. Continue through the hamlet and over river past the tiny chapel to Our Lady of the Snows *ermita N. S. de las Nieves* **[0.5 km]** (right) and up steeply on rough woodland path to re-join road at *rest area* **[0.9 km]** *[F.]* with unusual scallop shell motif. We next bypass *San Xil* **[0.4 km]** no facilities except drinks vending machine (left). From here we have a steep climb up by road to our high point today at **alto do Riocabo [1.7 km]** (910m). At this point leave the road onto forest track right> [!].

`3.5 km` Alto do Riocabo delightful new high level woodland path above Montán down through the hamlet of **Fontearcuda** and over the road **[3.2 km]** (*½ km detour to crystals studio at Mondaviega also Cafe+ CR Casa Campo €30 ℂ 616 821 385*). Cross road onto path over a stream back to the road and into *Furela* **[1.4 km]**:

`4.6 km` Furela *Casa do Franco* popular café-bar on slip road (if busy try next café). Continue over the road into the next hamlet:

`1.7 km` Pintín *[F.]* P* **Casa Cines** ℂ 982 167 939 welcoming pilgrim *café/bar.* Proceed s/o back over the main road to **Calvor [1.4 km]** *Alb.* Calvor *Xunta.[22÷2]* €6 ℂ 660 396 812 former school building located on the roadside. Continue over the road through the straggling hamlets of *Aguiada* and *Hospital* **[0.6 km]** bar *Taberna do Camiño.*

`2.0 km` Hospital site of a former pilgrim hosptial where todays pilgrims who took the **alternative route** via *Samos* join.

For **detour route ❷** via Samos turn <left at option point in Triacastela down past pilgrim monument and over river to join main road [!]. This a dangerous stretch of road – use the margins behind the crash barriers wherever possible. Continue alongside the road and cross over to take the access road down to the weir in:

`3.8 km` San Cristobo traditional village occupying a lovely position on the bank of the river Oribio with its ancient weir and mill buildings. Cross over the river onto a delightful track that winds its way through mixed woodland following the meandering course of the río Oribio to **optional detour [0.5 km]**

Detour Lusío ● ● ● ● path left for 400m detour to albergue in beautifully restored monastery building in Lusío. *Alb.* **Casa Grande** *Xunta.[60÷4]* €6 well restored mansion in this ancient hamlet (the property of Samos monastery). Return to option point to continue s/o along the woodland path before turning <left (*other path continues to Lastires*) over bridge by chapel and up to the main road **[1.2 km]** in:

1.7 km **Renche** *Bar* (often closed/ vending machine) continue down (sign Castres) over river again and up steeply to *Capela de Freituxe* [**1.5** km] to take a track back down and over the river again into *San Martiño* [**1.3** km] chapel and up steeply under main road through **tunnel** [**0.5** km] over secondary road onto track above Samos (good viewpoint here over the monastery and town) and down

steeply past **Casas de Outeiro** spa €75+ *©* 680 379 969 c/ Fontao. Café *A Lareira* by bridge in **Samos town centre** [**1.0** km]. *(For monastery albergue turn right along the river path and over next bridge).*

4.2 km Samos town wraps itself around the enormous monastery in this peaceful river valley where time seems to stand still.

❖ *Centre* café *España Alb.* ❶ **Val de Samos** *Priv.[48÷7]* €9 *©* 982 546 163. ❷ **Monasterio de Samos** *Conv.[70÷1]* €-donativo Entrance (and key) by petrol pumps. Basic facilities with 70 beds in one dormitory corridor. The simple austerity matches the surroundings and religious services take place throughout the day with Vespers and pilgrim mass at 19:30 (20:00 Sat / Sun) in the chapel. This is one of the of the largest and oldest monasteries in the western world founded in 6th century on the asceticism of the Desert Fathers, taking the Benedictine rule in 960. Regular tours take place daily 09:30-18:30 – monastery visit €3. ❸ **Albaroque** *Priv.[6÷1]* €9– €25 *©* 982 546 087 / 628 828 845 opp. the monastery. ❹ **Casa Licerio** *Priv.[20÷3]*+ €15–€30/40 *©* 653 593 814. *HsR*° **Victoria** *©* 982 546 022 and *HsR*° **Domus Itineris** *©* 982 546 088. The pre Romanesque (Mozarabe) 'Cypress' chapel (capilla *Ciprés* S.Salvador IXth) is located to the rear.

❖ From the centre follow main road out of town (signposted Sarria) passing *Hs*° **A Veiga** *©* 982 546 052 on track by road to picnic site by river and roadside chapel in Tequin *Teixos* [**1.3** km]. S/o main road and watch out for turn off right [**1.0** km] [!].

2.3 km **Cruce** *[the dangerous main road continues s/o into Sarria].* Cross road onto lane (sign Pascais) and turn off <left onto path [**0.7** km] and <left again by church [**0.7** km] back down to lane at **Gorolfe** [**1.1** km] with wayside chapel (see photo). *H* **Casa de Díaz** €30-70 *©* 982 547 070 Gorolfe Lugar de Vilachá 4 (*off* route). A short stretch of track joins to a quiet country road which we follow over the river (twice) shrine (left) in **Veiga** [**1.8** km] through **Sivil** s/o alongside river through woodland. The road undulates up and down with many turnings but waymarking is reasonable. We next arrive in the hamlet of **Souto de Perros** [**3.2** km] with wayside chapel **N.S do Camiño** and up through tunnel into **Hospital** [**0.4** km] where the other route joins at bar *Taberna do Camino*.

7.9 km **Hospital** where both routes join.

Continue on dedicated path parallel to the
road past **S. Mamed del Camino [0.7** km]
and *Alb.* **Paloma y Leña ♥** *Priv.*[20÷3]+*
€10–€40 ℰ 982 533 248 network* hostel
set back from the road (see photo) *'an oasis
of peace and tranquillity.'* All facilities and
meals available. *¿Porque no acqui?* Why
not indeed! The path continues bypassing
the hamlets of **San Pedro do Camiño** and

Carballal to *Café &* **Camping Vila de Sarria** *[12÷1]+* ℰ 982 535 467 (pilgrims
from €6) **[2.2 km]** opposite: *P** **Ana** ℰ 982 531 458 past *Casa Silva* (menú) to the
outskirts of Sarria **[0.7** km].

3.6 km **Vigo de Sarria** (Albergues Av. price €8-10) *Alb.●* **A Pedra** *Priv.*[14÷3]+*
ℰ 982 530 130 adj. *Bar.* **Turismo** ℰ 982 530 099 town map & list of hotels. Opp.
Alb.● **Oasis** *Priv.[27÷4]* ℰ 605 948 644. S/o into busy Calvo Sotelo *café/ Hs*
Cristal ℰ 669 799 512 and *Alb.●* **Alma do Camiño** *Priv.[96÷10]* ℰ 982 876 768
m: 629 822 036 c/ Calvo Sotelo, 199. *Alb.●* **Barullo** *Café* ℰ 982 876 357 Praza
de Galicia, 40. *Alb.●* **Credencial** *Priv.[96÷10]* ℰ 982 876 455 m: 639 722 878
Rúa do Peregrino, 50-bajo. *Alb.●* **Puente Ribeira** *Priv.[40÷4]* ℰ 982 876 789 m:
698 175 619 Rúa do Peregrino, Nº 23 - Bajo. Continue past *H***** **Alfonso IX** €85
ℰ 982 530 005 (right) and popular *H** **Oca Villa** €45 ℰ 982 533 873 (left 100m).
Turn right> in c/Benigno Quiroga and <left by *P* **O Camiño** €40+ ℰ 626 205 172
& •*Peregrinoteca* ℰ 982 530 190 a veritable Aladdin's Cave of equipment exclusive
to pilgrims presided over by José Mª Díaz. We now climb the ancient granite steps
Escalinata Maior to the central hub of pilgrim Sarria:

1.0 km **Sarria** *Centro [km. 111,5] rúa*
Maior. **Albergues ❶** – **❾** (Av. price €10).
❶ *Casa Peltre* *Priv [22÷3]* ℰ 606 226 067.
*P**Escalinata €20 ℰ 982 530 259. **Rúa**
Maior Nº64 ❷ *Mayor* *Priv.[16÷2]* ℰ 685
148 474. **Nº79** (right) **❸** *Xunta.[40÷2]* ℰ
660 396 813 (€6). S/o up **Nº62** (left) *H* **Aqua**
€35 ℰ 619 879 476. **Nº44 ❹** *O Durmiñento*
Priv.[40÷7]+ ℰ 982 531 099 roof terrace.
Nº65 ❺ *Casino* *Priv [28÷2]* ℰ 982 886 785.

Nº53 *Casa Barán* €75 ℰ 982 876 487. **Nº57**
❻ *Internacional* *Priv.[44÷4]+* ℰ 982 535
109 roof terrace. **Nº49 ❼** *Obradoiro* *Priv.[28÷2]* ℰ 982 532 442 garden terrace.
Nº31 ❽ *Los Blasones* *Priv.*[42÷4]* ℰ 600 512 565 rear patio. **Nº19** *P** **Mesón**
Camino Francés ℰ 982 532 351 (opp. Mesón O Tapas).

Next we pass the *Concello* and the tiny *Plaza de la Constitución* and **Nº10 ❾** **Don**
Álvaro *Priv.[40÷4]* ℰ 982 531 592 rear patio. **Nº4 ❿** *Matías* *Priv.[30÷1]+* ℰ
982 534 285 adj. rest' Matias Locanda Italiana. ● Other albergues: ● **Dos Oito**
Marabedís *Priv.[24÷7]* ℰ 629 461 770 rúa Conde de Lemos, 23 modern terraced
house. 300m further up ● **Barbacoa** *Priv.[10÷1]+* ℰ 619 879 476 c/Esqueirodos,1.
On *other* side of rua Maior; 400m down rua da Calexa ● **San Lázaro** *Priv.[30÷4]+*
ℰ 982 530 626 c/San Lázaro,7. ● **La Casona de Sarria** *Priv.[31÷5]+* €10-12+€35
ℰ 982 535 556 (Marcela) Rúa San Lázaro 24. Top of town (out of the bustle) ●
Monasterio la Magdalena *Priv.[90÷3]* Av. de la Merced, ℰ 982 533 568 'twinned'
with albergue Seminario Menor in Santiago.

SALIDA

Ponte Áspera

rio Celeiro

Camiño Francés

San Roque
Cementerio

5 Monasterio de la Magdalena
A Monasterio de la Magdalena
·credencial

A La Casona
San Lázaro

Estación Ferrocarril

Campo
da Feira

Fortaleza de Sarria
(Ruinas)

Parque
Do
Bosque

rúa José Antonio

Roma **H**

A Barbacoa

rúa do Castelo

Torre **4**

rúa da Merced

Cruceiro

rúa Calexa

rúa Ponrir

Casa
Matías **P**

Mar de
Plata **H**

Matias Locanda Italiana

El Salvador **2** ■**3** San Anton

Sarmiento

rúa Nova

rúa Calvo Sotelo

Dos Oito **A**
Marabedís

Matías**10**

Don Álvaro **9**

P Camiño Francés

8 Los Blasones

7 Obradoiro

6 Internacional

H Casa Barán

5 Casino

rúa Matías López

Plaza

Concello

O'Durmiñento **4**

**Estación
de Autobuses**
(Santiago via Lugo)

Aqua **H**

Mayor **2**

Maior

1 Santa Mariña
·credencial

3 Xunta

rúa Matías López

Casa Peltre **1**

Escalinata Maiór→

rúa Benigno Quiroga

Oca Villa **H**

P Escalinata

Peregrinoteca (equipamiento) © 982-530 190

P

O Camiño

rúa Diego Pazos

Ferreiro

SARRIA
(Pop. 13,500 – Alt. 455m)

Parque
O Chanto

rio Sarria

Malecón

Campo do rio

A Puente Ribeira

H Alfonso IX***

rio Sarria

rúa de Peregrino

rúa Calvo Sotelo

Credencial **A**

A Alma do Camiño

A Barullo

Cristal **P**

VIGO DE SARRIA

Turismo © 982-530 099

Oasis **A**

i

A Pedra

ENTRADA

O

Puesta
del Sol

S ——— N

Salida
del Sol

E

❑ **Other accommodation:** *P* **Matias Rooms** €25-40 Calle Rosalia de Castro, 19 (same ownership asAlbergue Matias ⓒ 982 534 285). In the 'new' town *P*ˢ **Casa Matías** €25 ⓒ 659 160 498 Calvo Sotelo,39 and to the rear in rúa Formigueiros *H*ˢ **Mar de Plata** ⓒ 982 530 724. Adj. railway station *Hr*ˢ **Roma** ⓒ 982 532 211 Calvo Sotelo,2. ❑ Variety of lively cafes around the rúa Maior. For a tranquil setting on the river try *O Chanto* perched on the río Sarria with access via delightful river path (see map).

SARRIA: with its Celtic origins was a major medieval centre for pilgrims with several churches, chapels, monasteries and 7 pilgrim hospitals. The ancient atmosphere can still be felt in the attractive old quarter that climbs along the main street *rúa Maior* passing the main ❑ **Historical monuments:** ❶ *Iglesia de Santa Mariña XIX* with its evocative pilgrim mural (*credenciales* issued after pilgrim mass daily at 18:00 (Sun 12:00). At the top of rúa Maior ❷ *Iglesia del Salvador XIII* with its tympanum of Christ in Majesty and the Tree of Life (mass Sun 18:00). Opp: ❸ *Hospital de San Anton XVI antiguo hospital de peregrino* (now courts of Justice). ❹ *Fortaleza de Sarria y Torres XIII* castle (ruins). The camino continues to ❺ *Mosteiro de Santa María Madalena (Convento de la Merced) XIII* with fine plateresque façade and now an albergue that issues *credenciales*. *Daily mass at 18:30 (Sun 13:00)*. The camino continues down to the medieval bridge *Ponte Áspera (Rough Bridge)* over the río Celerio.

The advent of the railway in the 19th century pulled the town centre eastwards leaving the ancient *camino real* largely intact. Sarria is a bustling modern town with a population of 13,500. It has become a major starting point for pilgrims with limited time but anxious to pick up a *compostela* at Santiago – starting from here will cover (just) the requisite 100 km to the cathedral – hence the profusion of pilgrim hostels in town. Note you now need 2 stamps *sellos* per day to obtain a compostela. Pilgrims arrive via the bus and rail stations and from this point the route becomes crowded with new arrivals. Many hostels provide a backpack *mochila* transport service.

Note for 'seasoned' pilgrims who commenced (for example) in St. Jean Pied de Port or further back in Le Puy, Geneva, Budapest? Beware of signs of irritation at the intrusion of new pilgrims on 'my' camino – remember that many of the new arrivals may be nervous starting out and the last thing they need is aloofness built on a false sense of superiority. None of us can know the inner motivation or outer circumstances of another. A loving pilgrim welcomes all they meet along the path with an open mind and open heart... without judgement of any kind.

REFLECTIONS:

❏ **To err is human, to forgive, divine.**
Alexander Pope

29 115.1 km (71.5 ml) – Santiago

SARRIA – PORTOMARÍN

⬚⬚⬚⬚⬚⬚	--- ---	12.1	--- ---	55%
▬▬▬▬	--- ---	10.0	--- ---	45%
▬▬		0.0		
Total km		**22.1 km**	(13.7 ml)	

◣ --- --- 23.6 km (+1.5 km)
Alto ▲ Alto Momientos 660m (2,165 ft)
< 🅰 🅷 > Barbadelo ❶ **3.6** – ❺ **4.5** km – Morgade **12.1** km – Ferrerios **13.5** km
Mercadoiro **16.9** km – Vilacha **20.0** km – *[Fontedeagra 20.5 km +0.5km]*

❏ **The Practical Path:** The majority of today's stage is on lovely woodland paths and gravel tracks *sendas*. Apart from the bare flanks around the high point on the Peña do Cervo at Momientos (above Portomarín) much of the remainder is along tree-lined roads. So we have good shade from the sun or shelter from the driving rain. We will pass through many small hamlets that seem to blend seamlessly one into the next. Several new cafés offer refreshment stops along the way.

❏ **The Mystical Path:** Two ancient Orders occupied opposite sides of this river but their strongholds are long gone – buried under the flood waters created by the dam to serve the insatiable demands of a new generation. We cannot live in the past and we try in vain to live with the idea of some future golden age. The only place we can truly inhabit is the present. The rest is fantasy – some painful, some pleasurable – both deceptive.

❏ **Personal Reflections:** *"... I reflect on the extraordinary revelation of the third secret of Fátima. We are all fallen angels struggling to find our wings so that we can fly back home to the Divine. If God is my Father what does that make me and, by extension, all my fellow brothers and sisters? We each share the same Identity and the same Inheritance. And so I come full circle, back to the place where I began and to the realisation that the only way out... is in. The only way off the mortal coil is through the total forgiveness of self, other and the world. That is why external authority must collapse. The Voice for God is within and urges each one of us, as children of one God, to become the authors of own awakening ..."*

0.0 km Sarria *Centro* from albergue ❶ in Sarria head up c/Mayor past the church of Santa Mariña with its sombre medieval pilgrim murals and past the town hall (left) *Casa do Concello* with basic tourist information. Next we pass the intimate

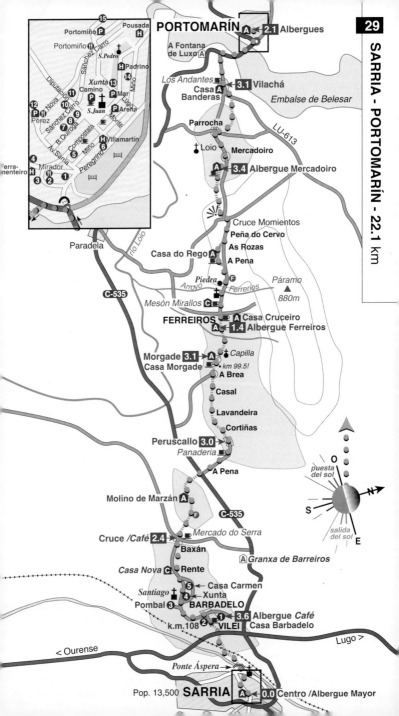

PORTOMARÍN

Portomiño
Portomiño
S.Pedro
Padrino
Xunta
Camino
Mar
Arena
Compostela
Miño
Villamartin
Mirador
Ferra-
nenteiro

Paradela

A Fontana de Luxo Ⓐ

Ⓐ 2.1 Albergues

Los Andantes 3.1 Vilachá
Casa Banderas Ⓐ

Embalse de Belesar

Parrocha

LU-613

† Loio Mercadoiro

Ⓐ 3.4 Albergue Mercadoiro

Cruce Momientos
Peña do Cervo
As Rozas
Casa do Rego Ⓐ A Pena

Piedra Ⓕ
Arroyo Ferreiros
Páramo
▲ 880m

Mesón Mirallos Ⓒ

FERREIROS Ⓐ Casa Cruceiro
Ⓐ 1.4 Albergue Ferreiros

Morgade 3.1 Ⓐ † Capilla
Casa Morgade • km 99.5!
A Brea

Casal

Lavandeira

Cortiñas

Peruscallo 3.0
Panadería

A Pena

Molino de Marzán Ⓐ

Ⓕ
C-535

Cruce /Café 2.4 Mercado do Serra
Baxán
Ⓐ Granxa de Barreiros
Casa Nova Ⓒ Rente
⑤ ← Casa Carmen
Santiago † ④ ← Xunta
Pombal ③ **BARBADELO**
① 3.6 Albergue Café
② **VILEI** Casa Barbadelo
k.m.108

< Ourense
Lugo >

Ponte Áspera →

Pop. 13,500 **SARRIA** Ⓐ 0.0 Centro /Albergue Mayor

O
puesta del sol
S
salida del sol
E

Praza da Constitución with its albergues, cafes and restaurants and towards the top of the street (left) Church of St. Saviour *Igrexa de San Salvador XIII[th]C* with its primitive Romanesque tympanum over the main door. Opposite was St. Anthony's pilgrim Hospice *Hospital de San Anton* (now courts of Justice) and here we turn right> to pass the ruins of the Sarria castle *Fortaleza de Sarria* (left) only one of

the 4 original towers remains. The castle was destroyed during the uprising of the peasantry against the aristocracy in the 15th century known as the *Irmandiños*. We pass a stone *cruceiro* (right) with fine views back over the town and up past the country market *Campo da Feira* (left) which has existed here since the 14th century and down to the plateresque façade of the ***Mosteiro da Madalena*** **[0.7 km]** (also provides *credencial*) originally instituted in the 13th century, later coming under the Augustinian rule. We finally head down past the cemetery and *Capela de San Lázaro* to cross the road and río Celeiro over the medieval **Ponte Áspera [0.5 km]** 'Rough Bridge' which describes its coarsely cut stone. A path now winds between river and railway before crossing the line in *Santi Michaelis* under road viaduct to cross a stream and climb up through delightful ancient woodland to join the road in **Vilei** an extension of **Barbadelo [2.4 km].**

3.6 km Barbadelo *Vilei Alb.* ❶ **Casa Barbadelo** *Priv.[68÷12]*+ €9-12 © 982 531 934 with garden and swimpool. ❷ **108 km** *Priv.[12÷5]*+ €8-29 © 634 894 524. ❸ **O Pombal** *Priv.[12÷1]* €9 © 686 718 732. 200m off route below *Igrexa de Santiago XII[th]C* Romanesque with a fine tympanum and statue of St. James. Pilgrim mass at 19:00 (check notice board). *[The area is known locally as Mosteiro in reference to a monastery founded here as*

early as the 9th century]. ❹ **Barbadelo** *Xunta.[18÷2]* €6 © former school house on **village green [0.7 km]**. Behind the albergue is a summer cantina and at the top of the lane (200m off route) ❺ **Casa de Carmen** *Priv.[26÷3]*+ €9-35 © 982 532 294 in restored 17[th]c farmhouse with terrace and private chapel *Capela de San Silvestre*. Continue to ***Rente*** **[1.0 km]** *CR* **Casa Nova** © 982 187 854 s/o along woodland paths through ancient oak and chestnut groves and cross main road **[0.7 km]**:

2.4 km Cruce *Café Mercado do Serra (right + 1.8 km Alb.* **Granxa de Barreiros** *Priv.[46÷8]*+ €10+18 © 982 533 656 *Ortoá LU-633)*. S/o past *[F.]* to *Alb.* **Molino de Marzán** *Priv.[16÷1]* €10 © 679 438 077. Cross road into **Leimán** and **Peruscallo.**

2.9 km Peruscallo *Panaderia Peruscallo*. S/o through **Cortiñas**, **Lavandeira**, **Casal** and into **A Brea [2.1 km]** passing (km 99,5) into **Morgade [1.0 km]**:

3.1 km Morgade *Alb.* **Casa Morgade** *Priv.[6÷1]*+ €10-28 © 982 531 250 with popular café (if busy continue to Ferreiros). Pass stone chapel and continue on track down (through!) the Ferreiros stream. This is rural Galicia at her best; green and often wet underfoot with the earthy smell of cow dung. Narrow laneways with granite stepping-stones raised above flood levels provide a gentle climb up to:

1.4 km Ferreiros *Mesón Casa Cruceiro* the traditional edifice overlooked by its ultra modern *Alb.* ❶ **Casa Cruceiro** *Priv. [12÷1]*+ €10-40 ⓒ 982 541 240. Just below the café (left) ❷ **Ferreiros** *Xunta. [22÷1]* €6 ⓒ 660 396 815 (Primitiva) former schoolhouse set in leafy glade. *[Ferreiros translates as blacksmith].* S/o

past **Mirallos [0.3 km]** *Mesón Mirallos* café (+ colchones €-donativo) adj. the Church of Santa María and just beyond the ancient ⊹ *Chalice Stone* up to the tranquil hamlet of **A Pena [0.4 km]** *Alb.* ♥ **Casa do Rego** *Priv.[6÷1]*+ €10 ⓒ 982 167 812 with a warm welcome in 7 languages! Café *menú* and outdoor terrace. Up steeply to **As Rozas [0.8 km]** *[F.]* and the high point *Pena dos Corvos 660m* at Cruce Momientos **[1.3 km]** with fine views over the reservoir as we begin our descent into the río Miño valley and **Mercadoiro [0.7 km]**:

3.4 km Mercadoiro *Alb.* **Mercadoiro** *& café Bodeguiña Priv.[32÷6]*+ €10-40 ⓒ 982 545 359. Popular café-restaurant with pilgrim menu in delightful hamlet with an official population of – one! Continue through **Moutras** and **A Parrocha**. *[off route left is the remote valley of Loio with the ruins of the Monastery of Santa María de Loio – birthplace of the Order*

of Santiago in the 12th century]. The route crosses several country lanes into:

3.1 km Vilachá *Alb.* **Casa Banderas** *Priv.[8÷1]*+ €10-40 ⓒ 982 545 391 Gordon Bell (one of the founders of the South African association) who also provides dinner. Snacks from adj. *Casa Susanna.* KM.94 *V.* pizzeria *Los Andantes* with plans for hostal. The route descends *very* steeply to the bridge spanning the deep Miño basin. *[Detour ½ km to Alb.* **A Fontana de Luxo** *€15+35 ⓒ 645 649 496 Fontedeagra,2.]* Cross bridge to **roundabout [2.0 km]** at Portomarín. *[To continue to Gonzar follow the road to the left over the second bridge (200m) see next stage].* Or take the steep staircase in front, part of the original medieval bridge across the river Miño. These lead up to the arch and *capela de Santa María de las Nieves* which, along with several other historic monuments, were all removed to the high ground around Portomarín when the dam was built across the river to create the Belesar reservoir in 1962. *[The original bridge was of Roman origin and joined the district of San Pedro, with links to the Knights of Santiago, with San Nicolás (headquarters of the Knights of Saint John). The river formed a major strategic boundary].* Climb the stairs for the first (lower) of 3 **albergues [0.2 km]** with fine views over the river and reservoir.

2.2 km Portomarín *(albergues Av.€10)* ❶ **Pons Minea** *Priv.[12÷1]*+ ⓒ 610 737 995 off Av. Sarria 11 (bajo). ❷ **O Mirador** *Priv.[27÷6]* ⓒ 982 545 323 with *bar/rest'* adj' ❸ **Ferramenteiro** *Priv.*[130÷1]* ⓒ 982 545 362. ❹ **Folgueira** *Priv.[32÷1]* ⓒ

982 545 166 Av. Chantada opp' the luxury *H**¨**Ferramenteiro* €80 ⓒ 982 545 361. The centre and main action is at the top end of town ½ km further on.

Continue up the cobbled main street *rúa Xeral Franco* with its handsome stone colonnades with various shops and cafés leading to the central square *Praza Conde de Fenosa* with choice of restaurants, bars and pensiónes. Here we also find the *Casa do Concello, Correos* and, overlooking all this activity is the austere Romanesque fortress church of St. John with links to the Knights of Saint John *Igrexa de San Juan / San Xoán* (also Saint Nicholas). It was painstakingly rebuilt from its original site now submerged under the waters of the Balesar reservoir and ascribed to the workshop of Master Mateo who carved the Pórtico da Gloria in Santiago. Built as both a place of worship

and defence, with its 4 defensive towers and battlements (crenellated parapet). The church has a single barrel vaulted nave and semicircular apse and prominent rose window *(see photo right)*. Daily mass at 20:00 (Sundays 12:30). Times may vary.

■ **Pilgrim hostels:** See town plan: *(albergues Av. €10)* ❺ **Pasiño a Pasiño** *Priv. [30÷6]* Ⓒ 665 667 243 Rúa Compostela 25. ❻ **Villamartín** *Priv.[20÷2]* Ⓒ 982 545 054 part of hotel Villajardín on rúa de Miño overlooking the river to the rear. **C**alle Benigno Quiroga **Nº16** ❼ **Casa Cruz** *Priv.[16÷1]* Ⓒ 982 545 140. **Nº12** ❽ **Novo Porto** *Priv.[22÷1]* Ⓒ 982 545 277. **Nº6** ❾ **El Caminante** *Priv.[12÷1]+* Ⓒ 982 545 176. **Calle Diputación Nº9** ●-10 **Ultreia** *Priv.[14÷1]+* Ⓒ 982 545 067 opp. **Nº8** ●-11 **Porto Santiago** *Priv.*[14÷1]+* Ⓒ 618 826 515 & small terrace off side entrance. ●-12 **Aqua** *Priv.[16÷1]+* Ⓒ 608 921 372 Barreiros, 2 (adj. Perez/ Guardia Civil). ●-13 **Portomarín** *Xunta.[110÷6]* (€6) Ⓒ 982 545 143 original hostel renovated with all mod cons + washing and drying machines at rear. ●-14 **Manuel** *Priv.[16÷1]+* (+€25) Ⓒ 982 545 385. ●-15 **Casa do Marabillas** *Priv.[20÷2]* €15 incl. Ⓒ 982 189 086 Camiño do Monte 3. ■ **Other Lodging:** €30+ *in addition to private rooms offered in albergues marked +*: Central square *Praza Conde Fenosa* with lively restaurants *P*' **Posada del Camino** Ⓒ 982 545 081. *P*''**Arenas** Ⓒ 982 545 386. Nearby in rúa de Miño 14 *H*'' **Villajardín** Ⓒ 982 545 054. **Rúa Fraga Iribarne Nº5** *P*' **Mar** Ⓒ 622 611 211 and at **Nº18** *Hs*''' **El Padrino** €60 Ⓒ 982 545 323 adj. Parque Antonio Sanz and Church of Saint Peter *Iglesia San Pedro* with fine Romanesque doorway. **Top of town Av. Sarria** *P*' **Portomiño** Ⓒ 982 547 575 reception at rest' *Portomiño* and *H*''' **Pousada de Portomarín** Ⓒ 982 545 200 (main road). *[Next albergue: Gonzar – 8.2 km].*

REFLECTIONS:

❒ **The foolish man seeks happiness in the distance;**
The wise man grows it under his feet.
———————————————————— *J R Oppenheimer*

30 **93.0** km (57.8 ml) – Santiago

PORTOMARÍN – PALAS DE REI

⫶⫶⫶⫶⫶⫶⫶⫶⫶⫶	--- ---	19.9	--- ---	*80%*
▬▬▬▬	--- ---	4.9	--- ---	*20%*
▬▬▬▬	--- ---	0.0		
Total km		**24.8** km	(15.4 ml)	

◣◣◣ --- --- 27.0 km (^450m +2.2 km)
Alto ◣ Sierra Ligonde 720m (2,362 ft)
< Ⓐ Ⓗ > Gonzar **7.8** km – Hospital **11.5** – Ventas de Narón **12.9** km –Ligonde **16.6** km – Eirexe **17.2** km – Portos **19.3** km – Os Chacotes **23.6** km.

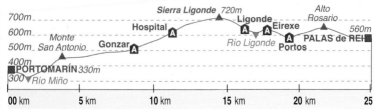

❒ **The Practical Path:** A day of varied terrain as we start by climbing up through woodland around the *Embalse de Belesar* to join the main road which we have to cross on several occasions before leaving it to climb the *Sierra Ligonde* descending to Portos which offers us the detour to Vilar de Donas. Then comes a gentler climb around the side of Rosary Heights *Alto Rosario* to drop down finally to Palas de Rei. Prepare for an early start if you intend to take the detour to Vilas de Donas.

———————————————————————————————————————

❒ **The Mystical Path:** Will you make time to detour to this mystical resting place of the Knights of Saint James? Here effigies of the knights in their armour are watched over by the beautiful frescoes that adorn the walls of this sacred temple dedicated to Saint Saviour. A pilgrim must travel on two paths simultaneously. The tourist will look for the stone altar – the pilgrim an altered state. The one seeks sacred sites – the other in-sight. Will you make time today to detour into the inner mystery?

❒ **Personal Reflections:** *"… The incessant rain pounds down as heavy as when it started a week ago. The country is awash; roads have turned to rivers; rivers to torrents. I sat for a while at the base of the ancient oak and felt its solid support and in the same instant knew that my period of silence was ended. I don't know how long I been in this altered state, induced as much by physical exhaustion as any ecstatic revelation. And I don't know how long they had been there but they helped me to my feet and we embraced in love and respect for the experiences we had each invoked; 3 pilgrims from 3 different countries with 3 different languages but part of one family. I found it hard to speak after such a long spell of silence but I managed to say 'bless you' realising that with every breath I send out positive or negative vibrations. Regardless of outer conditions I can choose to send out love. Until that moment I had not noticed the ancient wayside cross silently witnessing this loving reunion of fellow pilgrims …"*

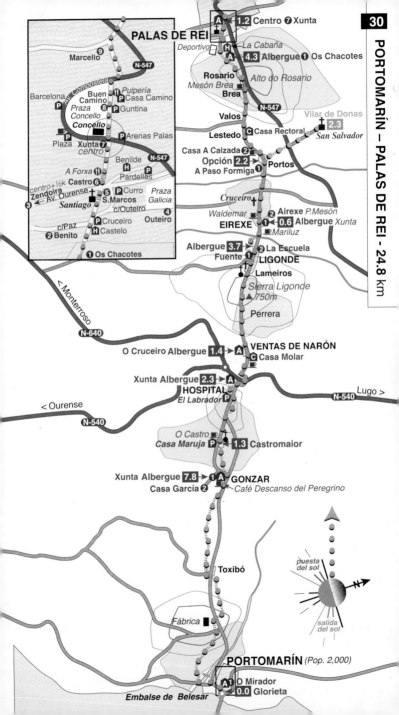

PALAS DE REI

Marcello ⑨

N-547

Barcelona

Av. Compostela

⟨ Monterroso

Buen
Camino ⑧

Pulpería
P Casa Camino
P Guntina

*Praza
Concello*
Concello

P

P Arenas Palas

Plaza

Xunta ⑦
centro

Benilde
H
Pardellas

N-547

A Forxa ⑪

Castro ⑥

centro+½k
Zendoira

⟨ Av. Ourense

③ ⟨

Santiago

P Curro
⑥ S.Marcos
c/Outeiro

*Praza
Galicia*

Outeiro ④

c/Paz

P Cruceiro

② Benito

H Castelo

① Os Chacotes

A **1.2** Centro ⑦ Xunta

Deportivo

H

A **4.3** Albergue ① Os Chacotes

La Cabaña

Rosario

Mesón Brea

Brea

Alto do Rosario

Valos

N-547

Vilar de Donas

✝ **2.3**

Lestedo

C Casa Rectoral

San Salvador

Casa A Calzada ②

Opción **2.2**

A Paso Formiga

① ⟨ Portos

Cruceiro ✝

Waldemar

② Airexe *P.Mesón*

EIREXE

① ⟨ **0.6** Albergue *Xunta*

■ *Mariluz*

Albergue **3.7**

Fuente ①

② La Escuela

LIGONDE

Lameiros

Sierra Ligonde
▲ *750m*

Perrera

O Cruceiro Albergue **1.4** → **A** **VENTAS DE NARÓN**

C Casa Molar

Xunta Albergue **2.3** → **A**

HOSPITAL

El Labrador **P**

⟨ Ourense

N-540

N-540

Lugo ⟩

O Castro ✝

Casa Maruja **P** → **1.3** Castromaior

Xunta Albergue **7.8** → ① **A** **GONZAR**

Casa García ②

⟵ *Café Descanso del Peregrino*

Toxibó

Fábrica ■

PORTOMARÍN *(Pop. 2,000)*

A ① O Mirador

0.0 Glorieta

Embalse de Belesar

*puesta
del sol*

*salida
del sol*

0.0 km **Portomarín** from albergue ❶ make your way back down to the main road and over the second (smaller) bridge over the the the río Torres [**0.4 km**]. We now continue up through dense woodland around St. Anthony's height *alto San Antonio* to join the pilgrim track *senda* by the main road at **San Mamed-Belad** [**1.8 km**] cross over by *Fábrica de Ladrillos* and re-cross by Coren fertilizer plant in **Toxibo** [**1.8 km**] after which we have a brief and delightful respite through woodland past *[F.]* to **Gonzar** [**3.8 km**].

7.8 km **Gonzar** popular (busy) *Café Descanso del Peregrino* on the main road and *Alb.* ❶ **Gonzar** *Xunta.[28÷1]* €6 noisy location on main road but recently refurbished. Around the corner (100m) *Alb.* ❷ **Casa Garcia** *Priv.[30÷5]+* €10–€35 ©️ 982 157 842 traditional village house with covered courtyard (see photo) in quiet location off main road also *Café-menú.* Continue and turn off <left onto minor road and then right> onto track before joining road into:

1.2 km **Castromaior** (originally a Celtic castro) *P° Casa Maruja* ©️ 982 189 054 *Café O Castro* Romanesque church of Santa María. Continue through the village criss-crossing main road and back to:

2.5 km **Hospital de la Cruz** where the N-540 cuts through this ancient village (its medieval pilgrim hospice no longer visible) but hospitality awaits at *Hs* **El Labrador** €30+ ©️ 982 545 303 & restaurant. *Alb.* **Hospital de la Cruz** *Xunta.[32÷1]* €6 another conversion of a school building by the main road (N-540 Ourense – Lugo) take the minor road flyover to the next village:

1.4 km **Ventas de Narón** *Alb.* ❶ **Casa Molar** *Priv.[18÷2]+* €10-30 ©️ 696 794 507 traditional stone house with restaurant and bar (see photo). *Alb.* ❷ **O Cruceiro** *Priv.*[22÷2]+* €10-30 ©️ 658 064 917 also with restaurant and bar. Tiny stone chapel *Capela de Magdalene* with picnic area adjoining. *[The area was scene of a fierce battle in 840 between Moor and Christian*

but there is nothing here now to disturb the peace beyond pilgrim chatter in the 2 cafés]. Now we start to climb the Sierra Ligonde to the highest point of today's route (720m) passing dog kennels *perreras Alejo* before dropping down to the ancient hamlet of **Lameiros** with the *Antiguo Hospital de Peregrinos* (now a private house – right) and just beyond the ancient *Casa da Carneiro* which provided hospitality to no less than the holy Roman emperor Charles V and King Philip of Spain while on his way to marry Mary Tudor.

3.7 km **Ligonde** equally ancient hamlet long associated with the camino with its *Cementerio de Peregrinos* and humble hospitality at *Alb.* ❶ **Fuente del Peregrino** *Priv.[20÷2]* €-donativo ©️ 687 550 527 basic facilities with communal meal prepared by voluntary hospitaleros. ❷ **Escuela de Ligonde** *Muni.[20]* ©️ 679 816 061 skillfully restored hostel with all facilities. *[Ligonde was formerly a significant medieval stop on the way. Charlemagne reputedly stayed here and other royal* *personages and it had a pilgrim hospice].* Igrexa de Santiago has a Romanesque porch. Opposite the Albergue is a short track down over the río Ligonde passing café-restaurant *Casa Mari Luz* (right) up past church and cruceiro into:

0.6 km Eirexe *Alb.* ❶ **Airexe** *Xunta.[20÷2]* €6 former school building at crossroads with all facilities. To the rear is ❷ **Eirexe** *Priv.[6÷1]+ –*€10 © 982 153

475 with bar-menú. At the crossroads is restaurant *Conde Valdemar*. Continue on quiet country road passing splendid 17th century wayside cross (left) by gnarled oak tree in the ancient hamlet of **Lameiro** with its diminutive capela San Marcos. We now climb gently to a crossing of 5 roads with fine views of the surrounding countryside before dropping down into **Portos** *Alb.* **A Paso de Formiga** (Ants Way!) *Priv.[8÷1]+* €10–€25 © 618 984 605. Continue s/o to:

2.1 km Opción *Detour* Portos *A Calzada / Alb.* **A Calzada** *Priv.[10÷1]* €10 © 982 183 744 separate stone pavilion at the rear. No kitchen but meals available at the popular café-restaurant with peaceful garden and picnic area.

Detour: Vilar de Donas recommended detour (4.6 km there and back) to this national monument and ancient seat of the Knights of Santiago. Closed Mondays and holidays (check in A Calzada for opening times). The Church of El Salvador is primarily 14th century but its origins go back to the formation of a nunnery here in the 10th century (hence the appellation Donas). The stone effigies of the knights and its unique frescoes (see photo under reflections) are hauntingly expressive. *Directions:* Turn right off the camino (opposite A Calzada) along quiet country lane across the main road [**1.1** km] (N-547 Palas de Rei – Lugo) passing rest area *área de descanco* (right) for remaining [**1.2** km] to:

2.3 km **Vilar de Donas – Igrexa San Salvador**. Take time to soak in its ancient history and to savour its treasures lovingly attended by the knowledgeable guardian. Return the same way.

From *A Calzada* continue along pathways into and through the hamlet of *Lestedo* [**0.6** km] *CR* **Rectoral de Lestedo** €60+ © 982 153 435 converted from an original pilgrim hospital, then priests house *casa rectoral* and finally to this modernised gem with rooms from €57. Dinner available. We pass village cemetery and then *Os Valos,* *Mamurria* and on to *A Brea* [**1.8** km] *Mesón A Brea* on the main N-547. A short woodland path at the back of the restaurant takes us up to *Alto Rosario* [**0.9** km]. *[Here (before the trees were planted) you could see the sacred peak above Santiago Pico Sacro and on entering the hamlet of Rosario pilgrims would start to recite the Rosary, hence the name].* We now pass through the hamlet which adjoins the main road before entering the suburbs of Palas de Reis and its delightful municipal parkland [**1.0** km] *Área recreativa de Os Chacotes*.

4.3 km Palas de Rei *Os Chacotes Alb.* ❶
Os Chacotes *Xunta.[112÷3]* €6 with 3 large
dormitories packed tightly with bunk beds.
Here amongst the peaceful parkland we also
find *H°°°* Complejo La Cabana ℂ 982 380
750 €35+ with rest'. S/o past sports hall into
town passing c/Paz ▲ (left 50m) *(Albergues
Av. Price €10 Pensions €30+)* to: ❷ Mesón
de Benito *Priv.[100÷7]* ℂ 982 103 386

menú €10. 300m further out ❸ Zendoira *Priv.[50÷4]+* €10-€35 ℂ 608 490 075
Amado Losada 10 (off Av.Ourense). ▲ Continue into town on rua Cruceiro past *Hs*
O Castelo ℂ 618 401 130 and ▼ *Café P* O Cruceiro ℂ 649 629 725. Here up right
on c/ Outeiro ❹ Outeiro *Priv.[50÷6]* ℂ 982 380 242 overlooking Plaza de Galicia.

▼ At *Café O Cruceiro* take the lane past parish church of **San Tirso** *[built in the 11th
century now only retaining its original Romanesque doorway]. [F.].* Down steps to
main road and ❺ San Marcos *Priv.[58÷7]+* ℂ 982 380 711 ultra-modern hostel adj.
P° Casa Curro ℂ 982 380 044 Av. Ourense. Cross road to: ❻ Castro *Priv.*[56÷6]*
ℂ 609 080 655 + café on corner. Sign for *Hr°°* Benilde ℂ 982 380 717 on rua do
Mercado adj. *P* Pardellas ℂ 982 380 181. Take steps down into rua Iglesia past
restaurant *A Forxa* with rear patio *(left)*.

1.2 km Palas de Rei *Centro* ❼ Xunta
[60÷7] €6 original hostel popular owing
to its central location directly opp. Town
Hall *Casa Concello* (see photo). ▲ Here
up (right) on main road *Av. Compostela*
Nº16 *P°°*Arenas Palas ℂ 982 380 326. ▲
down (left) Nº21 *P* Hostal Plaza ℂ 982 380

109 with internet café and beyond at Nº39
P Barcelona ℂ 982 374 114. ▲ Just over
the road on Travesía del Peregrino (off praza
Concello): ❽ Buen Camino *Priv.*[41÷8]* ℂ 982 380 233 network* hostel with all
facilities opp'. *P°* Guntina ℂ 982 380 080 and *P* Casa Camiño *Pulpería* ℂ 982 374
066. On the edge of town: ❾ A Casina di Marcello *Priv.[16÷2]* ℂ 640 723 903 c/
Camiño de abaixo. *[Next albergue: Mato Casanova – 6.3 km].*

❏ *Turismo* (Oficina Municipal) Av. de Compostela 28 ℂ 982 380 001 *Casa
Concello.* Note the regular Lugo – Santiago bus stops here.

❏ **Palas de Rei** straddles the camino and was a 'compulsory' stop in the *Codex
Calixtinus.* Little remains to remind us of its illustrious past but the name derives
from *Pallatium Regis* palace of the Visigothic king Witiza who reigned from 702
– 710. The Church of **Santiago de Alba** *XII°* has a Romanesque portal and scallop
shell motifs are visible in the town. Today, it is an administrative centre with good
modern facilities serving a population of 3,600 mostly engaged in the dairy industry
and the well known Ulloa cheese. ❏ **Detours** *Share a taxi?*: **Vilar de Donas** built
in twelfth century as a monastic church and linked to the Order of the Knights of
Santiago and the Templars. from this point (see mural right). **Pambre Castle** one
of the finest military castles of its era. Built in the fourteenth century by Gonzalo
Ozores de Ulloa on the Banks of the Pambre river. Check with the municipal office
or try the castle direct ℂ 628 159 469. Alternatively visit from albergues Casa
Domingo or A Bolboreta (see next stage).

REFLECTIONS:

❏ Walking, I am listening to a deeper way... all my ancestors are behind me. *'Be still, they say. Watch and listen. You are the result of the love of thousands'.*

Linda Hogan

31 68.2 km (42.4 ml) – Santiago

PALAS DE REI – RIBADISO (ARZÚA)

┄┄┄┄┄	--- ---	18.2	--- ---	71%
▬▬▬▬	--- ---	6.6	--- ---	26%
▬▬▬▬	--- ---	0.8	--- ---	3%
Total km		**25.6 km** (15.9 ml)		

▲ --- --- 26.5 km (+ 0.9 km)
Alto ▲ O Coto 515m (1,670 ft)
< ⒶⒽ > San Xulián **3.4** km – Casanova **5.7** km – O Coto **8.4** km –
Melide **14.5** km – Boente **20.3** km – Castañeda **22.5** km.

❏ **The Practical Path:** Today we cross 6 shallow river valleys and ¾ on pathways mostly through delightful woodland that helps to stifle the noise from the busy N-547 which we cross and re-cross all the way to Arzúa. Melide makes a good half way stop where we can sample the renowned octopus *pulpo Gallega* and explore the historic old town. Melide is also where pilgrims walking the Camino Primitivo (from Oviedo) join the main camino Francés.

❏ **The Mystical Path:** Will you see the tiny representation of Santiago in the flyover? He appears at the entrance and the exit, welcoming us and blessing us on our way. What does he represent to you and why do we follow his way? Is it to revere his relics that may lie in a silver casket two days ahead? Is that what brought you this far? Do you believe he chose to martyr his earthly body so we could venerate it? He has many names, but who was he really and what significance does he play in our story? What unknown hand beckons us to follow in the way of the true Master? Where will we find Him?

❏ **Personal Journal:** *"... In each moment I sense my guides setting up situations for me to learn the next lesson. I have an image of adoring angels urging me to learn through grace rather than grit. But the lesson will be integrated in perfect timing and with exquisite precision for the exact amount of sand required to produce the pearl. Not one grain too many, but, alas, not one grain too few. So my angelic escort set me up Toshio, just when I had lost my inner way and was confused as to my motivation. And he asks me three questions: each one a reminder of my reason for doing this pilgrimage and an invaluable aid to its accomplishment. How, in heaven's name, did they conceive of a Japanese Shinto grandfather to place on the earthly path of a lost Christian soul? ..."*

Milpes A   ARZÚA
            RIBADISO de Baixo
Los Caminantes 2   Xunta
                    3.1 Puente   río Iso
            N-547   Manuel
                    Portela
                    C Casa Garea
                      C Casa Milia
        La Calleja C
Albergue 2.2   A Santiago
                CASTAÑEDA

                                    río Boente
            Boente 2
Cruce X 3.3   1   Iglesia de Santiago
        El Alemán   Lugo >
        Raído   AC-840
        Penas
        Carballal   San Lázaro

                    2.5 Puente
            S.María
                    8   Camino Primitivo
                MELIDE
                    Sancti Spiriti
                    1.5 Centro Rotonda
                    San Pedro
                1 H Carlos
FURELOS   4.6 Puente Velha
                                río Furelos
        Polígono
        Industrial
        Gándarra
    N-547
        Disicabo
                    Sta.María XIII
        Lobreiro   río Seco
O Coto 2.7   C Casa de Somoza
        CORNIXA
                A CORUÑA
    N-547   LUGO
Ramil
Remonde
A Bolboreta A
        Casanova
        A 2.3 Albergue

        Casa Domingo A   Ponte Campaña Mato
Castillo
Pambre   SAN XULIÁN   N-547
    Albergue 3.4 A
    O Abrigadoiro   río Pambre
                río Roxán
                        CARBALLAL
            Ponterroxan   P
                        PALAS de REI
Centro 0.0 A   (Pop. 3,600 – Alt. 575m)

MELIDE inset:

H Sony
Pereiro 9   8   Xunta
Apalpador 7   H Chiquitín
                H S.Antón
            6 H Vilela
        Pz   5
        Const. M i
        Xaneiro
MELIDE
(Pop. 7,500)
                Qinzan
Estilo P   Rua Trek
        P/Coruña
        Alfonso II 4
Orois P r/A. Bovenda
        3 Cruceiro
parque P Berenguela
2 Arraigos
        r/Galicia
        Crucero
Ezequiel   S.Roque
Garnacha
    H Carlos
1 Melide   P Xaneiro-II

0.0 km **Palas de Rei** *Centro* albergue **❻** continue over the N-547 down rua do Peregrino and over the N-547 past monument and field of the pilgrims *Campo dos Romeiros* where medieval pilgrims gathered for the journey to Santiago and onto a path to cross the N-547 past *[F.]* and back down to the N-547 with *P* **Ponterroxan** €38 ℭ 982 380 132 and cross the river Ruxián and up into Carballal with its raised granaries *Horreos* back down to re-cross the N-547 again onto woodland path into:

3.4 km **San Xulián** (*Xiao*) **do Camiño** classical camino village with its tiny 12th century church dedicated to Saint Julian and *Alb.* **O Abrigadoiro** *Priv.[18÷3]* €10-12 ℭ 676 596 975 with dinner €10 and breakfast available. The path continues down to the Rió Pambre that we cross at Ponte Campaña-Mato **[1.0 km]** and *Alb.* **Casa Domingo ♥** *Priv.*[16÷3]* ℭ 982 163 226 network* hostel part of an old mill occupying a tranquil rural setting on the river Pambre with communal dinner. The route now climbs gently through ancient oak woods for **[1.3 km]** to Mato-Casonova:

2.3 km **Casanova** *Alb.* **Mato Casanova** *Xunta.[20÷2]* €6 ℭ the last Xunta hostel in Lugo (see photo) before we enter into A Coruña in this quiet rural location surrounded by woodland (no local facilities). We proceed up the country lane to junction (left) for *off route* (1½ km) the popular albergue and welcoming casa rural **A Bolboreta** *Priv. [8÷2]+* €13 incl. / €27 single / €37 double / Dinner €9. ℭ 609 124 717 a traditional stone house by Vilar de Remonde with possibility to detour to Pambre.

Detour: Castillo de Pambre. From *A Bolboreta* there is a 2½ km (5 km return) designated walk by medieval bridge passing an ancient Celtic Castro to the impressive 14th century Castillo de Pambre. Strategically situated on the río Pambre it has survived the advances of time and the Irmandiños revolt (the war in which the aristocracy were fighting the peasants rather than each other). The fight continues with disputes between private ownership and public access. Unlike its counterpart in Sarria, the four corner towers and inner keep are still proudly standing. 2 km further is the Palacio Villamayor de Ulloa one of the best-preserved Galician manor houses *Pazos*, family seat of the Ulloa's and setting for the novel *Los Pazos de Ulloa* by Emilia Pardo Bazán (only available in Spanish).

Continue up the Pass of the Oxen *Porto de Bois [scene of a bloody battle between warring nobility]* Hotel Pambre Balneario (left) the high point of this stage at 515m before crossing over the provincial border at scrap yard in Cornixa, past *café Campanilla* if busy continue to O Coto (700m).

2.7 km **O Coto** crossroads hamlet with several *cafés* vying for the breakfast trade. Also *P*** **Los dos Alemanes** €30-€40 ℭ 981 507 337 & *CR* **Casa de Somoza** €45+ ℭ 981 507 372 (prior booking). We now follow a delightful undulating track through woods to cross a medieval bridge into the quintessential camino village of *field of hares* **Leboreiro** no facilities but the Romanesque Church of **Santa María [0.8 km]** *XIIIth* with fine carved stone tympanum of Virgin and Child over the main door. The house opposite with armorial shield was formerly a pilgrim hostel donated by the Ulloa family. We now cross the medieval Magdalena Bridge over the río Seco into **Disicabo**. The path continues up towards the main road and over a footbridge to join a stretch of senda separating the N-547 from an industrial estate *polígono industrial*

Gándara [F.] Mesón Terra do Melide **[1.6** km]. Here the *Orde de Caballeros y Damas del Camino de Santiago* have erected a monument to themselves and a huge sword of Santiago leads us back through woodland down to **Furelos [2.2** km]:

4.6 km **Furelos** *Ponte Velha* medieval bridge into Furelos with *Igrexa San Juan.* No trace remains of the medieval pilgrim hospital but a house adj. the church is a museum. Bar *Farruco [F.]* From here we begin the climb up to Melide through modern suburbs past the first of 9 albergues *(Av. Price €10)* ❶ Melide *Priv.[42÷2]* €10 © 627 901 552 with front entrance on Av. Lugo. Continue s/o up to join main road opp. the Romanesque Church of *San Pedro & San Roque* beside its famous 14[th]c stone cross reputed to be the oldest in Galicia *Crucero do Melide* – Christ in majesty (see photo). We pass variety of pulperías, cafés & Parque S.Roque (left) to *Alb.* ❷ **Arraigos** *Priv.[24÷1]* © 646 343 370 Cantón de San Roque 9. Keep s/o to busy roundabout *Ronda de la Coruña.*

1.5 km **Melide** *Centro* *Alb.* ❸ **O Cruceiro** *Priv.[72÷12]* © 616 764 896 in the centre on Ronda de A Coruña 2 with neo-classical facade and all facilities (incl. lift to the upper floors!) ● 2 waymarked routes from the central roundabout through the old town as follows: (see map). ❶ Direct route via rua Principal and Plaza Constitución or ❷ via rua Convento to Concello and Turismo (museo) and rua S.Antonio with access to *Alb.* ❹ **Alfonso II El Casto** *Priv.[30÷2]+* © 981 506 454 Av. de Toques y Friol 52 (camino primitivo). ❺ **Vilela** *Priv.[24÷2]+* © 616 011 375 c/ San Antonio 2. ❻ **San Antón** *Priv.[36÷5]* © 981 506 427 m: 698 153 672 c/ San Antón 6 and at the end of the street (and town) ❼ **O Apalpador** *Priv.[30÷3]* © 679 837 969 c/ San Antonio 23 and the adj. ❽ **Melide** *Xunta.[156÷7]* (€6) all modern facilities in its cavernous interior (recently refurbished). Finally on c/Progreso 43 *Alb* ❾ **Pereiro** *Priv.[45÷4]* © 981 506 314. **Other Lodging:** *(Pensions €25-35)* *H*"**Carlos** © 981 507 633 lower end of Av. Lugo (opp' albergue 1). *Hs*"**Xaneiro II** © 981 506 140 Av. de la Habana. *P* Orois © 981 506 140 rua A.Bóvena. *P*' **Berenguela** © 981 505 417 off r/S.Roque. *P*'Estilo c/del Progreso. Opp. Xunta albergue *Pousada* **Chiquitín** © 981 815 333 Rúa San Antón 18 ultra modern, roof terrace to the rear. *H* **Sony** © 981 505 473 on N-547.

MELIDE: *Turismo* (9:00-15:00) Plaza Convento © 981 505 003 Casa Concello and administrative centre with (declining) population of 7,500. The old part follows its medieval layout of narrow winding streets with shops, bars and restaurants serving the regional speciality, octopus *pulpo.* For a local experience try *pulpería Garnacha* or *Exequiel* on Av.de Lugo. In *Plaza del Convento* we find the austere parish church, Sancti Spiritus, formerly a 14[th]c Augustinian monastery. Opp. is the original pilgrim refuge of 1502 *Antigo Hospital de Peregrinos* now a museum and Tourist information centre. Melide remains an important hub of the Jacobean pilgrimage and the point where pilgrims travelling down from Oviedo on the original pilgrim route *camino Primitivo* join the *camino Francés.* Today's pilgrim facilities include a •*Masaje y fisioterapia* (servicio al peregrino) in c/Lavadoiro,18 © 981 507 017 and pilgrim hiking gear at •*Rua Trekking* © 981 507 017 r/Convento (near popular restaurant *Casa Qinzan*).

We leave Melida via the western suburbs past *cementerio* **[0.4** km] over N-547 (sign San Martiño) past Romanesque *Igrexa Santa María de Melide XII* **[0.6** km] to leave the busy-ness of Melide behind and make our way into woodland and ***arroyo San Lázaro*** [1.5 km] (the ruins of the leprosarium no longer visible).

2.5 km **Puente *río San Lázaro*** we cross this small river via a stone causeway *[We cross several shallow river valleys during these final stages so our path is more undulating than the contour guide might suggest. Ultreya!]* Our way is now by a path that winds through shaded forest, oak and chestnut increasingly giving way to eucalyptus and pine. Continue through Carballal and the river beyond [1.6 km] through Parabispo over the río Raído with picnic area [2.2 km] passing Peroxa and café *El Alemán* down to the N-547 [1.1 km] at:

3.3 km Boente *Cruce Igrexa Santiago* with image of the Saint above the altar and convivial parish priest who offers a blessing to passing pilgrims. The hostels fronting the main road don't share the same positivity. *Alb.* ❶ **Os Albergues** *Priv.* *[28÷7]* €11 © 981 501 853 + *Os Mesón* bar menú. ❷ **Boente** *Priv.[48÷7]*+ €10+€35 © 981 501 974 + menú. We leave past Cruceiro and *[F.]* through underpass down into the Boente valley with shaded rest area (right), the delightful riverside setting somewhat marred by the noise of traffic. Up the other side we join minor road (N-547 in a cutting below) into Castañeda past café *No Camino* and the parish Church of Santa María to:

2.2 km Castañeda *Alb.* **Santiago** *Priv.* *[4÷1]*+ €10 +35 © 981 501 711 prominently located on the corner *A Fraga Alta* with attractive terrace bar and restaurant. *[It was here in Castañeda that the pilgrims would deposit the limestone rocks they had brought from Triacastela to be fired for the lime used in the building of the Cathedral at Santiago].* Just beyond the albergue we pass casa rural *CR* **La Calleja** © 605 787 382 with rooms

from €25 and down over river with shaded rest area [0.6 km]. From here we go around a wooded hill with track (right) *[leads to N-547 and casa rurales 400m off route: Garea* €35-40 © *981 500 400 and Milía* © *981 515 241].* We now climb to alto (440m) and cross a raised pass over the N-547 [1.0 km] through woodland to pick up minor road with café-bar *Manuel* [0.6 km] down to the beautiful medieval bridge over the río Iso [0.3 km] at:

3.1 km Ribadiso da Baixo *Alb.* ❶ **Ribadiso** *Xunta.[70÷3]* €6 © idyllic location right on the river Iso adjoining the medieval bridge. All facilities with toilets in a separate block to the rear. Pleasant space to relax on the river bank (weather permitting). This is a wonderful reconstruction of one of the oldest pilgrim hospitals still in existence with an award for environmental architecture. Adjoining bar and restaurant and *Alb.* ❷ **Los Caminantes** *Priv.[52÷3]*+

€10-38 (double room) © 647 020 600. *Alb.* ❸ **Milpes** *Priv.[38÷3]* €10 © 981 500 425 m: 616 652 276 with welcoming bar and splendid views of the surrounding countryside. Also *off route* modern *CR* **Vaamonde** © 981 500 364 in Traseirexe. *[Next albergue: Arzúa – 2.0 km].*

REFLECTIONS:

❒ **Let no one come to you without leaving better and happier.** *Mother Teresa*

---

32 **42.6** km (26.5 ml) – Santiago

RIBADISO – PEDROUZO *(ARCA / O PINO)*

....	--- ---	12.2 --- ---	*54%*
————	--- ---	8.2 --- ---	*36%*
————	--- ---	2.4 --- ---	*10%*
Total km		**22.8 km** (13.9 ml)	

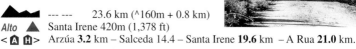

▲▲▲	--- ---	23.6 km (^160m + 0.8 km)

Alto ▲ Santa Irene 420m (1,378 ft)

< 🅰 🏠 > Arzúa **3.2** km – Salceda 14.4 – Santa Irene **19.6** km – A Rua **21.0** km.

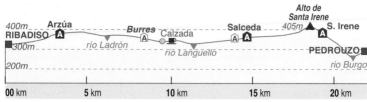

❒ **The Practical Path:** over ½ this stage is on natural pathways with good shade offered by the ubiquitous eucalyptus. We start with a steep climb up into Arzúa and end with a gentle climb around the alto de Santa Irene. In between we have a largely level path with just 3 shallow river valleys.

❒ **The Mystical Path:** The beautiful memorial to Guillermo Watt is timely. What plans have *we* made for our onward journey? Or are we too preoccupied with the dramas of this life to consider the next? To contemplate the impermanence of our earthly form can be revitalising, urging us to make every step a prayer for understanding, every breath a song of gratitude, every moment a chance to awaken from the dream that keeps us separate from our eternal Source.

❒ **Personal Reflections:** *"… The debate became heated, the only seeming accord being that the problems that beset our world were real and worsening. She had remained silent but now took the rare moment of quiet to state with utter conviction, 'There is only one solution'. Her words made us attentive – 'Allah'. The response was so unexpected. We had been looking for solutions on the level of the problem – our human condition of fear. She was a Sufi devotee. I laugh at the paradox that it took a Muslim woman walking an outwardly Christian path to point out to us the deeper truth that lay beyond. Whatever name we choose to describe the ineffable is immaterial. The only way out of our dilemma, is inward through Love …"*

0.0 km **Ribadiso** proceed up and through tunnel under the N-547 and veer right> past *Alb.* **Milpes** (see previous page) onto track parallel to the main road which we follow all the way into **Arzua** *suburbs* **[1.8** km] passing *Pr*** **Retiro** €48 ©️ 981 500 554 on *Av. de Lugo* and the first of 9 *Albergues (Av. Price €10)* **[0.6** km] *Alb.* ❶ **de Selmo** *Priv.[50÷1]* ©️ 981 939 018. ❷ **Santiago Apostol** *Priv.[72÷3]* ©️ 981 508 132 with all mod cons + lift! *P*Rua* ©️ 981 500 139. *Alb.* ❸ **Don Quijote** *Priv.*[50÷1]* ©️ 981 500 139 modern terraced building adj. ❹ **Ultreia** *Priv.*[38÷2]* ©️ 981 500 471 network* hostel in same modern block with all facilities and café &

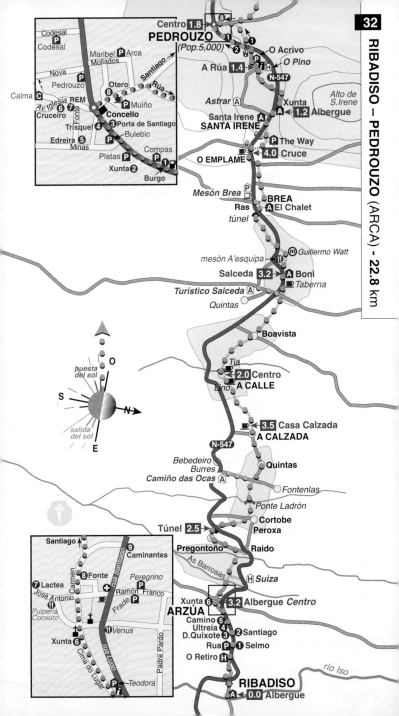

PEDROUZO
(Pop.5,000)

Centro **1.8**

Codesal
P Codesal

Nova
Pedrouzo

Maribel **P** Arca
Mollados

Calma **C**

Otero
8

Santiago
Rúa

Av. Iglesia **REM**
6 7
Cruceiro
Trisque **4** Concello
Edreira **5** Minas
Platas **P**
Xunta **2**
Burgo

P Muiño
3 Porta de Santiago
Bulebic
Compas
P
1

Centro **1.8**
8
1
1
2
8
O Acrivo
A Rúa **1.4** **P** *O Pino*
H
N-547

Astrar **A**

Santa Irene **A**
SANTA IRENE

Xunta
A **1.2** Albergue

Alto de
S.Irene

P The Way
4.0 Cruce

O EMPLAME

Mesón Brea
P

BREA
Ras **A** El Chalet
túnel

mesón A'esquipa **ⁿ**
m *Guillermo Watt*

Salceda **3.2** **A** Boni
Taberna

Turístico Salceda **A**

Quintas

Boavista

Tía
2.0 Centro
A CALLE
Lino

3.5 Casa Calzada
A CALZADA

N-547

Bebedeiro
Burres
Camiño das Ocas **A**

Quintas

Fontenlas

Ponte Ladrón

Cortobe
Túnel **2.5** Peroxa

Pregontoño Raido

As Barrosas

H *Suiza*

Xunta **6** **3.2** Albergue *Centro*
ARZÚA

Camino **5**
Ultreia **4** **2** Santiago
D.Quixote **3**
Rua **P** **1** Selmo
O Retiro **H**

ARZÚA (inset)

Santiago ↑

9
Caminantes

8 Fonte
7 Lactea
José Antonio
H
Pulpería
Conxuro

Peregrino
P
Ramón Franco
Frade **P**

11 *Venus*

Xunta **6**

Teodora **P**

RIBADISO
A **0.0** Albergue

río Iso

puesta
del sol **O**

S

salida
del sol **E** **N→**

❺ de Camino *Priv.[46÷4]+* ✆ 981 500 415. Continue towards the centre of town and **Plaza Mayor [0.6** km] *Turismo* adj. *P°°* **Teodora** ✆ 981 500 083 with popular restaurant. Turn <left into rúa Cima do Lugar adj. *Iglesia de Santiago y capela da Madalena* **[0.2** km]:

3.2 km **Arzúa** *Alb.* ❻ **Arzúa** *Xunta* *[46÷2]* €6 ✆ 660 396 824 restored town house in town centre. 50m beyond we come to a crossroads ❖ other albergues (all within a few hundred meters) compete for the lucrative pilgrim trade. Turn left for ❼ **Vía Láctea** *Priv.[120÷10]* €10 ✆ 981 500 581 rua José Antonio (just beyond pulperia *O Conxuro*). ❖ The camino continues s/o down rúa do Carmen with the traditional ❽ **da Fonte** *Priv.[20÷5]* €10-12 ✆ 981

501 118 Rúa do Carme, 18 a quiet 'backwater'. Continue up to the right to the main road Av. de Lugo (N-547) for: ❾ **Los Caminantes II** *Priv.[28÷1]* €10 ✆ 647 020 600 all facilities . **Other Lodging:** *Central* on rúa Ramón Franco N°22 *P°* **Begoña** ✆ 981 500 517 *(BBVA). P°* **Casa Frade** ✆ 981 500 019 / adj. *P°* **Casa Carballeira** ✆ 981 500 094 opp. *Hs°* **Mesón do Peregrino** ✆ 981 500 830 (mixed reports). Further out (+1.2 km) the modern *H°°* **Suiza** ✆ 981 500 862 on main road N-547.

ARZÚA *Turismo* Praza do Peregrino ✆ 981 508 056. The the last major centre of population (6,300) before we enter Santiago. The untidy development of the modern town is mirrored in the haphazard layout of the older central part and waymarking is also irregular. Off the central square (with variety of bars, cafés and restaurants) is the modern parish church dedicated to St. James with image of Santiago as both Moorslayer and pilgrim and just behind is the original 14th century Augustinian *Capilla de La Magdalena.* The town is known for its local cheese and the cheese fair *festa do queixo* held in March. The camino continues out through the old quarter of town down c/del Carmen (left of the main road) past fountain and over stream (site of San Lázaro hospice) onto a delightful track through ancient oak woods in *As Barrosas* (track to Hotel Suiza right) meandering over several small streams onto side road into Preguntoño to take path under the N-547:

2.5 km **N-547 túnel** we now alternate between country lanes & track bypassing the hamlets of **Raído, Fondevila, Cortobe,** and just beyond **Taberna Velha** *[½ km detour to: Alb.* **Camiño das Ocas** *Priv.[28÷5]+* €10 ✆ 648 404 780 *on the N-547 in Burres].* Continue over rio Ladrón into:

3.5 km **A Calzada** *Casa Calzada* popular track side café. Continue into:

2.0 km **A Calle** quaint village with traditional houses (cafes *Lino* & *Tia* await reopening) *[F.].* The camino wends its way over the stream through **Boavista** and shortly afterwards at a crossroads ❖ is detour to: *[Alb.* **turístico Salceda** *Priv. [8÷1]+* €12-40 ✆ 981 502 767 + bar/menú V. ½ km the **far** side of the N-547]. ❖ The camino continues s/o down to the N-547 at:

3.2 km **Salceda** on the N-547 with bar *Taberna Salceda* and *Alb.* **Boni** *Priv.[30÷6]* €10 ✆ 618 965 907. *Mesón A'esquipa / Bar Verde* with outdoor rest area. Continue on woodland path with monument (right) to pilgrim *Guillermo Watt* who died at this spot only a day away from his earthly destination. Take care as we crisscross the N-547 **[!]** into *Ras* where a pedestrian underpass *túnel* **[2.0** km] brings us safely into **Brea [0.4** km] El Chalet *Priv.[12÷2]+* © 659 380 723. *[Detour:* ❖ *left 100m far side of N-547 P Mesón Brea Bar S.Miguel © 981 511 040].* ❖ Continue s/o and back over the N-547 past 'rest' area up to crossroads **[1.6** km].

4.0 km Cruce *O Empalme O Ceadoiro* menú. Cross N-547 onto track through woods around *Alto de Santa Irene.* P The Way €12-15 en suite €45 © 628 120 202 Brea No 36. Continue down past *túnel* **[0.8** km] ❖ *[Detour to* ❶ *Alb. Santa Irene Priv.* [15÷2]* €13 © *981 511 000 network* hostel (see photo) rear garden & menú* €13. *Adj. capela Santa Irene (an early Christian martyr). 700m further on off route:* ❷ *Alb.* **Rural Astar** *Priv.[24÷2]* €10 © 981 511 463 m: 608 092 820. ❖ Continue s/o past pilgrim rest area *[F.]* **[0.4** km] to:

1.2 km Santa Irene *Alb.* ❸ Santa Irene *Xunta.[32÷2]* all facilities but directly on the busy main road (noisy). Continue down on woodland path through *túnel* **[0.8** km] down into **A Rúa [0.6** km]:

1.4 km A Rúa traditional hamlet with *Turismo Asoc. Hostelería Compostela* © 696 652 564 who provide general info. from Easter-Oct. and can pre-book hotels in Santiago. *[Just off route signposted (200m)* H⁺ **O Pino** © *981 511 035 on main road].* CR **Casa Gallega** © 981 511 463 opp. CR **O Acivro** single from €35 © 981 511 316 m: 609 105 948 with restful bar /restaurant and extensive garden. Continue over rio Burgo to climb steeply up to N-547 **opción [0.6** km]: Two options to access O Pedrouzo: ❷ turn left along the busy main road to *Alb.* ❶ *(Concello 1.0 km) or* ❶ take the recommended woodland access leading to the rear of the town and *Alb.* ❸ *(Concello 1.2 km).* For this latter route continue s/o over the N-547 onto woodland path merging into rua peregrino past Cultural/Sports hall to T-Junction ❖ *[waymarked path to Santiago turns right].* To access accommodation in Pedrouzo 200m turn <left into rua Concello passing the delightful P⁺ **O Muiño** (Mayka) © 686 419 046 with quiet garden to rear adj. *bar O Muiño* and *Alb.* ❸ **Otero** *Priv.[36÷2]* © 671 663 374 on c/Forcarei, 2. Continue s/o to Concello and centre of Pedrouzo:

1.8 km Pedrouzo *Centro (parish Arca municipality O Pino)* Satellite of Santiago straddling the busy N-547 with variety of shops and restaurants. *[Note: If you intend to make the Cathedral for 12 noon pilgrim mass you need to leave early in the morning].* Wide range of lodging mostly on the N-547 (see map). 8 albergues (Xunta €6 others Av.€10): ❶ **O Burgo** *Priv.*[14÷1]+* © 630 404 138 on main road adj. Repsol. ❷ **Arca** *Xunta.[120÷4] (down behind the supermercado off the N-457).* **Town centre:** ❸ **Porta de Santiago** *Priv.*[56÷3]* © 981 511 103 modern building with café and rear patio. Opp' ❹ **O Trisquel** *Priv.[68÷5]* © 616 644 740 corner of Rúa do Picon. ❺ **Edreira** *Priv.*[48÷4]* © 981 511 365 purpose-built network* hostel Rúa da Fonte 19. ❻ **Cruceiro** *Priv.[94÷8]* © 981 511 371 facilities incl. sauna on Av. Iglesia in modern block of apartments. Adj'. ❼ **REMhostel** *Priv. [40÷1]* © 981 510 407. **Other Lodging** €25-45: *Central* on N-547: Hs⁺⁺ **Plantas** © 981 511 378 adj. P⁺ **BuleBic** © 981 511 222. *Further out Av.Santiago:* P⁺ **Una Estrella Dorada** 630 018 363. P **9 de Abril** 606 764 762. *Nº13* P⁺ **Pedrouzo** © 671 663 375. *Nº23* P **En Ruta SCQ** © 981 511 471. P⁺**Codesal** © 981 511 064 rua Codesal. P⁺ **Maruja** © 981 511 406 rua Nova adj. parish church on rua Igrexa P⁺ **Casal de Calma** © 689 910 676. Near O Muiño (entrance/exit) on rua Mollados: Pr⁺ **Maribel** © 609 459 966 adj. P **Arca** © 657 888 594.

❏ **He went up into the mountain to pray... and the fashion of his countenance was altered, and his raiment was white and glistening.** *Luke IX, 29.*

33 19.8 km (12.3 ml) – Santiago

PEDROUZO (ARCA) – **SANTIAGO**

⸱⸱⸱⸱⸱⸱⸱⸱⸱⸱⸱⸱	--- ---	8.0	--- ---	40%
▬▬▬	--- ---	7.4	--- ---	38%
▬▬▬	--- ---	4.4	--- ---	22%
Total km		**19.8 km**	(12.3 ml)	

◣ --- --- 20.4 km (0.6 km)
Alto ▲ Monte do Gozo 370m (1,214 ft)
<🅐 🅗> Amenal **3.5** km – Lavacolla **9.6** –
Vilamaior **11.0** km – Monte do Gozo **15.3** km – San Lázaro **17.3** km.

(elevation profile)
300m — Amenal — Aeropuerto ✛ Labacolla — Vilamaior — *Monte Gozo* 370m — San Marcos — **SANTIAGO**
O PEDROUZO ARCA do PINO — *Río Labacolla*
200m — — — — San Lázaro 260m
100m —
00 km — 5 km — 10 km — 15 km — 20

❏ **The Practical Path:** The first part of this final stage is through the dense and ever-present eucalyptus. Make the most of their shade and the peace they exude. As we get nearer the city, asphalt and crowds begin to take over as busloads of pilgrims join the route for this one day into Santiago. If you are making for the pilgrim mass at 12 noon be prepared for large crowds and try and create an air of compassionate detachment. Be patient and prepare for the long slog up to Monte Gozo which, while surrounded by woodland, is all on asphalt.

❏ **The Mystical Path:** Will you stay awhile and lose yourself in the tiny grove of holm oak, itself almost lost amongst the mass of alien eucalyptus? Will you stop in Lavacolla, whose waters were used in the ritual cleansing of pilgrims prior to entering the holy City? Today the water is putrid but it is the symbolic purification that we seek so that we might glisten with the pure white light of Christ consciousness.

❏ **Personal Reflections:** *"... I had walked the equivalent of one day for each year Christ spent on earth. Here I was on the 33rd day but I could find no joy on this hill amongst the crowds huddled against the driving rain ... As I entered the cathedral I realised I had failed in my purpose. But in that same instant I realised I had been searching in the wrong place. A sudden rush of joy enveloped my soaking body. I knew the answer lay where the world of things ended and the unseen world began and I knew I had to go there. I hurried down the steps and out the city. I was alone but I had company. I did not know where I was going but I felt completely guided ..."*

0.0 km Pedrouzo *Centro* Turn up rua Concello past albergue ❻ and sports hall *polideportivo* **[0.5 km]** *(the waymarked camino joins from the right).* S/o past bar *Mirás* and <left into dense eucalyptus forest through San Antón down into the río Amenal valley over rio Xeimar and under N-547 *túnel* **[3.0 km]**:

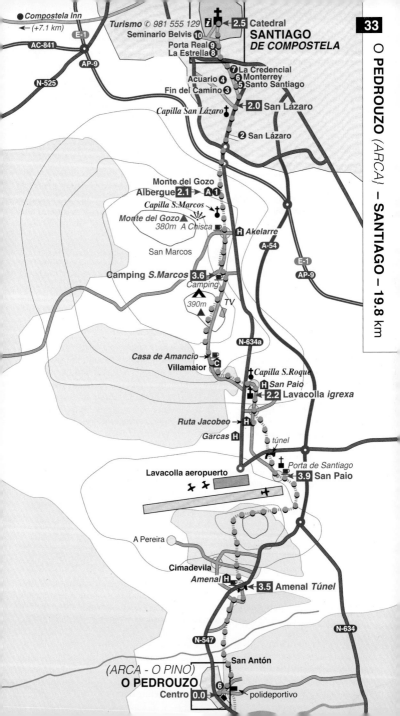

Compostela Inn
← (+7.1 km)

E-1
AC-841
AP-9
N-525

33

O PEDROUZO *(ARCA)* – SANTIAGO – 19.8 km

Turismo © 981 555 129   **i**   **2.5** Catedral
Seminario Belvis **10**   **SANTIAGO**
Porta Real **9**   *DE COMPOSTELA*
La Estrella **8**

La Credencial **7**
Monterrey **6**
Acuario **4**   Santo Santiago **5**
Fin del Camino **3**

Capilla San Lázaro   **2.0** San Lázaro

2 San Lázaro

Monte del Gozo
Albergue **2.1** **A** **1**
Capilla S.Marcos
Monte del Gozo ▲ *A Chisca*
380m   **H** *Akelarre*
San Marcos

A-54

E-1
AP-9

Camping *S.Marcos* **3.6**
Camping
▲ 390m   *TV*

N-634a

Casa de Amancio → **P** **C**
Villamaior   †*Capilla S.Roque*
H *San Paio*
2.2 Lavacolla *igrexa*

Ruta Jacobeo **H**
Garcas **H**   *túnel*

†*Porta de Santiago*
3.9 San Paio

Lavacolla aeropuerto
✈ ✈

A Pereira

Cimadevila
Amenal **H**   **3.5** Amenal *Túnel*

N-547
N-634

(ARCA - O PINO)
O PEDROUZO   San Antón
Centro **0.0**   **6**   polideportivo

`3.5 km` **Amenal** *túnel* *H°°* Amenal © 981 510 431 with popular *Café*. Continue up woodland path through Cimadevila. A wide forest track brings us around the perimeter of Santiago airport to roundabout. A dedicated pilgrim track alongside the motorway takes us down into a deep cutting at the end of the runway (see photo) to cross over an access road into:

`3.9 km` **San Paio** ancient hamlet with bar/restaurant *Casa Porta de Santiago*. We now enter the last recognisable stretch of the medieval 'Royal Way' *Real Camino* as we head uphill veering right> onto a natural path lined with remnants of the native deciduous woodland that once covered this area before eucalyptus was imported to fuel the pulp industry. Head downhill passing rear entrance to *H°°°* **Ruta Jacobea** © 981 888 211 (special pilgrim price) to:

`2.2 km` **Lavacolla** *Igrexa* *P°* San Paio © 981 888 205. Lavacolla is recognised today more for the name of the international airport than the place where medieval pilgrims came to wash *lavar* and purify themselves before entering the city. Modern Lavacolla now caters more for the business traveller than the pilgrim with variety of restaurants, bars and hotel. *[Short detour ● ● ● ● Capela San Roque (300m): If you continue down the steps past the bandstand you come to the little chapel dedicated to the pilgrim saint San Roque. While it may be closed it has a covered portico and sits in a shaded grove of trees where you can perform your own purification ritual in relative peace].* The path now continues around the side of the parish church to cross over the access road to the airport (N-634a) and over a small stream to head steeply uphill on dedicated track through crossroads at **Villamaior** [1.4 km]: *CR & Café* **Casa de Amancio** © 981 897 086. Continue on pilgrim track down over a stream with rest area up to our high point today at 396m *[not Monte de Gozo but the studios of Radio TV Galicia! A sign, perhaps, of how TV has come to dominate our lives].* Turn <left at T-jct *Camping* **San Marcos** *& Café* [2.2 km]:

`3.6 km` **Camping** *San Marcos*. Continue down side of RTVE into **San Marcos** with several *bars* and *cafés*. *[200m off route s/o H° Akelarre © 981 552 689 on the N-634].* Turn <left up rua San Marcos past *Café A Chica* and a short paved path brings us to the enchanting **capilla de San Marcos** in a glade of trees with *Cantina* and where, if it was not raining, medieval pilgrims espied the cathedral towers (the first one being crowned

'king' for the day) and giving rise to an exclamation, *'Monte do Gozo / Mount of Joy'*. Today, a monument to the visit of Pope John Paul II and Francis of Assisi stands sentinel atop the hill along with a statue of 2 pilgrims looking towards the cathedral now largely hidden by the sprawling suburbs of Santiago. Continue s/o downhill to:

`2.1 km` **Monte del Gozo** *Alb.* ❶ **Monte do Gozo** *Xunta.[400÷62]* €6 located on an elevated site overlooking the city. 400 beds in separate blockhouses containing rooms with 6-8 beds in each. Good modern facilities with *bar, restaurant* and large canteen on the main plaza. The hill itself has been reshaped by the bulldozer to provide a vast leisure complex for the city. The sprawling dormitory and recreational buildings are the price of an ever-increasing demand for accommodation. The tiny chapel of San Marcos is the only thing left on the hill that gives any sense of history to this romantic-sounding place. The route continues down the hill along Rua do Peregrino and down a flight of steps where we join the city traffic to pass over railway line and past statue of *El Templario Peregrino* (left) over A-9 autopista and roundabout into the wide N-634 and the modern city suburbs with prominent monument to notable historical figures connected with the camino (see photo). At the **2nd roundabout [1.3** km] on opp. side of the road behind *Museo Pedagóxico Alb.* ❷ **Residencia de Peregrinos San Lázaro.**[*80÷6*] *Xunta.* €10 (€7 subsequent nights) ⓒ 981 571 488 all facilities with garden area. Continue along the main road passing *Hˢ* **San Jacobo** ⓒ 981 580 361 over busy roundabout to pass the ancient chapel of *San Lázaro Santiago* [0.6 km] *[witness to the leprosarium that existed here in the 12th century, sufficiently far outside the medieval city walls to ensure contamination didn't spread inside].* 100m later we come to major crossroads (ruas S. Lázaro & Roma) and albergue option **[0.1 km]**

2.0 km San Lázaro *[albergues (Av.Price €10) in this area where you can unload backpacks and shower before visiting the city. Backpacks are **not** allowed in the cathedral].* ❖ *(200m left–signposted)* ❸ **Fin del Camino** *Asoc.*[*110÷6*] *(€8)* ⓒ 981 587 324 c/Moscova corner r/Roma, modern building behind the *Policía*. What it lacks in character it makes up for in the range of facilities *(bus 11 to Plaza Galicia).* ❖ Continue s/o into rua do Valiño **[0.3** km] and 'below' the park (steep steps left): ❹ **Acuario** *Priv.***[60÷9]* Rúa Estocolmo 2-b. ⓒ 981 575 438. S/o along r/ Valiño to ❺ **Santo Santiago** *Priv.*[*40÷3*] €10-12 ⓒ 657 402 403 adj. *H* **S.Lazaro** €35+ ⓒ 981 584 344. S/o into r/ Fontiñas Nº65 ❻ **Monterey** *Priv.*[*36÷3*]+ ⓒ 655 484 299 into Fonte dos Concheiros Nº13 (corner of r/Altiboia) ❼ **La credencial** *Priv.*[*36÷4*] ⓒ 639 966 704. S/o over ring road *Av. de Lugo* **[0.8** km] (main bus station *estación de autobuses* – up right) into *Rúa dos Concheiros [named after the stallholders who used to sell pilgrim shells **conchas**].* Continue up to Nº36 (left) **[0.2** km] ❽ **La Estrella** *Priv.*[*24÷1*] ⓒ 881 973 926 and just beyond **[0.1** km] Nº10 ❾ **Porta Real** *Priv.*[*24÷9*] €10-15 ⓒ 633 610 114. Continue to the top and St. Peter's cross *Cruceiro de San Pedro* **[0.1** km] which heralds our arrival into the old city with the spires of the Cathedral ahead.

❖ *Option:* For pilgrim hostel at Belvís 500m to our left *(signposted).* Access from the city centre is via rua Trompas (see city plan) ❿ **Seminario Menor La Asunción** *Conv.* [*177*]+ €10-15 ⓒ 881 031 768 Av. Quiroga Palacios. Depending on your time of arrival and intentions for the day you might consider going directly to the hostel (opens from 13.30 with lockers for backpacks) *Directions:*

Turn left and immediately right into rua dos Lagartos to join alt. route (from Praza da San Pedro) and continue around the walls of the convento de Belvís to the Seminario Menor which houses the main city hostel (Parque Belvís below). ❖ Continue down rua de San Pedro past the Church of San Pedro & Praza (left) and s/o to the famous Gate of the Way *Porta do Camiño* **[0.4**

km] which gives access to the wonderful old city. Up on the right overlooking the **Porta do Camiño** *Convento de Santo Domingo de Bonaval* housing the Pantheón and Galician museum, with the centre for contemporary Galician art opp. There is a quiet park behind the convent buildings to refresh body and soul from the rigours of city life. (See city map for directions to these and other places of interest.) We now proceed up Casas Reais and Rúa das Ánimas into Praza de Cervantes (with statue of the writer atop the central pillar) now we head down rúa da Azabachería (lined with jewellers selling jet *azabache* – see later) into Praza da Inmaculada (also called Azabachería) down under the arch of the **Pazo do Xelmírez** [0.3 km] to:

2.5 km **Praza Obradoiro** *Catedral*. Take time to *arrive*. We each experience different emotions, from euphoria to disappointment, on seeing the Cathedral. Whatever your individual reaction, honour and accept it. Gratitude for safe arrival is a frequent response but if you are overwhelmed by the crowds why not return later when you feel more composed and the Cathedral is, perhaps, quieter (open daily from 07:00 until 21:00). Whether now or later and whichever door you entered by, you might like to follow the timeworn pilgrim ritual as follows:

[1] Due to erosion it is no longer permitted to place your hand in the Tree of Jesse, the central column of the Master Mateo's masterpiece Door of Glory *Portico de Gloria*. But you can stop and admire the incomparable beauty of this inner portico carved between 1166 and 1188 (the exterior façade was added in 1750). The Bible and its main characters come alive in this remarkable storybook in stone. The central column has Christ in Glory flanked by the apostles and, directly underneath, St. James sits as intercessor between Christ and the pilgrim. Millions of pilgrims over the centuries have worn finger holes in the solid marble as a mark of gratitude for their safe arrival (the reason why it is now protected by a barrier). Proceed to the other side and **[2]** touch your brow to that of Maestro

Mateo whose kneeling figure is carved into the back of the central column (facing the altar) and receive some of his artistic genius in the ritual known as head-butting the saint *Santo d'os Croques* – touch your forehead to his and receive some of his inspiration. Proceed to the High Altar (right) to ascend the stairs and **[3]** hug the Apostle. Perhaps lay your head on his broad shoulders and say what you came here to say. Proceed down the steps on the far side to the crypt and the reliquary chapel under the altar. **[4]** Here, you can kneel before the casket containing the relics of the great Saint and offer your prayer …

    Pilgrim mass at 12 noon each day (doors may close 5 minutes before on busy days). The swinging of the giant incense burner *Botafumeiro* was originally used to fumigate the sweaty (and possibly disease-ridden) pilgrims. The ritual requires half a dozen attendants *tiraboleiros* to perform it so became an infrequent event but is used increasingly during mass these days. The seating capacity was extended in recent years from 700 to 1,000 so you might even find somewhere to sit but don't hold any expectations and remember – time itself is a journey.

REFLECTIONS: 'Time is the journey from ignorance to Gnosis. Time is imperfection longing to be the Good and progressively improving. Time is the relative reaching towards the Absolute.' *Jesus and the Lost Goddess*.' Freke.

4 squares surround the cathedral and provide access to it, as follows:

■ **Praza do Obradoiro**. The 'golden' square of Santiago is usually thronged with pilgrims and tourists admiring the dramatic west facing façade of the Cathedral, universal symbol of Santiago, with St. James looking down on all the activity from his niche in the central tower. This provides the main entrance to the Cathedral and the Portico de Gloria. To the right of the steps is the discrete entrance to the museum. A combined ticket will provide access to all rooms including the crypt and the cloisters and also to the 12th  century palace of one of Santiago's most famous individuals and first archbishop, Gelmírez *Pazo de Xelmírez* situated on the (left). In this square we also find the beautiful Renaissance façade of the Parador named after Ferdinand and Isabel *Hostal dos Reis Católicos* on whose orders it was built in 1492 as a pilgrim hospice. Opposite the Cathedral is the more austere neoclassical seat of the Galician government and town hall *Pazo de Raxoi* with its solid arcade. Finally, making up the fourth side of the square is the gable end of the *Colegio de S. Jerónimo* part of the university. Moving anti-clockwise around the cathedral – turn up into Rúa de Fonseca to:

■ **Praza das Praterías**. The most intimate of the squares with its lovely centrepiece, an ornate statue of horses leaping out of the water. On the corner of Rúa do Vilar we find the Dean's House *Casa do Deán* formerly the pilgrim office. Along the walls of the Cathedral itself are the silversmith's *plateros* that give the square its name. Up the steep flight of steps we come to the magnificent southern door to the Cathedral, the oldest extant doorway and traditionally the entrance taken by pilgrims coming from Portugal. The quality of the carvings and their arrangement is remarkable and amongst the many sculptured figures is one of St. James between two cypress trees. Continuing around to the right we come to:

■ **Praza da Quintana.** This wide square is identified by the broad sweep of steps separating the lower part *Quintana of the dead* from the upper *Quintana of the living*. Opp the Cathedral is the wall of the *Mosteiro de San Paio de Anteltares* (with museum of sacred art). The square provides the eastern entrance to the Cathedral via the Holy Gate *Porta Santa* sometime referred to as the Door of Pardon *El Perdón* only opened during Holy Years (the next in 2021). Adjoining it is the main  entrance to the Cathedral shop that has several guidebooks (in various languages) with details of the Cathedral's many chapels and their interesting carvings and statuary and the priceless artefacts and treasures in the museum. Finally, we head up the broad flight of steps around the corner and back into:

■ **Praza da Inmaculada (Azabachería)** to the north facing Azabachería façade, with the least well-known doorway and the only one that *descends* to enter the Cathedral. It has the most weathered aspect, with moss and lichen covering its bleak exterior. Opposite the cathedral is the imposing southern edifice of *Mosteiro de San Martiño Pinario* the square in front gets any available sun and attracts street artists. The archbishop's arch *Arco Arzobispal* brings us back to the Praza do Obradoiro.

The **Pilgrim Office** *Oficina del Peregrino* now at rua Carretas *below the parador* ℂ 981 568 846 open daily 09:00-21:00 (10:00-20:00 winter). The new office has tight security procedure (expect lengthy delays). It lacks the informal atmosphere of the former office in rua Vilar with its team of *Amigos*. However, providing you have fulfilled the criteria of a bona fide pilgrim and walked at least the last 100 km (200 km on bike or horseback) for religious/spiritual reasons and collected 2 stamps per day on your *credencial* you will be awarded the *Compostela* which may entitle you to certain privileges such as reduced entry fees to museums and a free meal at the Parador! If you do not fulfil the criteria you may still be able to obtain a ***certificado*** (€3) which is

essentially a certificate of distance travelled. The welcoming Companions meet in a room behind the adjoining pilgrim chapel (see below).

•**The Camino Chaplaincy** offers Mass in English daily at 10:30 & Sunday 09:00 May–Oct. in the cathedral *Capela N.S. de la Soledad.* •**Camino Companions** meet in the Pilgrims Office 9:00 & 14:30 daily May–Oct for reflection and integration (see camino companions facebook for updates). •**Pilgrim House** rua Nova 19 also offers a place of welcome and reflection 11:00–20:00 (closed Wed & Sun) under the care of Terra Nova USA.

❑ **Turismo:** ❖ r/Vilar, 63 Ⓒ 981 555 129 *June-Sept 09:00-21:00 / Oct-May 10-15 & 17:00-20:00*. ❖ *TurGalicia* r/do Vilar.43 Ⓒ 981 584 081 (10:00-20:00). **Luggage storage** *consigna* (Casa Ivar / camino forum) Ⓒ 603 466 490 Trv. Universidade 1.

■ *Albergues:* ❶ – ❿ (see previous pages) ■ *Centro €10-15:* ●11 La Salle *Priv. [84÷14]+* Ⓒ 981 585 667 c/ Tras de Santa Clara. ●12 Meiga Backpackers *Priv. [30÷5]* Ⓒ 981 570 846 C/ Basquiños 67. ■ *Centro Histórico:* ●13 O Fogar de Teodomiro *Priv.[20÷5]+* Ⓒ 981 582 920 Plaza de Algalia de Arriba 3. ●14 The Last Stamp *Priv.[62÷10]* Ⓒ 981 563 525 rua Preguntorio 10. ●15 Azabache *Priv. [20÷5]* Ⓒ 981 071 254 c/Azabachería 15. ●16 Mundoalbergue *Priv.[34÷1]* Ⓒ 981 588 625 c/ San Clemente 26. ●17 Roots & Boots *Priv.[48÷6]* Ⓒ 699 631 594 rua Campo Cruceiro do Galo. ■ *Otros:* ●18 La Estación *Priv.[24÷2]* Ⓒ 981 594 624 rua Xoana Nogueira 14 (adj. Estación de Tren +2.9 km). ● Compostela Inn *Priv. [120÷30]+* Ⓒ 981 819 030 *AC-841 (adj.Hotel Congreso +6.0 km)*.

■ *Hoteles €30–60:* Hs **Moure** Ⓒ 981 583 637 r/dos Loureiros. H **Fonte de San Roque** Ⓒ 981 554 447 r/do Hospitallilo 8. Hs **La Campana** Ⓒ 981 584 850 Campanas de San Juan 4. Hs **Estrela** Ⓒ 981 576 924 Plaza de San Martín Pinario 5-2°. Hs **San Martín Pinario** Ⓒ 981 560 282 Praza da Inmaculada. **Pico Sacro** r/ San Francisco 22 y **Pico Sacro II** Ⓒ 981 584 466. **La Estela** Ⓒ 981 582 796 r/ Raxoi 1. Hs **Barbantes** Ⓒ 981581 077 r/do Franco 3. **Santa Cruz** Ⓒ 981 582 362 r/do Vilar 42. Hs **Suso** Ⓒ 981 586 611 r/do Vilar 65. **San Jaime** Ⓒ 981 583 134 r/do Vilar 12-2°. A **Nosa Casa** Ⓒ 981 585 926 r/Entremuralles 9. Hs **Mapoula** Ⓒ 981 580 124 r/Entremuralles 10. Hs **Alameda** Ⓒ 981 588 100 San Clemente, 32. ■ *€60–90:* H **Rua Vilar** Ⓒ 981 557 102 r/Vilar 12-2° H **Airas Nunes** Ⓒ 902 405 858 r/do Vilar 17. **Entrecercas** Ⓒ 981 571 151 r/Entrecercas. **Costa Vella** Ⓒ 981 569 530 Porta de Pena 17. **MV Algalia** Ⓒ 981 558 111 Praziña da Algalia de Arriba 5. ■ *€100+* H**** **San Francisco** Campillo de San Francisco Ⓒ981 581 634. H****Hostal de los Reyes Católicos** Plaza Obradoiro Ⓒ 981 582 200.

❑ *Centro Histórico:* ❶ Convento de Santo Domingo de Bonaval XIIIth *(panteón de Castelao, Rosalía de Castro y museo do Pobo Galego)*. ❷ Casa Gótica XIVth *museo das Peregrinaciónes-1*. ❸ Mosteiro de San Martín Pinario XVIth *y museo* ■ *Prazo Obradoiro* ❹ Pazo de Xelmirez XIIth ❺ Catedral XIIth –XVIIIth *Portica de Gloria, claustro, museo e tesouro da catedral* ❻ Hostal dos Reis Católicos XVth *Parador* ❼ Pazo de Raxoi XVIIIth *Presendencia da Xunta* ❽ Colexio de Fonseca XVIth *universidade y claustro.* ❾ Casa do Deán XVIIIth *Oficina do Peregrino.* ❿● Casa Canónica *museo Peregrinaciónes-2.* 11● Mosteiro de San Paio de Antealtares XVth *Museo de Arte Sacra.* 12● S.Maria Salomé XIIth.

Santiago is a wonderful destination, full of vibrancy and colour. Pilgrims, street artists, musicians, dancers, tourists... all come and add to the life and soul of this fabled city. Stay awhile and visit her museums and markets. Soak up some of her culture or relax in the delightful shaded park *Alameda* and climb to the *capela de Santa Susanna* hidden in the trees or stroll up the Avenue of the Lions *Paseo dos Leónes* to the statue of Rosalia de Castro and look out west over her belovéd Galicia and... *Finis terrae.*

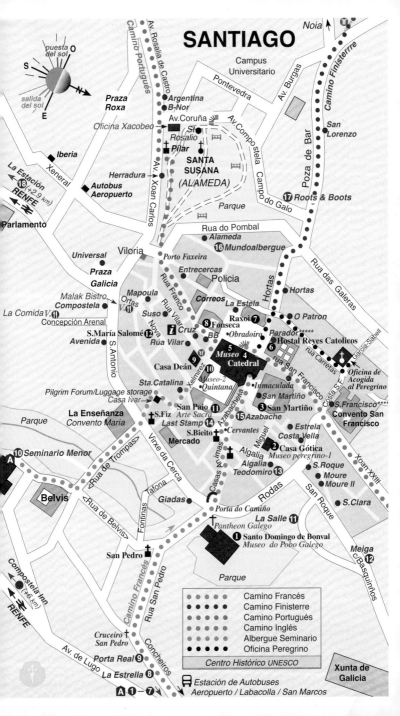

SANTIAGO

Campus Universitario

Pontevedra

Praza Roxa

Argentina
B-Nor

Av.Coruña

Oficina Xacobeo

Sta Rosalío

Pilar

SANTA SUSANA (ALAMEDA)

■ Iberia

Xeneral

La Estación
RENFE *+2.9 km

Parlamento

Herradura

Autobus
Aeropuerto

Parque

Av. Compostela

Campo do Galo

San Lorenzo

Poza de Bar

17 Roots & Boots

Rua do Pombal

Alameda

16 Mundoalbergue

Universal

**Praza
Galicia**

Viloria

Malak Bistro
Compostela
La Comida V.

Concepción Arenal

S.María Salomé 12
Avenida

S.Antonio

Porto Faxeira

Entrecercas

Policia

Mapoula
Orfas
V.

Suso

Nova

Rúa Vilar

Correos

La Estela

Cruz

Fonseca 9

BB

Raxoi 7

Obradoiro

8

Casa Deán

Museo-2
Quintana

Sta.Catalina

Pilgrim Forum/Luggage storage
Casa Ivar

La Enseñanza
Convento María

Parque

10 Seminario Menor

A

Belvis

Rúa de Belvis

Rua de Trompas

Virxe da Cerca

Tafona

Fontiñas

San Paio 11
Arte Sacra
Last Stamp 14

S.Fiz

S.Bieito
Mercado

Giadas

San Pedro

Compostela Inn
(+6 km)
RENFE

Cruceiro
San Pedro

Av. de Lugo

Porta Real 9
La Estrella 8

A 1 — 7

Rua San Pedro

Camino Francés

Concheiros

Hortas

Hortas

O Patron

Parador *****
Hostal Reyes Catolieos

Rúa San Francisco

Oficina de
Acogida
al Peregrino

S.Francisco****
Convento San
Francisco

Museo
5 Catedral 4

6

Inmaculada

3 San Martiño

San Martiño

Azabache 15

Cervantes

Costa Vella
Estrela

Algalia
2 Casa Gótica
Museo peregrino-1

Algalia
Teodomiro 13

S.Roque
Moure
Moure II

S.Clara

Xoan XXIII

Rodas

San Roque

Porta do Camiño

La Salle 11

Pantheon Galego

1 Santo Domingo de Bonval
Museo do Pobo Galego

Meiga
c/Basquiños 12

Parque

	Camino Francés
	Camino Finisterre
	Camino Portugués
	Camino Inglés
	Albergue Seminario
	Oficina Peregrino

Centro Histórico UNESCO

🚌 Estación de Autobuses
Aeropuerto / Labacolla / San Marcos

Xunta de
Galicia

puesta
del sol O

S

salida
del sol E

Av. Rosalía de Castro

Camino Portugués

Av. Burgas

Camino Finisterrre

Noia

Av. Xoan Carlos

Rúa Franco

Rúa Vilar

Hortas

Rua das Galeras

Casas Reais

Azabachería

Xelmírez

Costa S.F.

rúa Carretas

García-Sabell

18

11

The official literature for the last compostelan jubilee year *año jubilar compostelana* stated boldly on the front cover, 'A Road with an END' *Camino que tiene META*. That may be so – but it is not the end of the road.

Finisterre. Before you leave this corner of the earth why not visit the end of it *Finis Terra*: "... Finisterre is one of the great hidden treasures amongst the many Caminos de Santiago. Only a small proportion of pilgrims arriving at Santiago continue by foot to the end of the road. The way to Finisterre truly follows *the road less travelled* and *that* may make all the difference. We need to search out the waymarks to the source of our own inner knowing. The light, while obscured, lies hidden in our memory – it is no coincidence that the path to Finisterre ends at the altar to the sun *Ara Solis* and a lighthouse." From *A Pilgrim's Guide to the Camino Finisterre.*

ALBERGUE, HOSTAL AND HOTEL BOOKING SITES:
List of albergues open in Winter: http://www.aprinca.com/alberguesinvierno/
Albergues: www.onlypilgrims.com/en
Hostals: www.hostelworld.com
Paradores: www.paradores.es
Hotels: www.booking.com
B&Bs: www.airbnb:

PILGRIM AND BACKPACK TRANSFERS / STORES:
Camino Store and Information Pamplona: www.caminoteca.com/en
General Listing: www.amawalker.blogspot.co.uk
St. Jean / Biarritz: www.expressbourricot.com
Roncesvalles to Sarria: www.jacotrans.com
Sarria to Santiago: www.xacotrans.com

GROUP TOUR OPERATORS:
www.followthecamino.com
www.caminoways.com
www.spanishsteps.com

PILGRIM CONTACTS:

You can obtain further information and a pilgrim passport *credencial* from one of the English speaking organisations listed below which you are encouraged to join.

UK: The Confraternity of St. James, 27 Blackfriars Road, London SE1 8NY (0044-[0]2079 289 988) e-mail: office@csj.org.uk / *www.csj.org.uk* the pre-eminent site in English with an online bookshop.

IRELAND: The Camino Society Ireland. Based in Dublin: *www.caminosociety.ie*

U.S.A. American Pilgrims on the Camino. *www.americanpilgrims.com*

CANADA: Canadian Company of Pilgrims Canada. *www.santiago.ca*

SOUTH AFRICA: Confraternity of St. James of SA *www.csjofsa.za.org*

SANTIAGO:
Pilgrim Office *oficinadelperegrino.com/en*
Luggage Storage / Store / Forum *www.casaivar.com*
Tourism: *www.santiagoturismo.com*

There are a number of additional websites (in English) loosely connected with the Way of St. James or with the theme of pilgrimage that you may find helpful.

Camino News: Largest English online camino forum *www.caminodesantiago.me*

Walk Your Way: www.urcamino.com

Alternatives of St. James: *www.alternatives.org.uk* exploration of ways of living that honour all spiritual traditions. Based at St. James Church, London.

The Gatekeeper Trust devoted to personal and planetary healing through pilgrimage. *www.gatekeeper.org.uk*

The Beloved Community *www.sacredspaces.org* on-line courses in spiritual peacemaking and peace pilgrimages based in the USA.

Findhorn Foundation dedicated to personal and planetary transformation *www.findhorn.org* with daily reflections from 'Opening Doors Within.'

Lucis Trust incorporating the Arcane School of spiritual education and meditation and World Goodwill *www.lucistrust.org*

Paulo Coelho news and reflections from Brazilian author of The Pilgrimage *paulocoelhoblog.com*

Peace Pilgrim *www.peacepilgrim.com* audio and visual reflections of Peace Pilgrim's life and work.

The Quest A Guide to the Spiritual Journey. A practical home-study course for personal and spiritual discovery *www.thequest.org.uk*

BIBLIOGRAPHY: Some reading with waymarks to the inner path include:

A Course In Miracles (A.C.I.M.) *Text, Workbook for Students and Manual for Teachers*. Foundation for Inner Peace.

The Art of Pilgrimage *The Seeker's Guide to Making Travel Sacred*, Phil Cousineau. Element Books

Anam Cara *Spiritual wisdom from the Celtic world,* John O'Donohue. Bantam.

A New Earth *Awakening to Your Life's Purpose*, Eckhart Tolle. Penguin Books

A Brief History of Everything *Integrating the partial visions of specialists into a new understanding of the meaning and significance of life*, Ken Wilber.

Care of the Soul *How to add depth and meaning to your everyday life*, Thomas Moore. Piatkus

Conversations with God *Books One, Two and Three*. Neale Donald Walsch. Hodder & Stoughton

From the Holy Mountain *A Journey in the Shadow of Byzantium*, William Dalrymple. Flamingo

Going Home *Jesus and the Buddha as brothers*, Thich Nhat Hanh. Rider Books

Loving What Is *Four Questions That Can Change Your Life*, Byron Katie. Rider

Handbook for the Soul *A collection of wisdom from over 30 celebrated spiritual writers*. Piatkus

The Hero with a Thousand Faces *An examination, through ancient myths, of man's eternal struggle for identity,* Joseph Campbell. Fontana Press

How to Know God *The Soul's Journey into the Mystery of Mysteries*, Deepak Chopra. Rider

Jesus and the Lost Goddess *The Secret Teachings of the Original Christians*, Timothy Freke & Peter Gandy. Three Rivers Press

The Journey Home *The Obstacles to Peace*, Kenneth Wapnick. Foundation for A Course In Miracles

The Mysteries *Rudolf Steiner's writings on Spiritual Initiation*, Andrew Welburn. Floris Books

Mysticism *The Nature and Development of Spiritual Consciousness,* Evelyn Underhill. Oneworld

Nine Faces of Christ *Quest of the True Initiate*, Eugene Whitworth. DeVorss

No Destination *Autobiography (of a pilgrim),* Satish Kumar. Green Books. See also **Earth Pilgrim** *Conversations with Satish Kumar*. Resurgence.

Paths of the Christian Mysteries *From Compostela to the New World*, Virginia Sease and Manfred Schmidt-Brabant. Temple Lodge

Pilgrimage *Adventures of the Spirit*, Various Authors. Travellers' Tales

The Pilgrimage *A Contemporary Quest for Ancient Wisdom*. Paulo Coelho

Peace Pilgrim *Her Life and Work in Her Own Words*, Friends of Peace Pilgrim. Ocean Tree Books

Pilgrim in Aquarius David Spangler. Findhorn Press

Pilgrim Stories *On and Off the Road to Santiago*. Nancy Louise Frey.

Pilgrim in Time *Mindful Journeys to Encounter the Sacred*. Rosanne Keller.

The Power of Now *A Guide to Spiritual Enlightenment*, Eckhart Tolle. New World

Peace is Every Step *The path of mindfulness in everyday life*, Thich Nhat Hanh. Rider Books

Phases *The Spiritual Rhythms in Adult Life*, Bernard Lievegoed. Sophia Books

Sacred Contracts *Awakening Your Divine Potential*, Caroline Myss. Bantam

Sacred Roads *Adventures from the Pilgrimage Trail*, Nicholas Shrady. Viking

Secrets of God *Writings of Hildegard of Bingen*. Shambhala

Silence of the Heart *Dialogues with Robert Adams*. Acropolis Books

The Gift of Change *Spiritual Guidance for a Radically New Life*, Marianne Williamson. Element Books

The Inner Camino *A Path of Awakening*, Sara Hollwey & Jill Brierley. Findhorn Press.

The Reappearance of the Christ. Alice Bailey. Lucis Press.

The Road Less Travelled *A new Psychology of Love*, M. Scott Peck. Arrow Books

The Soul's Code *In Search of Character and Calling*, James Hillman. Bantam

The Prophet. Kahlil Gibran. Mandarin

Wandering Joy *Meister Eckhart's Mystical Philosophy*. Lindisfarne Press

Wanderlust *A history of Walking*. Rebecca Solnit. Verso

Who Dies? *An Investigation of Conscious Living and Conscious Dying*, Stephen and Ondrea Levine. Anchor Books

Whispers of the Beloved *The mystical poems of Rumi*. HarperCollins

RETURNING HOME: *Reflections ...*

When, after a prolonged absence, friends and family remark, *'you haven't changed at all'* I am hopeful they are either blind or following some meaningless social convention. I have spent the last 25 years of my life with the primary intention to do just that – to change myself. One of the more potent aspects of pilgrimage is the extended time it requires away from the familiar. This allows an opportunity for the inner alchemy of spirit to start its work of transformation. It's not just the physical body that may need to sweat off excess baggage – the mind needs purifying too. Our world is in a mess and we are not going to fix it with more of the same. We need a fresh approach and a different mind-set to the one that created the chaos in the first place. Hopefully, this re-ordering of the way we see the world will quicken apace as we open to lessons presented to us along the camino and begin to understand that... life itself is a classroom.

A purpose of pilgrimage is to allow time for old belief systems and outworn 'truths' to fall away so that new and higher perspectives can arise. We may also need to recognise that colleagues and partners at home or at work may feel threatened by our new outlook on life. Breaking tribal patterns, challenging the status quo or querying consensus reality is generally considered inappropriate at best or heretical at worst. The extent to which we hold onto any new understanding is measured by how far we are prepared to *walk our talk* and live our 'new' truth in the face of opposition, often from those who profess to love us. Christ was crucified for living The Truth.

These guidebooks are dedicated to awakening beyond human consciousness. They arose out of a personal existential crisis and the urgent need for some space and time to reflect on the purpose of life and its direction. Collectively we live in a spiritual vacuum of our own making where the mystical and sacred have been relegated to the delusional or escapist. Accordingly, we live in a three dimensional world and refuse to open the door to higher dimensions of reality. We have impoverished ourselves in the process, severely limiting our potential. Terrorised by the chaotic world we have manifested around us, we have become ensnared in its dark forms. We have become so preoccupied with these fearful images we fail to notice that we hold the key to the door of our self-made prison. We can walk out any time we choose.

Whatever our individual experiences, it is likely that you will be in a heightened state of sensitivity after walking the camino. I strongly recommend that you do not squeeze your itinerary so you feel pressurised to rush back into your work and general lifestyle immediately on your return. This is a crucial moment. I have often witnessed profound change, in myself and others, only to allow a sceptical audience to induce fear and doubt in us so that we fall back to the starting point – the default position of the status quo. Be careful with whom you share your experiences and stay in contact with fellow pilgrims who can support new realisations and orientation. Source new friends and activities that enhance and encourage the on-going journey of Self-discovery.

If you feel it might be helpful, please feel free to email me any time at *jb@caminoguides.com* – I cannot promise to answer all emails in writing but be assured they will all be noted and a blessing sent in return. I have developed great empathy and respect for my fellow pilgrims who have placed themselves on the path of enquiry. We are embarking together on a journey of re-discovery of our essential nature and opening up to knowledge of Higher Worlds. We have, collectively, been asleep a long time and while change can happen in the twinkling of an eye it is often experienced as a slow and painful process. It is never easy to let go of the familiar and to step into the new. How far we are prepared to go and how resolute in holding onto our newfound reality is a matter of our own choosing. There is little point in garnering peace along the camino if we leave it behind in Santiago. We need to bring it back into our everyday life. After the camino comes the laundry!

Whichever choice you make will doubtless be right for you at this time. I wish you well in your search for the truth and your journey Home and extend my humble blessings to a fellow pilgrim on the path. The journey is not over and continues, as you will have it be, dedicated to the sacred or the mundane, to waking or sleeping. To help remind us of our true identity, I leave you with the following words of Marianne Williamson, distilled from A Course In Miracles:

Our deepest fear is not that we are inadequate.
Our deepest fear is that we are powerful beyond measure.
It is our Light, not our darkness, that most frightens us.

We ask ourselves, who am I to be brilliant, gorgeous, talented and fabulous?
Actually, who are you not to be? You are a child of God.
Your playing small doesn't serve the world.
There's nothing enlightened about shrinking,
So that other people won't feel insecure around you.

We were born to make manifest the Glory of God that is within us.
It's not just in some of us; it's in everyone.
And as we let our Light shine,
We unconsciously give other people permission to do the same.
As we are liberated from our own fear,
Our presence automatically liberates others.

Before a new chapter is begun, the old one has to be finished.
Stop being who you were, and change into who you are.
Paulo Coelho – www.warriorsoflight.com

Stay in Touch:

The evolution of human consciousness is gathering apace. One manifestation of this is the increasing interest in taking time out to go on pilgrimage and nowhere is this more apparent than along the camino where facilities struggle to keep up with demand. Information garnered in one month may be out of date the next as old hostels close and new ones open up. Paths are realigned to make way for new motorways and budget airlines suddenly announce new routes (or with the advent of 'peak oil' – closing some). Whilst great care has been taken in gathering the information for this guide it also requires feedback from pilgrims who have recently walked the route to enable it to stay fresh and relevant to those who will follow on after us. Your comments and suggestions will be gratefully received and used to provide up-to-date advice on the free 'updates' page on **www.caminoguides.com** so if you would like to offer something back to the camino or simply stay in touch please e-mail me at:

jb@caminoguides.com

A tithe of royalties from the sale of this guidebook will be distributed to those who seek to preserve the physical and spiritual integrity of this route

Download our Mobile Application

Available on iOS, Android and Windows Phone 8

www.ecamino.eu

1 Camino Francés **790** km
  St. Jean / Roncesvalles – Santiago
• • • • • • • •

2 Chemin de Paris **1000** km
  Paris – St. Jean via Orléans & Tours
• • • • • • • •
  Alt. route from Chartres -
  Soulac – Tarnos 170km
• • • • • • • •

3 Chemin de Vézelay **900** km
  Vezélay – St. Jean via Bazas
• • • • • • • •
  Ext. to Namur (B) & Maastricht (NL)
• • • • • • • •

4 Chemin du Puy **740** km
  Le Puy-en-Velay – St. Jean
• • • • • • • •
  Ext. to Geneva, Konstanz, Prague

5 Chemin d'Arles **750** km
  Arles – Somport Pass
• • • • • • • •
  Camino Aragonés **160** km
  Somport Pass – Óbanos

  Camí San Jaume **600** km
  Port de Selva – Jaca
• • • • • • • •

6 Camino de Madrid **320**km
  Madrid – Sahagún
• • • • • • • •

  Camino de Levante **900** km
  Valencia (Alicante) – Zamora
• • • • • • • •
  Alt. via Cuenca – Burgos

7 Camino Mozárabe **390**km
  Granada – Mérida
• • • • • • • •
  (Málaga alt. via Baena)

8 Via de la Plata **1,000**km
  Seville – Santiago
• • • • • • • •

9 Camino Portugués *Central* **241**km
  Lisboa – Porto
• • • • • • • •
  Porto – Santiago

  Camino Portugués *da Costa* **372**km
  Porto – Caminho
• • • • • • • •
  A Guarda – Redonela

10 Camino Finisterre **87**km
  Santiago – Finisterre
• • • • • • • •
  via – Muxía – Santiago 114 km

11 Camino Inglés **110**km
  Ferrol – Santiago
• • • • • • • •

12 Camino del Norte **830**km
  Irún – Santiago via Gijón
• • • • • • • •

  Camino Primitivo **320**km
  Oviedo – Lugo – Melide
• • • • • • • •